■ Representing the Good Neighbor

Currents in Latin American and Iberian Music

Walter Clark, Series Editor

Nor-tec Rifa!
Electronic Dance Music from Tijuana to the World
Alejandro L. Madrid

From Serra to Sancho:
Music and Pageantry in the California Missions
Craig H. Russell

Colonial Counterpoint:
Music in Early Modern Manila
D. R. M. Irving

Embodying Mexico:
Tourism, Nationalism, & Performance
Ruth Hellier-Tinoco

Silent Music:
Medieval Song and the Construction of History in Eighteenth-Century Spain
Susan Boynton

Whose Spain?
Negotiating "Spanish" Music in Paris, 1908–1929
Samuel Llano

Representing the Good Neighbor:
Music, Difference, and the Pan American Dream
Carol A. Hess

Representing the Good Neighbor

Music, Difference, and the Pan American Dream

Carol A. Hess

OXFORD
UNIVERSITY PRESS

OXFORD
UNIVERSITY PRESS

Oxford University Press is a department of the University of Oxford.
It furthers the University's objective of excellence in research,
scholarship, and education by publishing worldwide.

Oxford   New York
Auckland   Cape Town   Dar es Salaam   Hong Kong   Karachi
Kuala Lumpur   Madrid   Melbourne   Mexico City   Nairobi
New Delhi   Shanghai   Taipei   Toronto

With offices in
Argentina   Austria   Brazil   Chile   Czech Republic   France   Greece
Guatemala   Hungary   Italy   Japan   Poland   Portugal   Singapore
South Korea   Switzerland   Thailand   Turkey   Ukraine   Vietnam

Oxford is a registered trade mark of Oxford University Press
in the UK and certain other countries.

Published in the United States of America by
Oxford University Press
198 Madison Avenue, New York, NY 10016

Library of Congress Cataloging-in-Publication Data
Hess, Carol A.
Representing the good neighbor: music, difference, and the Pan American dream /Carol A. Hess.
    p.   cm.—(Currents in Latin American and Iberian music)
Includes bibliographical references.
ISBN 978-0-19-991999-4 (hardcover: alk. paper)
1. Music—Latin America—20th century—History and criticism.
2. Music—United States—Latin American influences. 3. Pan-Americanism. I. Title.
ML199.5.H47   2013
780—dc23   2012028367

9 8 7 6 5 4 3 2 1

Printed in the United States of America
on acid-free paper

Publication of this book was supported in part by the Gustave Reese Endowment of the American Musicological Society.

Publication of this book was supported in part by the H. Earle Johnson Bequest for Book Publication Subvention of the Society of American Music.

For Robert M. Stevenson (1916–2012)

In memoriam

CONTENTS

■ LIST OF MUSICAL EXAMPLES

LIST OF FIGURES

■ ACKNOWLEDGMENTS

Many generous people have helped me write this book, proffering an abundance of practical and psychological support. My research has been aided by numerous individuals and institutions: Luiz Fernando Lopes, Emma Dederick, and Carmen Téllez (former director) of the Latin American Music Center at Indiana University; Thomas L. Riis, director of the American Music Research Center at the University of Colorado, Boulder; Jenny Romero of the Margaret Herrick Library at the Academy of Motion Picture Arts and Sciences; George Boziwick, Jonathan Hiam, and Charles Perrier of the New York Public Library for the Performing Arts; Patricia Baughman and Walter Svonchenko of the Library of Congress in Washington, D.C.; Jeffrey Wheeler of the Philadelphia Free Library; Nell Aronoff of the Library of the Museum of Modern Art (MoMA); Jean Henry of the Gallery Archives of the National Gallery of Art; Tom Akins, former archivist of the Indianapolis Symphony; Margaret Mair of the Hartt School of Music (University of Hartford); Norma Palomino and Valería Cancer of the Archive of the Instituto Torcuato di Tella (Buenos Aires); and Silvia Glocer of the Biblioteca Nacional (Buenos Aires). For many months the library staff at Michigan State University, especially Mark Andrews and Greg Lamb, satisfied my seemingly insatiable desire for difficult-to-obtain microfilms, while Mary Black Junttonnen of the Fine Arts Library (Music) was similarly helpful in many ways.

I was privileged to present in lectures and conference presentations various aspects of this book, sometimes in their earliest and roughest stages. Here I thank Enrique Sacau (Oxford University), Louise K. Stein (University of Michigan), Robert Addlington (University of Nottingham), G. Grayson Wagstaff (Catholic University), Thomas L. Riis (University of Colorado, Boulder), Jennifer Campbell (Central Michigan University), and Robert W. Blake (Center for Caribbean and Latin American Studies, Michigan State University). Colleagues from the American Musicological Society, the Society for American Music, the Society for Ethnomusicology, and the Society for Music Theory deserving of special thanks include Christopher A. Reynolds, Danielle Fosler-Lussier, Beth E. Levy, Richard Taruskin, Annegret Fauser, Eduardo Herrera, Erick Carballo, Anne C. Shreffler, Cristina Magaldi, and Leonora Saavedra, some of whose astute questions redirected my thinking. Robert M. Stevenson, to whose memory this book is dedicated, will always inspire Hispanists embarking on the many projects that still await us. I also thank Richard Crawford for his many acts of kindness to me over the years and for setting my historiographer's imagination on fire when he lectured on narratives of American music at Bowling Green State University (Ohio), where I taught from 1995 to 2006.

That institution's Mid America Center for Contemporary Music funded my research on a portion of chapter 5. Brief passages of this book have previously appeared in the *Journal of the American Musicological Society* 2013, vol. 66, no. 1 © 2013 by the American Musicological Society; and *Opera Quarterly* 2006, vol. 22, no. 3 © 2006 Oxford University Press. I am grateful to Michigan State University for sabbatical funding during spring semester 2008. Special thanks are also due the Argentine Fulbright Commission, which enabled me to teach a doctoral seminar at the University of Buenos Aires (UBA) in 2005. It was at the UBA that this book began to be written: I first tested some of its central ideas on my students there, a high-spirited and intellectually curious group with whom I have had the pleasure of staying in touch ever since, especially Silvia Glocer and Silvina Luz Mansilla. I am also grateful to Diana Fernández Calvo of the Instituto de Investigación Musicológica "Carlos Vega" of the Pontificia Universidad Católica Argentina (Buenos Aires), to the Ginastera scholar Pola Suárez-Urtubey, and to the composer Graciela Paraskevaídis.

Another Latin American colleague who has enhanced this book immeasurably through his astute and often impassioned ideas—and who was always willing to share them with me over hours of conversation—is the Venezuelan composer Ricardo Lorenz (Michigan State University). I can never fully acknowledge his contribution. Similarly generous with his insights was the conductor Raphael Jiménez (Oberlin College), whom I also knew at Michigan State, where he is much missed. I also thank Pablo Bagilet and Gwen Burgett-Thrasher for clarifying many percussion-related terms. Andrés Carrizo, Víctor Márquez, and David Gregory Byrne all worked hard on the musical examples; Alyson Payne and Monica Hershberger proved thorough and capable research assistants. Others graciously provided hospitality during my research travels: Andrew Byrne, Lynn Carter, and Immanuel Willheim (New York); Gretchen Horlacher (Bloomington, Indiana); Lois Lutes and Cristina Magaldi (Washington, D.C.); Raymond Hanson and Anne Koscielny (Hartford, Connecticut); David Gregory Byrne and Sylvia Desrochers (Los Angeles); and Maria Bambina Salinas (Argentina). I am also grateful to Suzanne Ryan of Oxford University Press, to Walter A. Clark, series editor of CLAIM, to Judith Hoover for her patient and attentive copyediting, and to the anonymous readers of the manuscript for their helpful suggestions. John Koegel, as usual, has been generous not only with practical advice but with his seemingly boundless knowledge of Latin American music. Any errors that remain are, of course, my own.

The affective ties strengthened over the course of a long writing project are surely the hardest to adequately acknowledge. As always, I thank Dorothy Weicker for her friendship and support over the years. Kevin Bartig, Justin O'Dell, and Marcie Ray, with whom I taught at Michigan State University, patiently tolerated my extended ruminations on George Orwell's observation that "writing a book is like having a protracted disease." Also blurring the distinction between "colleague" and "friend" are Elainie Lillios, Mary Natvig, and Robert

Satterlee, all from Bowling Green and always ready to lend a sympathetic ear. I am grateful to my new colleagues at the University of California, Davis, especially Dean Jessie Ann Owens and Christopher Reynolds, who released me from teaching responsibilities during fall 2012. *Como siempre,* I also thank Milton M. Azevedo.

There is also my family. While working on this project I had the pleasure of becoming acquainted with my first cousin once removed, David Stephenson, who introduced me to the 1922 textbook by my grandfather John A. Hess, which I cite in the introduction. The memory of my late parents, John A. Hess Jr. and Emily O. Hess, will always provide for me the surest example of the sort of optimism and energy needed for life's more mysterious challenges, such as writing a book. Part of my fascination with the period covered here is its many overlaps with my parents' era, which I, with the insouciance typical of youth, never discussed with them in sufficient detail. I am also blessed to be nurtured by family today. I daresay few musicologists have so regularly presented their work before a devoted band of relations, all of whom just happen to be in the same city in which the annual meeting of the American Musicological Society is taking place. They slip into my session and disappear just as discreetly the moment the Q&A ends, joining me afterward for a celebratory meal. At the 2006 meeting of the Society in Los Angeles, for example, I looked out from the podium to see two of my sisters, Bonnie Rose and Judith Byrne (Nancy Witt, my other sister, is missed in such gatherings), my nephews Andrew and David Byrne, and Sylvia Desrochers, now David's wife. I continue to hope that none of them will ever make me giggle or ask me a trick question. All have been profligate with their love and wacky humor over the years, and not just in relation to my writing this book. For these reasons and many more I can never thank them enough.

■ ABOUT THE COMPANION WEBSITE

The Companion Website to *Representing the Good Neighbor*, found at www.oup
.com/us/representingthegoodneighbor, contains several tables that complement the text:

Chapter Four

Figure 4c. Brazilian music at the 1939 World's Fair
Figure 4d. Music by Villa-Lobos performed at the 1939 World's Fair

Chapter Five

Figure 5b. "Festival of Brazilian Music," Museum of Modern Art. Program 1: The
Choros. October 16 and 17, 1940
Figure 5c. "Festival of Brazilian Music," Museum of Modern Art. Program 2:
Popular and Concerted Rhythms. October 18 and 19, 1940
Figure 5d. "Festival of Brazilian Music," Museum of Modern Art. Program 3:
Villa Lobos. October 20, 1940 (afternoon and evening)

Chapter Six

Figure 6b. Ginastera and the Inter-American Festivals, Washington, D. C.,
1958–65
Figure 6c. The Spanish avant-garde at the Inter-American Festival, Washington,
D. C., 1968

Chapter Seven

Figure 7a. Representative *Cantatas populares* by Chilean composers
Figure 7b. Formal Overview. *36 Variations on "The People United Will Never Be
Defeated!" by Sergio Ortega and Quilapayún* by Frederic Rzewski

■ EDITORIAL MATTERS

Throughout I retain diacritical marks in proper names even if sometimes they are omitted in the literature (i.e., Chávez). In the case of scholars with Spanish or Portuguese surnames who have apparently dropped diacritical marks, I continue this practice (i.e., Gonzalez).

If a work has been translated well into English, I cite the translation for readers unfamiliar with Spanish. When a foreign-language source is available in a good research library, I give only the English translation. For harder-to-find documents, such as newspaper reviews, I give both the translation and the original language. Unless otherwise noted, all translations are my own.

One thorny translation-related matter is the word *popular*. In Spanish it can mean "well-liked by a broad public," as José Ortega y Gasset so devastatingly explained in *The Dehumanization of Art*. It can also mean "of the people" or "made by the people"; consequently, what native speakers of English may call "folk music" may be labeled *música popular*. In English-language aesthetic discourse the term *popular* (as in "popular culture") is a matter of some contention. Does it approximate the second definition given above, that is, "made by the people"? Does it simply refer to wide favor? Anything not "high art"? Culture that is mass-produced or commercial? Throughout this book I have tried to situate each term as clearly as possible, referring to "folk music" when composers and critics themselves have done so and following suit with "popular." When necessary, as in the two chapters on the cold war, I specify "mass" or "commercial" music and contextualize the ideological agenda as appropriate.

Whether to give titles of works in the original language or in English is admittedly a judgment call, as is whether to include lengthy translations, especially of near-cognates, in the text. For clarity, I have given translations in most instances but have sometimes opted for custom and euphony.

■ Representing the Good Neighbor

Introduction

What do we in the United States know about Latin American art music, and how do we know it? This book takes as its point of reference the 1930s and 1940s, when at least the first part of this question mattered a great deal. It mattered because the United States, threatened by European fascism, renewed the enterprise known as Pan Americanism, a congeries of economic, political, and cultural objectives that first peaked in the late nineteenth century and was based on the premise that the Americas were bound by geography and common interests. With his inaugural address in March 1933, President Franklin D. Roosevelt outlined the essentials of the Good Neighbor Policy, promising to reverse U.S. interventionism in Latin America and to seek common ground north and south. Pan Americanism involved more than policies and programs, however. Rather, it upheld the "Western Hemisphere Idea," as one historian of the era called it. This Idea reflected north-south psychological and spiritual bonds, celebrating the identities of the individual American republics while subsuming them within a hemispheric framework. As such, it was invested with a "rational-mystical character."[1]

To help cement these affective ties, the Roosevelt administration assigned art music a significant role. Cultural diplomacy, then in its nascent stages in the United States, became a key element in the Pan Americanist project. Taking Latin America as something of a testing ground, the Division of Cultural Relations (established in 1938) sponsored a range of Pan Americanist musical activities.[2] Even more active, however, was the Office for the Coordination of Commercial and Cultural Relations between the American Republics (known as the OIAA after its cumbersome name was shortened in 1945), established under the Department of State and the Council of National Defense in the summer of 1940. Its Music Committee organized tours and exchange visits for composers and performers, sending Aaron Copland to Latin America in 1941; Carleton Sprague Smith, the musicologist and head of the Music Division of the New York Public Library, also visited Latin America under government auspices.[3] The Pan American Union, established during a prior wave of hemispheric solidarity, stepped up its musical activities under Charles Seeger, Music Division chief from 1941, who oversaw the publication of numerous scores and books on Latin American music.[4] Collaborating with other organizations, public and private, these entities organized national contests, music education projects, and concerts dedicated to Latin American music. Even Hollywood worked with the government, churning out dozens of Good Neighborly movies chock-full of lively dance sequences and percussion-heavy soundtracks, which sometimes left their mark on Latin-themed concert works by U.S. composers. Suffice it to say that in the 1930s and 1940s, the "golden age" of Pan Americanism, Latin American art music made itself felt in the United States to a degree unequaled before or since.

The Americanist musicologist Carol J. Oja has called Pan Americanism an "auspicious but little explored area of American musical history that is deeply enmeshed in national politics."[5] Although such "enmeshing" can be considered from several angles (including international politics), this book explores Pan Americanism vis-à-vis the question posed at the outset: What do we in the United States know about Latin American art music, and how do we know it? For when we compare Good Neighbor–era sensibilities in the United States with those of the latter part of the twentieth century, we behold nothing short of an epistemological chasm. In the former period, U.S. critics praised Latin American music for its cosmopolitan universalism, applauding points in common among U.S. composers and their southern neighbors. Since the cold war, however, critics and scholars generally became preoccupied with Latin American difference. Relying on the rhetoric of exoticism, essentialism, and nationalism, many even today see Latin American music as "particular and, thus, oppositional," to quote Ruth A. Solie in her pioneering study of musicology and difference.[6]

How did the phenomenon Kofi Agawu has called "embracing sameness" come to be forgotten in the post–Good Neighbor period?[7] What do the vicissitudes of memory—of a time when north-south amity was a national priority—tell us about the ways the history of American music has been written, a subject, some argue, that should be enlarged to encompass all of the Americas rather than just the United States? First, we examine some recent discursive trends. One U.S. scholar argued in 2005 that Copland was attracted to Latin American music for its "potential for transgression."[8] Another author proposes that Latin American music is "filled with irresistible exotic color"; indeed, terms such as *distinctive* and *characteristic* abound.[9] More than denoting particularity, they reflect a practice the Argentine historian Ricardo D. Salvatore calls "adjectivization," the reflexive layering on of descriptors.[10] In reading much of the literature on Latin American music from the past thirty-five years, we might even come to accept Roland Barthes's contention that music criticism generally depends on that "poorest of linguistic categories: the adjective."[11] It is difficult to see, for example, how our understanding of Latin American art music is enhanced by unelaborated descriptions of "unmistakably Mexican" or "genuinely Peruvian" features.[12] Often Latin American music is simply left for "unique," another vacuous but frequently brandished weapon in the adjectival arsenal.

As several of these examples show, adjectivization goes hand in hand with essentializing, which attributes unspecified—but somehow "unmistakable"—traits to a given country or region. Here we can consider Agawu's work on "African rhythm," a time-honored conceit, he argues, that has dominated scholarship on African music while discouraging critique such that the quality being essentialized can never be the subject of rational discourse or intellectual accountability.[13] This epistemological vacuum begets constructions of nationalism, which U.S. scholars have often taken as motive and marker for Latin American music, sometimes with Herderian fervor. According to this perspective, *national* takes over for the essentializing, exoticizing adjective. Opaque references to "national elements," "national effect," or "national character" surface repeatedly in what was for decades the only single-volume textbook on Latin American music in the United States, roughly one-third of which is devoted to nationalism or aspirations thereto. We read therein, for example, that "rhythmic-nationalistic elements" are present in the *Danzas humorísticas* by the Mexican composer Felipe Villanueva (1862–93), the duple-triple metric structures of which evince "the composer's awareness of the 'national' quality of hemiola."[14] Perhaps the author's scare quotes strike a vague blow at adjectivization? If so, they also fail to clarify, since hemiola characterizes any number of non-Mexican genres, including the *peteneras* (Spain), the *chacarera* (Argentina), the *pasillo* (Colombia), and certain styles of *música guajira* (Cuba). The easy adjective *national* thus denotes little more than difference, and a murky one at that.[15]

Compare this approach to the now-forgotten discourse of the Good Neighbor period. At this time, critics north and south *resisted* nationalism. In 1945 Nicolas Slonimsky published a book on Latin American music in which he managed to evaluate Silvestre Revueltas, Mozart Camargo Guarnieri, and Alejandro García Caturla without a single reference to nationalism; as we shall see, he considered other Latin American composers in terms of cosmopolitan (rather than local) trends as well.[16] Other critics fashioned some elaborate tropes to resist nationalism, urging the "long evolution" to universalism of musical style, as the musicologist Otto Mayer-Serra described this orientation from Mexico in 1942.[17] They updated European romanticism's rhetoric of organicism and universalism, with U.S. critics, especially, availing themselves of nonmusical metaphors. "Sublimation" proved apt for this purpose.[18] Borrowed from chemistry, this term denotes change (i.e., the "process of changing a solid directly to a vapor and the condensing of the vapor directly back to a solid") or purification (the "act of refining and purifying or freeing from baser qualities"), as explained in two roughly contemporaneous texts, one in chemistry and one in the burgeoning field of psychoanalysis.[19] Such evocative explanations extended handily to the presumably "base qualities" of musical nationalism and a host of related discourses, explored below. Although subtle hints of difference might surface, the unitary framework of the Western Hemisphere would prevail, in accordance with Pan Americanist ideology. Thus, in embracing sameness through sublimation, critics endowed the time-tested discourse of cosmopolitan universalism with a variety of New World tropes, often with Europe lurking in the background.

In comparing such representations with those of later decades, we might argue that avoiding nationalism during the Good Neighbor period was a fluke, a

politically motivated aberration that belied Latin American composers' true proclivities. After all, during World War II many north and south saw nationalism as
uncomfortably close to Nazi chauvinism. But Latin American composers found
plenty of other reasons to denounce nationalism. Some associated it with "reactionary" romanticism rather than the first-world modernism to which they
aspired.[20] Others warned that nationalism would relegate Latin American music
to the "periphery," thus separating it from the "central" (i.e., European) countries,
those that presumably produce universal music.[21] Such composers anticipated
by sixty years the exhortations of Mari Carmen Ramírez and Héctor Olea, two
Latin Americans important in the visual arts who urge that "stale remarks—such
as 'peripheral,' . . . 'exotic,' 'outsider'—be forgotten."[22] Regarding folk music, a
principal carrier of nationalism, those Latin American composers who drew
upon it warned of its potential for abuse.[23] Others frankly didn't care about folklore, rejecting it outright to avoid falling into the dubious categories of "travel
music" or "tourist nationalism," with their attendant connotations of commodification and easy pictorialism.[24] Others purported to sublimate folklore beyond
the point of recognition, especially during the cold war, when many in the United
States associated Latin American nationalism with communism.

These divergent views all suggest that U.S. scholars can benefit from listening to
those from what has come to be known as the periphery of music history, an idea I
have advanced in previous work.[25] For example, does discussing the Mexican composer Carlos Chávez under the rubric of "New World Nationalism" sensitively represent his position?[26] As Leonora Saavedra has shown, despite his status as the chief
representative of Mexican nationalism, Chávez actually held nationalism at arm's
length.[27] A corollary question to that posed at the outset thus arises: How does
whatever we in the United States know about Latin American art music square with
ways in which the same music is understood in Latin America? In incorporating
some opinions of Latin Americans in this book, I am well aware of my status as *la
gringa del norte*. I do not claim to "speak for" Latin Americans but rather to invite
dialogue. Much resentment is occasioned when U.S. scholars try to force Latin
American subjects into their own models, whether by overlooking Latin American
reaction to the "imperialist discourse" of Leonard Bernstein's *West Side Story* im-
puted by one Puerto Rican critic to this popular work, or by neglecting resistance
in Latin America to Copland's musical representations, as in his equally popular *El
salón México*.[28] Caution is especially important in light of the fact that traditional
models of political nationalism as proposed by Ernest Gellner, Anthony Smith,
and, more recently, Benedict Anderson rarely correspond to Latin America.[29] Yet
everything in these models *partly* applies, ensuring that Latin America can easily
become "the subject of a difference that is almost the same, but not quite," to cite
Homi Bhabha's well-known description of mimicry.[30] Hegemonic powers often
take advantage of the subaltern's impulse to mimic, of its vulnerability in negotiating the elusive play of sameness and difference. These habits have long affected
U.S.–Latin American relations.

Consequently universalism must be approached with care. Jacques Attali, for example, has maintained that the "will to construct a universal [musical] language operat[es] on the same scale as the exchanges made necessary by colonial expansion: music, a flexible code, was dreamed of as an instrument of world unification, the language of the mighty."[31] Universalism has also been attacked as a tool of bourgeois liberalism, despite its pretensions to inclusiveness.[32] No less a critic than Theodor Adorno has deemed "philistine" the notion that "art is a conciliatory force capable of smoothing over differences."[33] Did musical Pan Americanism "smooth over" difference with hegemonic intent? Did it promote nothing but mimicry of the so-called Colossus of the North? Rather than dismiss universalism as a critical sleight of hand or a utopianist illusion, this book weighs its potential. The Brazilian music specialist Cristina Magaldi has recently called for de-essentializing, arguing that essentializing, exoticist nationalisms are ahistorical since they imagine a music unaffected by cultural interactions.[34] Scholars outside of musicology too have proposed transnationalist and cosmopolitanist historical models, seeking process rather than essence on the premise that in a global community "cosmopolitanism is *there*—not merely an abstract ideal like loving one's neighbor as oneself, but habits of thought and feeling that have already shaped and been shaped by particular collectivities, that are socially and geographically situated, hence both limited and empowered."[35] As I argue here, musical Pan Americanism rested on these very precepts. Yet their impact on music historiography has been essentially forgotten.

To be sure, in probing their memory in this book, I am by no means suggesting that Pan Americanist sameness-embracing was uniformly benign. Rather, I bear in mind Foucault's reflections on "the overall 'discursive fact,'" as elucidated in his *History of Sexuality*. That is, I recognize the "fact" that Pan Americanism is "spoken about . . . discover who does the speaking, the position and viewpoints from which they speak, the institutions which prompt people to speak about it and which store and distribute the things that are said."[36] The wide-ranging "fact" of musical Pan Americanism served numerous interests. As noted, it enjoyed the support of the U.S. government, which threw its considerable weight behind Pan Americanism's cultural dimension during the Good Neighbor period. Yet a surprising number of composers and critics not connected with the apparatus of cultural diplomacy also responded to Latin American music during the 1930s and 1940s, some quite passionately. Those writing in the 1920s, moreover, anticipated Good Neighbor–period sameness-embracing. This book therefore concentrates less on official Pan Americanist cultural diplomacy and much more on what I call the edges of Pan Americanism, the sometimes quirky range of representations that spontaneously manifested themselves outside of the OIAA or the Division of Cultural Relations. Exploring these edges, which of course interacted with official Pan Americanism, enables us to appreciate more keenly the generous reach of Foucault's discursive fact.

These representations surface in the previously untapped primary source material on which I draw, namely, the hundreds of reviews of Latin American music by critics north and south. Several critics are of the first rank. They include Paul Rosenfeld, Olin Downes, Virgil Thomson, Colin McPhee, John Cage, Elliott Carter, Leonard Bernstein, Howard Taubman, Israel Citkowitz, Paul Henry Lang, Marc Blitzstein, Harold C. Schonberg, John Rockwell, Christian Wolff, Juan Carlos Paz, Francisco Curt Lange, and José Ardévol. I also acknowledge some of the central actors in musical Pan Americanism: Leopold Stokowski, Gilbert Chase, Henry Cowell, Paul Bowles, and Irving Lowens. As for Copland, widely recognized as the affable face of musical Pan Americanism, he makes only a cameo appearance in this book. I originally planned a chapter on Latin American reception to Copland's music from his OIAA-sponsored tour of 1941. After gathering reviews from only two countries, however, I realized that an entire book on Copland's Latin American experience was called for, on which I am presently at work.[37] To be sure, I do address the main points of Copland's Pan Americanism, including some of his Latin American–themed compositions, surely as telling a statement as any of his concert reviews or critical essays. I also consider analogous representations of Latin America by Gershwin, Cowell, and others. Complementing these figures in art music are Walt Disney and copywriters from the music publishing industry. If this roster of names reads like an assortment of rather strange bedfellows it only confirms that Pan Americanist culture was distinguished by the sometimes uneasy interpenetration of popular, elite, and commercial expressions.

To take in this range of cultural negotiations I have cultivated a Pan Americanist lens or perspective. Neither theory nor methodology, it seeks to register an array of representational practices of which musical discourse was only a part. This vast and far-reaching Pan Americanist "representational machine," as Salvatore describes it, operated in the visual arts, architecture, academic subjects such as history and anthropology, industry, advertising, and, of course, politics.[38] Thanks to this perspective, Chávez was discussed in *Vogue* magazine and Heitor Villa-Lobos in *Harper's Bazaar* alongside ads for Breck shampoo and Cartier wristwatches. In probing its extent, I bear in mind Néstor García Canclini's observation that representations are created and repeated through a network of policies and practices, which can shift and reconstitute themselves in the public imaginary in some surprising ways.[39]

Undergirding this representational machine were attitudes on modernism, race, primitivism, and gender. At first blush, all would seem more than capable of enshrining north-south difference. Critical debates over aesthetic modernism, for example, could easily have degenerated into misgivings over Latin America's "backwardness."[40] Race, described as recently as 2000 as a "specter [that] lurks in the house of music," manifested itself in musical representations of *mestizaje* (*mestiçagem* in Portuguese) or racial mixing, at odds with racial sensibilities in the United States and thus potentially explosive.[41] Gender too has long informed

U.S. views of Latin America, the "virgin" lands of which have been described in language redolent of defloration and rape.[42] Music critics have often articulated these tropes through the discourse of aesthetic primitivism, which, as Mariana Torgovnick has cautioned, often relies on us-them constructions as dictated by the hegemonic power.[43] Yet, as we shall see, U.S. critics imbued with the spirit of Pan Americanism reformulated these difference-charged tropes, often devising imaginative parallels in the process. Constructing what we might call rhetorical mirrors, they beheld not so much a titillating Other as a reflection of their own American selves.

■ THE NARRATIVE

Besides this introduction, *Representing the Good Neighbor* consists of an overview of Pan Americanism, six central chapters, and an epilogue. With the exception of chapter 7, all the central chapters discuss sameness-embracing as manifested in the U.S. reception of the so-called Big Three of twentieth-century Latin American art music: Carlos Chávez (Mexico), Heitor Villa-Lobos (Brazil), and Alberto Ginastera (Argentina). While offering much new information on these composers in the United States, this book is by no means oriented toward biography.[44] Rather, because these composers appear in surveys of twentieth-century art music and because their works are still the most frequently recorded and performed in the United States among Latin American composers, they are the logical subjects on which to train a Pan Americanist lens. Certainly this approach omits many aspects of musical Pan Americanism. It has not been possible to discuss, for example, other composers, figures such as Charles Seeger, or other government officials involved in music, or the role of new media such as radio and film, all of which would have made this book inordinately long. Through examination of the Big Three, we can trace the general shape of musical Pan Americanism: its roots in the aftermath of World War I and its apex during World War II. Their fortunes in the United States also hint at Pan Americanism's decline, a phenomenon manifested in the virtuosic piano work *36 Variations on "The People United Will Never Be Defeated!"* by the U.S. composer Frederic Rzewski, discussed in chapter 7, and which differs profoundly from prior Pan Americanist works by U.S. composers.

Rather than crafting some grand teleological narrative, I opt for a series of snapshots of Pan Americanist musical events, one of which launches each chapter. Examining these snapshots calls for broad contextualization of the representational machine's musical workings. Some that I select have been discussed by other scholars, mainly Americanist musicologists. That their conclusions often differ from mine suggests that our current understanding of "American" music can be enriched by looking beyond the borders of the United States. Over ten years ago Richard Crawford observed that "historians of American music have yet to agree what the history of American music *is*."[45] The moment is still ripe for discussion on this point and the prospects for reformulation still compelling. If we give up the practice of equating "America" solely with the United States, we will have no choice but to acknowledge the nearly two centuries of north-south debate over the nature and ownership of the vast territory known in both regions as "America."[46] We will have no choice but to assign historical importance to the music of the missions and brotherhoods of the Southwest or of the Florida settlements, which predated the New England colonies by a century. When we evaluate works by U.S. composers that evoke Latin America, such as *West Side Story* and *El salón México*, we will be more inclined to consider them through a Pan Americanist lens. Since roughly 2000, several positive steps, summarized below, have been taken in this direction. Yet as historians we cannot avoid asking why Anglocentric models prevailed as long as they did, nor why some scholars still cling to them.

In the snapshot that opens chapter 1, Ginastera and Chase reflect on these north-south differences apropos the naming of "America," a polite exchange I relate to the more tumultuous history of north-south relations. Central to this conflict is the famous 1891 essay *Nuestra América* (Our America) by the Cuban patriot José Martí, who energetically defended a broader, more equitable concept of "America" while rejecting U.S. political and commercial interventionism in Latin America. Just as incensed as Martí was the Uruguayan writer José Enrique Rodó, whose widely read essay *Ariel* of 1900 compared the muscle and materialism of the United States to Caliban, the formless monster of Shakespeare's *Tempest*. World War I, however, introduced new cultural priorities in the hemisphere, prompting U.S. intellectuals to look south rather than to exhausted Europe. By the mid-1920s U.S. composers, then debating the identity of "American" music, were ready to test in the musical sphere the premises of Martí's "our America."

Chapter 2 begins with a snapshot of the first of the Copland-Sessions concert series in April 1928, which showcased three works by Chávez. Critics connected these works to the Mexican Indian in a variety of ways. In a new reading of this event, I propose that these same critics did not applaud a primitive Other but embraced sameness through the universalizing discourse of classicism. Hearing not the influence of Stravinskian neoclassicism (as one scholar has suggested), they applauded what I call "ur-classicism," invested with the authority of an ancient past unique to the Americas yet redolent with universalist import, an idealizing trend already in motion in architecture, journalism, and especially anthropology. This classicizing bent, surprisingly powerful in the modernist ferment of 1920s New York, also surfaced in Mexico in the writings of José Vasconcelos, minister of education in Mexico from 1920 to 1924, some of whose ideas bear an uncanny resemblance to the perorations of Paul Rosenfeld, Chávez's most voluble and enthusiastic critic.

The snapshot launching chapter 3 catches the excitement generated by the 1932 premiere in Philadelphia of Chávez's explicitly Pan Americanist ballet *H.P.*

(Horsepower), with sets and costumes by Diego Rivera. Its conceptual premises would seem to be worlds away from those of ur-classicism: it treated interdependence between the technologically advanced North and the "natural" South. In depicting the North with modernist machine music and the South with salon-type, body-conscious Latin American dances, Chávez would appear to be exalting north-south difference, freighted in the discourse of race and gender. Yet *H.P.* seeks to embrace sameness. At all levels of the ballet, "dialectical indigenism" prevails, an interpretive model formulated by the cultural historian Jeffrey Belnap associated with complex codes and symbols in Rivera's murals and which, I argue, also informs Chávez's score.[47] In the end, dialectical indigenism proved unintelligible to most critics, and Chávez returned almost immediately to ur-classicism, composing the *Sinfonía India*, his best-known work, which inspired in the 1930s and 1940s sameness-embracing paeans from critics the stature of Colin McPhee and John Cage. Unlike critics from the 1970s, they found little to exoticize.

The snapshot for chapter 4 might well have been taken by the roving reporter Elliott Carter, who reflected on the musical dimensions of the 1939 World's Fair for readers of *Modern Music*. By now President Roosevelt's Good Neighbor Policy was in full swing, and Pan American amity was on display at the Fair, where Villa-Lobos's first significant performances in the United States took place. Critics detected three main facets of his musical personality. One, commercialism, was deemed vulgar. Another, which I call "unsublimated primitivism," evoked a savage Other and fulfilled expectations for "African rhythm," thus complementing then-current concepts of *American* rhythm, considered a shared hemispheric trait. In grappling with these issues, critics at the Fair largely overlooked Villa-Lobos's third style, universalism. Nonetheless it was the *Bachianas brasileiras*, which purported to link Brazilian folk music with the universality of Bach, that ultimately secured Villa-Lobos's reputation in the United States, as discussed in chapter 5.

That chapter examines the climax of north-south sameness-embracing, the period following the outbreak of World War II. An overview of Pan Americanist culture, including Latin American–themed works by U.S. composers, shows the extent to which these composers established a "brand" for Latin American music, one that often operated in tandem with the culture industry and thus reinforced "an image of Latin music as 'fun,' lightweight, and essentially trivial that has become a crushing stereotype," to recall John Storm Roberts's oft-quoted words.[48] I discuss the ways Virgil Thomson, as the newly appointed senior music critic at the *New York Herald Tribune*, laid the groundwork for Brazilian universalism by reviewing Villa-Lobos's music with antinationalist barbs that paralleled the sentiments of many Latin American composers and critics. During his sojourn in the United States during 1944–45, Villa-Lobos promoted his own universalist platform even as he flirted with Hollywood and the culture industry. The latter comes to light in *Magdalena*, his foray into the American musical, which I read in the context of Pan Americanism's abrupt deterioration during the early years of the cold war.

This new period in north-south relations is elaborated in chapter 6. Its opening snapshot captures the premiere of Ginastera's avant-garde and sexually explicit opera *Bomarzo* in Washington, D.C. in May 1967, which was greeted with a ten-minute standing ovation led by Vice President Hubert Humphrey. Eschewing the tourist nationalism U.S. critics had attacked in his earlier music, Ginastera came to pursue so-called cold war values, such as complexity and abstruseness, and proved so attuned to his era that one critic even tagged him a "musical Robert McNamara." A key factor in his success was sublimation, analyzed here in terms of Freudian psychoanalysis, then at the height of its popularity in the United States. Yet on the heels of *Bomarzo's* triumph in Washington, the Argentine military government throttled the opera's Buenos Aires premiere due to its sexual content. When *Bomarzo* was performed in New York a year later, critics effectively targeted difference by smugly expressing surprise over the Argentine government's action and implicitly proposing that censorship was fit only for "other countries." By this time the United States had resumed intervening in Latin America, shelving Good Neighborly promises to support anticommunist dictators.

As the cold war progressed and Pan Americanist accord became an ever fainter memory, musical priorities fractured. The opening snapshot of chapter 7 highlights a 1975 performance in New York City of *nueva canción*, a folkloric Latin American protest genre that arose during the 1950s and 1960s and was known in some countries as *música nacional*. Often explicitly anti-U.S., it asserted local or regional identity, especially in the face of the Dirty War (*guerra sucia*), the rash of atrocities and "disappearances" perpetrated throughout Latin America by various military dictatorships. It also attracted the U.S. composer and Marxist sympathizer Frederic Rzewski, whose fifty-minute virtuosic piano piece, *36 Variations on "The People United Will Never Be Defeated!,"* is rooted in the world of *nueva canción*. Unlike *El salón México* or Gershwin's *Cuban Overture*, with their snappy dance rhythms, *The People United* commemorates one of the bleakest moments in U.S.–Latin American relations: the CIA-assisted coup that brought Augusto Pinochet to power in Chile. By reading the variations through a Pan Americanist lens and drawing on theories of Freud and Paul Ricoeur, I propose that the work's unusual formal structure explicates processes of memory and forgetting, both central concerns in Latin America today. Memory and forgetting are also germane to the historiography of Latin American music in the United States, which, as noted earlier, ultimately forgot sameness-embracing in favor of fetishizing difference. A short epilogue revisits our initial epistemological question in terms of these concerns.

In remembering—rather than dismissing as utopian—that fleeting moment when Latin American music was hopefully applauded in the United States as a complement to our own, and when our vision of "American" music reached beyond the borders of the United States, we can consider the words of Fredric Jameson. He noted that even in the face of huge political differences it is possible to seek a way of talking that "neither reduces the 'third World' to some homogeneous Other of the West, nor . . . vacuously celebrate[s] the 'astonishing' pluralism of human cultures." Instead, Jameson proposes, we can let "differences . . . be measured against each other as well as against ourselves."[49] Jameson set forth these hopes in 1989 for comparative literature. This book invites musicology to contemplate the same.

1 The Roots of Musical Pan Americanism

In early 1964 the U.S. Hispanist Gilbert Chase and Alberto Ginastera corresponded on Chase's upcoming lecture series in Buenos Aires. Chase would speak on American music at the Centro Latinoamericano de Altos Estudios Musicales (Latin American Center of Advanced Musical Studies) in Buenos Aires, which Ginastera had directed since the previous year. In a delicately worded letter to his North American colleague of March 16, Ginastera wondered, however, whether his initial invitation had been clear. He observed, "[You] understood the word 'American' as we understand the word *estadounidense* [of the United States]," and explained, "In speaking of an American aesthetic, I was taking into account the whole continent from Alaska to Tierra del Fuego." He therefore asked that Chase's lectures comprise "fifty percent Latin America and highlight everything from the Mayan and Aztec ruins to the present musical generation of North and South America," diplomatically adding that Chase, with his consummate knowledge of "all America," would have no difficulty in meeting this request.[1] On April 2 Chase acknowledged this semantic-political problem. Promising to modify his lectures according to Ginastera's suggestions, he mentioned that he was well aware of the pitfalls of the term *American*, having addressed them in his book *America's Music from the Pilgrims to the Present*.[2] "We are not North Americans," Chase mused, "because so are Mexicans and Canadians." But he added, "If we don't call ourselves 'Americans,' in the national sense, we're left without any name at all. Sad fate for a great country!"[3]

Nearly three-quarters of a century before this gentlemanly colloquy, the Cuban patriot José Martí published the essay *Our America* (*Nuestra América*), which appeared almost simultaneously in New York and Mexico City.[4] In it Martí noted the vast populations outside U.S. borders who call themselves Americans and who reject both European and U.S. imperialism. Martí also offered his firsthand observations on the United States, having spent three years in New York as a founder of the Cuban Revolutionary Party.[5] He had seen, for example, the extent to which the United States was increasingly modeling itself on the British Empire, a goal it would fulfill in part through enhanced sea power and new colonies in the Caribbean.[6] In 1884 he warned his readers, "In our America it is vital to know the truth about the United States, . . . [a] nation of strapping young men . . . bred over the centuries to the sea and the snow and the virility aided by the perpetual defense of local freedom."[7] While Martí cautioned against exaggerating the faults of the United States, he also maintained that they should be seen for what they were. Shortly before his death in 1895, during the second war for Cuban independence, Martí addressed the United States in more dire terms, writing a friend, "I have lived in the monster and I know its entrails."[8]

Clearly in the naming of America we wrestle with questions of difference, of identifying an "us" and a "them." As Chase pointed out, English lacks an adjective that denotes "of the United States" and distinguishes U.S. citizens from other inhabitants of the Americas, as *estadounidense* (Spanish) and *estadunidense* (Portuguese) do. A term sensitive to history continues to eludes us. Is there a reasonable way, for example, to refer to those territories forfeited by Spain (ostensibly part of "our America"), only to be swallowed up by U.S. military or commercial zeal? The present-day U.S.-Mexican border is the result of both the Treaty of Guadalupe-Hidalgo of 1848, which marked the end of the U.S.-Mexican War, and the Gadsden Purchase of 1853–54, negotiated by the United States to expand its rail system. Vast swaths of what was once Mexico, including all or part of Arizona, New Mexico, Colorado, Utah, California, Nevada, Wyoming, Texas, and Kansas, were absorbed in short order by the United States. As the director of the Proyecto Latino de Utah, Tony Yapias, has noted, "no one asked Brigham Young for his papers" when the founder of the Mormon Church ventured westward to the Great Salt Lake.[9] Objections have been raised over the naming of America in *West Side Story*, in which the mordant song "America" clearly denotes the United States even as the Puerto Ricans who sing it hail from what is for all intents and purposes a U.S. colony.[10] However much residents of the United States are encouraged to attach inevitability or permanence to their nation's political borders—to the point of building fences along them—difference percolates within and without, even as assimilation and sameness-embracing beckon.

Pan Americanism proposes that the Americas are linked by common interests, or, as Chase put it, "common ideals of peace, friendship, and cooperation." Yet many Pan Americanisms exist, motivated by political, economic, commercial, cultural, and affective needs. This chapter surveys both the historical roots of this phenomenon and some of the means by which Pan Americanist ideas first insinuated themselves into musical life in the United States.

▪ HISTORICAL PREMISES

Although many U.S. scholars take the Monroe Doctrine of 1823 as a starting point for Pan Americanism, Simón de Bolívar, the Venezuelan liberator, floated the idea of Pan *Latin* American unity in 1815.[11] One consequence of his "Jamaica Letter" of that year was the Congress of Panama in 1826, at which representatives of the newly independent Latin American republics debated over whether to establish a confederation of American states. One sticking point was the role of the United States, whose delegates arrived only after the conference had ended. Some attendees argued for including it, whereas others insisted that any

U.S. presence would antagonize Great Britain, a necessary ally; Bolívar himself was in the latter camp.[12] Three years earlier the United States had rejected partnership with Great Britain through the Monroe Doctrine, which was conceived to stave off foreign encroachments into the newly independent Spanish territories.[13] In asserting that the United States and its vast new territories were unique in "the history of the world," the Doctrine also established a precedent for American (U.S.) exceptionalism.[14]

By the middle of the nineteenth century, buoyed by sentiments of Manifest Destiny, the Doctrine was rendered essentially meaningless in the territory grabs of the U.S.-Mexican War, itself rooted largely in notions of Anglo-Saxon superiority. The 1850 census itself averred that the primarily Teutonic and Anglo-Saxon population of the United States would, like its European counterpart, "fulfill its own destiny, in accordance with a system of laws as unalterable and supreme as those which control the physical universe."[15] Nineteenth-century U.S. academics, aware that Darwin himself privileged the Anglo-Saxon, extrapolated from this fact that Anglo-Saxon (Protestant) political institutions were superior to those of the Hispanic (Catholic) South.[16] These attitudes coalesced in 1904, when President Theodore Roosevelt expanded the Monroe Doctrine in a corollary that upheld the prohibition against European intervention in the hemisphere while allowing that in cases of "chronic wrongdoing or impotence" in Latin America, the "great free people" of the United States could intervene.[17]

In the glaring light of history, the Roosevelt corollary appears as little more than a gloss on existing practices. In early 1898 the rallying cry of the Spanish-American War ("Remember the Maine! To hell with Spain!") rang throughout a nation in thrall to the promise of world power. After easily defeating Spain, the United States essentially replaced one colonial power with another, making Cuba a U.S. protectorate through the Platt Amendment and squelching the ideals of Martí's followers.[18] Another result of the war was the annexation and direct rule of the Philippines by the United States, along with the ceding of Puerto Rico and Guam. Roosevelt's "taking" (as he himself put it) of the Panama Canal in 1903, effected by destabilizing the Colombian government, also extended U.S. power.

The "Big Stick" also prevailed in the commercial realm, motivated by no less fervent notions of Anglo-Saxon superiority.[19] President Chester A. Arthur investigated possibilities for trade in Latin America by sending to various countries a commission on which the Chicago journalist William Eleroy Curtis sat. Although Curtis spoke neither Spanish nor Portuguese, he saw fit to mete out judgments on the "Spanish-American race," elements of which he deemed "aggressive, audacious, and arrogant, quick to perceive, quick to resent, fierce in disposition, cold-blooded, and cruel as a cannibal."[20] Curtis's observations of 1888 confirm the enduring power of the centuries-old, anti-Hispanic Black Legend, initially crafted in the sixteenth century by Britain and the Netherlands to stem Spain's colonial might.[21] Most relevant here are the Legend's historical imbalances. In the United States, for example, historians and journalists have compared Spanish "plunderers" and "gold seekers" with English "nation builders" and "colonizers," overlooking the *overall* rapaciousness of the colonial period to proffer perfervid descriptions of "rapine and pillage" or "inconceivable brutality" under the Spanish flag, as proposed in an 1898 study by Henry Watterson.[22] As for Curtis, he was chosen to lead the Bureau of the American Republics, despite his antipathy toward his southern neighbors. This entity (the forerunner of the Pan American Union) was established at the First International Conference of American States, held in Washington in 1889 and where the main subject was commerce.

In the hopes of smoothing over any possible tensions, Latin American delegates were taken on a six-week tour of the United States, visiting industrial centers, universities, hospitals, and libraries and also attending concerts and plays. This intensive exposure to culture and ideas sparked optimism over hemispheric goodwill. James B. Angell, president of the University of Michigan, declared to his Latin American guests, "Whatever obstacles there may be to the exchange of material products of your countries and our country, there is no obstacle to the exchange of thought"; appealing to ideals of north-south amity, Angell added, "Are we not members of one intellectual household?"[23] In Milwaukee a local official claimed that the presence of the delegates, who were often met by curious and enthusiastic crowds at train stations, had "electrified the nation": "No civil event has for many years so engaged the whole people. The merchant in his store, the farmer at the plow, the brawny artisan and even the school-boy who dreams over the maps of the three Americas—all catch the inspiration of the new evangel, 'Pan-America.'"[24]

Some influential figures in the United States broke ranks with their government by favoring the Pan American "evangel" over U.S. imperialism. Having worked in a bobbin factory, Andrew Carnegie, the Scottish immigrant turned steel magnate, wondered why, in the aftermath of the Spanish-American War, the United States would "hang in the school-houses of the Philippines the Declaration of our own Independence, and yet deny independence to [Filipinos]."[25] In the election of 1900 William Jennings Bryan presented himself as an anti-imperialist, although he was easily defeated by the expansionist William McKinley. The Democrat Woodrow Wilson initially criticized interventionism, which many associated with his Republican predecessors. Yet in 1914 the chief representative of what came to be known as Wilsonian idealism ordered the occupation of the Mexican port of Veracruz (because of conflicts over an arms shipment) and three years later sent an expeditionary force of six thousand to quash Francisco (Pancho) Villa, among other incursions in the region.

Another project was dollar diplomacy, the effort to nudge foreign territories toward U.S. financial practices. Engineers of dollar diplomacy employed several strategies with respect to Latin America, which could include assuming debt to European nations, establishing U.S. financial institutions in Latin American countries, or imposing U.S. control on customs offices to ensure payments to U.S. lenders. For F. M. Huntington Wilson, the former assistant secretary of state in the Taft administration, dollar diplomacy rested on the science of Darwinism. In 1916 he declared:

> [The] march of civilization brooks no violation of the law of the survival of the fittest. Neighboring countries comprise an environment. The strongest will dominate that environment.... The biological law of the tendency to revert to the lower type as the higher attributes are disused is at work among nations; and nature, in its rough method of uplift, gives sick nations strong neighbors and takes its inexorable course with private enterprise and diplomacy as its instruments. And this course is the best in the long run, for all concerned and for the world.[26]

Others in the United States defended these weaker nations, believing that their peoples *could* flourish in modern economic systems. These individuals, many of them missionaries, initiated a service ideal, which exerted U.S. influence by spreading Protestant Christianity, teaching baseball (sportsmanship), or showing U.S. movies.[27] In short, attitudes in the United States toward Latin America during the first decades of the twentieth century rested on a mix of paternalism, exploitation, interventionism, and curiosity.

This complex of attitudes and behaviors served as the foundation of the Informal Empire, the pithy term used by Salvatore and others. If most Latin American countries were not bona fide colonies of the United States, many depended on the United States economically or were bound by political ties. This often uneasy relationship was reflected both in the discourse just excerpted and in material culture. At turn-of-the-century world's fairs, for example, natural resources—all potential commodities—dominated displays of Latin America. Burlap sacks overflowing with coffee beans, lengths of cured leather, quantities of tobacco, or *mate* might be assigned to a pavilion marked "Agriculture," where these items were guarded by a "native."[28] Ultimately, however, U.S. fairgoers reveled in their own "culture of abundance" (Warren Susman's term), eagerly comparing U.S. financial systems, Protestant Christianity, and the virtues of the free market with the workings of less favored countries.[29] As William Appleman Williams argues in *Empire as a Way of Life*, the mere perception of this difference is fundamental to imperialism.[30] Material and discursive practices such as these also recall the oft-cited observation of Edward Said that "the enterprise of having an empire depends upon the *idea of having an empire*."[31]

Certainly not all Latin Americans resented the United States. If Bolívar doubted its sincerity in the 1820s, President Domingo Faustino Sarmiento of Argentina, who visited the United States in the mid-1840s, was impressed with many aspects of its political life. Emperor Pedro II of Brazil, an admirer of Abraham Lincoln, toured the United States in 1876. Some Latin Americans wrote sympathetically of Pan Americanism. In the journal *Inter-America*, published by the New York–based Hispanic Society of America (founded in 1904 to promote the culture of Spain, Portugal, and Latin America), the Chilean jurist Alejandro Álvarez reminded his readers in 1923 that Pan Americanism was neither commercial nor military but rested on mutual history and destiny. Common interests included revolting against European powers, aspiring to democracy, and living under similar social and economic conditions. All, he urged, should inform policy and inspire hemispheric spirit.[32] From 1890 on, various north-south conferences were held on political, economic, legal, and scientific themes, often with the collaboration of universities.[33]

But for many Latin Americans, Martí's account of the "monster's entrails" resonated. Among those who inveighed against the United States was the Mexican author José María Roa Bárcena, who looked back on the U.S.-Mexican War as little more than a power play by the United States, "executed calmly and cold-bloodedly in a manner truly Saxon." (To be sure, he also criticized the lack of wherewithal on the part of his countrymen.)[34] In 1904 the Nicaraguan poet Rubén Darío penned his incendiary "To Roosevelt," a poem that condemns the twenty-sixth president as "the invader of our guileless America."[35] The writer José Ingenieros of Argentina, a country that by the 1920s was widely considered the equal of the United States for its natural resources, public education system, and stable democracy, held forth in 1922 in the *Revista de Filosofía* on financial imperialism in Latin America on the part of the United States, a "powerful neighbor and meddlesome friend" whose government had become increasingly dominated by corporations.[36]

Others addressed culture and sensibility. In 1900 the Uruguayan philosopher and literary historian José Enrique Rodó published *Ariel*, a slim volume that was widely read in Latin America into the 1940s. In it Rodó described a beloved teacher whom he calls Prospero, after the exiled master of the magic arts in Shakespeare's so-called New World drama, *The Tempest*. Prospero's students prod their enlightened master to explain their cultural heritage; in response, he takes as a point of comparison the United States, excoriating its obsession with material gain and "fervent pursuit of well-being that has no object beyond itself."[37] The Colossus of the North, Prospero warns, will obliterate Latin America's high culture of European inheritance no less crudely than Caliban, Shakespeare's formless monster, sought to spread his evil influence on the deserted island where the action of *The Tempest* unfolds. Preserving this high culture, which Rodó considered "Latin," was thus an urgent matter; since Caliban (the United States) showed no "inclination to aid in allowing excellence to rise above general mediocrity," it was up to Latin America to avoid cultural contamination. That task was entrusted to the graceful sprite Ariel, whose strong but subtle influence could safeguard the Latin spirit against the encroachments—political, commercial, but primarily cultural—of the North.

As several scholars have pointed out, *arielismo* is a natural response to U.S. hegemony.[38] But it also reinforces difference—between an economically and politically superior United States and a culturally superior Latin America, between "high" and "low" culture, and between elites and masses. Remarking on Rodó's confidence in hierarchy and privilege, Carlos Fuentes has declared *Ariel* "a supremely irritating book."[39] Another telling difference lies in readings of *The Tempest* in the United States. If it inspired *arielismo* for Rodó, the play struck Leo Marx as an archetype for *Moby-Dick, Walden,* or *Huckleberry Finn*. In his well-known essay *The Machine in the Garden*, Marx equates these independent protagonists who courageously seek redemption through nature, far from society's constraints, to William Bradford conquering the "hidious desert" filled with "wild beasts and wild men" as Bradford himself recalled of 1620.[40] Yet just as Prospero imposed his will, that very taming of the wilderness unleashed the violence of imperialism throughout the hemisphere.[41]

The idea of musical Pan Americanism took hold in the United States after World War I, albeit under a broader umbrella of general culture. Reeling from the catastrophe, intellectuals and artists concurred with Ezra Pound that civilization itself had been "botched" and Victorian notions of elite culture were suspect.[42] On the premise that "emotional and aesthetic starvation" were at hand, the writer Harold Stearns began holding meetings at his home in New York during the fall of 1920 to discuss the state of American civilization and explore ways to make "a real civilization possible."[43] A 1922 essay collection featuring Van Wyck Brooks, Lewis Mumford, H. L. Mencken, Elsie Clews Parsons, and others offers a compendium of their reflections. The composer Deems Taylor, for example, let loose an uninhibited screed on the lack of an authentic musical culture in the United States. He railed against "sterile" material and psychological conditions, along with a lack of "aesthetic emotions," which the music of a nation will ordinarily reflect. In contrast to France, Germany, or Italy, the United States lacked this collective aesthetic, because although a nation, it was not "also a race."[44] Confronting Anglo-Saxon superiority directly, Stearns boldly declared in his preface to the 1922 collection that "whatever else [U.S.] American civilization is, it is not Anglo-Saxon."[45] Both points would prove fundamental to musical Pan Americanism.

■ PAN AMERICANISM AND MUSIC: BEGINNINGS

For decades composers and critics had been thrashing out questions of U.S. musical identity. In December 1893 Antonín Dvořák's Symphony in E Minor ("From the New World") premiered in Carnegie Hall, the fruit of Dvořák's initial intention to write an opera or oratorio on Longfellow's *Hiawatha*, a project Richard Taruskin calls "a Herderian object lesson" to composers seeking a national voice.[46] As is well known, the symphony aroused controversy over ethnicity, identity, and musical models.[47] Less commented on is the fact that Latin America figured in the debate, albeit fleetingly. In a 1910 program note, the Boston critic Philip Hale lashed out at all those musics he considered unfit to serve as a foundation for a U.S. school of composition, targeting "Greaser ditties" along with "congo, North American Indian, Creole . . . and Cowboy ditties, whinings, yawps, and whoopings."[48]

What, exactly, were these "Greaser ditties" that so incensed Hale? The term *greaser* dates from the beginning of the twentieth century, when many Mexicans, working at loading pies onto the boats in California shipyards, absorbed the lard from the pies into their skin, becoming greasy.[49] After the Mexican Revolution broke out in 1910 and many feared the proximity of anarchic mobs just over the border, Hollywood was inspired to invent one of film history's first "bad guys" in the person of the greaser. This dark-skinned, mayhem-prone, and uniquely Mexican villain appeared in movies such as *The Greaser's Gauntlet* (1910), *The Greaser's Revenge* (1911), and *Licking the Greasers* (1914).[50] Of course, the greaser was hardly the only anti-Hispanic stereotype in the public imagination; buttressed by Black Legend sentiment, film directors, political cartoonists, and authors conjured up the wild-eyed radical, the bandit, the loose woman, or the somnolent Indian perpetually snoozing under a sombrero.[51]

As for music associated with "greasers," it is hard to know how broadly to interpret Hale's barb. Was he acquainted, for example, with the songs of the post–Gold Rush Southwest? The three-hundred-odd Spanish-language songs that Charles Fletcher Lummis recorded on wax cylinders in 1904 and 1905 would hardly seem to qualify as ditties, since many contain echoes of Donizetti; no less a musician than Lummis's assistant Arthur Farwell described the "charm, spontaneity, and grace" in this repertory, itself a testament to a long-standing oral tradition.[52] The burgeoning recording industry targeted middle-class Hispanics on both sides of the border, with companies such as Berliner, Zonophone, and Edison beckoning Latin American artists northward from the 1890s on. In turn-of-the-century New York City, the Cuban soprano Rosalía Gertrudis de la Concepción Díaz de Herrera y Fonseca (known more succinctly onstage as Rosalía Chalía) recorded Latin American popular songs; in 1912 she returned for additional sessions.[53] Eugenia Ferrer, Esperanza Iris, and María Conesa recorded songs such as "Los lindos ojos" by Manuel Ferrer (father of Eugenia) or selections from *zarzuela* (Spanish-language operetta), music that blurs the boundaries between art and popular music.[54] So too did the waltz "Sobre las olas," composed in 1888 by Juventino Rosas, an Otomí Indian who lived near Mexico City. Between 1890 and 1920 it was frequently recorded (including one rendering by John Philip Sousa) and figured at skating rinks and fairgrounds and in movies, sometimes under the title "The Loveliest Night of the Year," all with little material advantage for Rosas.[55] Other well-known Spanish-language songs were "La Paloma," by the Spanish composer Sebastián de Iradier, and "Estrellita" and "Perjura," by the Mexican composers Manuel Ponce and Miguel Lerdo de Tejada, respectively; in 1919 a collection titled *Canciones Mexicanas* was published in New York as an attempt to break into the Tin Pan Alley market.[56] During the 1920s "Estrellita" figured prominently in arrangements and was performed by art music luminaries such as Jascha Heifetz, reflecting the flexibility of genre, audience, and status just discussed.[57]

Spanish-language theater and its musical components have a venerable history in the Americas. The first opera performed in the Western Hemisphere was Tomás Torrejón y Velasco's *La púrpura de la rosa* (The Blood of the Rose),[58] on a text by Calderón de la Barca and mounted in Lima at the Viceregal Palace in 1701. The first opera by an American-born composer staged in the hemisphere was Manuel de Zumaya's *Partenope* of 1711.[59] Before the U.S.-Mexican War, Spanish-language theater was largely an ad hoc affair confined to what eventually became the southwestern United States. After 1850, however, when the Eagle and Merced theaters were built in Sacramento and Los Angeles, respectively, touring companies began making the arduous journey by stagecoach from Fort Worth to San Diego, some settling in cities such as Tucson and Santa Fe.[60] These troupes from Mexico, Spain, Cuba, and sometimes Argentina might visit New York, Philadelphia, Cleveland, Detroit, and Chicago before heading west to Los Angeles.[61] They also traveled the New York–Florida circuit, ending in Tampa or Miami and encompassing various points in between. Although theater in the Southwest generally emphasized a Mexican perspective, productions were often loosely billed as "Spanish," probably to diffuse anti-Mexican sentiment.[62]

In New York, with its smaller concentration of Mexicans, the Hispanic community was more international. Martí was only one of many independence-minded Cubans to reside there at the end of the nineteenth century. New York was something of a Mecca for Cubans and Puerto Ricans involved in such movements, and their efforts were sometimes supported with proceeds from theatrical performances. The Cuban composer and pianist Ignacio Cervantes lived in New York in 1875–79, also for political reasons. By the 1920s, however, most Spanish speakers in New York were from the erstwhile colonial power. The *colonia*, as this community was known, numbered around thirty thousand by the mid-1930s, mostly workers from northwest Spain. Some brought with them a love of zarzuela, their national lyric genre. In 1916 the Spanish-born actor Manuel Noriega moved to New York and produced zarzuelas in the Amsterdam Opera House, Carnegie Hall, and the Park Theater, accelerating a tradition that had begun at the end of the nineteenth century.[63] An especially successful zarzuela was *La Tierra de la alegría* (Land of Joy), with music by Quinito Valverde. A story of U.S. tourists in Spain, *La Tierra de la alegría* attracted plenty of attention in the press, and critics were much taken with the dancer "La Argentina." Works by the well-known Spanish theatrical team the Álvarez Quintero brothers, along with classic zarzuelas such as *Maruxa* (Amadeu Vives), *La corte de Faraón* (Vicente Lleó), and *Molinos de viento* (Pablo Luna), were featured at a variety of theaters as companies established themselves and a skilled community of actors and impresarios promoted zarzuela in the press. Not for nothing have the 1920s and early 1930s been called a "Golden Period of Hispanic Theater" in New York.[64]

Latin influence also made itself felt in jazz. In the first years of the twentieth century, Jelly Roll Morton experimented with what he called the "Spanish tinge," evocative of New Orleans (and palpable in the music of an earlier Creole, Louis Moreau Gottschalk).[65] Sheet music by Cuban, Spanish, and Mexican composers, especially the better-known tunes such as "La Paloma" and "La Golondrina," was available in music stores throughout the United States.[66] Potential for cross-over remained high. The Cuban composer Ernesto Lecuona, for example, composed cantatas and performed at Aeolian Hall in 1914 before organizing his rhumba band (*rumba* in Spanish).[67] The classically trained Catalan violinist Xavier Cugat also capitalized on the rhumba, conquering Hollywood. Another Latin American ballroom dance to dazzle the U.S. public was the Argentine tango, the suggestive steps of which were presented to U.S. ballroom enthusiasts in a wholesome, toned-down version by Vernon and Irene Castle in the 1914 revue *Watch Your Step* and which also inspired art music composers such as Igor Stravinsky, Conlon Nancarrow, and, as discussed in chapter 3, Chávez.[68]

By the 1920s the lines of debate over U.S. musical identity had been drawn.[69] Should composers embrace the African and native American legacy, as Dvořák had proposed? Aspire to European high culture, as had been done for much of the nineteenth century? Pay homage to the European heritage but adapt it to American circumstances through, say, folk music?[70] Or perhaps, as Copland later recalled, the most desirable alternative was to create a music that would "speak of universal things in a vernacular of American speech rhythms."[71] Insinuating themselves in these debates were questions of historical imperative, a topic Brooks explored in his seminal essay, "On Creating a Usable Past."[72] Marshaling well-nigh military language to attack "the professorial mind" (an "old guard" guilty of "cutting off supplies" to youth), Brooks noted the lack of cultural heritage in the United States. Much like Deems Taylor, he observed that the United States had no racial heritage on which to draw. Given this lacuna, Brooks called upon his compatriots to stimulate their historical memories to "discover, invent a usable past."

At the same time, an increasing number of Latin American art music composers began to come north. In 1920 Nino Marcelli, who was born in Rome but emigrated to Chile as a child, arrived in the United States, where he composed his *Suite Araucana*, loosely based on the Chilean epic that treats Araucana Indians' resistance to the Spanish invader; Marcelli eventually founded the San Diego Symphony.[73] During the 1910s and early 1920s, the Mexican composer Silvestre Revueltas studied in Texas and Chicago, leading a theater orchestra in Alabama before returning home in 1929.[74] The music of his compatriot Julián Carrillo, who lived in the United States from 1926 to 1928, became known thanks to events such as the 1926 concert sponsored by the New York–based League of Composers, which featured his microtonal *Sonata casi Fantasía*; a performance of his *Concertino* by the Philadelphia Orchestra followed a year later.[75] Just as Ponce's Mexican folk songs were applauded in New York, so too were some of his guitar pieces, introduced in the United States by the Spanish guitarist Andrés Segovia, who toured there for the first time in 1928.[76] As detailed in chapter 2, 1928 also saw the founding of the Pan American Association of Composers (PAAC), which showcased music of Chávez, Villa-Lobos, Revueltas, Alejandro García Caturla, Amadeo Roldán, and other Latin Americans.

Throughout the 1920s political relations between the United States and Latin America remained rocky. Intervening in Nicaragua, Haiti, and the Dominican Republic (besides Mexico, Cuba, Puerto Rico, and Colombia previously), the United States extended its hemispheric reach at what many considered an appalling rate. In 1928 Clarence H. Haring, a scholar from the Bureau of International Research of Harvard University and Radcliffe College, concluded, "The plain fact of the matter is that today we control the political destinies of Mexico, Central America and other nearby Latin regions as effectively as if we exercised a formal protectorate over the entire area."[77] The same author called U.S. ignorance of Latin America "nothing short of colossal."[78]

The foundations for musical Pan Americanism were thus rooted in a complex history. One scholar acknowledges the elasticity of broader Pan Americanism, noting that "with or without the hyphen," the concept has served as "a movement, a cause, a sentiment, a dream, a spiritual union, an advocacy, an aspiration, or a quasi-legal embodiment of a fraternity of the nations of the Western Hemisphere."[79] Among the many Pan Americanist musical ideologies discussed in this book, the notion of an American art music separate from that of Europe remains a central although controversial principle. The concept was shaped by a variety of forces. Many art music composers responded to commercial Pan Americanism, influenced by Latin ballroom dances, Tin Pan Alley, and the music of a spate of frothy Hollywood movies during the Good Neighbor period, with their catchy, percussion-heavy scores. During World War II patriotic Pan Americanism called upon north-south amity to eliminate Nazism in the hemisphere, resulting in musical curiosities such as Henry Cowell's *Fanfare for the Forces of Our Latin American Allies* and Clough Lighter's *Christ of the Andes Symphony*. Although socialist-progressive Pan Americanism attracted many composers, artists, and intellectuals, corporate Pan Americanism was effectively created by business and conservative constituencies; indeed, whatever the reservations of Rodó and Ingenieros, some projects by the magnates of industry complicate subsequent charges of political motives.[80] In sum, musical Pan Americanism reflected—and helped shape—a discourse embedded in government, business, humanitarian, and aesthetic interests. It was given voice through elite and popular cultural expressions, a potentially volatile mix of values explored in the rest of this book.

2　Carlos Chávez and Ur-Classicism

On April 22, 1928, at the Edyth Totten Theatre on West Forty-eighth Street, New York's musical public applauded the first of the Copland-Sessions Concerts of Contemporary Music.[1] As the next day's *New York Herald Tribune* reported, the series had been established "for the laudable purpose of presenting works chiefly by the younger generation of American composers . . . providing [them] with a means of testing their work in performance."[2] Venturing forth on this occasion were Theodor Chanler, Walter Piston, Virgil Thomson, and Carlos Chávez.[3] Then on his second trip to the United States, Chávez played his third piano sonata, a last-minute substitution for the sonata Roger Sessions had failed to finish on time; also featured were Chávez's three sonatinas (for solo piano, cello and piano, violin and piano).[4] The reception of these works was decidedly mixed. Although the anonymous reviewer for the *Tribune* noted a "sympathetic audience," that individual bestowed only tepid endorsement; despite the sonata's "vigorous and forthright" qualities, the work was judged "scarcely rewarding" and the three sonatinas even "less interesting."[5] Richard L. Stokes of the *Evening World* was downright scornful. "As for Carlos Shavez [*sic*]," he fulminated, "if there was any merit in his clangorous ineptitudes, it lay in the ability to get his sprawlings on paper at all."[6] W. J. Henderson of the *New York Sun* avoided comment on Chávez altogether.[7] Winthrop P. Tyron, however, admired the "uncompromising severity" of Chávez's music; of the sonata, moreover, he observed that it "affects the classic."[8]

Given this concentration of sonatas and sonatinas, we might imagine the concert to have been something of a showcase for neoclassicism. (Adding to this impression was Piston's *Three Pieces for Flute, Clarinet, and Bassoon*, itself a whiff of that icon of neoclassicist ideology, Stravinsky's Octet of 1923.) Certainly neoclassicism was generating plenty of discussion in U.S. musical circles during the 1920s.[9] But in the case of Chávez, those critics who admired his music—and there were a handful—heard something quite different. Some considered it primitive, the first time it was so perceived.[10] Even in the absence of programmatic referents, Downes sensed "Mexican Indian themes," which he found to be filled with "primitive joy, but without softness or mercy," such that the end result was "brutal." Carried away by notions of Indian brutality, Downes further conjectured that "if [Chávez] did not scalp, he tomahawked the keyboard" and that this approach, "as someone remarked, was counterpoint for you."[11] More matter-of-factly, Copland applauded Chávez's ability to echo the "ritualistic music of the Mexican Indian."[12]

These reactions, however, have little to do with the way Chávez presented himself in his own country, namely, as a cosmopolitan modernist. When his Sextet of

1919 was performed in Mexico City, he was upbraided for succumbing to the then-current influence of Debussy and Ravel; upon hearing Chávez's String Quartet of 1921, the critic for the Mexico City daily *Excelsior* attacked its "dissonances and absurd combinations."[13] Undaunted, Chávez defended modernism, sometimes aggressively, in numerous essays for the Mexican musical press.[14] He also contemplated strategies for forging a Mexican identity in modern art music, although here he was inclined to follow the lead of his compatriot Ponce, who considered *mestizo* popular song a more viable point of departure than "straight" Indian music.[15] In the United States Chávez's identity as a Mexican Indian culminated with his best-known composition, the *Sinfonía India* of 1936, understood as primitive and Other even today.

Tyron was not the only critic who found classic traits in Chávez's music, however. Others classicized Chávez's Mexican Indian musical persona and in doing so embraced sameness. They conferred on it universalism, timelessness, transcendence, authenticity, clarity, organicism (sometimes referred to as "wholeness"), objectivity, and the formal and affective restraint associated with absolute music, that is, values commonly understood as classic.[16] At stake here was a usable past. Much the way the Florentine Camerata invented its ancient roots, U.S. critics fashioned a narrative of an American music imbued with the authority of a venerable and ancient tradition equivalent to that of Greece and Rome.[17] These formulations, moreover, were echoed in anthropology, architecture, and the visual arts. Equally compelling was the conceit of the tabula rasa, a favorite Pan Americanist trope that signified all that was pristine, unprecedented, and hopeful in the Americas.[18] As the art historian E. H. Gombrich observes, "primitive," often understood in artistic discourse as "harsh" or "severe" ("brutal," for Downes), also means "close to origins."[19] Chávez's music suggested no less than a creation myth for American music, one in which the classic and the primitive merged. Ur-classicism, moreover, could encompass the entire hemisphere.

■ UR-CLASSICISM IN CONTEXT

Ur-classicism was the antithesis of *neo*classicism, equated in U.S. musical circles with Stravinsky and his followers, most of whom were based in France.[20] In accordance with the much-trumpeted conceit of "pure music," neoclassical composers drew (mainly) on eighteenth-century forms to purge their art of programmatic meaning, often sneered at as "literature," "philosophy," or "metaphysics" and associated with German music, especially that of the late nineteenth century.[21] (Bach was largely exempted from this anti-Teutonic fervor, with the result that some dubbed neoclassicism the "back to Bach" movement.) Neoclassicism's roots in the presumably French characteristics of wit, brevity, and refinement challenged not only German musical values, predictable enough in the aftermath of World War I, but also primitivism. Stravinsky, for example, vociferously disparaged that primitivist work par excellence, his own *Rite of Spring*. In the wake of its attention-grabbing premiere, the composer shunned the ancient Russia it depicted and tsk-tsked over its "wastefully large" performing forces, instead extolling the refinements of composers such as Mozart and Tchaikovsky, the latter often criticized as overly European.[22] Stravinsky also distanced himself from whatever nationalist or exoticist associations primitivism might accrue, insisting in 1924 to a Spanish interviewer, "To make Russian music it is unnecessary to sport a long boyar's beard and an oriental caftan."[23] Neoclassicism, on the other hand, was not only "pure" but cosmopolitan. Its modernity resided in the rejection of the immediate past (late romanticism), in flavoring eighteenth-century genres considered universal with contemporary-sounding harmonies or manipulating their traditional forms, often toward parodic or ironic ends.

Several U.S. composers were convinced that neoclassicism was tainted by the Old World. Dane Rudhyar held that it was "a strictly European attitude," adding, "The crux of the whole matter is whether or not one . . . wishes to identify oneself with the spirit of orthodox Europeanism."[24] For Cowell, neoclassicism was essentially a soporific: "easy to compose, easy to understand, easy to forget."[25] Farwell, calling on the glories of the Western canon, considered neoclassicism "devoid of vision or aspiration, [of] even a real knowledge of the principles of the great classic composers."[26] Others took a dim view of neoclassicism's quirky combination of historicism and modernism. Downes, for example, found "vain and artificial" the attempts by French composers to escape "fevered romanticism"; all told, he concluded, there was nothing new in "this business."[27] In 1928 the Russian composer Arthur Lourie (later an expatriate to the United States) argued in *Modern Music* that neoclassicism was little more than "a current formula."[28]

One entity that rejected Europeanism, orthodox or otherwise, was the Pan American Association of Composers, which addressed growing curiosity about Latin America by promoting recent music by composers of the Western Hemisphere. According to an early mission statement, the PAAC was open only to citizens of the Americas (North, Central, South); in addition to its founders Edgard Varèse (in the United States since 1915), Cowell, and Chávez, members included Rudhyar, Charles Ives, Ruth Crawford, Carl Ruggles, Silvestre Revueltas, Acario Cotapos of Chile, José André of Argentina, and Amadeo Roldán of Cuba.[29] Initially the PAAC attracted little notice in New York, its home base. Meetings were infrequent, partly due to the geographical distances separating its constituents and perhaps also to administrative ennui; as one member later complained, "There wasn't even any stationery."[30] Yet of the six composers most frequently performed in PAAC concerts—Ives, Wallingford Riegger, Chávez, Roldán, Villa-Lobos, and Alejandro García Caturla—four were Latin Americans. This level of attention to Latin American art music was unprecedented in the United States.

That the PAAC survived at all was largely thanks to no less a challenger to the European tradition than Ives. His financial support enabled Slonimsky, the

PAAC's unofficial conductor, to perform its aggressively modernist repertory in Europe; Slonimsky also conducted in Havana and New York, where he worked with a small but dedicated group of musicians.[31] Foreign critics excoriated the PAAC's performances as "pandemonium" or "cacophonous tumult," with one German reviewer dubbing Ruggles's *Sun Treader* a "Latrine-Treader" for its "bowel constrictions in an atonal, Tristanesque ecstasy."[32] Alfred Einstein considered the PAAC's repertory in terms of a creation myth (a decidedly negative one) since not only did the music eschew "almost any relation to the past," but it lacked "all capacity to create a new order."[33] In the United States critics concerned for their international reputation fretted over the PAAC's radical modernism. Confounded by Slonimsky's neglect of Arthur Foote, Deems Taylor, and Charles Martin Loeffler, Hale (previously exercised over "greaser ditties") held that the "wild-eyed anarchists" of the PAAC in no way represented current musical trends in the United States.[34] When the PAAC featured Latin American works with a classical bent, however, critics complained of staleness. In November 1933 a reviewer for *Musical America* found Villa-Lobos's Trio for Oboe, Clarinet, and Bassoon "a surprisingly academic work in strict sonata form, showing little originality and much imitation."[35] Clearly universalism and hemispheric identity were far from easy to reconcile.

Also expounding on the state of music in the Americas was Paul Rosenfeld, who, along with Copland and Downes, reflected on the Chávez works heard at the April 1928 concert. Rosenfeld devoted his career to defending artistic authenticity and what he called "wholeness" in publications such as the *New Republic*, *Scribner's Magazine*, and various little magazines, including the *Dial*. Cofounding with Van Wyck Brooks and Waldo Frank the short-lived journal *Seven Arts*, this energetic aesthete also published a host of books, some of which reprint his journalistic essays.[36] Rosenfeld was a champion of modern music who also revered the Western canon and devoted himself to exploring, often quite colorfully, the spiritual circumstances that shape art. His effusive language sometimes made him the object of attack. Edmund Wilson once scripted a dialogue between Rosenfeld and the U.S. author-critic Matthew Josephson, who takes a dig at Rosenfeld by observing, "The day for rhapsody as a substitute for exact aesthetic analysis has long gone by." Undismayed, Rosenfeld retorts, "The life of feeling is always real."[37] Perhaps it was this orientation that so aptly qualified him to translate Robert Schumann's writings into English.[38] As detailed below, Rosenfeld's panegyrics on Chávez were no less spirited than the ringing acclamation ("Hats off, gentlemen, a genius!") with which Schumann introduced Chopin to musical Europe.

Ever wary of criticism that "evidences an obsession with the means of music and a neglect of its substance," Rosenfeld charged full throttle into the ongoing debate on American music.[39] In an essay collection of 1929, he addressed several challenges its would-be creators faced, including communion with the American environment, the need for primordial sources, and, of course, substance.

Jazz, for example, promised "ready-made elysiums" but overlooked the "human environment."[40] In addition to these proto-Adornian reflections on music's dialectic with society, Rosenfeld also held forth on American music's raw materials. Just as Deems Taylor had lamented the absence of authentic musical roots, Rosenfeld targeted folk songs in this regard, which were not only too greatly influenced from without but constituted little more than "deteriorations of . . . primal ideas."[41] Bereft of the primordial, U.S. composers gravitated toward Europe for a usable past.

American composers needed to come to grips with the American environment, to "grasp [their] subject matter robustly, and play in the stream of things."[42] One of Rosenfeld's most cherished conceits, this energy-driven "stream" (elsewhere he refers to "the stream of the world") informs and interacts with human activity much like Henri Bergson's *élan vital*, the force behind the artistic impulse. (In the United States, where Bergson was extremely popular before World War I, the *élan vital* was sometimes tagged the "stream of life.")[43] Composers sensitive to this "stream" were connected to history, geography, and life itself, all necessary ingredients for authentic, original music. As for "things" (Rosenfeld sometimes referred to "thingness"), that equally potent concept smacks of an ur-nomenclature and first principles: an "old Adamic way of naming the individual things of the universe and releasing . . . the energy of meaning . . . gathered in the particularity of . . . things," as one scholar has described Walter Benjamin's epistemological stance.[44]

Chávez's music furnished the ideal pretext for Rosenfeld's ambitious platform. In his 1928 essay, "The Americanism of Carlos Chávez," Rosenfeld considers the works performed at the Copland-Sessions concert in terms of the composer's evolution.[45] He notes, for example, that the "objective form and virginal circumstance" (277) of Chávez's 1925 "Aztec" ballet *Los cuatro soles* (The Four Suns) were only intensified in the piano sonata.[46] "Virginal circumstance" is a key concept. As Rosenfeld proposes, Chávez conjured up these first principles through the vivid imagery his music suggested: of the "Mexican-American cosmos, the rocky, bare New World" (279) or of "his own high deserts" (273). Thus inspired by visions of a vacant and unencumbered terrain, Rosenfeld (who may have been the first to introduce the trope of "austerity" into Chávez criticism) rhapsodizes over its indigenous elements: "deeply affecting primitive singsong" that was "Amerindian in its rigidity and peculiar earthy coarseness," evocations of "Toltec divinities," and "savage, dusty" passages filled with the "echo of Aztec rattlings and scratchings."[47]

What of the classicism in Chávez's music that Rosenfeld calls both "intrinsic" and "veritable"? To be sure, he allows that "an amount" of Chávez's music was "incontrovertibly derived from eighteenth-century European classicism" and thus reflects "something beside" the aboriginal cultures of the Western Hemisphere (279). Yet this "amount" and this "something beside" (Rosenfeld discusses neither) are completely dwarfed by the "original aspects of [Chávez's] work," which are "numerous and preponderant" and, perhaps most significant, whose "pure, severe contours [and] stony corners . . . make us feel America" (279–80).[48] Dismissing with stinging scare quotes neoclassicism's much vaunted purity, Rosenfeld rejects the possibility that Chávez's works "embody a return, like the precise, architectural and 'pure' composition of the Strawinskies" (273), simultaneously exempting him from any charge of herd mentality. Rather, "veritable classic music," the fruit of "virginal circumstance" inherent in Chávez's music, discloses nothing less than the "form and expression of commencing cultures." Gathering momentum, Rosenfeld's breathless paean to "authentic expressive values" continues apace. By the time he exclaims—almost nine pages into his essay—"An original classical music!" it is quite clear that he has no truck with "neo" anything.[49]

These effusions relate directly to Pan Americanism, however. In proposing that Chávez rejected the European past to write on the blank slate of virginal circumstance, Rosenfeld calls to mind an observation of the political scientist Eldon Kenworthy, who identified one of Pan Americanism's core principles, namely, the idea that "the Western Hemisphere is a geographical *tabula rasa*."[50] According to this foundational myth, the pristine, wide-open territories of the Americas ("clean, free lands," as one of President Ronald Reagan's speechwriters would put it) symbolized resistance to external interests and the "freshness" of the New World, to use a term common in Pan Americanist discourse.[51] Visual counterparts to the blank slate abound. They include the vast and open prairies of the U.S. Midwest, the unbounded frontier, the pampas of the Argentine, and of course, Rosenfeld's "high Mexican deserts." Further, more than one history was formulated in terms of virginal circumstance. Perhaps the best known of these in the United States is the so-called frontier hypothesis of Frederick Jackson Turner, who proposed that westward expansion to open, untrammeled spaces was fundamental to U.S. character and behavior.[52] Because the geographical tabula rasa was isolated or barren, the capacity to brave unforgiving climes became a part of the American psyche. At the same time, the sheer newness of the tabula rasa implied malleability or plasticity: the potential to be formed in ways unimagined by previous civilizations.

In Latin America the concept of the tabula rasa has a longer history. Wiping clean the slate of indigenous culture, sixteenth-century Spanish and Portuguese colonists and religious orders brandished the tabula rasa as both philosophy and practice.[53] Over bitter protestations by Indians that the religion of their forefathers was being supplanted by "the worship of a wooden beam they call a cross," *conquistadores* demolished indigenous religious sites and replaced them with Christian monuments such as the cathedrals in Mexico City and Cuzco, built over Aztec and Incan structures, respectively.[54] As Drew Edward Davies has observed, edifices such as Mexico's Durango Cathedral were "developed, from the European perspective, on a tabula rasa."[55] The concept of a Latin American tabula rasa has also mattered to those with less evangelical zeal; in the twentieth century, as many avant-garde visual artists synthesized aboriginal civilizations and modernism, Latin America itself "functioned as a tabula rasa for artistic creation," as Mari Carmen Ramírez notes.[56]

The multifaceted concept of the tabula rasa is invariably complicated by tensions over identity and power, which have emerged at various points in the Pan Americanist project. For the nineteenth-century U.S. historian Francis Parkman, the American continent's untrammeled wilderness represented man's capacity to overcome the unfathomable.[57] Seventy years later, however, the Mexican historian Edmundo O'Gorman argued that the process of transforming an uncharted world found its logical terminus in U.S. individualism, which, in turn, fundamentally shaped U.S. imperialism in Latin America and diminished the indigenous presence.[58] Such debates played themselves out in the realm of culture. Thanks to social Darwinism, many in the United States of the late nineteenth century believed indigenous America to be an inadequate point of origin for U.S. culture. Editors of the *American Journal of Archaeology*, for example, situated ancient America at "a low stage of civilization."[59] Ancient Greece and Rome, on the other hand, furnished a wholly acceptable usable past given their presumed Aryan demographic, which presupposed "even balance [and] fair proportion," classic virtues members of the American Institute of Archaeology approvingly noted.[60] Such a legacy, however, was to be appreciated by the fittest rather than the first Americans. Had Rosenfeld enthused over the "rocky, bare New World" in 1900, likely no one would have questioned the term *New World*, as Gary Tomlinson has recently done, asking, "New to whom?"[61]

■ THE MEXICAN VOGUE AND CLASSIC VALUES

Certainly many in the late 1920s refrained from asking this question as well. But just as Rosenfeld and other New York intellectuals wondered over the fate of their culture, Waldo Frank considered the "lack of spiritual substance" in the United States by looking south in his 1919 book *Our America*.[62] As implied by the title (identical to that of José Martí's essay), Frank believed in the unity of the Americas. Such unity was critical, since substance and wholeness were to be found only through union with the Hispanic world, a point Frank argued in his *Virgin Spain* of 1926.[63] In *The Re-Discovery of America* (1929), Frank bemoaned the fragmentation of self, society, spirituality, and culture in the United States, lambasting the "practical men," Anglo-Saxons who "solve the question of life by begging it," such that the United States was "truly without contact with an organic whole."[64] In other words, Frank felt keenly the lack of something very much like Rosenfeld's "stream of things," with its promise of integration and spiritual plenitude.

The suggestion that organic wholeness, authenticity, and originality lay just across the Rio Grande not only intrigued public intellectuals such as Frank but was abetted by government, commerce, and popular culture. All interacted in the 1920s phenomenon known as the "enormous vogue of things Mexican," discussed in a *New York Times* article from which a study by the historian Helen Delpar takes its title.[65] It claims that the vogue came about "when people gave signs of being fed up with material comforts and turned . . . to primitive cultures."[66] Political relations with Mexico took a cordial turn; whereas U.S. businessmen with holdings in Mexico had feared radical politics in the aftermath of the 1910 revolution and greasers graced the silver screen, by the mid-1920s postrevolutionary fervor seemed to pose little danger. The former U.S. ambassador to Mexico James Rockwell Sheffield had been convinced of "the futility of attempting to treat with a Latin-Indian mind."[67] His successor, Dwight W. Morrow, a former J. P. Morgan banker, sought to mend this frayed relationship. One means to this end was art. Previously, Mexican artists and intellectuals had been leery of U.S. materialism and machine culture and looked to Europe for inspiration. Diego Rivera, for example, resided in Paris almost steadily between 1909 and 1920, where he experimented with cubism in works such as *Man with a Cigarette* (1913) and *Still Life with Gray Bowl* (1915).[68] Likewise, composers such as Ricardo Castro and Ponce also studied in Europe, whereas others, such as Gustavo Campa, were loyal to European models.[69] In the 1920s, however, as public art and *indigenismo* (glorification of Mexico's pre-Conquest past) took hold, the Mexican muralist movement was born. Ambassador Morrow and his wife made friendly overtures to various artists, commissioning from Rivera, who was now back home, murals for the Cortés Palace at Cuernavaca.

In the United States it was the classical properties of this art that critics often noticed. Walter Pach praised the "sure design" and "majesty of proportions" of pre-Columbian Mexican art in the *Dial* in 1920, the year Rosenfeld joined the magazine's staff.[70] Taking classicism as a point of departure, Pach also embraced sameness: defying the social Darwinist outlook of a few decades earlier, he argued not only that pre-Columbian works belonged in museums of art (rather than anthropology) but that they also reflected the "essential oneness" of the Americas.[71] Others embraced sameness with the broad brush of historical memory. In November 1922, when an exhibition of Mexican folk art opened at the Los Angeles Museum of History, Science, and Art, the Mexican consul Leandro Garza Leal declared that "the ideals of the Pilgrims were the same in basis as those of the Mexican Revolutionists, against the Spanish in 1810, against the French in 1863, against Díaz in 1910, and against Huerta in 1917"; like their northern brethren, Mexicans too "were fighting for life, liberty and the pursuit of happiness as they understood it."[72]

The idea that art could cement understanding between the United States and Mexico caught on. Artists such as José Clemente Orozco, Miguel Covarrubias, Jean Charlot (born in France but of Mexican descent), and of course Rivera all visited the United States. In October 1930 New York's Metropolitan Museum of Art mounted an exhibit of Mexican art that ran for four weeks and attracted more than twenty-five thousand viewers. After traveling to Boston, Pittsburgh,

Washington, Louisville, and San Antonio, the show had been seen by an estimated 450,000.[73] U.S. critics eagerly applauded tradition, balance, and order, which in turn represented unity within the larger whole of Mexican life. Reminding his readers that "the Western Hemisphere is indeed . . . very venerable," Edward Alden Jewell of the *New York Times* observed that "the [Mexican] glass blower is essential to the poet of fiery pigment; the humble weaver of thread and reed to the sculptor"; the show itself was "simple, orderly, and right."[74] The "beautifully balanced masses" of Orozco's murals, displayed at New York's New School for Social Research, won notice, as did the "organic unity" in his series *Epic of Civilization on the American Continent* (Dartmouth College), which found favor with no less a critic than Lewis Mumford.[75] Even more explicit classicizing is found in Orozco's *Prometheus* for Pomona College.[76]

Anthropologists also turned southward and also privileged classic values. Their foundational text was Franz Boas's *The Mind of Primitive Man* (1911), in which Boas defied the epistemological premise that one racial group was superior to another, urging the student of non-European cultures to cultivate a mindset akin to a tabula rasa and "divest himself entirely of opinions and emotions" of his own society.[77] Accordingly, his students delved into new concepts of culture, a central anthropological concern in the 1920s, an era George W. Stocking Jr. has dubbed the "classic" period of modern anthropology.[78] (Stocking also refers to several anthropologists who came of age at this time as "Apollonians.") Exploring these new concepts was Edward Sapir, whose influential essay "Culture, Genuine and Spurious" appeared in two parts in the *Dial* and *Dalhousie Review*.[79] In contrast to practices governed by material civilization, Sapir maintained, human activity undertaken within genuine culture possessed a spiritual meaning within a broader whole.[80] Exemplifying genuine culture was the American Indian (also the focus of much of Sapir's linguistic work). Unlike the urban telephone operator, who manipulates daily a technological system that "answers to no spiritual needs of her own," the Indian *lives* genuine culture. The salmon spearing he practices is "culturally higher" than the operator's tasks since "it works in naturally with all of the rest of the Indian's activities instead of standing out as a desert patch of merely economic effort in the whole of life." In other words, the Indian achieves harmony with the "stream of things."

Salmon-rich waters aside, anthropologists identified two principal sites for contemplating organic wholeness, timelessness, balance, and proportion: Mexico and what was once Mexico, the American Southwest, that is, Rosenfeld's "high deserts." In her influential *Patterns of Culture*, Boas's student Ruth Benedict reflected on the Zuni Indians, a "genuine" culture by Sapir's standards.[81] For Benedict, the Zuni were imbued with what she called "Apollonian" traits, that is, "delight . . . in formality" along with "measure and sobriety."[82] Robert Redfield, another of Stocking's Apollonians, spent a year in the Mexican village of Tepoztlán, where he admired Tepoztecan attunement to natural forces.[83] Many were also drawn to the sense of timeless transcendence in these cultures. Benedict, for example, observed that visitors to the Zuni pueblo were plunged into a "timeless platform outside today."[84] Similarly D. H. Lawrence, who visited Taos, New Mexico, in 1922, observed, "It has been [in existence] since heaven knows when."[85]

Nonanthropologists besides Lawrence were attracted to Mexico and the American Southwest in the 1920s. Carleton Beals, Mabel Dodge, Frances Toor, John Dewey, Katherine Anne Porter, John Dos Passos, Anita Brenner, and, of course, Frank visited this region, many marveling over the same values the Apollonian anthropologists studied.[86] Dodge discovered that in the pueblo, "virtue lay in wholeness instead of dismemberment."[87] Brenner observed that "nowhere as in Mexico has art been so organically a part of life"; much the way Rosenfeld cherished music that reflected "the stream of things," she found Mexican art to be infused with "a strong current of life."[88] Others responded to this perfectly calibrated equilibrium in well-nigh biblical language. Rivaling the famous passage from the book of Ecclesiastes, in 1927 the poet Witter Bynner praised the Mexican Indians' "proportioned sense of the values of life," which endowed them with "a power to work when work is necessary, a power to endure where endurance is necessary, a power to oppose when opposition is necessary, to smile and live and fight at happy intervals and to loaf magnificently when the earth commands."[89]

Architects were similarly inspired, as is evident in the so-called Mayan Revival style, popular in the United States during the 1920s and 1930s. (In fact, it intermingled Aztec and Mayan elements.) One of its most enthusiastic proponents was the architect Robert Stacy-Judd. A showman who dressed up in native costumes and sent home dramatic press releases from his on site research in Mexico, Stacy-Judd preached the virtues of Mayan architecture in ladies' luncheons and architectural meetings alike.[90] Among his projects were the Aztec Hotel (Monrovia, California), with its curlicued, glyph-filled façade. He also designed houses of worship, a Masonic temple, a medical complex, and private residences. Frank Lloyd Wright's Hollyhock House in Los Angeles featured an open-air theater presumably inspired by a structure at Yaxchilan; Mayan theaters (Los Angeles, Denver, Detroit) sprang up as well. Particularly spectacular was the Mayan Temple at the 1933 Chicago World's Fair, described in a postcard as "an exact reproduction in actual colors of the famous Nunnery at Uxmal . . . erected almost 1200 years before the Christian era."[91] The critic Edgar Lloyd Hampton exulted that Mayan architecture was "100 percent American," and a New York Times editorial called it "a new style which will be in every sense of the word indigenous in the New World (figs. 2a, 2b)."[92]

It was also classicized. In repudiating neoclassical and Beaux-Arts styles, Mayan architecture borrowed just enough of Art Deco's abstractions to appeal to modernist sensibilities without venturing into extremes associated with Dada, for example. As such, it managed to remind many in the United States of the Greeks. A pamphlet by the architect Sylvanus Griswold Morley that accompanied the opening of the Mayan-style Fisher Theater in Detroit in 1928 was titled "The Story of the Maya: The Greeks of the New World."[93] The U.S. artist Lowell Hauser proposed that just as the Greeks had been "the source of European cultures," the Mayans were the "fountain head" of native American culture; likewise Hampton claimed that Mayan sculpture "might have been from the chisel of a Phidias."[94]

This hunger for unity, organicism, balance, wholeness, and substance is surely attributable to cultural envy, giving rise to an us-them binarism.[95] If we in the United States of the 1920s were afflicted with what Stearns bluntly called "aesthetic starvation," then they (Mexican Indians) were nourished by the perfect integration of environment, work, art, religion, and human relations. If the United States lived by the artificial "metronome of human interests," to borrow Redfield's description of clock-obsessed culture, primitive Mexico responded to natural rhythms.[96] Cultural envy thus motivated the sales of the book *Mexico: A Study of Two Americas* by Stuart Chase, one of Redfield's many readers, who wrote of the "essential dignity" of the Indians (Mexico's "machineless men").[97] Some U.S. travelers to Mexico were so struck by these virtues that they even effaced the us-them binarism by identifying with the Mexican Indian. After visiting Mexico in 1932, Copland marveled over a "fresh and pure and wholesome" quality he found there, along with the ubiquitous presence of "Indian blood," sympathetically concluding, "I must be an Indian myself."[98] A similar awareness infuses Lawrence's novel *The Plumed Serpent*, published in 1926 in New York and likely familiar to Rosenfeld, since Lawrence was contributing to the *Dial* by that time.[99] In it, Kate,

Figure 2a Ventura Center for Spiritual Living (formerly First Baptist Church), Ventura, California. Special thanks to Reverend Bonnie Hess Rose.

Figure 2b 852 Jefferson Avenue, west elevation, detail of decorative Mayan relief. Miami Beach Art Deco Historic District, Miami, Miami-Dade County, Florida. Library of Congress, Prints and Photographs Online Catalogue.

a forty-something widow of an Irish political leader, goes to Mexico, where she is rejuvenated after joining a group seeking to revive an ancient Aztec religion. Like Mabel Dodge (who married a Pueblo Indian), Kate is attracted to Indian men; like Copland, she senses the ubiquity of Indian blood.[100] Reacting less to the sexual attractions of an exoticized Other than to her own benighted state, Kate seeks to fulfill independently of sex roles her authentic self, long repressed by Anglo-Saxon mores. A primitive dance that functions as a synecdoche for the cosmic whole renders irrelevant a host of constraining binarisms.[101]

Passion for Mexico in the 1920s also reflected growing interest in Latin America in general. During the war, as the study of German declined in the United States, Spanish-language instruction increased, and influential figures such as Columbia University's president Nicholas Murray Butler urged every U.S. citizen to learn Spanish as a second language.[102] The American Association of Teachers of Spanish and Portuguese was founded, partly in hopes that "young America, in turning to the study of Spanish, [would] not limit her interests to the merely commercial aspect."[103] The pedagogy of American history was reformulated when Herbert E. Bolton began lecturing on "Greater America" at the University of California at Berkeley.[104] Arguing that traditional pedagogy lacked "freshness," he promoted the "essential unity" of the Americas and, in his homespun way, summed up traditional history teaching: "Americans licked England; they licked the Indians; all good Indians were dead; the English came to America to build homes, the Spaniards merely explored and hunted gold; Spain failed in the New World; the English always succeeded."[105] Convinced that Spain had been a key player in the history of the Americas, in 1928 Bolton coauthored a textbook that covered non-English-speaking colonies along with the thirteen in the East, typically the sole point of reference for U.S. creation myths.[106] By embracing sameness, he also challenged his colleagues. In a widely used textbook of 1919, for example, the historian William Warren Sweet referred to Latin American "half-breeds" as "sentimental and impulsive" elites, descendants of the temperamental *conquistadores*.[107]

Wholeness, proportion, and organicism also had their political currency. U.S. progressives, whether moderate leftists or diehard communists, saw postrevolutionary Mexican society as a beacon for the United States, much the way the Peruvian Marxist José Carlos Mariátegui (to whom Frank dedicated *America Hispana*) considered the Incan Empire a model egalitarian society.[108] Leftist politics often intersected with art to the point that the two were practically synonymous. In 1927 John Dos Passos published in the communist journal *New Masses* "Paint the Revolution!," an article on Rivera's murals for the Secretariat of Education, commissioned by the postrevolutionary government of Álvaro Obregón. Dos Passos concluded that the Mexican muralist movement "wasn't a case of . . . a lot of propaganda-fed people deciding that a little revolutionary art would be a good thing, it was a case of organic necessity."[109] Conservative agendas were also satisfied by the Mexican vogue. Members of the monied class and the business community embraced Mexico through arts patronage. After the 1930 show at the Metropolitan

Museum, the *New York Times* reported that "a group of wealthy Americans" established the Mexican Arts Association at the home of Mrs. John D. (Abby Aldrich) Rockefeller, who after her first visit to Mexico declared it "the most paintable country" she had ever seen.[110] Also, the travel industry profited handsomely, offering package tours to Mexico so that visitors blissfully indifferent to the values of the Revolution could imbibe the hallowed atmosphere of Teotihuacán and Chichén Itza. By 1924 fifty thousand tourists a year were visiting the Grand Canyon thanks to the Santa Fe Railway and its energetic marketing of ancient grandeur.[111]

A striking symbol of Mexico's appeal to these divergent aesthetic, political, corporate, and social constituencies in the United States—and of their desire to display it—was the splashy pageant "Aztec Gold," held in May 1929 at Madison Square Garden. Before *tout* New York, this extravagant staging called on approximately one thousand participants to enact "a chapter from the ancient Mexican emperor's time, when Cortez [*sic*] entered the treasure land of the New World," as the *New York Times* reported.[112] Participants included artists such as Covarrubias, the sharp-tongued, left-leaning Orozco, and the avant-garde choreographer Ted Shawn, who by then had created what was billed as a "Toltec" ballet for Martha Graham, *Xochitl*.[113] Also featured, however, was Florenz Ziegfeld, hero of the Broadway spectacular, now playing a Hopi Indian chief.[114] William Randolph Hearst and Conde Nast, both members of the planning committee, represented business interests. Because "Aztec Gold" was a charity event for the Judson Health Center, New York's social register set showed up in droves, as the long lists of names in the dailies attest.[115] Society matrons and debutantes portrayed "divinities and symbolic figures . . . resplendent in plumed costumes," enacting roles such as Poison Arrow, Passion Flower, and Imperial Mother of Mexico. (Some evidently impersonated the Grand Canyon.) Besides these evocations of Mexico, however, Finance, Transportation, and Locomotion were represented; so too was Religion, in the person of Mrs. De Forest Manice Alexander and several choirboys from Grace Church.[116] As for music, the press reports on various selections: a "harvest dance," *Montezuma Comes* (presumably an ancient Zuni chant), and that exemplar of spiritual and musical wholeness, Gershwin's *Rhapsody in Blue*. No piano soloist is identified, but the orchestra was led by one Anna C. Byrnes, whose assumption of this traditionally male duty probably alluded less to cosmic erasure of male-female binarisms or ancient matriarchal powers than to the fact that charity work was one area in which women were permitted to take a leadership role. Thus did leftists, capitalists, artists, and entertainers share the same stage to revel in the spirit of ancient America.

■ ABSOLUTE MEXICAN MUSIC: CLASSICIZING THE AMERICAN PRIMITIVE

As these various constituencies worshipped the wholeness, substance, and timelessness of the Americas, musicians sought the same values. Indigenous music of the United States had been shelved as an *un*usable musical past, with Indianist works by Anthony Philip Heinrich, Edward MacDowell, and Farwell deemed largely unsatisfactory.[117] Certainly many composers idealized the North American Indian's "freedom of spirit, self-reliance and stoical courage, dignity" that Farwell described.[118] But the musical legacy of indigenous people in the United States had failed to inspire. Like the archaeologists of an earlier generation, Rosenfeld found in it nothing "save barbarism," and Copland, in his review of the April 1928 concert, observed that "[U.S. composers] cannot, like Chávez...lose [themselves] in an ancient civilization."[119] Eleven years later, a young Leonard Bernstein would approach the limitations of native music in his undergraduate thesis at Harvard, claiming that Indianism had failed U.S. composers largely "because it was not an organic fruition."[120] If an indigenous American past were to prove usable, it would have to originate elsewhere in the hemisphere.

Chávez's timing could not have been better. Although fortunate enough to have visited Europe, he found the musical scene there disappointing and at age twenty-four decided to seek his fortune in New York, arriving in December 1923. He remained until March of the following year but returned in September 1926, staying nearly two years.[121] The Mexican writer, poet, art critic, and diplomat José Juan Tablada bore witness to New York's growing importance. Resident there since 1914, Tablada wrote the column "New York, Day and Night" for the Mexico City daily *El Universal* and in 1926 explained, "Now the Mecca of music is no longer Paris, Milan or Berlin"; rather, he declared, "the center is here."[122] Chávez, fluent in English, took full advantage of that center. He gradually became acquainted with Cowell, Varèse, Sessions, and various members of the International Composers' Guild, under whose auspices his *Otros tres exágonos* (1924) for voice and chamber ensemble was performed in February 1925, something of a sequel to *Tres exágonos* of 1923.[123] By far his most important relationship was with Copland, whom he probably met during the autumn of 1926. In Copland, who became a lifelong friend, Chávez discovered a shared vision for American music.[124] It was on behalf of that vision that he became involved with the PAAC, serving as one of its vice presidents.[125] As discussed below, he also wrote articles for the U.S. musical press and worked on a variety of compositions while sojourning for long intervals in the United States.

Let us dig more deeply into reactions to Chávez's music performed in April 1928. As is clear from the remarks cited earlier, Rosenfeld found it the perfect repository for his quasi-Bergsonian outpourings. Yet despite its capacity to evoke images of "high deserts" and "Toltec divinities," Chávez's music contains no inherent programmatic qualities, Rosenfeld insists. Given Chávez's "original classical music, a music entirely free of literary associations and descriptive intentions," Rosenfeld argues, it would be nothing short of "insolence" to so interpret Chávez's works, since it is "undeniable that his music depends on programmes as little as does the mighty Bach's."[126] Rather, Chávez communicates "feeling through the play of sonorities and contrasting forms" alone, that is, through musical elements no less autonomous than the "tönend bewegte Formen" (sonically moving forms) to which Eduard Hanslick devoted so much attention.[127]

If Rosenfeld fell just shy of explicitly allying Chávez with absolute music, Copland did not. He arrived at this judgment in his 1928 essay, first making several related observations. Registering the young Mexican's independence, Copland notes that Chávez initially studied the European canon but eventually divested himself of its influence, wiping clean the slate, as it were, to compose "fresh, vital music [with] roots . . . firmly in an ancient culture."[128] Further, Chávez's music was "not a substitute for living but a manifestation of life." Through this ontological framework, Chávez displayed "his composer's gift for the expression of objective beauty of universal significance," writing fresh, original music that "propounds no problems, no metaphysics."[129] (In other words, it had nothing to do with German late romanticism, maligned for its excesses and extramusical baggage.) "Here," Copland concludes, "is absolute music if ever there was any."[130]

Absolute music had its detractors in the 1920s. In his 1925 essay, "The Tyranny of the Absolute," the German critic Adolph Weissmann dismissed the "self-revelations" of romantic music but maintained that even if it were possible to compose music free "from human bonds," it would end up a captive of its own dogma.[131] The "human bond" he most cherished was racial identity, a point he addressed in another essay, "Race and Modernity." Fearful that absolute music would obliterate "racial color," Weissmann urged composers to observe the requirements of modernity while acknowledging the "differentiating characteristics" that conferred authentic character on their works, insisting, "It is race which colors modernity."[132] The challenge of aesthetic modernism thus presented itself: to sublimate racial and nationalist markers—difference—while subtly communicating their essence in a universalist framework. Here Chávez succeeded admirably. For although he channeled the "ritual music of the Mexican Indian," he did so in such a way that "only its essence remained." Cowell felt similarly. In June 1928 in *Pro-Musica Quarterly* he declared, "Chávez is a composer of music," but to clarify this apparent tautology, he added that Chávez "is also a Mexican; but although his music may have been somewhat influenced by his nationality, his claim to recognition as a composer is not based on his country but upon the actual worth [of] his music itself."[133]

But could music be both classic and also of the New World? Here we return to Rosenfeld, whose perfervid assertions are often corroborated by the score. The attribute of intrinsic classicism most important to him (and to any number of scholars of classic-period music) was form. For Rosenfeld, form was less a set of procedures than a manifestation of what he called "plasticity," the capability of being shaped or formed. Through plasticity, Chávez united classic principles with primitive utterance, the latter according to various musical signifiers composers had marshaled since *The Rite of Spring*. These included quartal and quintal harmonies (piano sonatina, mm. 54–62; mm. 3–6 of the violin sonatina), long static pedals (cello sonatina, mm. 99–154); repetition (movement 1 of the piano sonata, closing idea); ostinati (piano sonatina, mm. 63–69); or short motives of narrow intervallic range (cello sonatina, mm. 84–93). Plasticity, however, enables these primitivist signifiers to be poured into classic formal structures. For example, Rosenfeld praises the "beautiful form of Chávez's habitual suspension, so accessory to the plasticity of his music, [which] occurs in the third bar of the piano sonatina, in the arrest of a bit of three-part counterpoint in quavers on a sudden crochet."[134] Surely Rosenfeld's enthusiasm stems from Chávez's establishing D minor, enhanced by passing motion in the soprano and the B-flat in the bass (m. 1); in m. 2, quintal harmonies weave around the C, holding steady in the alto so that on the downbeat of m. 3, the figure Rosenfeld describes as a suspension and singles out for special mention (the C) stands out in what would otherwise imply a G major first-inversion chord; the simultaneous transferred resolution (B, bass), along with the fact that the alto delays the leap up to G, interrupts the flowing eighth-note motion on a fleeting caesura (ex. 2a).

Plasticity generates not only phrases but large-scale form. The same C natural, after three bars of harmonic fluidity, reemerges as the basis of a six-bar ostinato (left hand, mm. 7–14, temporarily interrupted in m. 13), which is answered by the sustained E-flat in the bass (mm. 16–18). A reprise of the "arrested" counterpoint follows (m. 25), after which C is reaffirmed (m. 29), the conclusion of the first section. Two brief contrasting passages follow before the retransition (m. 54ff.) is launched. At its culmination, C, insistently repeated (mm. 61–69), abruptly yields to B; in a restatement of the ostinato initially heard in mm. 7ff., B-flat is bypassed to begin a scalar descent on F such that the piece ends not on C, but on A. As contrapuntal lines propel the harmonies and enable all manner of allusions to triadic harmonies to emerge from the thicket of sevenths and ninths, that third-measure suspended C remains integral to the note-to-note harmonic flux at the same time that it leads the listener to believe that it, rather than A, might be the pitch center of the compact little work, thus reenacting in new ways that essential ingredient of classic sonata form, the opposition of tonal centers and their ultimate reconciliation (ex. 2b).

To be sure, Rosenfeld recognizes such a thing as "objective form," that is, blueprints of musical design on which any number of composers have drawn. It is most conspicuous in the piano sonata, which, unlike the sonatinas, unfolds not in a single continuous flow but in four discrete movements, three of which allude to

Example 2a Carlos Chávez. Sonatina for piano, mm. 1–3. © Copyright 1930 by Boosey & Hawkes, Inc. Reprinted by permission.

Example 2b Carlos Chávez. Sonatina for piano, mm. 91–96. © Copyright 1930 by Boosey & Hawkes, Inc. Reprinted by permission.

Example 2c Carlos Chávez. Sonata for piano, mvt. 3, mm. 1–9. Reprinted by kind permission of Ediciones Mexicanas de Música, A.C.

traditional forms.[135] The second movement, which Rosenfeld labels a scherzo despite certain irregularities in the repeat scheme, requires sure octaves and hand-crossings at a brisk tempo. The third movement is a "disguised fugue . . . bald, excessively compressed, and wry"; packed into its scant thirty-three measures are three initial statements of a "subject," one that recurs throughout, sometimes in inversion (mm. 16–17, 20–21, 22–23), and concluding with a fortissimo statement (soprano) (ex. 2c).

Example 2d Carlos Chávez. Sonata for piano, mvt. 1, mm. 20–32 (second group and closing idea). Reprinted by kind permission of Ediciones Mexicanas de Música, A.C.

It is in the first movement of the sonata, however, that form wields the great-est influence. Only seventy-one measures long (Rosenfeld calls it "laconic"), the movement nonetheless encompasses two distinct groups in the exposition, the first harmonically dense (mm. 1–19) and the second leading off with a repeated rhythmic motive in two-voiced texture (mm. 20–26). A closing idea, resplen-dent in its austerity, consists of six measures of a sustained major ninth, with re-peated octaves in the bass, which Rosenfeld describes as "hollow," undoubtedly for their stark exposure and precisely calibrated decline in intensity.[136] The seven-and-a-half-measure stretch that follows consists of little more than an E-flat pedal, barely qualifying as a development. But both groups and the closing idea of the exposition return in the recapitulation (mm. 40–58), with the second group in a contrasting tonal area and a consonant major third replacing the major ninth that concluded the exposition. Admittedly the essential formal out-lines arose not from "the rocky, bare New World" but from Europe. Thanks to plasticity, however—the malleability of the tabula rasa—the Mexican composer had caught so authoritatively "the temper of life forced to adjust itself to . . . curi-ously cruel and splendid, profuse and irresponsive soil (ex. 2d)."[137]

We might argue that such readjustments of time-honored traditional forms are so freewheeling as to cast doubt on Chávez's credentials as an ur-classicist. Yet for Rosenfeld, authentic classicism *required* an original approach to established form. "Not only are no two fugues of Bach, no two sonatas of Beethoven . . . identical as wholes," he maintains, "but in many cases they radically vary the type to which they belong." Nor was traditional historical periodization a particular concern; unlike "the Strawinskies," obsessed with the ossified dictates of the eighteenth century, Beethoven, Schubert, and Wagner, Rosenfeld argued, all "established their own forms."[138] As a result, Chávez's works announced "an incipient Adam de la Hale, Josquin des Pres or Haydn of the fresh American world."[139] In availing himself of this flexible periodization, Rosenfeld had some distinguished predecessors. As Karol Berger notes, the fact that E. T. A. Hoffmann saw Haydn, Mozart, and Beethoven as "Romantic" was by no means incompatible with their status as "the new music's classic authors, its Homers and Virgils."[140] Rosenfeld's classicism beckons us into the realm not only of authenticity but of timelessness. Beethoven's late quartets and piano sonatas, Bach's fugues, and even *Tristan und Isolde*, he proposes, all give "the impression that these pieces existed since the beginning of the world."[141] Absolute music itself has traditionally been seen as timeless. As Daniel K. L. Chua observes, "Absolute music has 'no history.' It denies that it was ever born."[142]

Rosenfeld's musings on classicism had broader resonance even amid contentious debates over modernism in musical circles of 1920s America, in which classical ideals were surprisingly compelling. Many opposed classicism to neoclassicism. Lourie, for example, berated composers captivated by imitation, with the result that "the truly classical" was absent in their works.[143] Classicism could also counter neoclassicism's inherent faddishness by presenting itself as vital, a living thing. Just as Copland exalted Chávez's music as a "manifestation of life," Israel Citkowitz praised Walter Piston (for many the quintessential American neoclassicist) in terms of "living classicism," which defied the "criteria of neo-classicism." Indeed, these criteria also lacked timelessness, since despite "their appeal to a universality of musical values, [they] are strongly marked by the particular circumstances under which they arose."[144] Roy Harris, who once told Copland to "avoid neo-classicism like the pest that it is," nonetheless upheld classicism.[145] In the fall of 1931 he contacted Farwell, then writing an article on Harris for *Musical Quarterly*, to make sure Farwell would categorize Harris properly in this regard.[146] By then Farwell had conspicuously displayed his own enthusiasm for ancient tradition, not surprisingly with an indigenist slant. Surely his "California Masque," a pageant held at the Greek Theater of the University of California at Berkeley in 1919, was as impressive as "Aztec Gold." A dramatized account of the U.S. West's spiritual proximity to the ancient world, the pageant featured the toga-clad character California, surrounded by the muses; another role was Ancient Greece. Both presided over a harmonious array of ethnic groups, including "red," with "plaintive strain," and "black . . . redeemed from slavery's smart." Students and faculty participated in this massive event. (One wonders if Bolton was among them.) Just the Maya were considered New World Greeks, "California Masque" served as Farwell's assurance "that the western United States could take up the artistic mantle of ancient Greece," as Beth E. Levy suggests.[147]

In his *Musical Quarterly* article, Farwell identified Harris as an authentic ("straight-out") classicist. That he challenged "neo-classicists and all, from the primal standpoint of Bach and Beethoven," is confirmed by his Piano Sonata op. 1.[148] As in Chávez's sonata, with its "hollow octaves," Harris's op. 1 contains what Farwell describes as "bare octaves and fifths . . . bald and stark" (20); further, "organic growth" rather than objective form propels note-to-note movement. Like Chávez representing "commencing cultures," Harris was a "first-fruit" (19). Harris too conjures up austere open spaces, albeit of the U.S. West. Like Chávez's Mexican deserts, those regions are an aural equivalent of the tabula rasa. Harris even proclaimed himself the embodiment of the tabula rasa; after returning to the United States from studies with Nadia Boulanger, he suggested that Boulanger's teaching had left next to no imprint on his art, which had arisen through a far more mysterious combination of self and environment.[149]

Not only was American primitivism classicized. In January 1924 the Boston Symphony Orchestra under Pierre Monteux gave the New York premiere of *The Rite of Spring*. Although the U.S. premiere in Philadelphia two years earlier (under Stokowski) had been less than remarkable, New York readily made sense of the piece—in terms of classicism.[150] Although Downes acknowledged that the *Rite* was "filled with a primitive and at times vertiginous energy," much the way Cowell categorized Chávez as a "composer of music," Downes considered the *Rite* primarily as "music," that is, "not mere sound to accentuate or accompany something done in the theater."[151] W. J. Henderson of the *New York Herald* (not yet the *Herald Tribune*) found the score "powerful and often savage" but added, "[Stravinsky's] outline is sharp. His form is clear. His treatment is intelligible."[152] Pitts Sanborn, much taken with the *Rite*'s "great primal force," nonetheless pronounced it "clear as a Haydn piano sonata."[153]

How did Chávez address classicizing? Like Rosenfeld, he reflected on wholeness, form, plasticity (organic growth), and substance in print. A few weeks after the April 1928 concert, the first of his five articles for *Modern Music* appeared. Titled "Technique and Inner Form," it opened with a resounding paean to wholeness: "External and internal form cannot be separated; they are one." Maintaining that "external form unfolds from the center of a work of art," he added that "the whole inner substance . . . is nothing more than the external form."[154] Further, "the strength, the singular energy of these means lies precisely in the degree of perfection to which they develop all that is contained in the internal substance. Art is the result of converting internal substance into external form by tangible means."[155] Chávez's compatriots detected the influence of ancient Greece in the art of ancient Mexico. The art historian Manuel G. Revilla likened the "Hellenic elements" in the palace of Zayí (Yucatán) to Greek architecture, and Tablada praised the head of the moon goddess Coyolxauhqui as a "masterful work, worthy of being compared with any . . . Greek work."[156] Rivera, Indianist par excellence, also endowed the indigenous with classic trappings. In one mural of his well-known Secretariat of Education series of the mid-1920s, he depicts the Greek god Apollo with rays emanating from his head and presiding over identifiably Mexican figures, such as workers, *campesinos*, and Indians. With nine women (muses) witnessing Apollo's divine protection, the scene reminds the viewer of a classical tableau.[157] Comparisons with ancient Greece went only so far, with Alfredo Chavero seen as overly zealous in his classicizing.[158] Yet such enthusiasm confirms the attractiveness of the concept north and south as artists sought a usable past.

■ UNIVERSALIST STIRRINGS IN THE HEMISPHERE: ROSENFELD AND VASCONCELOS

Another key figure in Mexico was José Vasconcelos, minister of education during the presidency of Álvaro Obregón (1920–24), to whom many have attributed the surge of postrevolutionary *indigenismo*. *Indigenismo* made itself felt on any number of levels, whether in images of the native that now graced murals in public spaces or in the new government agencies established on behalf of the Indian. Yet this congeries of policies and attitudes was really the work of *mestizo* elites, who debated social policy in relation to class- and race-based identity and recognized that the Indian contribution to the Revolution had been diffuse and largely anonymous.[159] Still, officials such as Manuel Gamio, subsecretary and director of the Bureau of Anthropology in the Obregón administration (and former Boas student), declared in 1916 that although "the revolutionary movements never took shape or rose up in the heart [of the Indian population]," it was "in that population that it found its primordial origin."[160]

For his part, Vasconcelos remained loyal to the Western European tradition in his cultural policies. In 1922 he advocated less than enthusiastically the Department of Indigenous Culture, which he considered a provisional measure, since in the society he envisioned, all Mexicans would speak Spanish and remain mindful of their European inheritance even as they pursued an American identity.[161] Neither did Vasconcelos particularly warm up to Chávez's music. Contrary to any number of accounts, he did not support the 1921 ballet *El fuego nuevo* (The New Fire), which stalled and was eventually canceled. (It was performed only in November 1928, four years after Vasconcelos ended his term, by which time Chávez was directing the Orquesta Sinfónica de México.)[162] Neither does Chávez's name surface in Vasconcelos's extended essay of 1926, "Indología: An Interpretation of Ibero-American Culture."[163] In it, he surveys his administration's artistic accomplishments, including masques and open-air pageants that combined choral singing, dance, and Mexican popular music. As for concerts, Vasconcelos proudly recalled hearing the symphonies of Beethoven, Tchaikovsky, Brahms, and Mozart, along with selections by Wagner, Debussy Saint-Saëns, Strauss, Schubert, and Berlioz.[164] Of the Indianist works heard in these programs, there were exactly four. Some, moreover, would seem to fall short of the authenticity aesthetes and anthropologists of the era admired, such as the dance number with music by the Yucatecan composer Cornelio Cárdenas, in which brown-skinned performers darkened their faces in the manner of blackface minstrelsy.[165] Yet, undoubtedly mindful of postrevolutionary agendas, Vasconcelos maintained, "Our indigenous masses constitute an ancient and refined race."[166]

Vasconcelos described his aesthetic in terms of universalism. Reconciling difference, universalism would integrate "the flourishing of the native within the realm of the universal, and in the reunion of our soul with the vibrations of the universe," as he declared in his inaugural speech for the Secretariat building.[167] Passionately he urged his fellow Latin Americans to embrace this "philosophical movement founded in emotion," to "adopt universal and collective [artistic] forms" with "hearts on fire."[168] In his essay "Aesthetic Monism," which is peppered with references to "unity" and "synthesis," he even maintains that the universe consists of a single substance, with "the Whole greater than the sum of its parts."[169] Extending this scheme of wholeness further, he notes that "the object moves in unison with the spirit, it begins to sing, and walk toward the One."[170] This reference to "singing" hints at Vasconcelos's belief that music not only represents but brings to fruition this universalist agenda. Not surprisingly, his beloved Western canon was best suited to that end. Especially compelling was sonata form, with its capacity for "reconciliation" and "synthesis." Like Rosenfeld, Vasconcelos conferred special powers on form, noting that the sonata transcends its form such that "the Absolute overflows formal constraints."[171] More than any other composer, Vasconcelos held, it was Beethoven who achieved such transcendence.[172] Likewise, Vasconcelos argued, the cosmic synthesis inherent in great music was both metaphor for and realization of an authentic life-force—Rosenfeld's "stream of things."[173]

In fact Vasconcelos and Rosenfeld had much more in common. Both revered the eighteenth- and nineteenth-century Western canon. Both believed (as did Chávez) in a mysterious "substance," whether as an ingredient of authentic art or as a fixture of the universe. Both privileged emotion, Rosenfeld to his professional peril. Both also meditated on "the One." In Vasconcelos's case, that concept was a pillar of his universalizing agenda. For Rosenfeld, "the One" manifested itself in the music of Beethoven, a phenomenon he discusses in his review of Romain Rolland's *Beethoven the Creator* (the 1929 English translation of *Beethoven: Les grandes époques créatrices*).[174] The essay is less a review and more a pretext for Rosenfeld's lucubrations on sublimation. The second movement of the Piano Sonata in C minor (op. 111), for example, conveyed to Rosenfeld "the feeling of a will completely sublimated and transformed in sympathy with that of the One which is 'our peace'" (73).[175] The libido is "orderly and sublimated" (78). Through sublimating his energy, Beethoven arrives at "an increased elevation of the feeling of life, its essences, its ideas" (78). Sublimation is also tied to timelessness: in Beethoven's mighty hands, musical forms and procedures seem "as if, like rocks, they had existed since the beginning of things," embodying the "recaptured pristine unity with the whole of things" (70).

Yet through this ongoing sublimation, Beethoven also "communicates what seems to be racial experience," convincing the skeptical listener of "the existence of faculties such as that of race-memory" (70–71). Compare these remarks with Rosenfeld's assessment of the leader of "the Strawinskies," Stravinsky himself. In an archly titled article, "Igor, Tu N'est Qu'un Villain!," Rosenfeld accuses

Stravinsky of having "turned against his own roots."[176] Whereas Beethoven had managed to preserve "race memory" and Chávez had communicated the "essence" of the Mexican Indian within the classicist framework, Stravinsky produced nothing but a "defective classicism," one "neither Russian nor Western nor Stravinsky."[177] Registering "much talk of 'pure' musicality"—again brandishing scare quotes—Rosenfeld complains that *Oedipus Rex* "compel[led] no fresh experience," only "adventures in archaism" and "prim intellectualistic masks."[178] Chávez, on the other hand, had fallen into no such trap.

For Rosenfeld, this complex of agendas and idealizations inevitably leads to Pan Americanism. Chávez the intrinsic classicist was heir to the sole region of the American tabula rasa that could legitimately boast a viable indigenous tradition. If ur-classicism was both timeless and contemporary, so too was Mexico, the spirit of its ancient world blending harmoniously with its capital, Mexico City, "not at all the provinces and 'down there,'" Rosenfeld explained, but "a perfectly contemporaneous place on the edge of the future."[179] Reveling in this fusion of the modern and the classic, Rosenfeld announces Pan Americanism's universalist agenda, inextricably bound to classicism. "If we say, an original classical music," he exults, "we imply a Pan-American renaissance! The one is sign of the other."[180] Hailing Chávez as the embodiment of "rampant Pan-Americanism," Rosenfeld concludes, "the man himself is an environment."[181] That environment encompasses not just the stark Mexican deserts, redolent of the tabula rasa, but the entire hemisphere, giving "assurance that a Pan-American revival is indeed in progress."[182]

Not all of Chávez's contemporaries were moved to embrace sameness. Much the way Downes had expounded on the tomahawk and Indian "brutality," Barthold Fles, who interviewed the composer for *Musical America* a few months after the April 1928 concert, emphasized the "nearly savage primitiveness" of Chávez's music and without recourse to universalist or classicizing paradigms.[183] Nor can much classicizing language be teased out of Chávez's remarks to Fles. Rather than expounding on form, for example, he recalled going out to "the country" in Mexico, where he "often was able to observe and study primitive Indian festivals . . . the life that burns in [his] mind." Over four paragraphs are devoted to his "Aztec ballets," concentrating on the Aztec cosmology and Nahoa rituals in *El fuego nuevo* and *Los cuatro soles*, respectively. Was Chávez playing along with Fles's interest in the exotic? Or was he simply emphasizing the *ur* side of ur-classicism? As we shall see in chapter 3, the next big moment for Chávez in the United States, the 1932 premiere of his ballet *H.P.* (Horsepower), exposed the consequences of rejecting ur-Classicism.

In the meantime we can conclude that directly or indirectly, critics such as Rosenfeld, Copland, and Cowell grappled with the prefix *neo* writ large. In denoting the recent and the modified, *neo* rejected authenticity and wholeness. Ur-classicism, on the other hand, created conditions for absolute music that united the usable past of ancient America with the universal whole, all within the "freshness" the tabula rasa promised. To be sure, commentary such as that found in the *Musical America* piece suggests that Chávez capitalized on difference by strategically reveling in exoticist images of the primitivism. But it also pays to remember Torgovnick's observation that the discourse of aesthetic primitivism "tells us what we want it to tell us."[184] What was wanted at this moment in the United States went beyond tomahawks and difference. Just as Rosenfeld so passionately insisted as he unfurled the banner of Pan Americanism, Chávez's ur-classicism made listeners throughout the hemisphere "feel America."

3 The Good Neighbor Onstage

Carlos Chávez's H.P. and Dialectical Indigenism

On the evening of March 31, 1932, Chávez's ballet *H.P.* (Horsepower) premiered at Philadelphia's Metropolitan Opera House. Thanks to an energetic publicity blitz, a capacity audience of 4,500 flocked to North Broad and Poplar amid torrential rain.[1] There they would take in Chávez's latest score, along with sets and costumes by Diego Rivera and choreography by Catherine Littlefield, all under Leopold Stokowski's flamboyant direction. Some had already wearied of the buzz. The Philadelphia critic Henry C. Beck quipped that *H.P.* had been "ballyhooed and Barnum-and-Baileyed" and (in a nod to Stokowski's unerring gift for publicity) "Stokowskied" as well.[2] *H.P.* also aroused Pan Americanist expectations. As John Martin, dance critic for the *New York Times*, explained, its main theme was "the tremendous difference between the lazy tropical atmosphere of the South and the machine-mad confusion of the North"; also explored, Martin noted, were "the production of material in the South and the consumption of the same material by the North."[3] Yet according to the ballet's slim plot, "tremendous difference" was to be acknowledged, ameliorated, and ultimately neutralized. In the spirit of hemispheric solidarity Stokowski conducted gratis.[4] It helped too that he had recently returned from Mexico.[5]

Witnessing this display of Pan Americanist goodwill was the cream of Philadelphia society, including Kathryn O'Gorman Hammer (Mrs. William C. V. Hammer, director and general manager of the Philadelphia Grand Opera Company), Mr. and Mrs. Cyrus H. K. Curtis, and Mr. and Mrs. W. Curtis Bok (of newspaper publishing and philanthropic fame).[6] Press correspondents from various eastern cities attended, as did several "pilgrims," as Martin described those visitors transported from New York in Pullman cars hired especially for the occasion.[7] Among them were Copland, Rosenfeld, the composer Marc Blitzstein, the choreographer Doris Humphrey, the conductor Walter Damrosch, the publisher Alfred Knopf, the violinist Efrem Zimbalist, and Rivera with his wife, Frida Kahlo. Chávez, now on his third visit to the United States, was present too, having just shared a concert program with George Antheil (also at the premiere) sponsored by the Philadelphia Society for Contemporary Music.[8] Various players in the burgeoning Pan Americanist project attended as well: Mexican ambassador José Manuel Puig Casauranc and his wife; Harry L. Hewes reporting for the *Bulletin of the Pan American Union*; and members of the Rockefeller family. Surely the lead dancer Alexis Dolinoff exaggerated when he later recalled that "all the diplomatic corps and all the ambassadors . . . from all over the United States and from Mexico and from other parts of the world, too" were in the audience.[9] Still, a great deal was riding on the event.

Given the ballet's theme of north-south difference, the collaborators confronted a challenge. Could the glaring dissimilarity between the technologically advanced North and the "backward" South possibly be served up on the Grand Opera stage as anything other than a glaring example of what Anthony L. Geist and José B. Monleón have called "global *unequal* development"?[10] Despite these premises (and the attendant issues of exploitation and stereotyping, especially with regard to race and gender), the ballet's upbeat publicity proposed that it could. *H.P.* opens with "Dance of Man," a solo number by the protagonist (also called H.P.), a half-man, half-machine hybrid representing northern industrialization. A second tableau, with the unwieldy title "A Cargo Ship at Sea Symbolizing the Commerce between the North and the South," depicts a boat trip to balmy southern climes, during which a bevy of guitar-toting sirens and a school of fish find their way on board and entertain the crew. In the third tableau, "A Ship in the Tropics," the boat lands in a southern port, where natives and gigantic fruits (dancing roles) gambol about. After the crew load southern bounty on board, the boat heads back to what Stokowski described as the "prohibition and machine civilization" of the North, the site of the final tableau, "The City of Industry."[11] With the New York City skyline as a backdrop, H.P. leads a group of factory workers in a rebellion, a fleeting moment of anticapitalist subversion mysteriously resolved by what amounts to a happy Hollywood ending.

Critics found the politically charged ending unconvincing, however, as they did many other aspects of the explicitly Pan Americanist ballet, and consequently it has never been produced since that rainy evening in Philadelphia. Yet there is more to *H.P.* than this brusque dismissal suggests. Numerous iconographic correspondences between Rivera's designs for *H.P.* and other works of his confirm that the ballet is part of the larger trend in Rivera's work that Jeffrey Belnap has labeled "dialectical indigenism."[12] Dialectical indigenism affirms the coexistence of indigenous culture and machine technology in the modern age and, not unlike the "ballyhoo" surrounding *H.P.*, proposes that North and South are interdependent. It also helps explain why Chávez and Rivera, two Mexicans creating a work for U.S. consumption, would at first blush seem to accept U.S. imperialism. For dialectical indigenism is embodied in esoteric visual codes, which, Rivera claimed, revealed his Marxist principles. Likewise, hidden messages are embedded in Chávez's score. All can be viewed through a Pan Americanist lens to clarify the work's more perplexing features while highlighting some of the political pitfalls inherent in Pan Americanist sameness-embracing.

■ DIALECTICAL INDIGENISM IN POSTREVOLUTIONARY MEXICO AND THE UNITED STATES

According to his biographer Roberto García Morillo, Chávez initially discussed "something with machines" in the early 1920s not with Rivera but with the Mexican painter Agustín Lazo, his collaborator on *El fuego nuevo*.[13] Machine culture was then at its height, and its various manifestations—pile drivers, flywheels, the saxophone, Tin Pan Alley, the flapper, and depictions thereof—were identified with the Colossus of the North. R. J. Coady, editor of the little magazine *The Soil*, defined American (U.S.) art as "the aesthetic product of the human beings living on and producing from the soil of these United States."[14] He took pains to insist that such art was accessed not in museums but "in the spirit of the Panama Canal," the "East River and the Battery... from the ball field, the stadium and the ring."[15] Anything but a "delicate disease" (i.e., anything but European), U.S. art had "grown naturally, healthfully . . . out of the soil," manifesting itself in "the Sky-scraper... Rag-time... the 'By Heck Foxtrot'... Blast Furnaces," to give just a few examples from Coady's breathless catalogue.[16] The novelist and screen-writer Gilbert Seldes, on the other hand, condemned "artistic chauvinism" as worthy of aesthetic "Ku Kluxers," those who habitually overlooked mixed or hybrid cultures in the United States and elsewhere.[17] Despite his rabid Americanism, Coady claimed to believe in internationalism.[18] Yet a Klan-like attitude emerges in one of his vaunted "aesthetic products," the Panama Canal. The result of Teddy Roosevelt's rewriting of the Monroe Doctrine and destabilizing of the Colombian government, the Canal hardly grew "naturally out of the soil" but rather enshrines hegemonic ambition at the expense of a racially mixed nation.

Critics debated these same issues apropos machine music. In works such as Honegger's *Pacific 231* (1923), John Alden Carpenter's *Skyscrapers* (1923–24), Antheil's *Ballet Mécanique* (1923–25), Alexander Mosolov's *The Iron Foundry* (1926–28), Vladimir Deshevov's *Rails* for piano (1926), Prokofiev's *Pas d'acier* (1925–26), and Shostakovich's *The Bolt* (1930–31), mechanical noises, real or simulated, assaulted ideals of transcendence, beauty, and timelessness.[19] Machine music could inspire nihilism or emotion. If some composers allied themselves with Dada and its call to take on "the great destructive, negative work" that lay ahead, others equated machines with living beings.[20] Apropos *Pacific 231*, which depicts a train, Honegger declared, "I have always loved locomotives passion-ately since, for me they are living beings which I cherish, as others cherish women or horses."[21] Machine-oriented scores such as *The Iron Foundry* might herald the collective vigor of the new Soviet state or, as in *The Bolt*, awaken sym-pathy for desperate workers rebelling against the tyranny of mechanization à la Fritz Lang's 1927 film *Metropolis*.[22] In the United States, creative minds grappled with the meaning of machine music. The music critic Oscar Thompson specu-lated that it might evoke nothing but "savagery and relentless brutality."[23] Art critics digested European trends such as Dada, wondering if its negation of human feeling and decadence were compatible with national values.[24] Others associated mechanization with the skyscraper. For George Gershwin, the latter symbolized U.S. can-do optimism, affording a "tremendous emotional experience" with its pairing of "mechanism and feeling," thus countering Dada-tinged nihilism. Yet in blithely maintaining that current European composers "largely received their stimulus, their rhythms, and impulses, from Machine Age America," he committed the sort of artistic chauvinism against which Seldes cautioned.[25] The critic Gorham Munson, on the other hand, considered the skyscraper along the lines of the Apollonian anthropologists idealizing the wholeness of Mexican Indian communities. Coining the term *skyscraper primitive* in 1925, Munson urged his readers to "relate man positively and spiritually to Machinery as well as nature."[26] He linked this harmonious relationship of machine and man to the tabula rasa, situating the skyscraper primitives in "the childhood of a new age."[27] If the ideological roots of ur-classicism seem strangely similar to those of the skyscraper primitives, it is also worth remembering that the mechanical noises of machine music were often expressed through many of the signifiers of musical primitivism discussed in chapter 2: ostinati, repetition, driving rhythms, mixed meters, angular melodies, abrupt block juxtapositions, long pedals, melodic fragments of narrow intervallic range, and prominent percussion. Not for nothing did Antheil describe being "stunned by the machine-precision" in African music as he discoursed on "A Method of Negro Music."[28]

In Mexico some took a dim view of machine culture. The writer Salvador Novo, who has been compared to Oscar Wilde for his homosexuality and dandified appearance, found New York little more than a "brittle machine" (*una máquina deleznable*).[29] For others, the machine spelled U.S. hegemony. In 1921 Manuel Ponce lamented that the foxtrot and its "execrable" percussion section, itself a mechanistic "Yankee invention," had caused Mexican youth to "deliver themselves unconsciously into the arms of the conqueror, without considering that behind the invading dance from the United States, Uncle Sam's coattails were etched."[30] Likewise, the flapper's bob threatened to usurp the thick black braid traditionally worn by Mexican women, while chewing gum and English-language phrases encroached on daily habits. One symbol of northern brashness was jazz, as the waltzes and mazurkas of prerevolutionary Mexico yielded to the saxophone.[31] Further evidence that Mexicans were hardly the "machineless men" Stuart Chase extolled is found in the short-lived but intense movement known as *estridentismo*, established in 1921 and in which Chávez briefly indulged. *Estridentismo* partook of futurism, Dadaism, and *ultraísmo*, a related movement from Spain.[32] As the artist David Alfaro Siqueiros declared in his "Manifesto to the Artists of America" of 1921, "We must love our marvelous dynamic age! [We must] love the modern machine, dispenser of unexpected plastic emotions, the contemporary aspects of our daily life."[33] Siqueiros also marveled at the proximity between machine culture and that of indigenous Mexico, urging his fellow Mexican artists to pursue "synthetic energy" by studying the works of Maya, Aztec, and Inca painters and sculptors.[34] Charlot would later recall that in the 1920s, Mexican art students would return home from Paris and visit the National Museum of Mexico, where they observed that "the Aztec pyramids, spheres, cubes, and cones, far from retaining, as did the cubist ones, a whiff of classroom dampness," appeared as "cogs, pistons, and ball bearings that one suspected had cosmic function."[35] Depictions of machines surfaced in unexpected places.

A critic contemplating Orozco's rendering of Cortés in the Hospicio Cabañas (Guadalajara) found the conqueror's armor looking "a little as though it had been manufactured in Detroit," while "the massive bolts with which it is assembled add a striking, robot-like effect."[36]

The master of dialectical indigenism, of course, was Rivera. In his murals for the Secretariat of Education, several images of Pan American harmony emerge from this perspective.[37] In the series of murals on level 1, he depicts fruit-bearing, brown-skinned Zapotec women from the isthmus of Tehuantepec, the tropical region separating the Pacific Ocean from the Gulf of Mexico (Veracruz and Oaxaca states) and rich in natural resources.[38] Covarrubias considered the region emblematic, claiming it was both "a microcosm of the larger Mexico" and the site "where very probably man first evolved on the American continent from a nomadic barbarian into a highly civilized sedentary agriculturist."[39] Tehuantepec's women are unusual in that they engage in trade and avoid menial work, securing their place in exoticist fantasies through power and seduction while defying Western gender conventions. Level 1 also shows the darker side of the Americas. In "Exit from the Mine" ("Salida de la mina") workers submit to cruel authority, with one assuming the posture of the crucified Christ while being frisked by the *patrón*.[40] "The Yaqui Dance of the Deer" ("Danza del Venadito") hints at salvation, however. Rivera portrays the male dancer in the traditional butterfly-cocoon leggings and antler headgear, who dances before a community gathered around a bonfire and meditating on the life cycle.[41] Level 2 represents education and scientific advances. In one of its murals, Rivera depicts an electricity-producing machine dominated by two perfect circles and a lightning flash of power emanating from two poles, thus situating machines in the realm of human intelligence (fig. 3a).

On level 3, Rivera exposes Yankee imperialism. In the mural "Wall Street Banquet" a shifty-eyed Henry Ford sips champagne with John D. Rockefeller, J. P. Morgan, and other cronies in the presence of a safe, while a miniature Statue of Liberty festooned with ticker tape looks on vacantly. A flapper with bobbed hair and rolled-up hose reflects the brazenness of 1920s U.S. culture and the rapidly shifting gender roles of that era; besides downplaying their female bodies under straight, sack-like dresses, flappers smoked, swore, drank in speakeasies, and used contraceptives—in other words, they acted like men. Additionally, the flapper's mass-produced dress represented machine culture and the social havoc it may wreak, given that women no longer needed to stay home and sew their own clothes.[42] Above the sinister assembly the words of the revolutionary song "Corrido de Emiliano Zapata" appear on a banner: "thus the rich man, always thinking about how to double his money." Another section of level 3 offers a hopeful dialectical-indigenist view of Pan Americanism. Symbolizing the fusion of nature, humankind, indigenous culture, and technology, rural and urban proletarians join hands, with various contemporary heroes looking on, including Zapata himself. Figures from level 1 reappear, apotheosized. The Tehuana woman

Figure 3a Diego Rivera, "The Dance of the Deer." ©2012 Banco de México Diego Rivera Frida Kahlo Museums Trust, Mexico, D.F./Artists Rights Society (ARS), New York.

ascends, displaying her tropical fruit against the backdrop of an industrial skyline and glorifying the triumphant interrelation of mechanization and the tropics. Also reappearing is the Yaqui deer dancer, now with a partner, the two interlocking in complementary movements that unfold beneath the motif of a snake biting its own tail, an infinity sign that represents the timelessness of indigenous culture.[43] The natural bounty, the urban skyline, the Tehuana woman, and the Yaqui dance are all elevated in a new cosmogony brought about through the cleansing processes of the Revolution.

In the United States, the Secretariat murals won praise for crystallizing the "reconciliation of the spirit of man and the machine," as the journalist Ernestine Evans put it.[44] Rivera revisited this theme in *Detroit Industry*, the series of murals commissioned in 1931 by Edsel Ford for the newly founded Detroit Institute of Arts. In one panel, stooped and dejected auto workers symbolize exploitation by the machine. In another, they energetically work the stamping press (used to make fenders and shown in the lower right of fig. 3b), which Rivera equates in proportion and volume with Coatlicue, the Aztec goddess of war and creation, again showing the interrelatedness of mechanization and the indigenous heritage.[45] Rivera's ideal of Pan Americanism emerges in the ample, brown-skinned woman on the east wall who clutches fruit to her perfectly rounded breasts and signals the natural abundance of her tropical environment, with its profligate fruits, flowers, and minerals. Her rounded, seemingly jointless form recalls pre-Columbian sculpture, just as her white, golden-haired counterpart on the opposite end of the wall symbolizes the Anglo North (figs. 3b, 3c).

In *Detroit Industry*, Rivera also promotes *mestizaje* (miscegenation). Four monumental figures, each representing one of the four principal racial groups (white, African, Asian, Native American), are stationed over two walls of the gallery. Gazing impassively down at viewers, they embodied the postrevolutionary ideal Vasconcelos articulated in his 1924 essay, "La raza cósmica" (The Cosmic Race).[46] An advanced, still-unrealized race would arise through the mixing of all existing races, he argued, the origins of which would be Latin America. Given the history of racial policy and outlook in Latin America, Vasconcelos's essay, despite its mystical tone and murky essentializing, is not wholly irrational. In contrast to the United States, where race has traditionally been seen as biological and immutable, racial categorizations in Latin America are far more fluid, determined not solely by "blood" or color but by context, including social factors such as upward mobility, which may differ from country to country.[47] Certainly it was an ample racial taxonomy that identified the inhabitants of the Spanish Empire, with possible classifications including Indian, black, *lora*, *coyote*, *lobo*,

Figure 3b Detail of Rivera's *Detroit Industry*. Detroit Institute of Arts, USA. Reproduced by permission of Bridgeman Art Library.

Figure 3c Coatlicue, Aztec goddess of war and creation. Reproduced by permission of Bridgeman Art. Reproduced by permission of Corbiss Images.

color quebrado, mulatto, *pardo*, *morisco*, mestizo, and *zambaigo*, several of which denoted color despite the fact that color had no legal standing.[48] Whiteness has traditionally promised respectability and access to political power, whereas blackness is considered the least desirable category. In Mexico, *mestizos* such as Benito Juárez and Porfirio Díaz could rise to political power, however, and during the Revolution the cult of the *mestizo* gathered momentum.[49] Differing attitudes toward race between the United States and Latin America nonetheless drove one more wedge between the two regions. Vasconcelos pointed out as much by challenging the legacy of Herbert Spencer, whose works were widely read in the United States until World War I. Condemning *mestizaje* (known as "hybridity" in the United States), Spencer considered human hybrids "inferior to 'pure' races."[50] So did his heir, the eugenicist Madison Grant, who argued in *The Passing of the Great Race* (1921) that "the result of the mixture of two races, in the long run, gives us a race reverting to the . . . lower type," such that "the cross between a white man and an Indian is an Indian; the cross between a white man and a negro is a negro."[51] This extreme version of binarist thinking—white versus "other"—helped enable the myth of racial purity in the United States.[52] In *Detroit Industry*, Rivera gave these issues pride of place through the four imposing figures.

These conflicting attitudes toward race have affected perceptions, north and south, of that mythical zone of Latin America, the tropics. The North, bedazzled by the South's natural resources, has long portrayed tropical abundance in terms of excess. Colonial-era Europeans reported "coconut palms, fifty to sixty feet high . . . sweet-smelling flowers as big as your hand," while Carmen Miranda's oversized cornucopia headdresses are but a twentieth-century version of the fruits and vegetables artistically rendered by Europeans, such as Jacopo Ligozzi's *Mirabilis Jalapa* (Peruvian Miracle).[53] In the "banana republics," the term O. Henry coined, "many thousand bunches of bananas, so many thousand oranges and cocoanuts" promised exceptional profits for U.S. businessmen, and the lazy pace of life made time itself seem "redundant."[54] Whatever the promise of economic gain for Latin America, however, it was responsible U.S. managers who would oversee the processing and distribution of raw materials and supervise the local workers fundamental to the enterprise, the attitude O. Henry so scathingly described.[55] Thus an international economic system was established through which wealthy countries maintained their position at the core of development while creating peripheral economies. Refusing to concede that some countries must be poor for others to be rich, Latin American social scientists and economists eventually conceived of the dependency theory to challenge these practices.[56]

The tropics also suggested ways of being. Vasconcelos attributed bodily ease (*soltura*), imagination, and ampleness of thought to denizens of the tropics, qualities he compared unfavorably to the "Yankee," who was "a victim of his own characteristics."[57] In the North, however, the tropics have come to emblematize Latin America to the point of fantasy and have been held responsible for irrationality, incapacity for democracy, and "hot-blooded" behavior.[58] The tropics have also seduced the North, promising sexual license and sultriness with the result that gender has figured prominently in the discourse of the colonialist-commercial system undertaken in the region.[59] In the presumably feminine (subaltern) tropics, women worked in the field, factory, and bedroom (as prostitutes for male workers hired by the male administration), whereas first-world women were targets of advertising, perhaps most conspicuously via that creation of United Fruit, the cartoon figure Chiquita Banana, with her cheery, syncopated jingle.[60] Also ensuring that the North was gendered male was the day-to-day business of dollar diplomacy, which emphasized duty, authority, pragmatism, single-minded efficiency, individualism, and professionalism.[61] Northern masculinity was even set forth in the Monroe Doctrine, which sought to preserve inter-American relations via "a frank, firm, and manly policy."

Directly or indirectly, dialectical indigenism dealt with these issues. But what of its political orientation? When Rivera began to accept commissions from wealthy patrons in the United States, Mexican communists criticized him for selling out to corporate America. Siqueiros, for example, taunted him as "Picasso in Aztecland," a dig at U.S. Pan Americanism, which many Latin Americans found opportunistic and insincere.[62] Rivera insisted that he was motivated not by high commissions but by the unprecedented chance to "infiltrate" his works with anti-imperialist messages. Here his corporate patrons cut him plenty of slack, either out of respect for his talent or because his iconography completely escaped them or because they hoped Rivera would renounce communism. Mrs. Rockefeller's assistant Frances Ford Paine, for example, opined that "'Reds' would cease to be 'Reds' if we could get them artistic recognition."[63] Only when he inserted an image of Vladimir Lenin in the Rockefeller Center murals, which was removed in 1934, did he go too far.

Whether or not we believe the smooth-talking Rivera, dialectical indigenism played well north and south as the need for hemispheric bonding began to take hold. In 1928 President Herbert Hoover toured Latin American to begin smoothing over the effects of interventionism under his predecessor Calvin Coolidge. In Honduras, he used the term *good neighbor*. (President Bartolomé Mitre of Argentina used it in 1865.)[64] As discussed in chapter 2, intellectuals and artists glorified Mexico and embraced the idea of a Western Hemisphere culture. The thought processes underlying some artifacts of this period are striking. Whereas Gershwin enthused over the skyscraper as a marvel of technology and a repository of human endeavor, Rivera and John Alden Carpenter used it to symbolize the oppression of workers, with Carpenter calling it "huge and sinister."[65] It could also fulfill the requirements of dialectical indigenism, however. Just as architecture critics compared Mayan architecture to that of ancient Greece, the "vertical lines" of the urban skyscraper were seen to "embod[y] Mayan principles of construction."[66] Even Stokowski sensed the indigenous influence on the urban North. Two years before the premiere of *H.P.*, he remarked that although the New York skyline had "sprung from [U.S.] soil," it was "more Aztec than anything else."[67] Other critics compared the graded levels of the setback skyscraper with the stepped pyramids of ancient Mexico, parallels that could be savored at 2 Park Avenue, a 1927 setback skyscraper by the architect Ely Jacques Kahn that the Mexican architect Francisco Mujica singled out for particular approval.[68] Thus dialectical indigenism was transplanted to Park Avenue— minus the Revolution.

■ *H.P.* AND "YANKEE PALATES" IN 1926

In the early stages of his work on *H.P.*, Chávez not only discussed with Lazo the possibility of a ballet for the U.S. public but also brainstormed with the poet and essayist Octavio Barreda, who wrote Chávez in February 1925 from New York. Some of Barreda's ideas were unabashedly opportunistic:

> On the way home in the subway I was thinking of a ballet. It would be called *Suave Patria* and it would take place on 15 September [Mexican Independence Day], with fireworks, parades, patriotic speeches, etc. I don't have it too well crystallized yet . . . but it would be a certain success for its novelty and exoticism (both conditions for triumph). . . . *Suave Patria* could [also] be titled *Marihuana:* in this case [the hero] is a soldier at night, taking a hit in the barracks, which leads to a parade of our usual stuff.

Or, in lieu of "our usual stuff" (i.e., novelty and exoticism), Barreda proposed setting the work "in a factory, with shrieks of machinery, anvils, saws, a workers' riot and the final lynching of the owner, whom they press and turn into something useful, such as cufflinks, sausages or condoms; anything that all the workers could share amidst general merriment, clacking and hammer-blows."[69] Perhaps digesting these anticapitalist sentiments, Chávez also speculated on northern tastes with the poet José Gorostiza, who seems to have been as pragmatic as Barreda. Gorostiza sent Chávez an outline of a possible scenario for an Aztec ballet, with sets to be designed by Rufus Tamayo and Rivera, adding that it could be modified and even "falsified to suit Yankee palates."[70] By the following year, Chávez was collaborating with that master opportunist, Rivera, and had begun work on the score. He announced as much in a program note for an International Composers Guild concert in November 1926, when the "Dance of Men and Machines" (eventually the music for the final tableau) premiered at New York's Aeolian Hall, unstaged and with chamber-orchestra scoring. The performance, which Eugene Goossens conducted, came about thanks to Varèse, one of the Guild's directors.[71] Eager to make his mark in New York, Chávez presented himself as a cosmopolitan modernist with machine music his principal offering.[72]

In his program note, however, Chávez elaborated further. He stated that "Dance of Men and Machines" was part of a work in progress, the final form of which would involve Rivera's designs and "suggest objectively the life of all America."[73] Both visual elements and score, Chávez explained, would "have their own proper and autonomous life."[74] He also alerted listeners to the presence of "Indian tunes [*sones mariaches*]," that is, one of two types of *son*, a genre central to Mexican popular music. Indian *sones* normally consist of one or two short phrases repeated at some length on instruments.[75] Chávez cautioned, however, that in "Dance of Men and Machines" the Indian *sones* appeared "not as a constructive base"; further, "all the conditions of their composition, form, sonority, etc. by nature coincide with those in [his] own mind, inasmuch as both are products of the same origin." In other words, any nationalist intent critics might be tempted to read into the score on the basis of the *sones* was a matter of pure happenstance. So too was Chávez's realization of these materials:

> Thus it happens that in this music of mine certain treatments of the strings, the lack of vibrato indispensable to the quality of the sound, the scraping bow, a certain insistence of the shrill instruments in their high registers, certain rhythms, simple and exhausting at the same time, certain deformations of a natural feeling for pure tonality, and the structural characteristics (horizontal rather than vertical) are some of the particularities which reveal the spirit of my country.[76]

Chávez's hopeful prognosis for a "final form" notwithstanding, there is no definitive text for "Dance of Men and Machines." The Music and Dance Division of the New York Public Library holds several manuscript sources, including versions for full and chamber orchestra and an incomplete piano reduction.[77] Although performance indications (and even pitches) are occasionally unclear, we can nonetheless reflect on whether the score confirms or contradicts Chávez's stated intentions.[78] With its fusion of indigenous, popular, and modernist elements, "Dance of Men and Machines" challenges any narrow understanding of Mexican nationalism. The scraping bow to which Chávez refers emerges in passages marked "raspar, *sul ponticello*," and *col legno*; melodies harmonized in thirds and sixths evoke Mexican popular music, as does the solo trumpet, the most prominent instrument in the mariachi ensemble (m. 54). The portion marked "American Dance" (m. 139ff.), however, features that hallmark of the primitive, a pentatonic fragment, here played by piccolo and flute and accompanied by repeated-note motives in the strings.[79] Indigenist and modernist elements sometimes coexist in the same passage: in accordance with the norms of musical primitivism, the repeated notes of the fragment in the second violins at m. 98 never exceed the range of a perfect fifth but conclude with a brief flourish of duple-triple metric alternation, an emblematic gesture in Latin American popular music (m. 102). Grating against this melody, however, is the flute at the interval of a major second, a level of dissonance incompatible with popular music. So too are the unpitched slides in the low brass à la Varèse (m. 150).

A rather different American tune also asserts itself as part of this hemispheric synthesis. Probably as a gesture to his New York public, Chávez inserted into the introduction (an interlude in the ballet version) a motive from "Sidewalks of New York," a 1904 song in brisk waltz time that recalls childhood innocence in the bustling metropolis. Chávez may have had in mind the "Dance" portion of Copland's *Music for Theatre*, the B section of which features this tune in an "angular, mechanized 5/8," as Howard Pollack notes.[80] With an over-the-bar syncopation, Chávez adjusts the waltz melody to duple meter, which the solo trumpet blasts out *fff*, silencing the rest of the orchestra.[81] What strikes the ear in the context just described, however, is the near-pentatonicism of the melody. But for the C-sharp and the C-natural (the latter a jazz-tinged lowered seventh tacked

Example 3a Carlos Chávez. Interlude, "Dance of Men and Machines," *H.P.*, "Sidewalks of New York" motive.

on to the original melody), the "Sidewalks" fragment is rooted in the pentatonic scale, confirming the inseparability of the northern metropolis—down to its sidewalks—and the southern primitive (ex. 3a).[82]

Whatever his eagerness to associate himself with modernism, Chávez recoiled from contemporary aesthetic debate, maintaining in his program note that his aim in *H.P.* was not "to relate the spirit of the work to the aesthetics of machines." In fact he did take a position. Not for Chávez the nihilism of Dada. Like Honegger, Chávez humanized machines:

> I do not consider [machines] objectively except for the sake of the vitality they possess. Machines are disciplined energy; they are a true product of will applied to intelligence and of intelligence applied to will. In other words, they are a human product in which emotion, like an autogenous solder, has welded intelligence and will together. . . . For this reason I see in a machine a human process, multiple and congealed.[83]

At least one critic of the 1926 performance was persuaded, with the reporter for *Musical America* noting approvingly that in *H.P.* "machines function, not as machines, but as animated mechanisms endowed with gleams of intelligence."[84] Such receptivity was rare, however. Although Chávez's compatriot Tablada dispatched to *El Universal* a sanguine account of "total triumph" before the "most sophisticated New York public," the "Dance of Men and Machines," which came at the end of a long program, proved too much for many critics, some of whom were not exactly fans of machine music in the first place.[85] Upon hearing it, Henderson tartly recommended that some composer "make a piece out of the Interborough power house [with] Carl Ruggles chant[ing] the voltage."[86] Downes, who deeply admired *Pacific 231*, confessed that he didn't know whether to take *H.P.* seriously, especially given its "mangled . . . Mexican ditties," at which, he claimed, the audience "laughed."[87] Even the loyal Rosenfeld initially devoted only a sentence to "Dance of Men and Machines" in a brief write-up in the *Dial*, calling it "strongly Varesian" and "genial."[88] In a later essay, he expanded on these modernist traits, applauding "the brilliance of its elevenths and thirteenths; the shrilling reedy clarinets, brittle, percussion-like pizzicati; and the thoroughly contrapuntal treatment of orchestral timbers [*sic*]."[89] Other New York modernists were equally impressed. In 1929 Cowell recommended "Dance of Men and Machines" to Slonimsky for a PAAC concert, and in 1933 Harris wanted to include it on a concert sponsored by Pro Musica, another musical society.[90] No New York critic perceived any outlines of dialectical indigenism, however, and certainly no political meaning was teased out of the score. At this time, Chávez was imbued with the precepts of the Mexican Revolution and considered the musician an "intellectual worker" charged with serving society.[91] These sentiments peaked with the compositions *Corrido de "El Sol"* and *Llamadas: Sinfonía proletaria*, both from 1934; he also worked on incidental music for the play by the communist writer Mike Gold, *Fiesta!*[92] Chávez, who never trumpeted his leftist politics to the extent that Rivera did, eventually inched to the right, however. The bewildering premiere of *H.P.* in its full ballet version almost seems to foretell this shift.

■ H.P. ONSTAGE: POLITICS OR *PORQUERÍA*?

For the much "ballyhooed" event, it fell upon Chávez and Rivera to unite the thorny topics just detailed in a coherent synthesis to the Rockefellers, Philadelphia Old Money, officials associated with Pan Americanism, and the general public. An additional challenge was the fact that the two were not foreigners exoticizing Latin America but Latin Americans shaping north-south images for northern consumption and bent on success in the Colossus of the North. Mainly, Chávez expanded on the strategies he had tested in 1926, depicting the North through machine music (tableaux 1 and 4, "Dance of Man," "Dance of Men and Machines") and the South through various Latin American dances and genres (tableaux 2 and 3, "Boat to the Tropics" and "The Tropics"). As Chávez completed the score, Littlefield set about the choreography, casting King Banana, the American Flapper, First Native, and the Red Snapper, along with other fanciful entities such as the Ventilator, Tobacco, and Cotton.[93] Of the creative trio, Rivera enjoyed the highest profile. His one-man show at New York's Museum of Modern Art had opened in late 1931, drawing 56,757 visitors and breaking previous attendance records at the museum.[94] In that exhibit, Rivera exalted the machine in *Pneumatic Drilling* and *Electric Power* but "infiltrated" an anticapitalist message in *Frozen Assets*, in which the urban skyline tops a morgue to send the macabre message that workers' bodies must be sacrificed to the temples of capitalism erected on their remains.[95]

As Rivera's designs for sets and costumes appeared in the press on the eve of the premiere, Chávez talked up the production with Linton Martin of the *Philadelphia Inquirer*.[96] The composer discussed his approach for capturing musically the "life of all America":

> *H.P.* is a symphony of the music that is in the very air and atmosphere of our continent…a sort of review of the epoch in which we live.…The tangos, huapangos, jazzes, and chanteys that are heard in *H.P.* have been written into the orchestration in the same natural form in which they are played at the fairs, popular saloons, public fiestas, or the plazuelas. *H.P.* contains expressions that are natural to our daily life, without attempting to select the "artistic."[97]

Besides showcasing these musical *objets trouvés*, the score addressed north-south difference as embedded in the plotline. Chávez explains:

> The sailors of North America find themselves intrigued and intoxicated by their own imagination of what the glamorous tropics hold for them, and finally the complete captivation of the machine-minded civilization by the allure and charm of the natural things in the universe. As the ship leaves the north, inhibitions tend to vanish under the warmer sun and above the bluer waters, until the southern port is reached. In this episode the [score] departs from the abstract musical setting and becomes frankly languorous and sensuous. It again grows abstract as the ship returns northward, the voyagers resume their mannered inhibitions, and the measured cadence of the machine rises as the curtain descends.

Thus the feminine South falls under the masculine northern gaze of sailors consumed with desire for the tropical Other. Yet at journey's end, the northerners resume their repressed way of life. Are they simply behaving like Vasconcelos's Yankees, "victims of their own characteristics"? Or was their exposure to the tropical Other such a profoundly transformative exercise in sameness-embracing that it brooked no further discussion? The production only obscured these questions. Nonetheless (and despite some discrepancies in press reports and other documents) its essentials can be reconstructed. First, the public would have read in Philip L. Leidy's notes in the Grand Opera program what amounted to a sugar-coated explanation of the dependency theory. For Leidy, the ballet "symbolizes the relations of the Northern regions with those of the Tropics and shows the inter-relationship of the industrialized United States with its southern neighbors who produce raw materials"; the ballet also "depicts the fact that the North needs the Tropics, just as the Tropics need the machinery of the North, and attempts to harmonize the result."[98] (Naturally no mention is made of exploitation of cheap labor or other structures of colonialist dominance.) Also greeting the Philadelphia audience was a proscenium arch. It featured a giant electric battery on the right and a horse and a palm tree on the left, with the letters "HP" mediating these symbols of the mechanical and the natural, which an unidentified critic for the *Los Angeles Times* dubbed "harmonization." Harmonization was called into question, however, by the position of the dancers flanking opposite sides of the stage. The same critic observed that those on the right typified the North's technological supremacy and those on the left "the tropical countries."[99] Next came the "Dance of Man," featuring the half-human, half-machine representative of northern machine culture, the protagonist H.P. A photograph of Dolinoff in the title role appeared in dailies on the East and West Coasts, showing gaskets connecting the various joints of his well-formed body.[100] Grasping a length of bolts, H.P. assumes a warrior-like stance while the firmness of his torso conveys groundedness even as the stiff bend of his elbows suggests inflexibility, perhaps of metal parts. Dolinoff himself recalled, "[I had] pistons on my head and on my legs and my arms (figs. 3d, 3e)."[101]

Figure 3d　Diego Rivera, *H.P.* proscenium frame. ©2012 Banco de México Diego Rivera Frida Kahlo Museums Trust, Mexico, D.F./Artists Rights Society (ARS), New York.

Chávez represents H.P.'s mechanical persona through the musical equivalent of dialectical indigenism: the ostinati, mixed meters, driving rhythms, block juxtaposition, and repeated melodic fragments of primitivism that are also the stock in trade of machine music. The numerous themes are often layered polyphonically, as in the ascending line in the cellos (doubled in winds) in the opening bars, noisily juxtaposed against *moto perpetuo* strings, and a theme in the brass (reh. 1) produces dissonances against the C-G open fifth in the tuba and low strings, with a thrice-repeated descending scale with parallel fourths cutting through the clatter.[102] As in "Dance of Men and Machines," Chávez incorporates "mangled Mexican ditties," some short-lived, such as the motives in trumpets (opening) or in the oboe (reh. 2), and others more substantive, such as the melody in the trumpet at reh. 6. When the popular tune evaporates (reh. 12), repeated slides in the low brass lead to a section in which wood block and snare take center stage. At reh. 17, the horns initiate a whirring trill and the violins begin circling around G, and by reh. 22, the Indian drum punctuates melodies of narrow range in the woodwinds and brass, the latter treated with dissonant, non-imitative counterpoint reminiscent of ur-classicism. A restatement of the machine music of the opening concludes the movement, all in the space of six breathless minutes (ex. 3b).

Tableau 2, "The Boat to the Tropics," opens with the "Danza Ágil" (Agile Dance), the static harmonies of which counter the dissonant "Dance of Man" and allow the sailors to demonstrate their physical coordination in a relaxed

Figure 3e Alexis Dolinoff as H.P. Jerome Robbins Dance Division, The New York Public Library for the Performing Arts, Astor, Lenox and Tilden Foundations.

dance filled with hemiola-laden passages. The flute and piccolo line leading into reh. 54 circles around A in a fourth- and fifth-based melody, suggesting Aztec *pitos* (clay flutes). In fact, the entire section serves as a prelude to the "Sirens' Tango," which represents the "nonchalance, sensuality, and seduction" described in the Grand Opera program and embodied by the sirens' sudden presence on the ship.[103] Fragments of its theme surface three times (reh. 49, mm. 1–4; rehs. 84 and 86, low brass) before the tango proper begins. Musically speaking, it raises several questions. Given the tango's origins in Buenos Aires, the genre is hardly a product of the tropics. Also, not only is Chávez's tempo too slow for the

Example 3b Carlos Chávez. "Dance of Man," *H.P.*, mvt. 1, mm. 44–51 (rehs. 12–14). © Copyright 1969 by Hawkes & Son (London), Ltd. Reprinted by permission.

(continued)

Example 3b (*continued*)

dance's usual urgency, but his instrumentation has little to do with the traditional tango ensemble of piano, violins, string bass, and bandoneón (button accordion), the plangent quality of which nearly defines the genre. Instead Chávez calls for saxophone, the instrument that replaced the waltzes and mazurkas of Porfirian Mexico, thus marking his tango as jazz-tinged (a mixing Astor Piazzolla would later explore). The percussion is also incongruous. At reh. 94 Chávez introduces claves, associated mainly with Afro-Cuban music; later we hear *güiro* and Indian drum, neither of which is especially prominent in the dance halls of Argentina, the whitest country in Latin America. Although one might suspect that Chávez is indigenizing the tango, the oddly prominent snare drum eliminates this possibility.[104]

These anomalies make sense in terms of musical *mestizaje*, however. The "Sirens' Tango" closely resembles the *danzón*, a genre that came to Mexico through Cuba, with its strong tradition of African influence.[105] The *danzón* does use the *güiro*, and its *timbales* (salsa drums) have a metallic ring not unlike Chávez's snare drum. The rhythmic cells in the "Sirens' Tango" (*güiro* and claves), also associated with the *danzón*, can be found in works such as "La Comparsa," the well-known *danzón* by Ernesto Lecuona. Similar cells appear in "northern" ragtime as well, which involves a syncopated melody against a steady *oom-pah* accompaniment. (A central difference between a rag and a *danzón* is the syncopated accompaniment of the latter.) The *danzón* and the rag are also related formally: each involves a free arrangement of sections such as ABCDCD or a similar combination. Various art music composers have been attracted to the *danzón*, including Arturo Márquez of Mexico, who composed the multisectional "Danzón no. 2," which uses claves and timbales in a symphonic format, and Copland, whose foray into musical *mestizaje*, *Danzón cubano*, relies on the rhythmic cells and syncopations demanded by the genre (exs. 3c–3f).[106]

Elsewhere in the "Sirens' Tango," Chávez hews more closely to the tango's norms. The motive introduced in the English and French horns (reh. 97) echoes a phrase of "Adios, muchachos" by Julio Sanders, a tango known in the United States since the 1930s, when it was performed (in English) by the Italian tenor Nino Martini.[107] In the "Sirens' Tango" it leads into a B section in the parallel major, common in any number of tangos (and in other Latin American popular genres as well). The prominent solo violin line of the B section is also closer to the tango's origins. Thus, in combining *danzón* and tango, Chávez fashions a hybrid form that reaches across boundaries of genre, region, and race in a manner analogous to the fluid processes of racial identity.

If tableau 2 represents travel to the gendered tropics, by tableau 3 viewers have definitively arrived at the isthmus of Tehuantepec, with its defiant, capable women and rich natural resources immortalized in the Secretariat murals. Just as in O. Henry's banana republics, time is "redundant": as the program explained, the "natives are . . . whiling away their time in dance."[108] Displaying the bodily ease to which Vasconcelos alluded, Tehuana women move about gracefully, reveling in tropical abundance as a gaggle of gigantic pineapples and coconuts appears onstage led by the equally large King Banana, whose phallic presence barely registers on the crowded stage. As for the music, we first hear a *huapango*, a lively dance based on alternating two- and three-beat patterns and often performed on a wooden platform (*tarima*) and subject to numerous regional variants.[109] (Like the *danzón*, the *huapango* has been adapted for concert music, most famously by José Pablo Moncayo in 1941.) As in the "Agile Dance," we find

Examples 3c, 3d, 3e Carlos Chávez. "Sirens' Tango," *H.P.*, mvt. 2 (rhythmic cells).

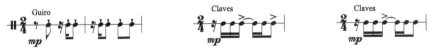

Example 3f Ernesto Lecuona. "La Comparsa," mm. 1–4 (basic rhythm).

plenty of metric friction; here, however, the hemiola is more generously laced with percussion, including maracas, *güiro*, and the claves so prominent in the "Sirens' Tango." Surfacing briefly (rehs. 165, 168, and 187) is a pentatonic fragment, one that occurs in nine of Chávez's works as well as in several Mexican folk songs;[110] a *son*-like popular melody harmonized in thirds and sixths (reh. 172) adds to the mix of styles as well. All become unglued in a dissonant section at reh. 188, which may allude to the *desplante*, the section of the *huapango veracruzano* during which dancers can rest or exchange good-natured insults. The *desplante* itself derives from the Spanish *fandango*, as Paul Bowles pointed out in an article for *Modern Music*. In the same essay, he bemoaned the terminological confusion in Mexican popular music, noting that due to its sheer variety, style labels are used "with complete interchangeability," with the term *fandango*, for example, appearing "in connection with the playing of Sones, Huapangos . . . called *Rondeñas, Malagueñas*, and so on."[111] As we have seen, the vocabulary of racial categorization was equally daunting.

The "Agile Dance" also draws on *mestizaje* through the extended marimba interlude with solo violin (beginning reh. 175). Associated with Guatemala and the Mexican state of Chiapas (just east of Oaxaca), the marimba was brought to the Western Hemisphere by Africans but was so thoroughly adopted in Chiapas, Oaxaca, Guatemala, Nicaragua, and the Ecuadorian-Colombian Pacific littoral that many accept it as Amerindian. Debates over the marimba's African roots have been tinged with racism, but because it has adapted so completely to the region, T. M. Scruggs calls the marimba a "shared instrument."[112] Accordingly, Chávez assigns all three percussionists the same marimba for this prominent solo, in which harmonically static passages with concatenating melodic lines (reh. 180–82) recall the *son jarocho* (a *son* from Veracruz state).[113] After interjections in the low brass and a new *son* melody (reh. 185), the *desplante* unwinds in a protracted cadence for the full orchestra (reh. 193), in which alternating tonic-subdominant harmonies and offbeat accents imitate the rapid strum of repeated chords on the *jarana*, a small guitar used in the *huapango*. To the uninitiated ear, the passage suggests a giant, accordion-like machine, as if mechanization were growing naturally out of the tropics. Additional folk-like fragments, along with a sustained countermelody, pile up, with a modal shift (two bars before reh. 201) leading into the next section.

In the second half of tableau 3 Chávez represents the female South with a *sandunga* (variant: *zandunga*), a triple-meter, multisectional dance from Tehuantepec with a prominent marimba part, often doubling the melody line.[114] The adjectival form of the word not only conveys grace, charm, and vivaciousness but can enhance a description of an inviting young woman.[115] The *sandunga* is also associated with the cycles of nature and procreation and traditionally figured in Tehuantepec weddings, part of which involve presenting the bride with flowers.[116] Several creative minds have seen the *sandunga* in this light. In his unfinished film *¡Que viva México!* Sergey Eisenstein treated the matriarchal society of Tehuantepec in a section entitled "Sandunga," which depicted "semi-animal, semi-vegetable and biologically unconscious existence," as he stated; likewise, in sketches for the project, the director likened the earth's abundance to a naked female with a voluptuous body.[117] The *sandunga* even found its way to Walt Disney. In his Pan Americanist cartoon feature *The Three Caballeros*, an early attempt at combining live actors with animation, an airy soprano voice-over sings the *sandunga*'s lyrics of desire while an oversexed Donald Duck joins hands with a young woman (a live actor), accentuating the difference between erotic fantasy and the reality of the body as a thicket of garish blue petals gyrate in time with the omnipresent rolls of the marimba.

In *H.P.*, Chávez quotes liberally and literally from existing *sandungas*.[118] But just as he tinkered with convention in the "Sirens' Tango," he alters the instrumentation here, minimizing the emblematic marimba and assigning it largely accompanimental status. Chávez's *sandunga* also proclaims hybridity, albeit from a surprising source: Europe. Through *Fortspinnung*, the baroque process of continuing a melody through the working-out of material, Chávez reinforces several cadence points, such as at reh. 205, where a D-minor triad is spun out in the woodwinds along with its dominant, or the extension at reh. 207 in the strings, a procedure not uncommon in folkloric *sandungas*.[119] Chávez intensifies this resource in the final cadence, not only drawing on *Fortspinnung* but augmenting the note values and calling on the full orchestra to inject into the tropical paradise the exuberant style of a Stokowski Bach transcription. He also inserts a dissonant F-sharp in the glockenspiel, which pierces through the D-minor triad, reverberating in the dark at the Philadelphia premiere during the scene change for the final tableau, "City of Industry (ex. 3g)."

With that mocking sonority, Chávez introduces the workers' rebellion, led by H.P. himself.[120] When the houselights dimmed, the public beheld a bleak skyline almost identical to that in *Frozen Assets* of Rivera's MoMA show, accompanied here by a *fff* trumpet blast of the "Sidewalks of New York" motive. The workers encounter an American Flapper, clearly an allusion to "Wall Street Banquet" of the Secretariat murals. Unlike the powerful Tehuana women, however, the Flapper is ineffectual, for her efforts to quell the demonstration come to naught. Throughout the final tableau, the dialectical indigenous "Dance of Men and Machines" accompanies dance sequences by H.P. and by the *corps de ballet* with a great deal of nervous energy. Interpretations of the scene conflict, however. According to the Grand Opera program, the "sullen and unruly" workers rebel

against the despotism of Machinery, as Capitalism, represented by a large stock ticker, becomes panic-stricken. The workers revolt and open a Safe, representing the wealth of the world, out of which come finally all the Natural resources of the Earth; gold, silver, cotton, iron, etc., and the fruit and produce of the soil. The workers resume their toil as the sun sets on a resumption of the more normal activities of Man and a return to simpler methods of labor and living.[121]

Example 3g Carlos Chávez. "Sandunga," *H.P.*, mvt. 3, mm. 412–20. © Copyright 1969 by Hawkes & Son (London), Ltd. Reprinted by permission.

This was risky subject matter to offer the likes of Rockefeller in 1932, one of the worst years of the Depression. Consequently another program was hastily printed up after the event as a souvenir and reproduced in the *Bulletin of the Pan American Union* with an eye to damage control. It squelches any threat of class struggle or political discontent, observing merely:

Man collects the raw materials of the earth; gold, silver, cotton, tobacco, and the
machinery which enables him to dominate his surroundings, and satisfy his desire

and needs. The world at work, dominated by the stock ticker, denoting increasing wealth. Mankind's struggle for its welfare revolts against mere material values, reverting to an insatiable desire for the natural products of the earth. Men and raw materials dance and blend into the rhythm of H.P. as the Ballet ends.[122]

In the souvenir program, workers are no longer bent on dismantling capitalism but merely question slavery to materialism. Rather than a safe forcibly opened the Safe, it is eliminated so that the Earth's bounty can simply be "collected." The stock ticker (like the Safe and the Flapper, an allusion to "Wall Street Banquet") no longer symbolizes a corrupt and powerful few but prosperity for humankind. Last, the horde is apotheosized: rather than revealing the rage of the underclass, it now represents "mankind" and "Man," who seek only to satisfy basic human needs. In short, the rescripting of the final scene promoted the sort of Pan Americanism its U.S. architects conceived rather than that of "Red" ideologues.[123]

The final scene also left critics scratching their heads. Several make no mention whatsoever of a revolt, much less defiant anticapitalism. Not even Blitzstein, whose communist sympathies surely would have endeared him to the workers' plight, sensed any such meaning. The reporter for the *Philadelphia Record*, for example, described only "drab, colorless men and women" who open a vault "in the middle of their sooty parade."[124] John Martin bypassed any question of an uprising, claiming that the finale was impossible to follow even with the synopsis and, in the second of his three pieces on the ballet, essentially threw up his hands to conclude that *H.P.* was "entirely without plot."[125] If Oscar Thompson sensed that "something like a revolt" took place, the few critics who perceived anticapitalist intent collectively rolled their eyes.[126] One described the final tableau as "a sinister tocsin telling us that we are disintegrating, that hustle, bustle, ticker tape . . . are driving us to Hell."[127] Robert Reiss, in a piece entitled "*H.P.* Presentation Is Swell Occasion but Lacks Timely Proletarian Touch," wisecracked:

> One felt a little sorry there were no representatives of the proletariat present . . . since the ballet was designed by a Mexican Communist, Diego Rivera. . . . It was understood that [the management of the Philadelphia Grand Opera] had been asked to import a couple of hard-boiled proletarians from the Labor Temple just to give the occasion a dash of the real thing . . . but the proletarians didn't know what it was all about.[128]

Part of the confusion lay in the difficulty of interpreting H.P.'s costume. Only a viewer intimately familiar with the Secretariat murals would connect the pistons on Dolinoff's ankles to the butterfly-cocoon leggings of the Yaqui deer dancer. Yet it is precisely this reading, which privileges the indigenous dance of kinship and community, that elucidates the mysterious final scene, for as Belnap points out, no representative of U.S. machine culture would lead a rebellion against U.S. machine culture. Piston-cocoon leggings and all, H.P. represents the resilience of indigenous values in modern technology, much the way the stamping press in *Detroit Industry* symbolized in an equally recondite allusion the enduring presence of Coatlicue.[129]

If plot, sets, and costumes were deemed incomprehensible, so too was Chávez's score. Critics heard his stylistic mixing not as a celebration of *mestizaje* but as a muddle. One problem was the fact that by 1932 machine music had started to run its course. The premiere five years earlier of Antheil's *Ballet Méca-nique*, with its ten pianos, a propeller, pianola, and siren, had irritated critics and lacked even *scandale* value.[130] The machine music in *H.P.* annoyed the antimod-ernists and frustrated the forward-looking. Leading the former was Henry C. Beck (or rather, his "lowbrow" alter ego, Beck C. Henry), who found "patches of tamale here and there but mostly . . . that clashing of sound, that mixture of racket, that bedlam that belies what music really is, which so delight the fol-lowers of Dr. Stokowski."[131] Mary F. Watkins, reporting for the *New York Herald Tribune*, applauded Chávez's references to indigenous music but also accused him of indulging in "a great deal of noise."[132] Linton Martin, on the other hand, deemed *H.P.* about as "revolutionary as your grandmother's lace ruffles."[133] Thompson too noted the ballet's anachronistic bent, calling the American Flapper the "sole survivor of the flapper age."[134] He was hardly more encouraging on Chávez's score, observing that although it "resolves itself into rhythm for dancing, plus scenic sound" with all the "melodic basis . . . of a Sunday band con-cert in the park," Chávez the modernist, "could not permit this kind of thing to dominate his ballet" and therefore "subordinates his tunes to a heaping of rest-less idioms, now atonal, now polytonal, now plain tonal," such that "the ear is confronted with every sort of scoring. . . . By turns it is harsh, truculent, steely, pulsatile, violent, muffled—and it must be confessed, sometimes confused."[135]

Blitzstein reflected on machine music and north-south identity. Certainly he acknowledged portions of the score in which a "charged, fighting music breaks through . . . till the sound almost cracks."[136] Yet the reason *H.P.* as a whole failed to live up to these isolated moments was the work's "strange, unreferable finality like the sort found in all 'local-color' art."[137] In Chávez's case, local color was complicated by his "characteristic" classicism, the very quality that had won him favor with the New York modernist crowd. As an innate classicist, Chávez composed music that was "hard, not soft, literal, brutal and unperfumed," thus forcing listeners to confront "the paradox of a 'Southern' composer dealing most successfully with the 'Northern' aspects of his theme" and representing far less convincingly his own languorous South.[138] North and South could not meet even in the same person. Even more objectionable were the other produc-tion elements. According to Blitzstein, the "enormous papier-maché pineapples, cocoanuts, bananas, and palm trees" were nothing but "the amiable products of a child's imagination [and] took up so much room that . . . the Big Fish got in the way of the Grand Pineapple, and the stage was invariably messy and ugly to look at."[139] Thus Chávez's score accompanied the spectacle of tropical abun-dance deteriorating into clutter, a problem Littlefield's casting, which relied on locals, only exacerbated. The choreographer had hired a "crowd of insipid blonds pretending they were Indians from Tehuantepec," as Frida Kahlo commented to a friend. In the end, Kahlo complained, *H.P.* was a "god awful mess" (*porquería*).[140]

Could any critical approach possibly distance Chávez from the pathetic image of the Grand Pineapple losing its balance in the tropics? Enter Paul Rosenfeld. Shortly after the premiere, he published a quick write-up for the *New Republic*, praising the "feeling of sun, of abundance and young strength" in *H.P.* but questioning, ever so gently, some of Chávez's representational strategies, such as incorporating into the *sandunga* "the severe style of a Bach two-part invention."[141] Weeks later these brief observations crystallized into an essay for *Modern Music*. In it, Rosenfeld came surprisingly close to articulating the values of dialectical indigenism. He writes, "*H.P.* begins with the dance of man in Aztec fire and splendor, in the youth and fullness of his naked powers; . . . celebrates Indian adjustment to the bitter conditions of the harsh unfriendly old continent: peace, union, equilibrium with its virginal and unfriendly forces; and final light, mobile, impassive superiority to them. The man has his motor within him, and is automotive."[142] To be sure, Rosenfeld imagined not a Yaqui protagonist but the more familiar Aztec, the object of so much idealization during the Mexican vogue. As in contemplating ur-classicism, Rosenfeld is much taken with the indigenous presence, so much so that here he situates the machine music in "Dance of Man" not in the contemporary industrialized North it actually represents, but in the same "virginal circumstance" from which ur-classicism had sprung: the "old continent," or ancient America. Just as Stokowski imagined the New York City skyline as "more Aztec than anything else," Rosenfeld, struggling to make sense of the work in Pan Americanist terms, understood its references to mechanization in terms of the indigenous heritage.

Rosenfeld also subverted gender, challenging the convention of the feminine, submissive South. For despite *H.P.*'s origins below the Rio Grande, the protagonist is exuberantly male. Chávez's music was "a dance of the male on the American soil," of a male who is "good humored, robust . . . ultimately detached: in the plenitude of liberated energies, in joyous reserve, in derisive impenetrability."[143] Further, this blend of Eagle Scout, noble savage, and Mister Machine was a specimen of health and vigor, enjoying the "fullness of naked powers." These characteristics are also a harbinger for the rest of Chávez's music, which, in accordance with the masculinist discursive practices of the era, Rosenfeld does not hesitate to gender.[144] The "Dance of Man," for example, hints at "the masculine quality of [Chávez's] fuller, later pieces," which in turn constitute "a rhythmic expression of masculine completeness and independence on the American soil."[145] Unlike Blitzstein, who found Chávez's "hard, not soft, literal, brutal and unperfumed" (northern) music to be a "paradox," Rosenfeld concluded from it that Chávez had transcended geography and gender stereotypes, eschewing the restraints of the South to become one of "us."

In thus exalting the primitive man, Rosenfeld reinforced H.P.'s—and Chávez's—non-European status. Such moves were familiar to Rosenfeld. For example, he was no fan of Edward MacDowell, whose works amounted to little more than "an assimilation of European motives, figures, and ideas" and who was guilty of writing music that "minces and simpers, maidenly and ruffled."[146] The primitive man was an especially attractive figure in the United States in the post-Victorian period, during which exaggerated masculinity served as one more means of throwing off the restraints of a past largely unusable for its undue refinement and timidity.[147] Corroborating this new understanding of manhood were Teddy Roosevelt's strenuous physical activity, so-called Muscular Christianity, and the popular Tarzan stories. In part, this phenomenon stemmed from fear, as threats to Anglo-Saxon manhood seemed to be coming from all quarters: women, immigrants, African Americans, and, as Nadine Hubbs points out, homosexuals. Cultivating the "mobile, impassive superiority" Rosenfeld extolled was especially crucial during the Great Depression, when so many men were deprived of their hunter-gatherer status. Gilbert Seldes even came to believe that male desperation emerged in the "plaintiveness, the self-accusation, the emasculatory atmosphere of the American songs" of the era";[148] other songs mask angst with humor. In "Find Me a Primitive Man" from the 1929 Cole Porter musical *Fifty Million Frenchmen*, a young woman is on the prowl not for "the kind that belongs to a club but the kind that has a club that belongs to him."

Unfortunately, in *H.P.* rugged virility missed the mark. Just as the American Flapper was ultimately powerless, the ballet's protagonist lapsed into impotence. Thompson reported that while dancing, H.P. "cast behind himself a shadow much larger than he," a lighting scheme that only emphasized limitation and smallness of stature.[149] Martin noted that pitting the 114-piece orchestra against "one human figure" effectively reduced H.P. to a cipher, who barely got the opportunity to dance in any case.[150] H.P.'s frustrated movements recall Adorno's remarks on the semi-mechanical Petrushka: pathetically trapped in his body and manifesting the alienation of self from society so characteristic of modernity, he represents the "distorted, conspicuous, individual delivered up to the others."[151] In 1932 such existential despair was only too real for those emasculated by economic distress, which many blamed on industrialization and mechanization, the very attributes of the industrialized North H.P. celebrated.

Still, like any 1930s Hollywood musical, in which all tensions are resolved in a splashy production number, *H.P.* ends on a cheery note. Thompson, who had glimpsed "something like a revolt," observed that this "something" was followed in short order by "a new day," adding that all of a sudden "H.P., Flapper, Bananas, Pineapples, Cocoanuts, Sailors, and Stevedores [were] apparently on the best of terms." With the workers' dust-up assuaged and the dangers of anticapitalism neatly squelched, *H.P.* effectively trivialized exploitation, racial identity, and the constraints of geopolitical gender stereotyping. Clearly the ballet's failure to convey the message of hemispheric cooperation, the virtues of which had been trumpeted for so many weeks, was due in large part to dialectical indigenism's elusiveness. For some peculiar reason, its essential principles were grasped only by Chávez's devoted admirer, Paul Rosenfeld.

■ RETURN TO UR-CLASSICISM

Almost immediately after *H.P.*'s thwarted premiere, Chávez refocused on ur-classicism. He asserted its principles in his first symphony, the *Sinfonía Antígona* of 1933. Originally conceived as incidental music for an adaptation of Sophocles' tragedy by Cocteau, the *Sinfonía Antígona* is one of several Chávez works inspired by Greek antiquity. These include the 1956 cantata *Prometeo encadenado* (Prometheus Bound) and the 1957 work for solo oboe, *Upingos*, incidental music to Novo's adaptation of Euripides's *Hipólita* (Hippolytus).[152] With its quartal and quintal harmonies, some based on Dorian and Hypodorian modes, the symphony strikes an overtly classic pose.

To be sure, initial reaction to the U.S. premiere in June 1934, conducted by the Spanish pianist-conductor José Iturbi (not yet of Hollywood fame), was less than encouraging.[153] Taking up the banner of absolute music, Chávez insisted in his program note that despite its theatrical origins, the *Sinfonía Antígona* should be understood as a symphony rather than as a symphonic poem, a remark to which Howard Taubman, recently hired at the *New York Times*, reacted. Like those critics who had found Chávez's music severe or "scarcely rewarding" in 1928, Taubman believed that the composer had so exaggerated the symphony's abstract qualities as to render the Greek heroine "bloodless."[154] The work fared better in 1936, when Chávez performed it in Boston, perhaps because, as a conductor, he approximated Rosenfeld's primitive man. Critics observed, for example, that he was "of the sturdy, athletic type," and "tall, well-built."[155] They also remarked on the naturalness of his habit of conducting without a baton, with one reviewer noting the ability of the "dark, spare musician of almost Indian aspect" to coax "freshness" from his players.[156] Yet just the right touch of intellectualism accompanied Chávez's primitive aura, as can be seen in the October 1936 issue of *Vogue* magazine, which features a photograph of the bespectacled composer against the backdrop of a Mexican pyramid, contemplating with furrowed brow the essence of ancient America.[157]

Boston Post critic Warren Storey Smith considered the power of the *Sinfonía Antígona* via the "rhythmic, harmonic and melodic elements essential to the early theory of Greek music."[158] Downes marveled at the symphony's "savage" quality, but instead of invoking tomahawks and scalping, he linked "savagery" to a classic value, specifically, "clearness of line."[159] In 1937, when Chávez conducted the *Sinfonía Antígona* with the New York Philharmonic-Symphony Orchestra,

Francis D. Perkins of the *New York Herald Tribune* found "considerable dignity" in the work, and a Philadelphia critic observed that the symphony "reeks with the background of classicism, for which the composer is renowned."[160] As might be expected, Rosenfeld enthused over the *Sinfonía Antígona*, upholding it as "classic music in the grand severe style" and, forgoing the vivid imagery of "high Mexican deserts," used some form of the word *austere* six times in as many pages.[161]

The next big moment in Chávez's career in the United States was the premiere in 1936 of *Sinfonía India*, his best-known work. Just as Willa Cather was inspired to write about Nebraska from her Greenwich Village apartment, Chávez completed the *Sinfonía India* far from his source of inspiration, during one of his many visits to New York. More has been written on the *Sinfonía India* than on any other composition by Chávez, with its Indianist elements commanding the most attention.[162] These include native melodies and indigenous percussion instruments, such as the *teponatzli* (two-keyed xylophone), the *huehuetl* (drum), a string of deer hooves, a water gourd, and *tenebari* (butterfly-cocoon rattles), the latter used in the Yaqui deer dance.[163] The main classicizing element is its one-movement symphonic format, for which the experienced listener instinctively takes sonata form as a point of reference.[164] Yet even the Indian themes unite Europe and the primitive Other. As Saavedra observes, many of the melodies available to Chávez at this time were tonal rather than pentatonic, ensuring that even in his best-known Indianist work Chávez draws on *mestizaje*.[165] As we have seen, he had done precisely that on a grand scale in *H.P.*

Much of the U.S. media drew attention to these Indianist traits. In an article on Chávez in the *New York Times*, Taubman noted that the composer's compatriots, Daniel Ayala and Blas Galindo, were composers "of full-blooded Indian descent" and that among the new generation of Mexican composers (Luis Sandi, José Pablo Moncayo, Silvestre Revueltas, and Francisco Contreras) most have at least some Indian ancestry. For Chávez, Taubman observed, it was "a source of pride . . . to know that he is even partly of Indian extraction" and heir to its heritage.[166] Chávez himself reported for *Modern Music* on various Indianist projects undertaken by his composition class in the National Conservatory in Mexico City, resulting in works such as Sandi's *El Venado* (The Deer) and Ayala's *U Kayl Chaac*.[167] In *Musical Quarterly* Herbert Weinstock dwelt on Chávez's ability to transmit to his listeners the essence of ancient America, a result of finding "in his own blood" communion with Mexico rather than Europe.[168] In keeping with the spirit of dialectical indigenism, however, Chávez also sinks "his roots firmly in the soil of Mexico" while drawing "nourishment from Philadelphia . . . and New York as well."[169] A less nuanced attempt at public relations came from the creator of dialectical indigenism himself: Rivera bluntly declared in *Musical America*, "In Mexican music there are only Carlos Chávez and the Indians."[170] Chávez, however, took pains to emphasize common ground between Indian music and the Western classical tradition. To the *New York-World Telegram* he remarked that in Indian music the same basic principles apply . . . as in the classic symphony, for example. A classic symphony with regard to form, consists of an inter-relation of two themes of different character. . . . Occasionally a . . . [primitive] song will show that it has only one theme. But the primitive people made up the deficit by supplying another song to complement the first. And there you have your two themes all over again. "Primitive" music is really not so primitive. It is ancient and therefore sophisticated.[171]

Thus the Indian music of ancient America is not so very different from those sonata forms perfected by Haydn, Mozart, and, of course, the universal Beethoven, whose music, as Rosenfeld once mused, seemed to have existed "since the beginning of the world."

Several critics of the *Sinfonía India* embraced sameness. Shortly after the premiere in January 1936, with Chávez conducting the CBS Radio Symphony, Colin McPhee noted select classical attributes, such as "sharp and clear" outlines.[172] Although he found the work to exude "primitive energy," however, McPhee insisted that it had "nothing of the exotic."[173] Maud Cuney-Hare probably had the *Sinfonía India* in mind when she wrote in 1936 in her study of African American music that Chávez was the Mexican composer "who alone writes universally."[174] In 1942, at the height of the Good Neighbor period, John Cage held that the *Sinfonía India* "could very easily become our Pan-American *Bolero*" and invoked absolute music by adding that in quoting Indian melodies, Chávez had availed himself of an "essentially musical" source, one that "relies completely on musical elements which never call for literary explanations but speak in terms of rhythm and sound." Further, Cage proposed, in "hearing this *Symphony* for the first time one has the feeling of remembering it. . . . The *Sinfonía India* is the land we all walk on, made audible."[175] Ur-classicism, which united ancient America in universal terms, thus offered North and South a common usable past.

Throughout the 1930s the "enormous vogue of things Mexican" gradually wound down, in part due to political tensions between the United States and Mexico.[176] Some in the United States believed that President Lázaro Cárdenas (1934–40) veered dangerously close to communism, even if the Mexican Left attacked what they perceived as his coziness with the bourgeoisie.[177] During the Spanish Civil War (1936–39), Mexico challenged the official neutrality of the United States by aiding the left-leaning Spanish Republic, alone with the Soviet Union. In March 1938 the Mexican government nationalized foreign-owned oil companies, causing a furor in business circles in the United States and straining Roosevelt's Good Neighborly intentions, already articulated in 1933.

As a representative of Standard Oil, Nelson A. Rockefeller (son of John D. Rockefeller Jr. and Abby Aldrich Rockefeller) shrewdly combined art, business, and politics, traveling to Mexico to negotiate personally with Cárdenas. Although Rockefeller was unsuccessful, it is worth noting that he presented himself not as the U.S. capitalist par excellence but as the recently installed president of

MoMA.[178] In May 1940, the same year G. Schirmer brought out Chávez's *Ten Preludes* for solo piano, the museum presented the exhibit *Twenty Centuries of Mexican Art*.[179] The exhibit involved concerts of Mexican music, affording one more opportunity to contemplate sameness and difference. It also yielded an opening vignette for Robert M. Stevenson's still authoritative *Music in Mexico* of 1952. Perceiving the Pan Americanist enthusiasm of the day, Stevenson observes that "the music chosen by critics and public . . . was that which was thought to show the least traces of European influence."[180] Among the works performed were an eighteenth-century mass and arrangements of popular genres, including *sones mariachi* and a *huapango*, along with Yaqui music from Sonora state. Chávez and his research team arranged popular genres into sonata or variation form. Since the idea that primitive music could coexist with time-honored "universal" models had been current for over a decade, Chávez was hardly breaking new epistemological ground when he declared Blas Galindo's *Sones Mariachi* a "highly developed, true sonata movement," in which the Indian element, "far from losing character, has been intensified."[181] There was also Chávez's own chamber work, *Xochipili*, in which he attempted to re-create the essentials of Aztec music by replicating the complexity of the Western art music tradition.[182] A hint of the *mestizaje* so unsuccessfully realized in *H.P.* insinuated itself when Chávez acknowledged that a major feature of Mexican music is "crossbreeding."[183] In sum, the MoMA concerts hardly suggested nationalism; in fact, just as in 1928, Mexican music had provoked universalist stirrings on the part of listeners and participants alike.

Another reason the Mexican vogue lost steam was that the Good Neighbor Policy, directed at all of Latin America, diminished interest in the specifically Mexican. Pan Americanist sameness-embracing now shifted to other sites and implied a host of new propositions. One, the Amazon jungle, was related to the much-debated music of Heitor Villa-Lobos, performed at the 1939 New York World's Fair. Sustaining not a reformulation of but a *crisis* of primitivism, it is the subject of the next two chapters.

4 Caliban and Unsublimated Primitivism

Villa-Lobos at the 1939 World's Fair

On April 30, 1939, the World's Fair opened in New York, taking as its theme "The World of Tomorrow." Symbolizing this forward-looking orientation were the modernist Trylon and Perisphere, the former an obelisk of some 700 feet, and the latter an 180-foot ball. Fairgoers attuned to recent trends in art admired qualities one critic tagged as "abstract purity" and "universal appeal" in these structures, both of unelaborated white.[1] The Perisphere, moreover, did double duty, serving as an enclosure for Democracity, a diorama of an urban center of the future in which technology and democracy would ensure a better life for all.[2] Affirming the role of the United States in this democratic utopia was the sixty-five-foot statue of George Washington, who had been inaugurated 150 years earlier.[3] Much of the Fair's architecture proclaimed with equal vigor the virtues of the so-called American (U.S.) way of life, including the free enterprise system. Most explicit here was the National Cash Register Building, atop which a gigantic cash register loomed over the proceedings in all its prosaic glory (figs. 4a, 4b).

The music of the Fair complemented these varied perspectives on "The World of Tomorrow." Its official march was "Dawn of a New Day," which Gershwin had not lived to complete but which Kay Swift assembled from three of his unpublished melodies, with lyrics by his brother Ira.[4] The African American composer William Grant Still wrote *Song of the City* for the Democracity exhibit, drawing on what he called his "universal style" (i.e., lacking African American signifiers) and depicting life in the futuristic metropolis with a massive choir that "reached out of the heavens" and rose to "diapasonal heights," as the guidebook exulted.[5] At the Ford Pavilion, Ferde Grofé and three colleagues demonstrated the Hammond Novachord and organ. Copland's score for the puppet play *From Sorcery to Science* enlivened the Hall of Pharmacy, and in his *Railroads on Parade*, Kurt Weill called for orchestra, chorus, and fifteen historical locomotives.[6] By night, fairgoers lingering at the Lagoon of Nations could thrill to Robert Russell Bennett's *The Spirit of George Washington*, a medley of national airs scored for concert band enhanced with red, white, and blue spurts of water manipulated by technicians behind a console. At the Hall of Music, the cognoscenti could sample live concerts of art music.

A trenchant reaction to this omnium-gatherum of musical styles came from Elliott Carter, who reported on the Fair for *Modern Music*. He saw fit to "deplore the conscious writing down to popular taste" in Bennett's homage to the first

Figure 4a Trylon and Perisphere, New York World's Fair, 1939. Manuscripts and Archives Division, The New York Public Library, Astor, Lenox and Tilden Foundations.

president, and he sniffed at the ubiquitous loudspeakers emitting throughout the fairgrounds everything from "soupy" Strauss waltzes to selections from *Schéhérezade* and the *L'Arlésienne* suite. These, he believed, forced upon fairgoers the "expression of jollity and merriment," as if some "huge Walt Disney monster [were] pouring out his weepy soul in a slightly inarticulate voice."[7] Still, other music redeemed these lapses into crass commodification. Those fleeing the omnipresent Walt Disney enjoyed unfamiliar works in the Hall of Music such as *Symphonie Concertante* by the recently deceased Karol Szymanowski of Poland or *Variations on an Original Theme* by Jonel Perlea of Rumania. Other art music concerts were dedicated to entire countries, including two all-Brazilian programs on May 4 and 9. Carter found these "showy, torrid," and the "most fun" of any musical event the Fair had to offer (fig. 4c, website).[8]

Brazilian composers represented were Burle Marx (who also conducted), Carlos Gomes, Francisco Mignone, and Oscar Lorenzo Fernandez. It was Heitor Villa-Lobos, however, who "made the deepest impression," as Thompson wrote

Figure 4b National Cash Register Building, New York World's Fair, 1939. Manuscripts and Archives Division, The New York Public Library, Astor, Lenox and Tilden Foundations.

in the *New York Sun*.[9] Other critics, including not only Carter but Rosenfeld, Perkins, Samuel Chotzinoff, Edward O'Gorman, Irving Kolodin, Jerome D. Bohm, and Downes, all seemed to concur, to judge from the amount of space they gave his works.[10] Downes, who was in charge of the Fair's music, devoted two columns to the Brazilian concerts, along with a lengthy piece on Villa-Lobos alone for the Sunday section of the *New York Times*.[11] For all intents and purposes, the Fair was Villa-Lobos's U.S. debut. Only a handful of his works had ever been performed in the United States, and his reputation rested largely on "hearsay," as Rosenfeld acknowledged.[12] Some of this talk was less than encouraging. In January 1930, New York's Schola Cantorum offered *Choros* no. 10 for chorus and orchestra (the title refers to a Brazilian urban popular genre, discussed below). The aggressively primitivist work caused Downes to suspect that

Villa-Lobos was too much the showman, "always yelling and beating his drum," to find favor with the public.[13] In March 1932, the *Quarteto simbólico* for flute, saxophone, celesta, harp (or piano), and female voices figured on a League of Composers program and fared even worse. For Israel Citkowitz, the piece amounted to little more than travel music of a distinctly commercial bent, perhaps on the level of a Hollywood film:

> Here was music distinctly of accompaniment-to-a-travelog-film order, both in the nature of its content and its way of progressing. Local color was plentiful. The meandering of the instrumental sections suited perfectly a scenic anthology by the camera. Even the placing of the women's voices, coming arbitrarily and too fragmentarily, considering the length of the work, suggested that the women of the village were singing at sundown and that the camera-man happened to be around.[14]

Yet Villa-Lobos had his supporters in the United States. One was Martha Graham, who choreographed several of his scores in *Primitive Canticles* and *Primitive Mysteries*, part of her campaign to promote American dance.[15] Another was the Wisconsin-born pianist, teacher, and writer Irving Schwerké, who reported on Villa-Lobos for the *League of Composers' Review* from Paris, where the composer spent much of the 1920s. In his essay "A Brazilian Rabelais," Schwerké expounded on the composer's larger-than-life musical personality, calling special attention to his "lawless rhythm."[16]

At the Fair critics digested an unprecedented quantity of Villa-Lobos's music but concentrated on two orchestral works: "The Hillbilly's Little Train" (the final movement of the *Bachianas brasileiras* no. 2) and *Choros* no. 8. The former struck some as hackneyed, perhaps even an example of what Carter called "writing down." The latter both repelled and attracted critics, with some questioning its scope, intensity, and form, while others hailed it as "a *Sacre du printemps* of the Amazon." Downes, now inclined to evaluate more thoughtfully Villa-Lobos's "yelling and beating his drum," dubbed this primitivist score "Caliban, if you like, and the jungle (fig. 4d, website)."[17]

To be sure, by equating Villa-Lobos's music with the feral, deformed character in *The Tempest*, Downes unwittingly put his finger on the polemic over sensibility, power, race, and resistance in Latin America that Rodó initiated with his essay *Ariel* nearly four decades earlier. Yet neither Caliban nor jungle thickets had much to do with the image Brazil was trying to promote at the Fair. Keenly aware of the need to present their nation as something other than one more impoverished Latin American country, Brazilian fair planners sought to appear unified, forward-looking, and armed with the full credentials of universalist modernism.[18] In doing so they were fulfilling the cultural program of the Brazilian president-dictator Getúlio Vargas, in power as of 1930. Not only did Vargas substantively affect Villa-Lobos's career, but his coziness with Hitler and Mussolini made him a special target of U.S. diplomacy. Thus official Brazil's vision of "The World of Tomorrow" hewed far closer to the aesthetic modernism symbolized by the Trylon and the Perisphere than to either Caliban-like primitivism or unseemly commercialism. This chapter situates Villa-Lobos within these agendas in Brazil, all of which figured in his reception in the United States and interacted with the goals of Pan Americanism, which by now was a national project.

■ FROM "HALLUCINATED CITY" TO DEMOCRACITY: VILLA-LOBOS AND BRAZILIAN MODERNISM

Born in Rio de Janeiro in 1887, Villa-Lobos came of age in an environment scholars have labeled "a culture of imitation."[19] As in the United States, the culture being imitated was European, specifically French or Italian. The most frequently cited example of musical Europhilia in Brazil is the 1870 opera *Il Guarany* (*O Guarani* in Portuguese) by Carlos Gomes, born in 1836 in Campinas (São Paulo state). The libretto (based on the eponymous 1857 novel by the Brazilian author José de Alencar) recounts the love of a Guaraní Indian for the daughter of an aristocratic Portuguese colonial. It thus glorifies one of Brazil's foundational myths, *mestiçagem*, or the mixing of the nation's Indian, European, and African populations. Gomes emphasizes this point in the *bailado* (ballet), which calls for native percussion instruments.[20] A far greater portion of the score of *Il Guarany* could pass for early or middle-period Verdi, however. For example, in the multisectional Overture (known as the *Protofonia*) homophonic textures, dotted rhythms, and tuneful diatonicism prevail, with a graceful trumpet descant in the reprise of the principal E-major melody putting an Italianate seal on the work. Still, *Il Guarany* received full exoticist billing when it premiered at La Scala in 1870, with the title translated as *Guarani, storia del selvaggi del brasile*, and Gomes himself described in the press as "a savage who can write opera."[21] In the 1920s, when Brazilian intellectuals in Rio de Janeiro and São Paulo began debating possible ways to free themselves from European influence and forge a national artistic identity, they disparaged Gomes as too internationalized.[22]

At critical points in his career, Villa-Lobos played the "savage" card, whether in his own relentless and often imaginative public relations campaign or through his music. He frequently proclaimed his fascination with the jungle, the influence of which he claimed to have absorbed during his travels there.[23] He was equally fascinated by the *sertão*, the northeastern backlands of Pernambuco, Paraíba, Rio Grande do Norte, Alagoas, Ceará, and Sergipe, one of the poorest regions in Brazil. Yet because the *sertão* had little hold over the international public's imagination, it was Villa-Lobos's jungle-themed works, such as the 1917 ballets *Uirapurú* and *Amazonas* (both stimulated by the presence of the Ballets Russes in Rio during World War I), that were among the first of his compositions to win wide acclaim. *Uirapurú*, in which rather conventional nineteenth-century harmonies, opulent orchestration, and glowing colors coexist with driving rhythms reminiscent of early Stravinsky, especially expanded his horizons. Villa-Lobos was also considered a radical, however, especially after critics greeted his Rio de Janeiro debut in November 1915 with irritation.[24] In addition, he was stimulated by Artur Rubinstein and Darius Milhaud, both of whom traveled to Rio, the latter as secretary to French minister Paul Claudel during 1917–18. Another influence was Brazilian popular music. Principally a cellist, Villa-Lobos could also get along reasonably well on the guitar, which he played in a *roda de choro*, the customary ensemble for the urban genre on which he would repeatedly draw.[25] The *roda* (circle) normally involved members of the guitar family, including the *cavaquinho* (a small, four-stringed guitar), flute, and *pandeiro* (tambourine); to these standard instruments ophecleide, tuba, and cornet were sometimes added, and in the 1920s saxophones became common. *Choro* players generally improvised, fashioning a contrapuntal texture dominated by independent melodic lines against the main melody, sometimes with rhythmic ostinati.[26] In the 1930s, Brazilian intellectuals conferred a privileged status on the *choro*, believing that it fused popular and elite expression under the hospitable embrace of *mestiçagem*.[27]

In February 1922 several of these intellectuals and their counterparts in the fine arts organized their resistance to the "culture of imitation" by mounting the Week of Modern Art, hosted by the coffee boomtown of São Paulo and coinciding with the centennial of Brazilian independence. Although the lectures, readings, concerts, and art exhibits preached no single aesthetic, upheaval and change were the watchwords. Participants sought nothing less than to generate "the birth of art in Brazil," as the author José Pereira da Graça Aranha declared in his inaugural speech, "Aesthetic Emotion in Modern Art."[28] Others preached liberation from academicism and nineteenth-century belle-lettrist formalism, matters on which the poet, ethnographer, and musicologist Mário de Andrade was especially vehement. Reveling in the creative power of the unconscious, Andrade penned *Cidade Desvairada* (Hallucinated City), a series of short poems filled with terse but lyrical reactions to the randomness of urban life, with its "goose-fleshed streets" and trolleys that "swish like a skyrocket . . . spitting out an orifice into the whitewashed gloom."[29] Throughout the week, canvases by Anita Malfatti, Emiliano Cavalcanti, and Vicente de Rego Monteiro hung in the belle époque Teatro Municipal, their bold, raw colors and formal freedom scandalizing the *paulista* establishment.[30]

Music was also represented during the Week of Modern Art, with Villa-Lobos deemed the composer best suited to carry the defiant torch of Brazilian modernism. Most of his works performed at the event were not new: the *Characteristic African Dances* (*Danças características africanas*) are from 1915, and both the Sonata no. 2 for Cello and Piano and String Quartet no. 3 are from 1916, although the *Quarteto simbólico* (Citkowitz's "travelog music") dates from 1921.[31] Imbued with the crusading spirit of the event, however, Villa-Lobos's contemporaries greeted these works as pioneering.[32] In the case of the string quartet, with its marked references to Debussy's and Ravel's works for the same medium (considered advanced in Brazil of the 1920s), such an assessment was not unreasonable. More fanciful rhetoric surrounded the *Characteristic African Dances*, however, originally for solo piano but performed in Villa-Lobos's arrangement for octet (string quintet, flute, clarinet, and piano). Despite the restrictive title ("African"), he added in his catalogue the subtitle "Dances of Mestiço Indians of Brazil" and claimed that he had been inspired by the Indian themes from the Brazilian state of Mato Grosso. The African presence was manifested in the titles of the three individual dances ("Farrapós," "Kankukús," "Kankikis"), along with the work's "harmonic atmosphere," which Villa-Lobos claimed he had realized with "scales [used in] African instruments."[33] At the Week of Modern Art the poet and diplomat Ronald de Carvalho situated the *Dances* in a narrative of Brazilian racial harmony, announcing in the newspaper *O Estado de São Paulo* that Villa-Lobos's music was "one of the most perfect expressions of [Brazilian] culture," representing not merely "Portuguese, African, or Indigenous temperament," nor the "simple symbiosis" of these ethnicities, but, like Vasconcelos's cosmic race, "a new entity . . . in a cosmic milieu."[34]

In fact the score resembles nothing so much as a harmonically and rhythmically tame evocation of *négritude*, similar to that of Debussy's unpretentious little piano piece *Le petit nègre*. Availing himself of the washes of sound, added-note chords, and whole-tone harmonies associated with French impressionism, Villa-Lobos defies expectations of complex "African" rhythm by deviating only occasionally from a simple, usually quadruple division of the beat. Surely it was this persistent rhythmic pattern that prompted an early publisher of the piano version to insert the word *Rags* in the subtitle.[35] When Stokowski performed the orchestral version of the *Characteristic African Dances* in Philadelphia in November 1928, Linton Martin praised the work's "racy rhythms and its exuberant syncopation with a frank flair for decidedly Gershwinish jazz."[36] Impressionist-tinged harmonies were surely an odd means of expressing *mestiçagem*; further, if any jungle was evoked it was one without the slightest hint of Caliban (ex. 4a).

In considering *mestiçagem*, Brazilians often focused on their country's substantive African population. During nearly four hundred years of slavery, interracial sexual relations were not uncommon in Brazil, and in areas where there were no white women, concubinage (*mancebia*) was permitted. Even the Church approved of mixed-race marriages in some circumstances. When the slaves were liberated in 1888, they were a far more visible presence than their counterparts in the United States, as were mixed-blood individuals.[37] Various cultural phenomena reflect this proximity. *Umbanda* (often called *macumba*), a ritual originally practiced by slaves to contact the dead, uses African musical practices such

Example 4a Basic rhythm, *Characteristic African Dance* no. 1 ("Farrapós").

as call-and-response singing and prominent drumming but also incorporates images of Catholic saints renamed as African deities, and it is not uncommon for whites to participate. In the 1920s, Afro-Brazilian performers of popular music such as Pixinguinha (Alfredo da Rocha Vianna Jr.), Antônio Lepes de Amorim Diniz (Duque), and Ernesto Joaquim Maria dos Santos (Donga) were becoming increasingly known nationally and worldwide, with critics of their performances often taking their race into account.[38]

Although the racial fluidity just described may seem enlightened, many who waxed enthusiastic over "symbiosis" and "new entities" did so from a fundamentally racist perspective. Just as Vasconcelos's cosmic race implied eventual assimilation, so too did the Brazilian theory known as *branqueamento* (whitening), which peaked between abolition and World War I.[39] Its proponents held that "inferior" races could eventually be overwhelmed by an ongoing infusion of European blood. *Branqueamento* was often shaped to suit political agendas. For example, some Brazilians claimed the United States was politically and economically stronger than Brazil because its dominant Anglo-Saxon population had resisted miscegenation. Teddy Roosevelt seemed to agree; when visiting Brazil in 1914, he observed that "the Negro question" would disappear in Brazil "through the disappearance of the Negro himself… through his gradual absorption into the white race," a remark that circulated in the Rio de Janeiro press.[40] Certainly many Brazilian elites and intellectuals were squeamish about publicly advocating the gradual annihilation of Africans. Euphemisms such as *fusion, synthesis*, and *symbiosis* (the term applied to Villa-Lobos's music) afforded a softer vision of *branqueamento*, promising a society free of racial strife, since, after all, everybody would be white.[41] After World War I, the more outspoken advocates of *branqueamento* toned down their rhetoric, and Brazil's problems were increasingly attributed to poverty rather than blood.[42] Of course, racial tensions persisted. When the *choro* musician Pixinguinha was applauded in Paris during a 1922 tour, many elites were pleased by the international recognition but concerned that Europeans might believe Brazil was primarily black.[43] Graça Aranha, who in 1922 so compellingly launched the Week of Modern Art, worried that in fetishizing blacks and Indians, his compatriots had created a "jungle of myths," one that could be cleared only by reinvigorating Brazil's Luso-Portuguese heritage and which, like Rodó's *arielismo*, was essentially Latin.[44] Indeed, most Brazilian intellectuals conceded that a new national art required a proper relationship with universal (European) culture. In 1924 Mário de Andrade, the painter Tarsila do Amaral (known as Tarsila), and the poet-novelist Oswald de Andrade (no relationship to Mário) launched the movement known as Pau-Brasil (Brazilwood). Stimulated by travels to the baroque cities in the state of Minas Gerais, they came to see their country as both exotic and of a piece with its colonial past, in effect seeing Brazil through European eyes.[45] In his *Brazilwood Manifesto* of 1924, Oswald de Andrade addressed this healthy friction between "the forest and the school." The forest could encompass certain types of Brazilian food, for example, or the vernacular of Brazilian (rather than continental) Portuguese, along with local practices such as carnival and *mestiçagem*, whereas the school stood for erudition, sometimes false and often but not always imported.[46] In his *Manifesto Antropófago* (Cannibalist Manifesto) of 1928, he even advocated cannibalism—of Europe. Just as the Tupi-Guaraní Indians had devoured Portuguese missionaries, Oswald argued, modern-day artists should ingest European techniques, schools, and theories and transform them according to Brazilian reality.[47] In reconfiguring European primitivism, Latin America enjoyed several advantages. Unlike Picasso, inspired by African masks torn from their true context, Brazilian artists could find artifacts of folk and tribal culture ready at hand, some even surviving in urban environments, albeit in diluted or recontextualized forms.[48] Aesthetic cannibalism thus empowered the subaltern to transform both self and other.[49] Still, latter-day cannibals vacillated, as Oswald's quip "Tupi or not Tupi?" suggests. Was cannibalizing the "school" a form of cultural suicide? Of receptivity to a vast array of artistic influences?[50] Such questions energized Brazilian creative artists negotiating their standing in local and international culture.

Another strand of Brazilian modernism made no secret of its cosmopolitan roots. In 1928, the Casa Modernista, designed by the Russian-born, Italian-trained Giorgi Warchavchik, went up in São Paulo. Its sleek, unadorned lines affirmed Le Corbusier's concept of buildings as "machines for living" and the universalist aspirations of the so-called International style.[51] Ultimately, universalism would win Villa-Lobos favor in the United States.

▪ *CHOROS* NO. 8 IN PARIS

In the 1920s Villa-Lobos mulled over these modernist agendas—but from afar. Roughly a year after his music was hailed as a near-perfect expression of national culture, he took off for Paris, subsidized by the wealthy Guinle family.[52] He was less interested in studying than in enhancing his reputation as an enfant terrible. (His possibly apocryphal remark, "I am here not to study but to show what I can do," would be frequently repeated in the U.S. press.)[53] Far more than Gomes seventy years earlier, Villa-Lobos was known as a savage. Colorful jungle-related tales swirled around him: the French publication *Intransigeant* described his capture by cannibals, who tied him to a pole and danced around him in gleeful anticipation of a feast of juicy human meat.[54] He rejected the refined impressionism of the *Characteristic African Dances* and the sensuous orchestration of *Uirapurú*, employing instead forces on the scale of Stravinsky's "wastefully large" orchestra in *The Rite of Spring* in *Choros* no. 10, to which he added a chorus.[55] In *Choros* no. 3, a smaller-scale work, he paid homage to the Indians of Mato Grosso and Goîa.[56] Villa-Lobos also glorified the primitive in *Three Indigenous Poems* (*Três Poemas Indígenas*) for voice and orchestra and in his Nonet of 1923, discussed in more detail in chapter 5. These works were performed at the Salle Gaveau over two concerts (October 24, December 5) in 1927. In reviewing them, Lucien Chevalier was moved to embellish the tale of Villa-Lobos's capture by cannibals, noting that after this ordeal the composer emerged in a state of "unconscious receptivity" that sensitized him to his own soul, which Chevalier described as "frequently savage, harsh, tumultuous," but also "sometimes incoherent."[57] Henri Prunières compared Villa-Lobos to Gauguin in Tahiti and proclaimed that the Salle Gaveau concerts were "the first time one heard in Europe works from Latin America that bring with them the enchantments of the virgin forests, the broad plains, of an exuberant nature, prodigious in fruit, flowers, in dazzling birds."[58]

Thus the jungle secured Villa-Lobos's reputation in Paris, where audiences were then applauding difference as manifested in Josephine Baker and Joe Alex's *Danse du sauvage*, part of the popular *La Revue nègre*.[59] With its formal freedom, the *choro* was an apt vehicle for *sauvagerie*. (Villa-Lobos composed seven of his fourteen *choros*, not all of which are primitivist, in Paris.) In *Choros no. 8*, which dates from 1925, Villa-Lobos played up primitivist associations for all they were worth. The work employs an arsenal of Afro-Brazilian percussion instruments: *chocalhos de metal* (a shaken rattle), *puita* (friction drum), *matracá* (clapper), and *caraxá* (handheld shaker, also called *caraxa*), along with *reco-reco* and *caracachás* (both types of scrapers). Complementing the Afro-Brazilian percussion are timpani, bass drum, cymbals, tam-tam, triangle, and celesta, requiring a total of eight players. The two pianos, scored as part of the ensemble rather than soloistically, occasionally recall the piano writing in *Petrushka*, with thickly voiced parallel chords played at a wrist-stiffening clip; elsewhere (reh. 48) a sheet of paper is inserted between the strings of the first piano. As for the rest of the orchestra, Villa-Lobos adds piccolo, English horn, four clarinets, bass clarinet, alto saxophone, contrabassoon, four trombones, tuba, and two harps to the standard complement of strings and winds. The listening experience is marked with sudden, seemingly arbitrary shifts from one episode to the next, as in the opening bars, where wind and brass instruments emit individual lines of widely spaced intervals in free counterpoint over the dry ostinato of the *chocalho* and *caraxá*; forty-five seconds later, multiple lines explode into *fortissimo*. At reh. 7 Villa-Lobos abruptly erects a wall of sound in which the offbeat thuds of the *puita* culminate in another *fortissimo*, with random countermelodies hurled out in contrary motion (vlns. and trombones, reh. 7 + 4) and punctuated by glissandi in the celesta and piano 2. Likewise, at reh. 28 + 4, the buzzing of repeated notes across several sections prepares a round of glissandi in saxophone and horns, all marked "sauvage (see ex. 4b)."

Choros no. 8 explicitly glorifies *mestiçagem*. According to a prefatory note in the published score (Max Eschig, 1928), the work "represents a new form of musical composition, in which different aspects of Brazilian music are synthesized, Indian and popular, having as their principal elements Rhythm and whatever typical Melody of popular character, which appears from time to time accidentally, always transformed according to the personality of the composer," thus ensuring that rhythm is fundamental and melody incidental or random ("accidental"). In fact, Villa-Lobos serves up primitivism and practically nothing else. Most of his motives are of narrow melodic range, often extended with repeated pitches (reh. 4 + 3, reh. 40–42), and others circle around a single pitch (vln. 1, reh. 45). These fragments pile up noisily, as at reh. 6, where a motive introduced in the strings is immediately answered by a new motive in the low brass and another in the low strings (3 mm. before reh. 7). Pedal points and ostinati ensure slow-moving, sometimes deadening harmony. The few allusions to popular Brazilian melodies, limited to the dance-like passage in the English horn at reh. 10 + 4 (reprised at rehs. 11 + 3 and 41 + 1) and the euphonious

Example 4b Heitor Villa-Lobos. *Choros* no. 8, reh. 28 + 4ff. Reprinted by kind permission of MGB Hal Leonard.

(*continued*)

Example 4b (continued)

hiatus at reh. 31, are swallowed up in the onslaught of volume, contrapuntal density, and a seemingly infinite supply of motives.

Several of these strategies dominate the final pages of *Choros* no. 8. A theme in the violins circles around A-flat (reh. 48) against a heavily accented ostinato in piano 1, whereupon new motives accumulate (clarinet and contrabassoon, reh. 48 + 5) and the percussion instruments, led by the *reco-reco* (reh. 53), gradually enter, culminating in a quadruple forte of the full ensemble in the final bars. Yet the volume level unexpectedly fades, as brass and the keyboard instruments alone sustain the last chord while the rest of the orchestra falls silent. As with the ambivalent conclusion of *The Rite of Spring*, which one early critic found "lacking in the feeling of finality" (and with which Stravinsky was never entirely satisfied), *Choros* no. 8 ends "not with a bang but a whimper," to recall T. S. Eliot's oft-quoted words (ex. 4c).[60]

Yet for all its enthralling primitivism, "le fou huitième" gave the French critics pause when it premiered in 1927 at the Salle Gaveau. Writing in *Paris Matinal*, Florent Schmitt, like Chevalier, evaluated Villa-Lobos's soul, and applauded in *Choros* no. 8 "fantasy mixed with savagery . . . a stylized expression of the primitive instincts of a man who is honest and of noble soul, a man who has not sold

Example 4c Heitor Villa-Lobos. *Choros* no. 8, reh. 54 to end. Reprinted by kind permission of MGB Hal Leonard.

(*continued*)

Example 4c (*continued*)

his soul."[61] Apropos the "howls of rage" he heard in the orchestra, however, Schmitt wondered if "the absolute limits of superhuman dynamic tension [had] been reached," a state of affairs, he believed, that the public would ultimately deem either "infernal or divine."[62] By assaulting his listeners with *bruitisme* and "lawless rhythm," Villa-Lobos invited them to flirt with the primitive, racially marked Other even as his mode of expression teetered on the edge of an existential abyss, a crisis of primitivism in which the voice of the savage could never be wholly articulate.

■ BRAZIL AND THE GOOD NEIGHBOR POLICY

Villa-Lobos returned to Brazil in June 1930 for some conducting engagements, his persona as a savage well established. But when he was evicted in absentia from his Paris apartment for failure to pay the rent, he decided to remain in Rio de Janeiro.[63] A few months later a military intervention over a disputed election brought Vargas to power, who initially served as the civilian head of a provisional government (1930–34) and in 1937 ascended to president-dictator of the authoritarian Estado Novo (New State).[64] Centrist, corporatist, nationalist, anticommunist, and supportive of the Church, the Vargas regime has been compared to the fascist states of Europe. Shortly after Vargas came to power, Roosevelt introduced his Good Neighbor Policy, the culmination of prior Pan Americanist initiatives and the benefits of which Villa-Lobos would enjoy—after adjusting his image, that is.

Even if the concept of the Good Neighbor was not original with Roosevelt, it was under his administration that it captured the public imagination. Granted, some credibility problems had to be finessed: as assistant secretary of the navy under Wilson, Roosevelt had helped effect the U.S. occupations of Haiti, the Dominican Republic, and Veracruz, although he opposed intervention in Nicaragua. The empire-conscious language of earlier periods was revamped, with references to "half-breeds" and "sick nations" excised in favor of phrases such as "hemispheric cooperation" and "extending the area of freedom."[65] In his inaugural address of March 1933, Roosevelt explained the concept, describing the good neighbor as one "who resolutely respects himself and, because he does so, respects the rights of others."[66] Latin Americans soon appreciated this new perspective. In December 1933 delegates at the Seventh Pan American Conference in Montevideo were pleasantly surprised when Secretary of State Cordell Hull promised that the United States would renounce military interventionism in the region; in addition, the Platt Amendment was revoked (the United States retained Guantánamo), and Panama ceased to be a protectorate.[67]

Also in 1933 Roosevelt marked Pan American Day with a speech before the Governing Board of the Pan American Union. In focusing on "the essential qualities of a true Pan Americanism," Roosevelt touched on culture, noting that besides finding "its source and being in the hearts of men," it "dwells in the temple of the intellect."[68] As we have seen, various intellectuals and artists were already drawn to Pan Americanism. But now that policymakers were pursuing Pan Americanist objectives, the very meaning of culture began to loom large. The Division of Cultural Relations, for example, opted for universal culture, as did several private foundations and government organizations, including the Carnegie Endowment for International Peace (one "peace palace" of which was the Pan American Union).[69] Established in 1938, the Division was headed by Ben Cherrington, a professor from the University of Denver who confirmed the Division's penchant for universalist discourse by simply declaring, "Culture is in its essence cosmic."[70] With this outlook, it was easy to overlook the fact that Pan Americanism itself is an intrinsically regionalist, pan-nationalist concept in that it privileges a bounded geographic area encompassing over twenty countries, three principal language groups (in addition to indigenous languages), and a multitude of cultural expressions.[71] As it turned out, since cultural diplomacy in the United States was then in its nascent stages, Latin America proved something of a testing ground, given the Division's emphasis on the region.[72]

As war threatened ever more ominously, Pan Americanism became less the province of artists and intellectuals and more a network of governmental, commercial, and entertainment industry interests, all of which helped ensure that the Good Neighbor Policy had tremendous mass appeal.[73] For example, months after Roosevelt's inauguration speech, the musical *Flying Down to Rio* was released, which recounts the adventures of a U.S. band on tour in Rio de Janeiro. RKO produced the film in collaboration with Pan American Airways, then the only airline flying to South America and on whose board of directors sat Merian Cooper, production chief of RKO.[74] *Flying Down to Rio* reinforces racial stereotypes; one dance sequence proclaimed Brazil's multiracial society with so much abandon that the Production Code Administration attacked its "sex suggestiveness," which it largely blamed on the "entire colored troup [sic]."[75] But it also broke new ground in that the Latin American musicians have an edge over their U.S. counterparts in several musical situations; further, the Brazilians use Portuguese, by no means a given in Hollywood. As if to complement *Flying Down to Rio*, the Roosevelt administration promoted tourism at the Pan American Conference in Montevideo, a "perfectly safe" topic, as Roosevelt advised Hull.[76]

Culture was especially high on Vargas's agenda. Although not especially interested in the fine arts himself, he was extravagantly likened to Pericles, Louis XIV, and Cósimo de Médici, with one official claiming that Brazil had been saved from cultural disaster thanks to Vargas's "clear, optimistic, and brilliant vision," which in turn reflected "tranquility, equilibrium, and the truest principles of Brazilianness."[77] Although Brazilianness (*brasilidade*) was the centerpiece of Vargas's cultural program, it was less than precisely defined. Certainly unity was paramount, as evidenced in the ceremonial burning of flags from each Brazilian state at the foot of the national flag, a gesture intended to repress regionalist stirrings in the Estado Novo.[78] Music could also promote Brazilian unity. Each night, the overture to Gomes's *Il Guarany* announced *A Hora do Brasil* (Brazilian Hour), the radio program of government-generated news, which often surged from loudspeakers in public places.[79] Calling on an Italianate operatic overture to represent Brazilianness may reflect ignorance on the part of cultural officials.[80]

But it may also underscore the idea that diverse ethnicities had fused into a single Brazilian people, perhaps one dominated by European blood. Indeed, Brazilian-ness under Vargas was largely white. Many spoke openly in favor of allowing blacks to become "absorbed by the white race's superior capacity for stability and assimilation," as one deputy put it, drawing on earlier precepts of *branquea-mento*.[81] The French anthropologist Claude Lévi-Strauss, on a fieldwork trip in Brazil, came close to being arrested by Vargas's plainclothesmen for having himself photographed with Brazilian blacks and giving the impression that Brazil was inhabited by Africans.[82] When Orson Welles arrived in 1942 to make a movie about carnival in Rio, the regime opposed the project because it emphasized samba's African roots and its popularity among impoverished Afro-Brazilians living in the *favelas* (hillside shantytowns) of Rio.[83] To be sure, in some public discourse *mestiçagem* was seen as a national strength, and Vargas himself made gestures on behalf of Afro-Brazilians.[84] For example, he supported samba and admired Carmen Miranda, with her dress and idioms of Bahia, the northeastern state sometimes called the "Africa of the Americas."[85] Yet while some Brazilians applauded Miranda's African-tinged performance art, others attacked her "vulgar negroid sambas."[86]

The jungle and the *sertão* were also subject to Vargas's cultural campaign. Rather than glorifying their primitivism, he set about to civilize them. Thanks to a plethora of newsreels depicting his visits there, he could almost give the impression of being in many remote places at once.[87] *A Marcha para Oeste* (The March to the West) of 1940, for example, shows him traveling "through regions where Brazil still retains its primitive jungle," thus confirming the breadth and thoroughness of his mission.[88]

It was through architecture that the Vargas regime made its strongest mark on culture, however. The simple lines and unadorned surfaces of the International style, debated in the 1920s, were deftly co-opted on behalf of Brazilianness. Lauro Cavalcanti explains in his ironically titled 2003 book, *When Brazil Was Modern: Guide to Architecture 1928–1960*, that the unmarked nature of the International style enabled it to pass for "unmistakably Brazilian and, at the same time, universal."[89] The sleek designs inspired by Le Corbusier were nonetheless enhanced with presumably Brazilian features, such as landscaping with local plants. The young architect Lucio Costa, appointed to reform the curriculum at the National School of Fine Arts in Rio de Janeiro, was the leader in establishing this Brazilian-universalist aesthetic.[90] It culminated in Brasilia, begun during Vargas's second term and called a "utopian city."[91]

Some intellectuals, such as the writer Jorge Amado, were silenced or harassed in the Estado Novo. Moderates and leftists of various stripes, such as the painter Cândido Portinari and the architect Oscar Niemeyer (both future communists), received contracts and positions, however, olive branches the Ministry of Culture held out to a potentially contentious constituency.[92] Other positions were filled by rightists or at least the politically malleable. Among the latter was

Villa-Lobos, who vaguely expressed admiration for Mussolini's leadership and in 1931 was appointed Head of Musical and Artistic Education (*Superintendência de Educação Musical e Artística*).[93] Like Costa in architecture, he was expected to revamp curricula and inculcate Brazilianness. He elaborated on that topic in numerous essays, some of which appeared in the national press. (As Simon Wright notes, Villa-Lobos's writing on matters musical and political abruptly ceased after Vargas's overthrow in 1945.)[94] Under Vargas's able guidance, Villa-Lobos maintained, music would promote unity since it "integrates the individual into the social fabric of the country."[95] Especially suited to this end was folk music, which Villa-Lobos called "racial music."[96] The "Rabelais of music" pursued these goals in his usual supersized fashion, organizing gargantuan choruses of thirty to forty thousand voices, which were sometimes accompanied by orchestras of a thousand players.[97] Villa-Lobos also saw to it that pamphlets on music were flung out of airplanes to enhance the "social-civic-artistic" sensibility of the populace.[98] Another state-oriented project was Villa-Lobos's score for Humberto Mauro's 1937 film *O descobrimento do Brasil* (The Discovery of Brazil). Like Vargas confronting Brazil's primitive jungle, the film depicts the Portuguese explorer Pedro Álvarez Cabral gazing for the first time upon the Tupi Indians in the wild.[99]

In his compositions Villa-Lobos sought to elevate folk ("racial") music. Much the way Brazilian architects were expected to achieve the "unmistakably Brazilian and, at the same time, universal," Villa-Lobos channeled "racial music" into what is surely the most blatantly universalist opus by any Latin American composer, the *Bachianas brasileiras*. Composed between 1930 and 1945, the exact time frame of the first Vargas regime, the nine-work series drew on Brazilian music to honor Johann Sebastian Bach, whose music was, Villa-Lobos explained, "a kind of universal folkloric source, rich and profound . . . linking all peoples"; in addition, Bach's music flowed from "the astral infinite to infiltrate itself in the earth as folk music . . . dividing itself among the various parts of the terrestrial globe, becoming universal."[100] With this rhetorical maneuver Villa-Lobos accomplished several things. First, he allied himself with numerous scholars and musicians worldwide who have endowed folklore with universal significance, many citing commonalities of function, subject matter, or musical traits among various folk or traditional musics.[101] He also reshaped Max Weber's "universal polyphony of folk music"; whereas it had yielded to the cold "rationalization" of Western European art music, the essence of Brazilian folk music would be preserved, thanks to the uncanny relationship between it and Bach, which Villa-Lobos himself had discovered.[102] He also tapped into then-current concepts of musical evolution, according to which the progression from primitive to folk and popular musics culminated in Western art music (note the singular) via an unbroken line, yielding a universal patrimony of masterpieces. To be sure, anthropologists in the first half of the twentieth century challenged this largely nineteenth-century view.[103] But musicians, critics, and music appreciation teachers found the idea of a universal music attractive.[104] So too did government officials during the Good Neighbor period.

Frequently and expansively Villa-Lobos recounted the experiences that enabled him to imbibe the universal spirit of Bach from the most distant corners of his native land. No longer does the composer suffer at the hands of cannibals. Rather he uncovers incontrovertible evidence of the Western tradition's presence in folk and primitive cultures. For example, in the heavily supervised biography by Paula Barros (Gerard Béhague calls it "practically an autobiography," thanks to the composer's constant interventions) we read that on a visit to the *sertão*, the composer chanced upon "modulations and countermelodies in the manner of Bach" (not to mention "melodic cells with characteristics of rhythmic accentuations and an extreme affinity with elements of works of Beethoven").[105] Like Vargas and Cabral, Villa-Lobos civilized the "forest."

The famous opus enhanced Villa-Lobos's international reputation as well. By inserting a Brazilian element into the ongoing debate in the United States over classic values, he could ensure that the *Bachianas* would be received as something other than tepid neoclassicism. Also, in 1933–34 the pianist Edwin Fischer released his powerfully idiosyncratic recording of the *Well-Tempered Clavier*, and in April 1936 Pablo Casals began his landmark recording of the six suites for unaccompanied cello. In the United States Bach especially gained ground. Besides the three preludes and fugues with which she often opened her recitals, Myra Hess regaled audiences there with her signature encore, her transcription of "Jesu, Joy of Man's Desiring" from Cantata BWV 147 (*Herz und Mund und Tat und Leben*) such that audiences from New York to Boston to Lincoln, Nebraska, would shout for "more Bach!"[106] In 1935, when music lovers worldwide marked the 250th anniversary of Bach's birth, the number of radio broadcasts of Bach skyrocketed in the United States, as did record sales, eventually surpassing those of Beethoven.[107] All the while, Stokowski was turning out orchestral transcriptions, including "Jesu, Joy," "Sheep May Safely Graze" (from Cantata BWV 208), and the Toccata and Fugue in D Minor (BWV 565).[108]

Illuminating this phenomenon was Paul Rosenfeld, tireless advocate of "substance" and "intrinsic classicism." In July 1940, by which time Hitler had invaded Poland, Finland, Denmark, Norway, Luxembourg, the Netherlands, and France, he published the article "Bach Conquers Musical America." In it, Rosenfeld declared that Bach's music was "one of the great expressions of artistic impersonality. Not in the least that it is unlyrical! Only . . . it never seems to sing the sorrow and joys of an individual. . . . Invariably it says 'we,' not 'I.'" The ideal of a universalist, collective transcendence was doubly comforting in war; as Rosenfeld sadly acknowledged, Bach's "greatest gift" was "the evocation of a peace of which the world knows nothing."[109] If Bach had "conquered" musical America, then perhaps Villa-Lobos, with his ideological platform so perfectly timed with these sentiments—and with the vision of Pan American unity ever more compelling to the U.S. public—could do the same.

■ CALIBAN UNBOUND: VILLA-LOBOS AT THE FAIR

For Brazil, the 1939 World's Fair was a prime opportunity to showcase the Estado Novo. But how best to make the case that Brazil was "economically united, homogeneous, and indivisible in its productive capacities," as one memo circulating among Brazilian fair planners had it?[110] Aesthetic modernism was pressed into service. The Brazilian pavilion, with its flat roof, ribbon windows, non-load-bearing walls, and *brise-soleil* louvers designed by Costa and Niemeyer, perfectly realized the Estado Novo's aesthetic.[111] Since not all fairgoers could be expected to appreciate modern architecture, however, other ways of asserting universalist-Brazilianness had to be conceived. For example, exhibiting the country's abundant natural resources would show its readiness to aid in the war-time economy, even as Vargas continued to vacillate between the United States and the Axis Powers. But the mode of display had to be modernist. In lieu of "natives" presiding over burlap bags bursting with coffee beans, Brazil's chrome, ore, nickel, palm oil, and manioc were exhibited in simple, streamlined arrange-ments. Coffee, its most appealing product, also figured; within the pavilion's plate-glass walls, young women *de boa aparência*—a code word for "white," as Daryle Williams points out—served coffee while visitors enjoyed Brazilian pop-ular music provided by Romeo Silva's band.[112] More than just another one-crop Latin American economy, Brazil hospitably offered its natural resources to first-world consumers within a universalist-modernist framework.

The planning and execution of the Fair as a whole were ripe for international conflict. Nazi Germany, which New York's mayor Fiorello LaGuardia called "a museum of horrors," was not represented, although Italy and Japan were.[113] As for the Western Hemisphere, the Pan American Union Building displayed the flags of the twenty-one American republics. The Venezuelan pavilion housed the "Altar of the Good Neighbor," which contained a lock of the first U.S. president's hair, given to Bolívar by Lafayette.[114] In light of Bolívar's conviction that the United States was ever "to plague America with torments," this gesture was less than clear.[115] Other disagreements touched on national concerns. If in Victorian-era fairs the United States had reveled in empire and acquisition, in 1939 these themes were muted while urgent international alliances hung in the balance and the ravages of the Depression confirmed that economic plenty was closed to much of U.S. society. Looking to the future—a "usable future," as Francis V. O'Connor has quipped—was science, with its presumed neutrality.[116] Science was not only the backbone of exhibits on transportation, communication, and nutrition, but it literally lit up the Fair: on opening night, Albert Einstein, in the United States since 1933, turned on the switch that illuminated the main build-ings.[117] But even in the face of this Genesis-like gesture, science and its vaunted ideological purity had to compete with industry. To waylay potential charges of blatant commercialism, consumerism was dressed up in euphemism. Who, after all, in Depression-era America would oppose the vision of prosperity promised by the World of Tomorrow, a direct result of "today's modernizing," as California's governor Frank Merriam had it?[118] Consumerism, it was tacitly argued, could be as enlightened as science, promising a future filled with time-saving machines that would facilitate civic, educational, and artistic pursuits for all.

It could also be crass. Imperialist yearnings of previous decades found new life in the ever-expanding reach of U.S. corporations and products. In the World of Tomorrow, mass consumption rather than military aggression would conquer new territories. Like O. Henry's natives, inhabitants of these territories would both provide raw materials and become eager consumers of U.S. products, fulfilling the notion that "empire as a way of life is predicated on having more than one needs."[119] These practices, as realized at the Fair, illuminate Walter Benjamin's description of world exhibitions as "phantasmagoria," capable of creating frameworks that obscure the true value of commodities.[120] The National Cash Register Building was surely the most blatant example of this tendency. But apropos similar displays, architecture critics complained that the Fair glorified advertising and consumerism over science, aesthetics, and even democracy.[121] A reporter for *Architectural Review* argued that too many of the Fair's buildings betrayed "the commercial expediency that dominates so much of American life."[122] Frederick Gutheim went so far as to lament that the only architectural style represented at the Fair was the "Corporation Style," which he defined as a "bastard dialect of architectural larceny and advertising."[123]

Challenges to the "Corporation Style" presented themselves, however, albeit mainly from outside the United States. Among them was the Brazilian pavilion, which won accolades for "purity," "finesse," and its "excellent refutation of the dogmas of the industrial designers."[124] One critic praised the pavilion's "subtlety of design" but suggested that it was "perhaps a building for architects rather than for the less perceptive public."[125] No less a figure than Philip L. Goodwin of the American Institute of Architects commended Brazil's "courage to break away from the safe and easy path."[126] Perhaps moved by Good Neighborliness, Goodwin also hailed the *brise-soleil* as a Brazilian invention, calling it one of Brazil's "great, original contributions." To be sure, he acknowledged that the idea of using external blinds to control heat on glass surfaces had originated with Le Corbusier; still, Goodwin insisted, it had been the Brazilians who first translated the idea into practical use.[127] In short, by "cannibalizing" a European trend, the Brazilian modernism on display at the Fair surpassed even the culture of the technologically advanced United States.

The two all-Brazilian concerts shed light on some of the aesthetic positions Villa-Lobos had already tested in Brazil and Paris while also exposing an epistemological conundrum: the limits of aesthetic primitivism. As noted, the two Villa-Lobos works that piqued the most critical interest were "The Hillbilly's Little Train" from *Bachianas brasileiras* no. 2, the first orchestral work in the *Bachianas* series, and *Choros* no. 8, the work Paris had called "le fou huitième." In *Bachianas* no. 2, any links to the cantor of Leipzig are utterly unrecognizable.

Neither does Villa-Lobos's approach to the work suggest any sustained communing with "the astral infinite." He dug up four miscellaneous works he had composed in 1930 (three for piano and cello, one for piano solo), orchestrated them, and christened each with a generic baroque title and a Portuguese one, his practice for nearly all nine of the multi-movement *Bachianas*.[128] In September 1938 he presented the four recycled works as a set at the International Society for Contemporary Music in Venice, where Raymond Hall of the *New York Times* heard nothing of Bach but plenty of jungle or, as he put it, "a panorama of tropical nature and native ritual."[129]

In fact, *Bachianas* no. 2 refers not to the jungle but to the *sertão*, as is clear from the Portuguese titles taken in their totality: "The Song of the Rogue" ("O canto do capadócio") for movement 1 (Prelude); "The Song of Our Land" ("O canto da nossa terra") for movement 2 (Aria); "Memories of the Backlands" ("Lembrança do sertão"), for movement 3 (Dance); and "The Hillbilly's Little Train" ("O trenzinho do caipira") for movement 4 (Toccatina).[130] In no. 3, "Memories of the Backlands," Wright even hears echoes of Euclides da Cunha's 1902 novel *Os sertões* (Rebellion in the Backlands), the tale of an uprising by impoverished *sertanejos* during the 1890s.[131] It follows, then, that the musical language of *Bachianas brasileiras* no. 2 looks backward. In contrast to the *bruitisme* and orchestral "howls" of *Choros* no. 8, its four movements are stubbornly tonal, with the first three unfolding in ternary form and their large-scale sections delineated by movement to the relative minor or major. No. 2, "The Song of Our Land," is considered a *modinha*, a sentimental art song some scholars trace back to the eighteenth century and traditionally accompanied by the guitar. Homophonic texture prevails, enlivened by isolated flashes of color, as in the saxophone solo in movement 1, itself enhanced with leaps of tritones, sixths, and sevenths, along with glissandi (mm. 1–15). (According to Burle Marx, Villa-Lobos was so fond of the saxophone that he used it in Beethoven symphonies if he lacked a bassoon.)[132] Despite their programmatic titles, the first three movements lack pictorial or mimetic elements.

By contrast, the last movement unabashedly imitates a rustic train. In the introduction Villa-Lobos manipulates syncopations, duple versus triple divisions of the beat, rests, and a gradual diminution of note values such that the mechanically limited vehicle, initially awkward and uncertain, gathers the necessary speed to begin its journey. Trills and string harmonics replicate metal-on-metal friction, clarinet glissandi suggest the wail of the whistle, and the flutter-tonguing of the flute evokes escaping steam. The main melody, a nonmodulating, sequence-driven, stepwise tune in C major, proceeds in regular, four-bar phrases, the last of which is reiterated. Throughout, the percussion (*chocalhos*, *reco-reco*, piano, celesta, timpani, tambourine, and ratchet) comment discreetly. The main theme verges on the trivial; even a Villa-Lobos enthusiast such as Béhague refers to its "banal village-band type melody."[133] In the coda, the train slows down— the ride totals just over four minutes—and a final C-major chord briskly asserts a happy ending, *a tempo*. Thus, unlike the brash assertion of machine culture in *Pacific 231* or *H.P.*, "The Hillbilly's Little Train" is a relic from a backward region, a world very much at odds with modernist-universalist Brazil (ex. 4d).

If their counterparts in architecture lambasted the easy commercialism of so many of the Fair's buildings, music critics verged on proposing that "The Hillbilly's Little Train" represented a *musical* "Corporation Style." Some, of course, found its mimetic elements "appealing" or "droll" (hardly high praise for a modernist).[134] Yet most concurred with Oscar Thompson, who observed that these elements served largely to offset "a rather commonplace melody."[135] Downes compared the more sophisticated locomotive of *Pacific 231*, performed on the Swiss program, and found it by far the superior work.[136] For Rosenfeld, "The Hillbilly's Little Train" was nothing short of "vulgar."[137] Yet perhaps influenced by the freewheeling mix of aesthetic modernism, science, and blatant consumerism around them, critics seemed ultimately to accept the "Little Train" on its own terms. Just as Homo Spectator roamed the fairgrounds at will, exercising his prerogative as a consumer to survey all that the "society of the spectacle" had to

Example 4d Heitor Villa-Lobos. "The Hillbilly's Little Train" ("O trenzinho do caipira"), *Bachianas brasileiras* no. 2, mvt. 4, mm. 1–2. Reprinted by kind permission of MGB Hal Leonard.

(*continued*)

Example 4d (continued)

offer, music critics essentially shrugged off "The Hillbilly's Little Train" as an inferior commercial product.[138] It was enough for Rosenfeld, for example, that the
plucky "Little Train" "merrily sings its music-hall ditty as it climbs—carries us
among the coffee plantations of the high tropics," just as the endearing *Little
Engine That Could* triumphed in the children's story so popular in the 1930s.[139]
However trite Villa-Lobos's musical resources he had managed to endow backwardness with colorful effects, resulting not in high art but in an ingratiating,
picture postcard–style commodity congenial to a mass public increasingly avid
for attractive representations of Latin America. We should hardly be surprised
that when the creator of Carter's ubiquitous Walt Disney monster—Disney
himself—visited Rio de Janeiro in 1941, he discussed with Villa-Lobos the possibility of using "The Hillbilly's Little Train" in an animated feature.[140] (The
project never came to fruition.) In short, Villa-Lobos's intention to project the

Example 4d (continued)

"universal folk" and the "astral infinite" in *Bachianas brasileiras* no. 2 was eclipsed by the values of the culture industry.[141]

Choros no. 8, on the other hand, defied any hint of consumerism. Just as it made the Parisian critics hesitate, the work stunned U.S. critics with its density of texture, sheer volume, and array of primitive percussion instruments. Many were fascinated by the ways in which the work represented the primitive jungle, with Rosenfeld waxing euphoric over the "feeling of wild tanglewoods, fantastic vegetation and animal life, damp and drowsy heat."[142] Less exuberant temperaments reacted similarly. Marx noted that Villa-Lobos drew on an "almost impenetrable forest of . . . ever-changing ideas," while Downes simply affirmed, "The

music is . . . the jungle."[143] Through all these jungle metaphors, "spontaneity" figures prominently. Marx, for example, described the composer's "continuous,
spontaneous, abundant pouring forth" of musical ideas, adding that Villa-Lobos
"creates like a god."[144] Yet his natural gifts were not always properly channeled.
Edward O'Gorman complained that *Choros* no. 8 was "eight times louder, eight
times longer" than necessary, and Marx feared that Villa-Lobos would become
"entangled" in his own ideas.[145] Others would have preferred a more clearly articulated form, with Perkins considering it "undefined" and Thompson complaining of "virtual negation of form."[146] Rosenfeld, who called the composer an
"amazing involuntary force," tentatively suggested that Villa-Lobos's multiple
ideas and "lush and overelaborate instrumentation" staggered under their
own weight in *Choros* no. 8.[147] In contrast to the stark deserts of Chávez's ur-
classicism, tempered by universal forms and lofty visions of wholeness, Villa-
Lobos offered up a thicket of exotic vegetation to be hacked through by intrepid
souls undeterred by "straight" primitivism. Although no critic referred explicitly
to sublimation, it was clear enough that *Choros* no. 8, with its random flow of
ideas, its raw materials immune to refinement, its unleashing of the primitive
id, were worlds away from that concept.

U.S. critics also considered rhythm. Perkins, for example, found it "pervasive,
complex and weighty" in *Choros* no. 8.[148] Downes too addressed complexity,
proposing that the "often strange and primitive" percussion instruments, more
than mere color, enhanced the rhythmic intricacies of the score, and added that,
as "with [Villa-Lobos's] savage music," "the savage may be very complicated in
his rhythms."[149] As Agawu has noted, associating rhythmic complexity with
primitive musics is a long-standing trope, one often framed as difference and
thus a barrier to the Western mind; Erich von Hornbostel even described one
passage in African music as "syncopated past [Western] comprehension."[150]
Rhythmic complexity was hardly neutral. In his widely read study *Primitive
Music: An Inquiry into the Origins and Development of Music, Songs, Instruments,
Dances, and Pantomimes of Savages* the Austrian scholar Richard Wallaschek opposed the "mere craving" for rhythm to the "desire for tones and melody" exhibited by connoisseurs of Western European art music.[151] Primitive rhythm in art
music lent itself to a narrative of degeneracy. The British critic Cecil Gray condemned as an "obsession" the rhythm in *The Rite of Spring*, which he likened to
the music of "the most primitive and uncultured races," and advised readers to
"consult Professor Sigmund Freud's treatise on the 'Resemblances between the
Psychic Life of Savages and Neurotics'" (the subtitle of *Totem and Taboo*).[152] In
addition, rhythm portended an insuperable dark force to which the body was
infinitely susceptible, a theme the anti-jazz constituency in the United States
took up, with one wag proposing that "jazz put the sin in syncopation."[153]

Rhythm was nonetheless an important element of the ongoing quest for an
American musical identity. Was American rhythm essentialized to the same
extent as African rhythm, and if so, what can we learn about perceptions of

north-south difference vis-à-vis rhythm? Virgil Thomson noted certain "characteristic [rhythmic] traits that can be identified as belonging to this continent only," some of which were "probably" shared by "our South American neighbors." Although he described these traits only vaguely, he emphasizes naturalness and bodily (even sexual) ease, referring, for example, to "a quiet, vibratory shimmer, a play of light and movement over a well-felt but not expressed basic pulsation, as regular and varied as a heartbeat and as unconscious . . . lively but at ease, quiet, assured, lascivious."[154] For Roy Harris, American rhythm married freedom to inevitability: it was "less symmetrical than the European rhythmic sense"; Americans, moreover, "do not employ unconventional rhythms as a sophistical gesture; we cannot avoid them."[155] Harris also believed rhythm held the key to the tabula rasa of the American continent, seeking with the composer Arthur Berger the origins of American rhythm, a project Martin Brody describes as an "American Dream of a primal, prehistorical sonority."[156]

Copland developed his ideas on American rhythm over several years. In a frequently quoted lecture he gave during his tenure as Norton Professor of Poetics at Harvard (1951–52), he left no doubt of either its geographical reach or its source. As opposed to Europe, art music composers in the Americas "learned [their] rhythmic lessons largely from the Negro," Copland asserted, adding, "The rhythmic life in the scores of Roy Harris, William Schuman, Marc Blitzstein, and a host of other representative American composers is indubitably linked to Negroid sources of rhythm."[157] In fact, Copland had privileged American rhythm even earlier, and in less overtly racialist terms. In 1941, on his goodwill tour of Latin America, he explained to the Buenos Aires press, "Musical works written in the United States of recent times have a particular rhythmic structure. It's an influence that's perceptible in all of us [U.S. composers]. . . . Rhythmic complexity is one of the principal characteristics of our music."[158] Was pervasive rhythmic complexity a sign of American sympathy toward African music? If so, could it serve as a north-south bond? Copland left the matter sufficiently open so as not to have to enter the realm of cultural miscegenation, offering instead "an incongruous trope of nature versus culture," that is, the familiar idea that body-oriented African rhythm would serve Western composers only insofar as it can be "entirely sublimated into the body of mature musical forms."[159] To be sure, African American musicians themselves were not necessarily concerned with rhythm, complex or otherwise. In a 1939 essay, R. Nathaniel Dett allowed that rhythm connected U.S. blacks with their African forebears but mentioned it only in passing, having rejected at the outset of his essay the discourse of difference according to which "Negro melodies are neither too wild, strange, exotic or unusual" for conventional musical notation.[160] Cuney-Hare also dismissed the notion of a music motivated by bodily impulses, arguing that African American composers have dedicated themselves to writing music that is "apprehended by the intellect and emotions rather than by the physical and sensational."[161]

The young Leonard Bernstein did not shy away from either the body or the effects of "Negro" rhythm on U.S. art music. Indeed, he viewed it as part of a universalizing project, as he explains in his 1939 senior thesis at Harvard, "The Absorption of Race Elements into American Music."[162] For universality to be achieved, however, "race elements" had to "lose their Negro quality."[163] Bernstein hears its traces in some surprising contexts, such as "The Alcotts," Ives's evocation of the famous New England family in the third movement of the *Concord* sonata, in which Ives absorbs and transforms these rhythms to make them universal.[164] Yet universalism cannot erase the Americanness of the *Concord* sonata, which, paradoxically, is confirmed by the body: even if the listener is completely unaware of "Negro rhythm," the third movement of the *Concord* sonata "*feels* American."[165] Bernstein developed these ideas further in a 1959 telecast, drawing on metaphors of blood and its transformative power to explain the creative processes of U.S. composers. Although "jazz [i.e., Negro rhythm]," he proposed, "entered their blood stream," music "came out" in "new, transformed ways, not sounding like jazz at all, but unmistakably American."[166] In other words, once Negro rhythm is absorbed into the blood and mixes with non-Negro blood, its essential qualities are sublimated. All the while, Bernstein drags us to the edge of an epistemological abyss: absorption, blood, and loss, all premises on which he builds his ideas, are uncomfortably close to those of *branqueamento*, the ultimate absorption of an "inferior" race through an infusion of "superior" blood. In light of his championship of civil rights throughout his career, Bernstein's words expose a glaring rift between rhetoric and practice.[167]

They also echo some nonmusical matters that had percolated in psychological circles since Freud first lectured at Clark College (Massachusetts) in 1909. His followers in the United States pursued with particular interest the concept of sublimation, some relating it to sexual behavior (discussed in chapter 6) and others to communal well-being. One of them, Isador H. Coriat, wrote in 1920 that the cohesion of a given society depended on the extent to which the instincts of individuals could be repressed.[168] Given Freud's notion that the primitive mind was a point of departure for the modern self, a "necessary stage . . . through which every race has passed," it was entirely logical for composers and critics to consider that great indicator of musical primitivism, rhythm, and speculate on its potential for sublimation.[169] Accordingly Cowell declared that, far from displaying neurosis in *The Rite of Spring*, Stravinsky had struck a blow for progress: his music was a "further step in cultivating complexity" because, among other reasons, he had used rhythm, along with other "barbaric" elements, in a "highly sublimated" way.[170]

In the case of *Choros* no. 8, no hint of sublimation can be teased out of critical discourse. Rather, in the tangled jungle of Villa-Lobos's teeming imagination, so fecund in themes, volume, and texture, critics, whether intrigued or offended, encountered at every turn the "mere craving" of the savage. In fact, any rhythmic complexity in *Choros* no. 8 was more "fantasized than heard," to borrow Lawrence

Kramer's crisp phrase.[171] The knuckle-twisting section showcasing the two pianos (rehs. 22–27) does involve a clash of duple and triple values, along with mixed meters; similar metrical relationships prevail in the countermelody to the insistently repeated theme at reh. 3, and sextuplets and septuplets occasionally grate against triple and duple divisions of the beat (reh. 5 + 3). Yet over the twenty-minute piece, such moments are rare, as is the urge to rebar. In sum, U.S. critics *expected* to hear savage rhythms in a work such as *Choros* no. 8 and to implicitly acknowledge it as a racial Other.

That racial Other remained "not wholly articulate," a point Downes addressed at greater length than his colleagues. In calling forth Caliban, Downes effectively ruminated on the challenges of representing musically Freud's concept of the primitive, the "necessary stage" before sublimation enables high civilization. Just as *Choros* no. 8 suffers from lack of form, Caliban too is formless, "not honored with a human shape" (I.ii 283–84). Just as Villa-Lobos is confused by his own proclivities for excess, Caliban hears "a thousand twangling instruments" that "will hum about [his] ears" in confusion (III.ii 142–43). Just as *Choros* no. 8 is "not wholly articulate," Caliban, upon meeting Prospero, is unable to communicate. Once enslaved, however, he learns Prospero's language and proceeds to curse his master (I.ii 363), perhaps a parallel to the "howls of rage" Villa-Lobos assigned his mammoth orchestra. Caliban, on whom "nature, nurture can never stick" (IV.i. 188–89), is ultimately incoherent, even as he learns the conqueror's language. Likewise, Villa-Lobos risks becoming entangled in his own spontaneity. The "we" and the primitive Other can never meet on common ground.

Acknowledging difference so blatantly had little place in the Pan Americanist project. If in 1900 Rodó equated Caliban with U.S. materialism and lowbrow culture—the equivalent of the National Cash Register Building or the commodified "Walt Disney monster"—decades later the Cuban postcolonialist scholar Roberto Fernández Retamar analyzed *The Tempest* in an essay Fredric Jameson called "the Latin American equivalent of Said's *Orientalism*."[172] Retamar defends the degraded Caliban as a slave "in the hands of Prospero, the foreign magician," just as the masses, the "barbarians, peoples of color, underdeveloped . . . [of the] Third World" were enslaved and robbed of their territories; like them, Caliban yields to the colonizer's language and frames of reference.[173] With the unfathomable jungle as the background for the primitive id in all its riotousness, Villa-Lobos set in bold relief the cul de sac with which aesthetic primitivism is freighted: Is sameness-embracing with the incoherent Other possible? Music flowed from Villa-Lobos's "unconscious," music Downes believed the composer heard "with a pair of ears as keen and unspoiled as those of a wild animal."[174] Insusceptible to sublimation and unmediated by universality, it is a poor vehicle for sameness-embracing.

It is often remarked that Caliban is Shakespeare's anagram for "cannibal."[175] Villa-Lobos, the self-styled "savage" in Paris and enfant terrible turned folk universalist in his native land, had cannibalized a variety of strategies à la Oswald de Andrade to present himself at the World's Fair. Whereas critics did not trouble to poke holes in his cosmic pretensions and benignly dismissed "The Hillbilly's Little Train," the jury was out on *Choros* no. 8. On another work, they were strangely silent: the vocalise for soprano and eight cellos, *Bachianas brasileiras* no. 5, which would eventually become Villa-Lobos's most recorded work. The Brazilian soprano Bidu Sayao performed its first movement, Aria, on the May 4 concert.[176] Villa-Lobos doubles the wordless soprano line by one of the eight cellos, while the other seven cellos interweave a delicate accompaniment of pedal tones and pizzicati, emulating the picked style of playing common in Brazilian guitar technique, which includes the *violão* and *cavaquinho*. As Béhague aptly observes, the return of the main melody, which the soprano performs *bocca chiusa*, creates a new timbral unity and assures that "the soprano and the cello voices become one."[177] Several critics had no comment whatsoever. For his part, Thompson remarked only that it was "effective," whereas Perkins found the connection with Bach to be "rather remote."[178] Only Downes sounded the universalist note to which Villa-Lobos aspired, praising the "beautifully chiseled" line and reminding readers that Bach was the "most universal of geniuses."[179] After the Brazilian pavilion and the rest of the Fair had been taken down, Villa-Lobos's primitive jungle, with shades of Calibanesque Otherness, receded to make way for universalism. The next chapter contextualizes some of the ways Pan Americanism smoothed his way.

5 The Golden Age

*Pan Americanist Culture, War, and the Triumph
of Universalism*

In 1941, with the world at war, the U.S. government sent Walt Disney and his team of researcher-animators to Latin America to find material for the cartoon feature *Saludos amigos!*[1] As one official reasoned, because of Disney's worldwide popularity, it would follow that Latin Americans would favor his "message of Americanism" over Nazi rhetoric, then making inroads in the hemisphere.[2] Some were surprised by Disney's new status as war-time diplomat. Even his characters seemed to be on the same footing as Nazi cultural officials; as the film critic Theodore Strauss joked in the *New York Times*, "Who would have thought in the dim primordial past of five years ago that Donald Duck would be giving the retort perfect to Herr Doktor Goebbels?"[3]

In movies such as *Saludos amigos!* Disney made no bones about these objectives. A 1942 document from the Disney Production Archive in Burbank, California confirms that such films were conceived to purvey both "direct and indirect propaganda" about and to Latin America.[4] *Saludos amigos!*, released in North and South America in 1942, crammed a variety of characters and situations into a breathless succession of four "movements," as one critic called its contrasting sections. The score emphasizes Latin American folk genres, such as the *triste* (the lament of the Argentine gaucho) and the *cueca* (the national dance of Chile), some jazzed up in Charles Wolcott's arrangements.[5] More recent music included the 1939 song by Ary Barroso, "Aquarela do Brasil," and the opening credits, a soaring proclamation of hemispheric amity sung by a unison male chorus in Spanish-inflected English. Although in the United States *Saludos amigos!* largely succeeded as both entertainment and education, the degree to which its cuddly cartoon characters promoted hemispheric understanding in Latin America remains a matter of speculation.[6]

Far less circulated was the 1942 documentary *South of the Border with Disney*, an account of the research undertaken for *Saludos amigos!* According to its opening credits, *South of the Border* chronicles the ways in which the visit yielded "a better understanding of the art, music, folklore and humor of our Latin American friends and a wealth of material for future cartoon subjects." Of course, the documentary is more than that: Julianne Burton-Carvajal maintains that it glorifies the rapaciousness of colonization and marvels over the ease with which raw materials of Latin America could be refashioned for ends far different from those dictated by local practices.[7] Be that as it may, the documentary is mainly about the war. Whereas *Saludos amigos!* makes no mention of international events, *South of the Border with Disney* confronts Nazi aggression head-on, referring in the Uruguay sequence, for example, to the *Graf Spee*, the Nazi warship that was scuttled in the waters off Montevideo after being pursued by the British.

Not all Latin Americans favored going to war. Argentina, for example, hesitated for years, prompting many in the United States to insist that the country harbored fascists by the thousands.[8] Brazil's loyalties were an open question during the filming of *South of the Border with Disney*, and perhaps for this reason, the Brazil sequence leads off. It opens in medias res, with the narrator announcing, "And here's the studio we set up in Rio de Janeiro, Brazil." Disney and his team are hard at work in a hotel suite, where white-jacketed waiters serve coffee and several conversations take place at once along with what seems to be a samba demonstration. Then the camera cuts from this creative ferment to the streets, where festivities for Brazilian Independence Day (September 7) are in full swing. Waves of Brazilian armed forces pass before the viewer, as if choreographed by Leni Riefenstahl. The mounted artillery and the Naval Fusiliers (Fuzileiros Navais) file by; the First Cavalry Regiment, also known as the Independence Dragoons (Dragões da Independência), also pass, their uniforms designed for the Imperial Honor Guard of Pedro I (reigned 1822–31) and revived by Vargas for a touch of pomp.[9] "This really was an impressive sight," the narrator intones à la Edward R. Murrow as the brass helmets of the Dragoons gleam in the sunlight. "All day long they marched. Every branch of the armed forces. . . . It made us realize that Brazil was not going to be caught napping in the midst of a world at war but was prepared to meet any emergency." Accompanying the Technicolor waves of armed forces is a peppy, foursquare march. As its trio section begins, the scene shifts to a stadium, probably Maracaná. "[Here] we heard the children of Rio—thirty thousand of them, singing patriotic songs," remarks the narrator. "And leading this enthusiastic chorus was Dr. Heitor Villa-Lobos, one of Brazil's outstanding composers. The famous musician devotes much of his time to the musical education of Brazil's children, and his efforts have been highly successful." For all of six seconds the camera rests on the Head of Musical and Artistic Education as he shapes the "social-civic-artistic" sensibility of Brazilian youth. His features obscured in shadow, Villa-Lobos waves two gigantic sticks as row upon row of white-clad children sing what is surely a patriotic or folk song. No singing is audible, however, and Villa-Lobos marks a meter in conflict with the soundtrack such that when the music abruptly shifts into a hymn-like melody, Villa-Lobos's arrhythmic beat surges on, unchanged.

This fleeting and imperfectly coordinated sequence neatly crystallizes the seemingly random links among business, popular culture, government propaganda, and art music that helped shape impressions of Latin America in the United States at the height of the Good Neighbor period. This chapter discusses the ways in which Villa-Lobos's status in the United States solidified during the war years, often called the "golden age of Pan Americanism."[10] First, however, we survey Pan Americanist culture and its effects on U.S. composers, who effectively "branded" Latin American music through their own Latin American–themed works, ensuring that epithets such as "travel music" or "rum-and-coca-cola school" circulated in the United States even while many Latin American composers pursued cosmopolitan universalism.

▓ PAN AMERICANIST MUSICAL CULTURE IN THE UNITED STATES

For years, U.S. visitors to Latin America had reported on Nazi Germany's finesse with the airwaves and the press, especially in Brazil and Argentina. Few were so determined to squelch Axis infiltration as Nelson A. Rockefeller. He first became interested in Latin America as a minor stockholder in Standard Oil's Venezuelan subsidiary, when he took the trouble to learn Spanish and sought ties with various communities in Venezuela. After the European war broke out, he discussed with Roosevelt's confidante Harry Hopkins the idea of forming an agency to encourage educational, scientific, and cultural ties with Latin America. (As the scion of a prominent Republican family working in a Democratic administration, Rockefeller also sought the blessing of fellow Republicans such as Wendell Willkie.)[11] In August 1940 such an agency, eventually known as the OIAA, was established with Rockefeller at its helm.[12] With its fifty-nine committees, the OIAA was mainly charged with countering Axis propaganda in Latin America and presenting the United States in a favorable light. On matters of culture, however, Rockefeller parted company with his colleagues in the Division of Cultural Relations. Rejecting their preference for universal (i.e., European) culture, he made regionalism his mission, promoting the United States as a model for Latin Americans with such zeal that the OIAA was accused of fomenting "hemispheric cultural autarchy."[13]

The OIAA, which received $3.5 million in its first year alone and a staggering $38 million in its second, sponsored art exhibits and contests for Pan American poetry and essays; a prize for a Pan American novel was awarded in New York on April 14, 1941 (Pan American Day), which NBC covered in a special broadcast.[14] As for film, Rockefeller appointed John Hay ("Jock") Whitney, a vice president of the MoMA, to head the OIAA's Motion Picture Section. (It was Whitney who brought Disney into the Pan Americanist fold.) To clean up stereotypes and geographical inaccuracies (especially important for movies that would be shown in Latin America) Hollywood's Production Code Administration hired a special consultant, Addison Durland.[15] Raised in Cuba and bilingual, Durland checked Spanish and Portuguese spellings and excised images of excessive poverty and indolence he believed would make Latin America look "too much like a slum."[16] Good Neighbor films thus ensured that the U.S. public saw their southern neighbors not as primitive Others but as well-heeled residents of modern cities who enjoyed all the latest amenities. Nor would U.S. viewers imagine them to be anything other than white: Latin American elites were reluctant to suggest that their respective countries were populated by blacks or that their dances derived from Africa, as the Brazilian historian Pedro Calmon cautioned Durland.[17] For all intents and purposes, Durland and his agency practiced censorship. According to a 1947 report, the OIAA implemented strategies to "establish a voluntary censorship over all United States motion pictures insofar as relationships with the other Americas was concerned."[18] With censorship holding sway, the happy Hollywood ending remained a predictable outcome for these frothy productions, one often enhanced with a percussion-heavy production number. As the lyricist and producer Arthur Freed declared, "I believe that hemispheric solidarity, good neighborliness, and the like is [sic] only a background reason for the flood of South American features. . . . The actual reason is South American music. . . . The rhumba stuff is jumping into the number one position in American taste."[19] Surely this wildly popular repertory, now a box-office draw, helped create the impression that Latin American music was "fun" and "lightweight."

Besides Disney, the government sent numerous representatives of U.S. culture to Latin America on what came to be known as goodwill tours. They included Waldo Frank, Douglas Fairbanks Jr., Lincoln Kirstein and the American Ballet Caravan, and Copland, who visited nine Latin America countries between August and December 1941.[20] The last two were sent by the OIAA Music Committee, which was chaired by Carleton Sprague Smith, the musicologist, flutist, and chief of the Music Division of the New York Public Library.[21] Unofficial cultural diplomats relied on private funds; among these were Stokowski, who formed his All-American Youth Orchestra especially for a Latin American goodwill tour in 1940, and Arturo Toscanini, who toured the same year with the NBC Symphony amid accusations that he was insufficiently American to represent the United States.[22] Other activities not officially associated with the OIAA included composition contests, such as that sponsored in 1942 by the Fleischer Music Collection in Philadelphia, along with various initiatives in musicology, radio, and music education.[23]

What sort of music would best inculcate hemispheric solidarity? However compelling Chávez's ur-classicism, it reached mainly the New York modern music crowd. H.P., with its abstruse allusions, had missed the mark, as had Villa-Lobos's unsublimated primitivism. Although it took no official position, the Music Committee effectively came to conclude that the music best suited to winning hearts and minds in the Americas should be accessible and identifiably Latin American. The pianist and author Arthur Loesser of the Cleveland Institute of Music urged committee members toward this ideal, writing Smith in April 1941 to discuss a nationwide project in which U.S. orchestras would commission works from Latin American composers. Loesser offered potential awardees the following advice:

Do not interpret the commission as an opportunity to show off the extreme limits of your imaginative horizons. South American rhythms are swell, and Indian percussion instruments are fine, provided they are not too hard for our boys to learn how to play. But webs of atonal dissonant counterpoint are definitely *out*. Nothing remotely resembling Hindemith, Schoenberg, post-Sacre Stravinsky, or Bartók will do. Here I am not speaking as myself but as a representative citizen of a fairly progressive middle-western large city.... The titles of the compositions are important. *Variations on an Original Theme* is not particularly calculated to arouse an interest in South America. But a title like *Anaconda* or *Commodore Rivadavia* is intriguing and will start a burgeoning of program notes, with consequent fixation of attention.[24]

Copland, a Music Committee member, concurred. He implicitly endorsed OIAA regionalism by arguing that, musically speaking, "the [Latin American] countries that have developed most quickly are those with the richest folklore," a conclusion his 1941 tour only confirmed.[25] Not surprisingly, Copland praised composers such as Mozart Camargo Guarnieri for his "profoundly Brazilian" works and Ginastera for his command of "local melodic phraseology," while dismissing Latin Americans who aggressively pursued international modernism, such as the Argentine serialist and antinationalist Juan Carlos Paz, for example.[26] Copland himself had only recently decided to tone down the dissonant language of his Piano Variations (1930) and *Short Symphony* (1932) to express himself "in the simplest possible terms."[27] This new style, which might involve folklore (as in *El salón México*), more or less coincided with Charles Seeger's campaign to communicate with the masses through folk music. Arguing on its behalf at the height of the Depression, when communism beckoned U.S. workers as never before or since, Seeger urged his fellow composers to cut through the "prejudices of music-professionalism" with its stultifying mix of "pride and plain hokum," exhortations that resonated in a political as well as musical sense.[28]

Clearly, in his remarks on Latin America, Copland was promoting his own aesthetic. But as we have seen, these formulae did not always serve Latin American composers well, some of whom aspired to cosmopolitan universalism. What about composers from the United States representing Latin America, now such a timely subject? What if, in avoiding the "webs of atonal dissonant counterpoint" against which Loesser warned, they went too far, lapsing into lighthearted travel music? Given the power of the culture industry and the Latin-tinged popular music streaming out of Hollywood, the risk was significant.

▪ U.S. COMPOSERS REPRESENT LATIN AMERICA

Freed's enthusiasm over "the rhumba stuff" was no idle observation. Not that his terminology was all that precise: as Roberts points out, most pieces marketed in the United States as rhumbas resembled the Cuban *son*, a multifaceted genre in duple meter that combines African and Hispanic influences.[29] Certainly the glitzy nightclubs that came to be associated with rhumba (the ballroom dance) were a far cry from the original *rumba*, which lower-class blacks performed in nineteenth-century Cuba, often as an emotional outlet.[30] (The term *rumba* can also connote the event itself.) In the commercial rhumba, the lilting melody of the typical *son* is offset by a prominent percussion section, which normally included claves, *güiro*, conga drums, maracas, one or more cowbells, bongos, and *timbales*. Besides climbing record sales, evidence of the rhumba craze is apparent in the movie *Weekend in Havana* (Twentieth-Century Fox, 1941), in which Alice Faye and Cesar Romero sang of the dance's "enchanting rhythm" and "primitive beat" in the song "Romance and Rhumba."[31] Symphonic composers who caught the rhumba fever included Harl MacDonald (Symphony no. 2, 1934) and Morton Gould (*Latin American Symphonette*, 1941).

Probably the best-known symphonic rhumba is Gershwin's *Cuban Overture*, which he initially called *Rhumba*. Unabashed travel music (it has been called "a charming little travel piece"), the work came about when Gershwin visited Cuba in February 1932, where he evidently lived it up on the golf course, at the beach, and in nightclubs, often in the company of attractive women.[32] In Havana's dance orchestras he heard claves, maracas, bongos, and the *tres* (a three-course, six-string guitar associated with Cuba) and returned to the United States with several percussion instruments in hand, determined to re-create some of these sounds.[33] Gershwin was then exploring Joseph Schillinger's mathematically based compositional method, which may have affected his manipulations of the song "Échale Salsita" by the Afro-Cuban musician Ignacio Piñeiro, quoted in inversion, augmentation, and canon.

Still known as *Rhumba*, the work premiered at an all-Gershwin concert on August 16, 1932, at Lewisohn Stadium in New York. Although it was hailed as the "novelty of the evening," critics were less than impressed. Pitts Sanborn found that even "rich sonorities, fascinating in the interplay of rhythms and its characteristic turns of melody" did not save *Rhumba* from dullness.[34] For Taubman, despite "maracas, gourd, bongo and other Cuban instruments, [*Rhumba*] was merely old Gershwin in recognizable form."[35] All critics, however, were staggered by the huge throng, estimated at seventeen thousand, with four thousand turned away.[36] Apropos these vast numbers, Henry Beckett of the *New York Evening Post* sermonized that while putting Gershwin "in a class with Rudy Vallee, Edgar A. Guest, the writer of verses, and Jimmy Walker, the Mayor" might be unjust, the composer was still no "match for Beethoven and Wagner." He added as a parting shot, "Popularity is a doubtful criterion of value, that adulation often goes to the mediocre."[37] By November, Gershwin had christened the work *Cuban Overture*, that is, as a symphonic work. It was heard at the Metropolitan Opera at another all-Gershwin program, which included the Piano Concerto and *An American in Paris*. Downes alone praised the composer's learned qualities, noting "polytonality—combinations of keys, boldly employed," and "canonic treatment of certain motives."[38] Oscar Thompson commented on the "various exotic and esoteric instruments [he] would not be so foolhardy as to attempt to name" (several of the "thump and rattle variety") but doubted that any of the Gershwin works performed, all "flings in a borderland idiom," would sit well with the cognoscenti.[39] Thus, in blurring the boundaries between symphonic music and commercial idioms, the *Cuban Overture* assumed its place in the canon of what Michael Steinberg has called "high-class pops music."[40]

Another rhumba fan was Gershwin's teacher, Henry Cowell.[41] Having helped found the Pan American Association of Composers (PAAC), he worked during the Good Neighbor period for the Music Division of the Pan American Union on the Editorial Project for Latin American Music, charged with making available to U.S. performers scores by Latin American composers.[42] During this period Cowell also composed the brief and strongly tonal *Fanfare to the Forces of Our Latin American Allies*, in which he inserted a Mexican-sounding theme. (Copland's *Fanfare for the Common Man* grew out of the same project, which Eugene Goossens of the Cincinnati Symphony Orchestra initiated in 1942.)[43] Besides *Grandma's Rhumba* (for band), Cowell composed a rhumba in his seven-movement suite, *American Melting Pot* for chamber orchestra (1940), a survey of influences on music in the United States. "Rhumba with Added Eighth" takes its place with "Chorale (Teutonic-American)," "Air (Afro-American)," "Satire (Franco-American)," "Alapna (Oriental-American)," "Slavic Dance (Slavic-American)," and "Square Dance (Celtic American)." Its humorous countermelodies and transparent woodwind writing, along with frequent pentatonic and modal melodic turns that hint at an Orientalist version of ragtime, create an unusually placid rhumba. Another anomaly is the percussion: but for brief wood-block episodes, there is no showcasing of scrapers, maracas, or claves that so attracted Gershwin. "Rhumba with Added Eighth" was first performed in October 1941 by the National Youth Administration Orchestra of Philadelphia under Louis Vyner at the Mountain State Forest Festival in West Virginia, and in May 1943 the Orchestrette of New York (initially an all-female ensemble known as the Orchestrette Classique) performed it at Carnegie Chamber Music Hall.[44] On that occasion, a critic for the *New York Times* suggested that the suite as a whole failed to enhance the music of the world, and Cowell eventually withdrew the work.[45]

Given the popular orientation of these representations, it is hardly surprising that when an arch-modernist such as the Ukrainian émigré composer Leo Ornstein experimented with the Latin idiom, he eschewed his customary free dissonance.[46] His solo piano piece "A la Mexicana," brief and harmonically conventional, is built on an incongruous *habanera* rhythm and nowhere suggests radical modernism. Another émigré composer, one with strong conservatory credentials, was the Alsatian-born Jean Berger. Having lived in Rio de Janeiro before emigrating to the United States in 1941, he took full advantage of Pan Americanism. With sonatas, art songs, and works for mixed chorus to his credit, Berger now began cranking out sambas by the dozen as a freelance arranger of Brazilian music for CBS and NBC radio. Two of his songs appeared in Charling Music Corporation's "Good Neighbor Series." In one, "Querita," he collaborated with the lyricist Bob Russell, acclaimed as "especially adept at writing lyrics that convey the mood of South American music." In fact the title "Querita" is pure invention, substituting for the standard *querida* (dear) much the way Frito-Lay coined the term *bandito* (the Spanish word is *bandido*). All the requisite characteristics of a Latin song are present: a syncopated bass line with a chordal accompaniment, alternating metric units of two and three, and an ingratiating melody. As for the cover art, whoever purchased the sheet music would behold a map of North and South America in red set off from a red field by an aureole of white. A blue banner sprinkled with stars announces "The 'Good Neighbor' Series," with an insert stretching from somewhere in Peru to northern Brazil that ambitiously claims, "This series is a collection of songs that capture the authentic flavor of all the Americas." The exclusively red, white, and blue color scheme, however, suggests which party had the upper hand (fig. 5a).

Surely the work by a U.S. composer that has come to represent Latin America most widely to the U.S. public is Copland's *El salón México*. He completed it in 1936, just before the golden age of Pan Americanism. As one of Copland's first attempts to deliver on his promise to express himself "in the simplest possible terms" it was thus a critical point in his career. Several critics were less than sympathetic to this new orientation. The pianist John Kirkpatrick noted that some critics expressed "anxiety . . . suspecting more concession than conviction."[47] As is well known, *El salón México* was inspired by Copland's 1932 visit to the eponymous dance hall in Mexico City, which he undertook with the aid of a guidebook by Anita Brenner, one of the U.S. pilgrims to Mexico during the vogue years. So was Frances Toor, who compiled one of the two anthologies in which Copland found his folk tunes. (The other was by the literature professor and author Rubén M. Campos.)[48] Important early performances include the premiere of the two-piano version (October 1935) at New York's New School for Social Research and the performance of the orchestral version in Mexico City (August 1937) with Chávez conducting. (Chávez repeated the work a few weeks later in one of his free concerts for workers.)[49] New York digested *El salón México* when Adrian Boult conducted it with the NBC Symphony in a May 1938 radio broadcast. A performance at the London ISCM followed in June, and that autumn the Boston Symphony Orchestra featured *El salón México* in Boston and at Carnegie Hall.

A few early critics heard travel music, some less than appreciatively. Marc Blitzstein dismissed *El salón México* as "a good chance for musical reportage . . . wasted in up-to-the-minute travel-slumming music."[50] Gilbert Chase too described the work as "a deliberate attempt to write 'tourist music,'" one that situated Copland in the same category as Rimsky-Korsakov and Chabrier.[51] Other early critics had no particular reservations about tourist music, with Downes warding off the suggestion that the work was intended as authentic,

Figure 5a "Querita," by Jean Berger and Bob Russell. Charling Music Co., New York.

proposing that it was Mexican only in the sense "that a Frenchman's music would be American if he had gone to the Casino in Harlem and later composed about it."[52] Few critics found *El salón Mexico* particularly modern. Sanborn noted an "attractive, if rather surprisingly decorous score."[53] Its main appeal lay in the orchestration and in Copland's manipulation of the folk melodies, often humorous and with witty interruptions.[54] Here, form was critical. Most reviewers concurred with J.D.B. (surely Jerome Bohm), who commended Copland for successfully negotiating the potpourri, that dubious aesthetic category Adorno would come to associate with "atomistic listening," with all its baleful effects on the attention span of the musical public, a constituency whose needs, Bohm believed, Copland had calculated in *El salón México*.[55] "Mr. Copland's potpourri on Mexican themes," Bohm observed, "is skillfully orchestrated and effective in an obvious way and at least serves to reveal that although he has created such things as the granitic piano variations, he has not forgotten the practical value of stereotyped diatonic harmonies."[56]

In *El salón México* Copland met his intended goals. Whatever the stigma of travel music, he explicitly allied himself with it, as is clear from his program note for the Boston Symphony performance in November 1938. "No doubt," he wrote, "I realized that it would be foolish for me to attempt to translate into musical sounds the more profound side of Mexico: the Mexico of the ancient civilizations or the revolutionary Mexico of today. In order to do that one must really know a country. All that I could hope to do was to reflect the Mexico of the tourists."[57] He embraced the potpourri with equal enthusiasm. Rather than promoting "atomistic listening," he found it an effective approach to working with folk music:

> The use of folk material in a symphonic composition always brings with it a formal problem. Composers have found that there is little that can be done with a folk tune except repeat it. Inevitably there is the danger of producing a mere string of unrelated "melodic gems." In the end I adopted a form which is a kind of modified potpourri, in which the Mexican themes and their extension are sometimes inextricably mixed for the sake of conciseness and coherence.[58]

In sum, as with other representations of Latin America by U.S. composers, *El salón México* is a "borderland fling," to borrow Thompson's phrase. In depicting Latin America, U.S. composers rejected the modernist strategies of central Europe and reached out to a mass audience, sometimes in the face of criticism from some of their peers. They affixed to their works picturesque titles appropriate to the Latin American idioms they showcased, filtering dance rhythms, prominent percussion, folk music, and flashy trumpet "licks" through their own perspectives. In short, they adhered to the very norms Loesser recommended to the OIAA music committee.

■ FOLKLORE CULTS AND THE DEMISE OF UNSUBLIMATED PRIMITIVISM

The horizon of expectation just sketched was also the backdrop for Villa-Lobos's ascent in the United States. The limitations of unsublimated primitivism were soon clear. In April 1940 an audience that included personnel of the Pan American Union and the Pan American Society heard *Choros* no. 10 in Carnegie Hall, with Hugh Ross and the Schola Cantorum performing that gigantic work for orchestra and chorus, along with Mignone's *Maracuta de Chico Rei* (like *Choros* no. 10, a repeat from the World's Fair), Burle Marx's *Pater noster*, and *Sinfonía*

Bíblica by the Argentine composer Juan José Castro.[59] In *Choros* no. 10, Villa-Lobos intended to depict the "eternal rhythms of nature and humanity," with the "Brazilian heart palpitat[ing] in unison with the Brazilian earth."[60] To achieve this goal, the composer marshaled forces comparable to those for *Choros* no. 8, approximating its scope, volume, and texture. Instead of wallowing in "virtual negation of form," however, Villa-Lobos marks the work's various sections with choral interjections, some set contrapuntally (reh. 6ff.) and presumably based on Amerindian chants. All culminate in the song "Rasga o coração" (Break the Heart), heard at five measures after reh. 9. Its telluric vibrations hail not from some cosmic realm, however, but from the commercial music industry of Rio de Janeiro. "Rasga o coração" is a schottische by Anacleta de Medeiros (1866–1907), with lyrics by Villa-Lobos's old friend and *choro* musician Catulo da Paixão Cearense.[61] Soaring above the birdcalls and the random sounds of nature, the suave urban melody boldly insinuates itself into the jungle, calling into question Caliban's overweening power.

Reaction was mixed. Downes observed that the composer "writes like a real savage with uncivilized keenness of sensation," whereas Perkins commented only briefly on "exotic colors."[62] Colin McPhee was unimpressed. Having praised "primitive energy" in Chávez's *Sinfonía India*, he found Brazilian primitivism to fall short, confessing to readers of *Modern Music* that he departed from Carnegie Hall with "the feeling of emerging from a jungle of tangled vines and fantastic foliage," from an "atmosphere, torrid and suffocating [and] too much for many people."[63] *Choros* no. 10 was largely to blame. Despite certain remarkable features, such as "brooding, animal mutterings . . . like nothing one has heard before," McPhee concluded, one was "definitely conscious that something vital was lacking, some real point of gravity." He also took aim at folk music—or what he believed to be folk music—that is, "Rasga o coração":

> Suddenly the chorus enters, chanting barbaric syllables to a wild dynamic rhythm. The tension is so great that one wonders how it can possibly be maintained. . . .
>
> Bit by bit a Portuguese[-language] folksong creeps in, sugary and banal beyond words. The rhythmic pattern, so forceful and exciting at the beginning, suddenly loses its vitality, becomes automatic, a mere guitar-strumming. There is a terrific let-down and the energy appears so suspect that we feel perhaps we were deceived from the beginning. The ending of the work in a super-brilliant, strident chord from the chorus only confirms this.[64]

McPhee could hardly have been expected to know that "Rasga o coração" was a published work and not the voice of the Brazilian folk. In identifying the "sugary and banal" melody as a folk song, he called into question a core element of Villa-Lobos's aesthetic program. The final "super-brilliant, strident chord," a grandiose, Hollywood-ending gesture, may have tipped the balance. "What is the matter with all this music?" McPhee railed. "Why are we not satisfied?"[65] The jungle betrayed both incoherence and a dearth of vital ideas.

At the next big event for Villa-Lobos in the United States, the Festival of Brazilian Music, which took place in October 1940 at the MoMA, New York's critics reflected further on folk music, banality, and unsublimated primitivism. Like the concerts of Mexican music there the previous May, the Brazilian programs were paired with an exhibit, this time a one-man show that featured Cândido Portinari, another Latin American "Red" artist under the Rockefeller family's watchful eye.[66] It was hardly the moment was for a cultural diplomacy disaster. Vargas had recently received a $20 million loan from the (U.S.) Export-Import Bank to construct steelworks plants in Brazil; an advantageous trade deal with the United States had also been signed.[67] Yet he was still unwilling to commit himself: as Jerry Dávila points out, a 1939 Brazilian history textbook upheld both European fascism and the New Deal "as the zeniths of civilization."[68]

Casting a broad net, the MoMA concerts showcased art, folk, and popular genres (the last understood as commercial dance music, to judge from Burle Marx's program notes). According to Marx, Brazilian art music is rooted in these influences: "To appreciate Brazilian art music of today, a survey of its sources is helpful. They lie in the popular and folk music of the country. . . . The examples selected [for the MoMA programs] are such that even a layman can feel the connection between the folk source and contemporary Brazilian [art] music."[69] As at the Fair, Villa-Lobos dominated. Ten of his works appeared on the first two programs, and a third was dedicated solely to his music. His various styles were well represented. Caliban surfaced in the choral work "Xango" (described in the program as a setting of "an authentic *macumba* theme"), in the Nonet for chamber orchestra and chorus, and in the piano piece *Rudepoema* (Savage Poem), performed by Artur Rubinstein, who also played the suite *O Prole do Bebe* (The Baby's Family). Universalism emerged in *Bachianas brasileiras* no. 1 (for cello ensemble) and in the Aria of no. 5, the latter a repeat from the Fair. Several *Choros* were also performed. Critics noted the salient points of Villa-Lobos's works, comparing them with those of his compatriots (Guarnieri, Mignone, Ernesto Nazareth, and others were also on the program) and also considered the future of Brazilian music (fig. 5b, website).

Leading the charge was Virgil Thomson, newly repatriated from Nazi-occupied Paris and appointed chief critic at the *New York Herald Tribune*.[70] Thomson was familiar to U.S. readers of *American Mercury*, the *New Republic*, and *Modern Music*; his book *The State of Music* was also beginning to be reviewed.[71] Years later he looked back with relish on the MoMA concerts. "In my second week [on the *Tribune*], reviewing two Brazilian programs at the Museum of Modern Art," he wrote, "I poked fun at . . . folklore cults in general, at all music from Latin America, that of Villa-Lobos in particular, and found an error in the museum's translation of a title from the Portuguese."[72] In fact in none of his reviews does he address "all music from Latin America," much less poke fun at it. Neither was he all that hard on Villa-Lobos.[73] "Folkloric cults" were another matter. Because Thomson had been based in Paris since 1925 he had experienced Depression-era enthusiasm for folklore only from afar. If Seeger had cut through anti-folkloric snobbery, Thomson attacked folklore for its dubious musical results and the puffed-up nationalist sentiments he believed lay behind it. In his first review of the Brazilian concerts, "Heavy Hands across Caribbean," he jests, "Folk-lore is supposed to be an especially virtuous form of music and composers who use it for art purposes are often considered with a respect they would never receive if they took the trouble to write their own tunes. . . . This reviewer . . . thinks music is music, no matter who wrote it, and that a dumb tune is a dumb tune, no matter how anonymous its origins."[74] To be sure, Thomson was not necessarily suggesting that Brazilian folk music consisted of nothing but "dumb tunes." But its essential characteristics were hardly inspiring. Like "American rhythm," it could be explained in racialist—and equally questionable—terms:

> Brazilian folk-lore and popular music have the gentle monotony of all things Portuguese. That monotony is not really boring; it is too subtle and refined to be boring. But it is as far from the passionate flaming of things Spanish as a Portuguese *fado* is from a *jota* or a *canto flamenco*. Its Indian elements are flat and static like all things Indian. And its negroid substratum is no more or less negroid than our own barrel-house blues and Scotch-African spirituals. The Negroes seem always in this hemisphere to have acted as musical soil and fertilizer. They have never yet been either the seed or the final flower of anything.[75]

If Brazilian folk music was inherently deficient as raw material, more serious was the use to which it might be put. For Thomson, "folklore cults" veered perilously close to nationalism, a particular danger for Villa-Lobos:

> Villa-Lobos places himself among the provincials, the local-color boys, by occupying himself so exclusively with musical nationalism. He classifies himself thus with de Falla and Smetana and Dvorak and Kodaly and the early Bartók. Fine composers enough these though none of the first water and all of them harder and more penetrating than Villa-Lobos. But all together they constitute a League of Minor Musical Nations as pathetically out of date today as Geneva itself.[76]

So cosmopolitan was Thomson that he later argued that writing American music was "simple," for "all you have to do is be an American and then write any kind of music you wish."[77] Yet folklore in and of itself did not necessarily lead to blatant flag-waving. A few weeks later, Thomson reviewed Harris's relatively abstract *American Creed* and observed, "Musical material, even folklore material, is as international as musical form and syntax, [such] that localism is no more than one man's colorful accent." He praised Harris for avoiding such accents and addressing musical problems such as form. But the threat of musical nationalism lurked. Of Harris's descriptive prefaces Thomson scolded:

No composer in the world, not even in Italy or Germany, makes such shameless use of patriotic feelings to advertise his product. One would think . . . that [Harris] had been awarded by God, or at least by popular vote, a monopolistic privilege of expressing our nation's deepest ideals and highest aspirations. And when the piece so advertised turns out to be mostly not very clearly orchestrated schoolish counterpoint and a quite skimpy double fugue (neither of which has any American connotation), one is tempted to put the whole thing down as a bad joke.[78]

Only in the second of his reviews of the MoMA concerts did Thomson get down to discussing actual compositions, that is, the direct consequences of Villa-Lobos's "occupying himself so exclusively with musical nationalism." Although Thomson singled out *Choros* no. 4 (for three horns and trombone) and the Nonet for "folklorish pretensions," he also saw the innate value in both works. Surely due to the spiky, independent lines, angular melodies, the parody of a walking bass, and offbeat accents in *Choros* no. 4, Thomson found it "a perfectly good wind instrument piece of the witty sort [that] could have been executed with deadly seriousness at any of those concerts devoted to what used to be known as Contemporary Music" (in other words, at the sort of event not generally associated with the Minor Musical Nations).[79] Thomson condemned as "tommyrot" the subtitle of the Nonet ("An Aural Impression in Miniature of the Whole of Brazil"), which he placed on the same level as "Roy Harris's preposterous pantheistic prefaces to his symphonic scores." Yet the Nonet redeemed itself, albeit for surprising reasons. "Not being familiar with any part of Brazil, let alone the whole of it," Thomson remarked, "I cannot say whether Senhor Villa-Lobos's aural impression of it is true and resembling. I can certify, however, that the work is a good and true musical likeness of Paris, France in 1923, where (and when) the Nonetto was composed."[80]

Few higher compliments were possible from a Francophile such as Thomson. As Suzanne Robinson has observed, he was "transparently pro-French," publishing numerous Sunday columns in the *Herald Tribune* on French composers and surrounding himself with French-trained U.S. composers, mainly former Boulanger students.[81] Still, one has to wonder whose Paris of 1923 Thomson had in mind. In the Nonet, Villa-Lobos employs (albeit in reduced forces) the same "instruments typiques brésiliens" with which he had besieged Florent Schmitt and Lucien Chevalier in the 1920s. Neither the *puita*, the two *reco-recos*, the *chocalhos*, the persistent repeated rhythms, the *bocca chiusa* Indianist chants, nor the frenzied finale exactly conjure up the French capital. Rather, the Frenchified Brazilian forest Thomson heard in the Nonet echoes Milhaud's ballet *L'homme et son désir* (1918), equally rich in extended percussion episodes, interwoven random melodic lines, prominent percussion, and wordless chants.[82] In sum, Thomson heard Villa-Lobos's music through his habitually pro-French ears, hearing not a trace of folkloric nationalism in the mix. Surely for these reasons, he deemed the Nonet the best of Villa-Lobos's pieces performed at the MoMA, with the urbane *Choros* no. 4 a close second.

Accordingly, Thomson considered Villa-Lobos in relation to German music, the undue influence of which he despised. (Shortly after the MoMA concerts, Thomson would describe the first movement of Beethoven's *Eroica* as a "dud.")[83] Villa-Lobos's music, on the other hand, was "as Latin as one could imagine anything being. Portugal and Spain and France are all there, and a little, O, ever so little of lighthearted Italy. His Germanism goes no farther than an occasional title about the 'soul of Brazil.'"[84] Thus, with its Latin credentials, Villa-Lobos's music offered charm and facility despite the occasional whiff of folkloric-nationalist bombast. Conspicuously lacking in transcendence, it can nonetheless be listened to on its own modest terms:

> [Villa-Lobos's] harmonizations are . . . far from banal though they are never profound and rarely distinguished. His formal structure, [which] is loose and lackadaisical, doesn't need to be anything else when the music is so easygoing. His instrumentation, his orchestral fancy, is the most charming thing about his work. No more profound or penetrating than his harmonic structure, it is none the less full of bright and welcome "effects" . . . all the more welcome in music that has so little of formal progress or of contrapuntal perspective to hold it together.[85]

Thomson hardly "poked fun" at Villa-Lobos, as he claimed. Indeed, however obscure his praise (and however dubious his observations on race), Thomson ultimately embraces sameness, welcoming the Brazilian composer into a loosely defined federation of Latin *sensibilté*. Perhaps, Thomson seems to speculate, Villa-Lobos is even one of "us."

Another work that stood out at the MoMA concerts was the Aria of *Bachianas* no. 5, which Downes alone had admired at the Fair. Now he compared the work with actual Bach compositions, perhaps the first critic in the United States to attempt this interpretive leap:

> The soprano solo of "Bachiana" no. 5 has an astonishing relation, in its first and last parts, to the style of solo passages in the cantatas and passions of the Leipzig master. These resemblances are not incongruous with the change of expression of the middle part. It is indeed as though Villa-Lobos had caught in an [*sic*] curiously personal way a reflection of the Bach manner, which does not weaken his own creative position and makes for an uncommonly felicitous piece.[86]

Tellingly Downes omits any mention of folk music's role in the Bachian project. He did, however, revisit Caliban and unsublimated primitivism apropos *Rudepoema*, described in the program as "perhaps the most difficult piano composition ever written." Like *Choros* nos. 8 and 10, the roughly contemporaneous *Rudepoema* (it dates from 1921–26) surges along with dense textures and prolonged *forte* passages, its form largely indiscernible. This time, however, the excesses of the jungle and Caliban's formlessness did not sit at all well with Downes, who found the twenty-minute work overly long, lacking in development, and written in such a way that the piano had to "be beaten as a madman would beat his drum."[87] The unsublimated jungle was wearing thin for other critics as well. Perkins, who covered the final concert for the *Herald Tribune* instead of Thomson, noted in *Rudepoema* "diffuseness of form."[88]

But no critic was more incensed than McPhee. In a review entitled "Jungles of Brazil," he lambasted Villa-Lobos's music, which had increasingly proved disappointing over the course of the three concerts. He assailed the program booklet, in which the public read of Villa-Lobos's boast to his Parisian colleagues that he had come to Paris not to learn but to show others what he could do, a stance McPhee found preposterous. As for *Rudepoema*'s status as one the most challenging piano works ever composed, McPhee scoffed that "it was also surely one of the worst."[89] He isolated the problem as an "overwhelming sonority of sound" behind which Villa Lobos "takes refuge, concealing himself within an elaborate acoustic jungle like some wild animal, invisible beneath a tangle of ferns and creepers. He has a wealth of material . . . and no idea what to do with it."[90] Caliban had degenerated into incoherence after all. McPhee then proceeded to attack the Brazilian concerts in their entirety, taking Chávez's MoMA programs as a point of comparison:

> There was more musical interest in any single piece on the Mexican program than in all the Brazilian programs put together. What was impressive about the Mexican [event] was the sureness of approach, the originality, the awareness and fine manipulation of sonorous material. The Brazilians, on the other hand, lack direction; their exoticism is sentimental and extravagant, their feeling for timbre haphazard and of the lush-impressionist school.[91]

Ever deaf to the ideals of Pan Americanist solidarity, McPhee declared, "These concerts succeeded in pleasing neither the general public nor those interested in the progress of contemporary music." Other critics largely agreed. Thomson confined his remarks to Villa-Lobos, omitting mention of any other composer. (Like several of his colleagues, he singled out the singer Elsie Houston, commenting that "her numbers were the only ones that held the complete attention of the rather choice but skimpy audience.") Oscar Thompson tersely dismissed as little more than "incongruous popular music" a *Choro* by Oswaldo "Vadico" Gogliano, which Romeo Silva conducted "gourd in hand," and Downes found the art songs set by Guarnieri, Fernandez, and Mignone derivative.[92]

Clearly a new direction was in order. Brazilian music as a whole, permeated with folklore and "sentimental and extravagant exoticism," was on shaky ground. Whether Villa-Lobos could potentially redeem his country depended on several things. Caliban and the jungle seemed an increasingly risky proposition, and folkloric or "tourist" nationalism were equally undesirable. Under these circumstances, it was the *Bachianas*—or at least their universalist dimension—that could save Villa-Lobos. In pursuing universalism, moreover, he enjoyed the support of many of his Latin American colleagues equally unwilling to be typed as "local-color boys."

■ NATIONALISM: THE "GREATEST FOE"

That musical nationalism was suspect in the United States can be seen in sober articles such as "War, Nationalism, Tolerance," published in *Modern Music* in late 1939. Its author, the Jewish musicologist Alfred Einstein, had recently arrived in the United States, fleeing his native Germany in 1933 and living in England and Italy before settling in Massachusetts to teach at Smith College and at the Hartt College (now School) of Music in Connecticut.[93] Meditating on recent events in Europe and their effect on music, Einstein deplored nationalism's legacy. He allowed that nineteenth-century nationalism had imparted "color, charm and fresh character" to music. But ultimately "blood and soil" cannot constitute creativity; rather, he declared, "the greatest foe of freedom, independence and truth in art—and in science—is Nationalism."[94] Roger Sessions, long a champion of universalism, linked such tendencies more explicitly to German chauvinism, arguing that Goebbels's nationalist rhetoric was "the basis of polemics, slogans, and theories" that were becoming ever more widespread.[95] What if such tendencies reached the Americas? Sessions was pessimistic on this point. In "On the American Future," he considered music in the United States, bemoaning the spread of "nationalism and cultural isolationism," and bleakly added that to preserve "the values which totalitarianism aims to destroy" would require a long and sustained struggle.[96] Clearly the "foe" was no abstract concept.

Farwell also considered musical nationalism a "dangerous subject" and, like Sessions, brought the matter home.[97] In 1939 he invoked Emerson and Whitman, enthusing that the former had declared, "One day we shall cast out the passion for Europe with the passion for America," and the latter, "I hear America singing," dryly adding that when the poet "pictured himself as listening to America singing, he was assuredly not thinking of it as singing 'Die Wacht am Rhein' or the 'Marseillaise.'"[98] Farwell could hardly have known that in calling forth those two selections he was anticipating that famous contrapuntal clash in the 1941 movie *Casablanca*. But whatever his reservations about nationalism, Farwell also cautioned against universalism. Old saws such as "Music is the universal language" (Henry Wadsworth Longfellow, *Outre-Mer*, 1833) may inculcate sensations of unity, he argued, but they also fail to promote critical analysis. Even in works widely recognized as universal, national essences are inevitable; like Weissmann, Farwell held that to "'purify' . . . music of [the] racial and national elements of which it is redolent, [to] abstract it entirely from recognizable humanity" effaces its power (1236). For Farwell, true universalism, rather than the "'universal' illusion under which the musical world has so long been laboring" (1237), is the apex of a five-rung schema: (1) music of "people who have no national life in our sense of the subject," that is, primitive cultures; (2) music of peasants from countries with an established cultural identity; (3) composed music that quotes folk songs; (4) composed music not based on quotation but subtly evocative of a given people; and (5) music by composers who "transfigure and beautify the national soul, [giving] it to us in its most exalted aspect." To this highest order belonged Haydn, Mozart, and Beethoven, all of whom absorbed the essence of their national song (1237–38). Clearly folk music is central to Farwell's scheme. But fifth-order composers enter the lofty realm of universalism only by "spontaneously or consciously refining and sublimating" folk music (1238). U.S. composers, Farwell maintained, are just as capable of sublimation, for once they draw "spiritual strength from union with the soul of the people from whom they sprang" and "exalt that soul, in their expression to a height which commands the highest and widest admiration which it is in the power of their general culture sphere to give," they will have created universal music (1238). The only thing missing in Farwell's grand design is an account of the "astral infinitus." But for that, he essentially described Villa-Lobos's sublimation of Brazilian folk music through the language of Bach.

To be sure, any number of Villa-Lobos's Latin American colleagues who pursued universalism sought to reformulate folklore along similar lines. But many associated folklore with nationalism, rejecting it outright, especially during the 1930s and 1940s, when the nationalist movements that had surged in musical circles at the beginning of the century were losing momentum. Neoclassicism proved especially attractive, perhaps due to its ideological similarities with *arielismo*, the European orientation of which was far less objectionable than in the United States. Even after the carnage of World War I, when muralists in Mexico and Indianist novelists in Bolivia and Peru renounced notions of European cultural superiority, neoclassicism beckoned composers.[99] Ponce, for example, composed *Prelude and Fugue on a Theme of Handel* and *Preludes and Fugues on a Theme of Bach*; sonata form and the baroque suite figure in his *Classical Sonata for Guitar* (1928) and *Suite in Antique Style for Strings* (1933), respectively. Although these are just a few of Ponce's stylistic forays, they nonetheless show neoclassicism's appeal, even for one so widely associated with Mexican nationalism.[100] In Uruguay, Guido Santórsola (born in Brazil) experimented with neoclassicism, as did his younger colleague Héctor Tosar, albeit to a lesser degree. The Venezuelan composer Juan Bautista Plaza wrote two-part inventions and *diferencias*, works that have been described as "neo-Baroque" and "reminiscent of Bach and Hindemith"; he also wrote several fugues, including the *Fuga-Canción Venezolana*, the purported Venezuelan elements of which are not all that evident, "even to Venezuelans."[101] In Cuba the Barcelona-born José Ardévol (he settled on the island in 1930) resisted the image of the rough-hewn autodidact bonding with the Indians, registering instead "the poverty of aboriginal artistic manifestations."[102] Among his works are six *Sonatas a tres*, three *Ricercare*, and two concertos grosso, along with other works rooted in eighteenth-century forms. An influential teacher, Ardévol considered neoclassicism a pedagogical tool that would enable his numerous students to resist *localismo*.[103] He presented himself as such in the United States, publishing a piano sonata with a dissonant, two-voiced fugue in Cowell's *New Music*.[104] The Chilean composer, diplomat, and university administrator Domingo Santa Cruz, founder of the Bach Society in Santiago, composed a *Sinfonia Concertante*, a string quartet, and *Five Short Pieces for String Orchestra* that so thoroughly represent his neoclassical bent that Slonimsky called him the "Chilean Hindemith."[105] In Argentina, Jacobo Ficher composed a neoclassical oboe sonata and his second symphony, which Lazare Saminsky admired, and Juan José Castro, who warned against the "abuses of folklore," wrote numerous neoclassical works.[106] Luis Gianneo composed *Sinfonietta: Homage to Haydn*, and José María Castro (Juan José's older brother), Honorio Siccardi, and Ginastera all composed children's pieces, recalling Stravinsky's largely neoclassical forays into that genre.[107] (José María Castro's "Estudio," from *Diez Piezas Breves*, for example, relies on Alberti bass, sequence, and the humorous repetition of motives similar to those found in *Pulcinella's* more harmonically static passages.)

One of the most outspoken antinationalist Latin American composers was Juan Carlos Paz. Born in Buenos Aires in 1901, he studied composition with Vincent d'Indy at the Schola Cantorum. He experimented with neoclassicism and jazz (as a way to "desensitize music") and eventually turned to serialism, composing works such as *Composition on the Twelve Tones*, *Ten Dodecaphonic Pieces*, and the *Three Inventions in the Twelve-Tone System*.[108] Among his international credits was the 1937 performance of his *Passacaglia* under Charles Munch at the ISCM (Paris), probably the first twelve-tone work by a Latin American ever to be heard abroad.[109] In an interview with Saminsky for *Modern Music*, Paz fulminated that when the Argentine composer succumbs to nationalism "his language seems dead, his folkloric style superficial, his creative impotence only too obvious and pathetic."[110] Elsewhere he described nationalism as "puerile" and seldom hesitated to attack his compatriots if he felt they had let themselves be seduced by what he called "easy folklore."

■ VILLA-LOBOS IN THE UNITED STATES

In August 1942 the blandishments in *South of the Border with Disney* came to fruition, and Brazil declared war on Germany, Japan, and Italy. (Brazilian troops went to Italy in July 1944.) The *New York Times* proclaimed, "Brazil at War Stirs Latins," and the music industry capitalized on the newly consummated alliance.[111] To give just one example: in 1943 G. Schirmer published Berger's song "They All Dance the Samba." By advertising it as a "gay and delightful song" in which "the laundress, the fisherman, the little baker's wife, and the tired businessman . . . 'join together [and] dance the samba from the evening till dawn,'" Schirmer portrayed Brazil as one big, unified—and happily dancing—family, conferring harmony and order on the new alliance.[112] Elsewhere Schirmer encouraged an antinationalist stance. The collection for solo piano, *Latin-American Art Music for the Piano by Twelve Contemporary Composers*, appeared in 1942 and was edited by Francisco Curt Lange, a German-born musicologist resident in Uruguay since 1930. In his 1936 essay, "Americanismo musical," Lange had preached a vague nationalism by expounding on the "spiritual forces" of the Latin American continent and the "expression that emanates from each one of its countries."[113] During the golden age of Pan Americanism, however, he changed his tone. In his preface to the collection, Lange now attacked nationalism on several grounds. Declaring that "nationalism in music is, without exception, reactionary in origin," he observed that its appearance on the musical scene "is of comparatively recent date; its duration is in many cases ephemeral, quite as often inconsistent; and seldom can it serve as a true justification for principles."[114] The piano collection drove these points home. Among the works by Argentine, Venezuelan, Brazilian, Chilean, Mexican, Peruvian, and Uruguayan composers, only a handful are folkloric, such as the *huayno* (an Andean genre), the dance portion of *Himno y danza* by the Peruvian composer Andrés Sas. But many more bear generic internationalist titles, such as Ponce's *Deux Études pour piano* (dedicated to Rubinstein) and René Amengual Astuburuaga's *Burlesca*. Pride of place is given to Villa-Lobos. In his preface, Lange devotes two full columns to the composer's universalist schemes, greater space than that allotted any other composer. He explains that Villa-Lobos drank from

> a spring, deep and freely-flowing, of universal folk-lore, a compendium of all the popular elements of sonority of all countries, which yet—in spite of that universality—flows directly from the folk, making Bach an intermediary between all peoples. For Villa-Lobos, the music of Bach comes from the infinity of the spheres, to imbue the earth as folk-music; and this cosmic phenomenon is reproduced in the various lands throughout the terrestrial globe, thus tending to become universal.[115]

We can practically hear Thomson clucking "Tommyrot." The sample of Villa-Lobos's sublimated folklore Schirmer offered was *Bachianas brasileiras* no. 4, movement 4. Like *Bachianas* no. 2, no. 4 began as a set of independent pieces, which Villa-Lobos orchestrated as a set in 1941 in addition to making a piano arrangement. Unlike *Bachianas* no. 2, no. 4 refers more explicitly to Bach; Villa-Lobos later stated that of the whole series, no. 4 was the closest to Bach, a statement that went beyond Villa-Lobos's usual hype.[116] In the first movement, Preludio/Introducão, Villa-Lobos alludes to *A Musical Offering* (mm. 1–2); in the second, Chorale/Canto do sertão, he writes "like an organ" at the climactic toccata-like passage starting at m. 71.[117] To universalize the utterances of the great Lutheran organist he chose a Portuguese title that refers to the religious song of Catholic *sertanejos* (people of the backlands), punctuating it with a recurring B-flat. The repeated pitch represents the monotone singing of the araponga bird, perhaps to recall Villa-Lobos's days of stumbling upon Bachian melodic cells in the wilds of the Brazilian jungle.[118] In the third movement, Aria/Cantiga, Villa-Lobos suggests a type of song from northeastern Brazil that he believed approximated the "serene pace" of similar works by Bach.[119] Movement

4 is entitled Dança/Miudinho, the latter a dance and ostensibly a far cry from venerable baroque allusions. Yet the long diatonic pedals, the right-hand, broken-chord figurations, the melodic pitches resulting from step-wise voice-leading within the arpeggiations (in a near-constant *moto perpetuo* style with unisons marking the final cadence) all suggest a fanciful rendering of organ-toccata style. At the very least, the *miudinho* might have convinced intermediate-level piano students in the United States familiar with the two- and three-part inventions or the *Notebook for Anna Magdalena Bach* that Bach's style and spirit could be mysteriously transferred to twentieth-century Brazil and that sameness across the Americas could be embraced through the universal language of music (ex. 5a).

Universalism was Villa-Lobos's motto during the first of his many trips to the United States, which took place in 1944–45.[120] Getting him there was by no means easy, despite interest on the part of many in official circles, including Henry Allen Moe of the Committee for Inter-American Artistic and Intellectual Relations and secretary of the Guggenheim Foundation, who oversaw Copland's trip.[121] Villa-Lobos rubbed several cultural diplomats the wrong way, however. When Lincoln Kirstein passed through Brazil with his American Ballet Caravan in 1941 he wrote, "Heitor Villa-Lobos could not conceivably [have] been more trying. . . . I thought him personally a cagy old goat with well-calculated hysterics. He . . . wants to come to the U.S. but bad. His terms—fare back and forth; 18 concerts in 6 weeks, only his works; $2,000 a performance and only Boston, Philadelphia and so forth orchestras, period."[122] Other times Villa-Lobos seemed indifferent to the prospect of a U.S. visit, but in other instances he laid down puzzling terms, such as refusing to accept government sponsorship.[123] As his six seconds of on-screen fame in *South of the Border with Disney* attest, he was known in the United States for his work with children's choruses. But according to Dean John W. Beattie of Northwestern University, who toured Latin America under State Department auspices as part of a music education team, Villa-Lobos knew "nothing of either child psychology or correct vocal methods"; also, "the tone quality he wants and gets is terrible."[124] Thanks to his reputation as a composer, however, the visit was expedited, and after considerable wrangling, Villa-Lobos arrived in Los Angeles in November 1944 under the auspices of the Southern California Council of Inter-American Affairs (the music section), the Motion Picture Academy, and Occidental College.[125] He conducted the Werner Janssen Symphony at the Philharmonic Auditorium in several of his works, including Symphony no. 2 (subtitled "Ascension") and *Choros* no. 6, for which Universal Studios fashioned special square drums.[126] He also lunched with Jerome Kern, Joe Green, and Mario Castelnuovo-Tedesco at the Beverly Hills Hotel, where he received a tribute.[127] Constantly at his side was his translator, the Brazilian author Érico Veríssimo, then a visiting professor at the University of California, Berkeley, and dispatched on short notice for what was evidently a challenging assignment. Tensions between the two larger-than-life Brazilians surfaced at the ceremony at Occidental College on November 21, where Villa-Lobos received

Example 5a Heitor Villa-Lobos. Dança-Miudinho. *Bachianas brasileiras* no. 4 (solo piano version), mvt. 4, mm. 11–26. Copyright © 1948 (Renewed) by Music Sales Corporation (ASCAP). International Copyright Secured. All Rights Reserved. Used by permission.

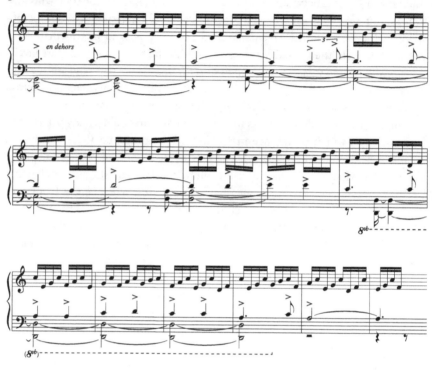

an honorary LL.D. Translating Villa-Lobos's acceptance speech, Veríssimo was unable to resist embellishing the composer's remarks. When Villa-Lobos declared that he had "learned the song of liberty" in the Brazilian rain forest, Veríssimo added, "and I believe it, because today liberty in Brazil exists only in the rain forest," a dig at Vargas's Estado Novo and Villa-Lobos's exalted place within it.[128] Fortunately a generous portion of the ceremony was given over to music, with the London String Quartet performing Villa-Lobos's third string quartet and the Occidental Women's Glee Club his *Canção de Saudade* for female voices.

In December Villa-Lobos traveled to the East Coast, where four concerts of his music were scheduled for New York (January 28, February 8, 9, and 12) and two for Boston (February 23 and 24), where he conducted at the invitation of Koussevitzky.[129] He also gave several interviews, now without Veríssimo's glosses. Chatting in French with the staff of the *New Yorker*, he addressed topics as wide-ranging as his fondness for vanilla ice cream, his expertise at billiards, and his prodigious knowledge of movie westerns, acquired during his early years of playing the cello in cinema orchestras.[130] Elsewhere, he reflected on nationalism.

In an interview with Downes, Villa-Lobos showed that, like Farwell and Thomson, he was ever alert to its peril. "Patriotism in music, and capitalizing upon it," he cautioned, "is very dangerous." Indeed, he added, "you cannot produce great music in that way."[131] A month later he was quoted in *Musical America* as saying, "Folklore cannot be exploited . . . in a blindly nationalistic way . . . for it belongs to the universal expression of the artist in all lands."[132] In fact, while in the United States, Villa-Lobos denounced nationalism to the point of predictability. Irving Gifford Fine, who reported on his concerts in Boston, wrote that he "obliged everyone by ringing the now familiar charges on nationalism."[133]

Another forum for Villa-Lobos's universalist agenda was a concert at the City Center of Music and Drama on February 12 in New York. With Cowell's *Fanfare for the Forces of Our Latin American Allies* as a curtain raiser, Stokowski led the City Symphony in one of his own Bach transcriptions and the "Pastorale" Symphony of Beethoven, the latter the embodiment of universalism and "sublimated vital energies," as Rosenfeld believed.[134] Villa-Lobos conducted *Uiraparú*, the glittering account of the jungle from early in his career, and *Bachianas brasileiras* no. 7, composed in 1942 and first performed in Rio de Janeiro in March 1944, both unknown to the New York public. Critics found *Uiraparú* pleasing enough, with Downes detecting "outbursts of sensuous song."[135] Paul Bowles, one of Thomson's composer-hires at the *Tribune*, noted a "nineteenth-century predilection for musical picture making" and, invoking one of his boss's least favorite composers, labeled Villa-Lobos "a southern Sibelius." In sum, *Uiraparú* was no more and no less than a piece of "color music," as Bowles called it: ingratiating but conventional, its sanitized jungle raising none of the vexing questions associated with Caliban's domain.[136] *Bachianas* no. 7 was another matter. Rather than "color," transparency prevails. In movement 1 (Preludio/Ponteio) a sequential theme emphasizing chromatic upper and lower neighbors of the fifth-related triads on which it rests (reh. 2, oboe, mm. 14–18) stands out in relief over an accompanimental figure in violin 1, the string-crossings of which are undoubtedly intended to recall passages from Bach's unaccompanied suites, sustained here by a tonic pedal, all followed by "pastoral" oboes (reh. 4) (ex. 5b).

Movement 2, Gigue/Quadrilha caipira, seeks to combine the baroque gigue with the atmosphere of rural Brazil, and movement 3, Tocata/Desafio, alludes to *Fortspinnung*. It is in the final fugue, however, that Bach is most present. The twelve-bar subject, announced in the cellos, contains a chromatically inflected sequence (mm. 5–6, 7–8, 9–10). Entering at the fifth, the violas offer a real answer over a rhythmically supple countersubject; unlike most baroque fugues, subsequent entries occur at the fifth as well (D-A-E-B), with a fourteen-measure extension leading to a dominant pedal that brings back the now-distant tonic. So expansive is the subject that the exposition (along with the extension) occupies sixty-two bars of the 149-bar movement. Yet the movement is informed by a restraint worlds away from Villa-Lobos's "continuous, spontaneous, abundant pouring forth." Only in a brief, final effusion, which involves a French-sixth

Example 5b Heitor Villa-Lobos. Preludio/Ponteio. *Bachianas brasileiras* no. 7, mvt. 1, mm. 14–18. Reprinted by kind permission of MGB Hal Leonard.

chord built on the lowered second of D minor (E flat-G-A-C sharp), played *fortissimo* by the full orchestra, does Villa-Lobos abandon this circumspection. With pounding timpani à la Bach-Stokowski he concludes the fugue with a triple-*forte* Picardy third, honoring the formulas of the baroque on which Bach himself drew and the bright D-major sonority affirming, to paraphrase Oswald de Andrade, the triumph of "the school over the forest." Thus the incoherent Caliban yields to the language of universalism and takes up civilized practices (ex. 5c).

Few critics found the piece convincing, however. Downes, Villa-Lobos's great champion in the United States, seemed to take the work seriously, or at least its

Example 5c Heitor Villa-Lobos. Fuga/Conversa. *Bachianas brasileiras* no. 7, mvt. 4, mm. 1–17. Reprinted by kind permission of MGB Hal Leonard.

intention: to recognize "the universal spirit . . . of the great Bach."[137] But he also heard "disproportions" and "naïvete." Bowles was both bored and perplexed, complaining that unlike *Uiraparú*, *Bachianas brasileiras* no. 7 offered "no way to pretend that frogs are croaking and crickets are chirping"; rather, the material of the over-long work was neither "folk music presented straight, nor yet transformed, but beaten willy-nilly in with some Bach-like figures and poured all unmixed into the large bowl of French impressionism."[138] Thompson, who found *Bachianas brasileiras* no. 7 rather timid, was nonetheless bemused by the fact that "many persons in the audience . . . left the hall whistling the theme of the fugue," concluding that even in his contrapuntal forays, "Mr. Villa-Lobos is always some-where near the popular."[139] On this point the critics agreed: Bowles found that much of the material came "unashamedly from popular sources," and Downes noted passages that seemed "astonishingly popular for the Bach idea." Like Gersh-win, Villa-Lobos offered a "borderland fling," albeit an even more extreme version.

The "astonishingly popular" also reared its head in another work, one in which we might least expect it. Just as he had heard Paris 1923 in the primitivist Nonet, Thomson took an outlier position on *Choros* no. 8 and its successor, no. 9, when Villa-Lobos conducted both works at Carnegie Hall with the Philharmonic-Symphony (February 8). Most critics reiterated the familiar themes of excess and incoherence.[140] Thomson, however, far from rejecting Cal-iban, situated Villa-Lobos's *sauvagerie* in Hollywood. Whereas he had earlier confessed his lack of familiarity with Brazil, he now miraculously found himself competent to opine on his South American neighbor's homeland—and its potential for embodying the values of the culture industry:

> *Choros* no. 8, last heard here at the World's Fair, sounds to me like rural Brazil, like rivers and plains and mountains and Indian villages and jungles. The jungles seem to have lots of trees in them, big ones and small ones, also some lurid snakes and wild animals. Certainly there are birds around of all sizes. And I thought I spotted . . . a sturdy stock of American canned nourishment and a few reels of the best Hollywood sentiment.[141]

Choros no. 9, also for large orchestra, not only furnished "quite a lot more Holly-wood sentiment," with its soaring violins and "general gaiety," but also recalled Citkowitz's barb of 1932 on Villa-Lobos's "travelog music." Thomson wrote, "It is all very pleasant and it is loosely enough constructed so that one doesn't have to pay attention all the time. . . . If one felt at the end like a tourist who has seen much but taken part in little, one was grateful for the trip, all the same. One could almost hear the voice of the travelogue saying, 'Now we are leaving beau-u-u-tiful Brazil.'" As it turned out, Thomson hit the mark, anticipating a growing (but by no means exclusive) trend in the reception of Villa-Lobos's music in the United States. As universalist rhetoric and pleas for hemispheric bonding lost their urgency after the Allied victory, the Brazilian composer increasingly tested the mass audience. In a sense, his travel music came full circle, albeit with nu-merous vicissitudes along the way.

■ "THE BRAZILIAN *OKLAHOMA!*"

Shortly thereafter, Villa-Lobos tried his hand at the genre some scholars call "the American musical."[142] *Magdalena*, a tale of the Latin American jungle, which opened in Los Angeles on July 26, 1947, with Villa-Lobos's score and choreogra-phy by Jack Cole, was quickly acclaimed as "the Brazilian *Oklahoma!*"[143] In fact, *Magdalena* is not Brazilian at all but Colombian, with its action unfolding on the

shores of the Magdalena River "deep in the South American jungle," as one an-
nouncement had it.[144] It was the brainchild of George Forrest and Robert Wright,
a team that specialized in inventing lyrics for other composers' music, a skill they
honed to perfection in *Kismet* (Borodin), *Czaritza* (Tchaikovsky), *The Great
Waltz* (Johann Strauss Jr. and Sr.), and *Song of Norway* (Grieg), using melodic
fragments by these composers and cobbling them together with original music.[145]
Like these works, *Magdalena* was thus a potpourri, the same genre Copland had
negotiated in *El salón México*. It is also rife with stereotypes. Appearing in quick
succession are the Latin American dictator Carabaña, his voluptuous paramour
Teresa, childlike Indians (the Muzos), a temperamental, violence-prone young
man (Pedro), and, in contrast to the "whore" lover, a docile young "madonna"
(predictably named Maria), who will convert the young man and the rest of the
tribe to Christianity. Accompanying the action was the political reality of 1947:
three months before opening night in Los Angeles, Colombia's liberal leader Jorge
Eliécer Gaitán was assassinated in broad daylight in downtown Bogotá, unleashing a riot in which two thousand people were killed. After order was restored by a
repressive government, rural violence expanded into an undeclared civil that
would eventually claim over 200,000 lives, known as *la violencia*. *Magdalena* is set
in the teens, a period that is also significant in U.S.-Colombian relations. In 1913,
for example, Teddy Roosevelt published his autobiography, in which he justified
U.S. appropriation of Panama by describing the Colombian government as "utterly impotent" and "wicked and foolish."[146] Elsewhere he commented that any
Latin American country that "misbehaves" should be "spanked."[147]

As Bertolt Brecht famously declared, "Good or bad, a play always includes
an image of the world. . . . Art is never without consequences."[148] Despite its
initially successful runs in Los Angeles, San Francisco, and New York, we can
safely consider *Magdalena* "bad." For one thing, Villa-Lobos underwent sur-
gery for cancer of the bladder while at work on the score and as a result was
probably unaware of what *Magdalena* actually entailed. As for "consequences,"
beneath *Magdalena*'s exuberant surface lurk questions frequently asked in the
United States about Latin America. Chief among them: Why dictatorships and
not democracies? Carabaña confirms the widespread suspicion in the United
States that tropical climates cannot sustain democratic institutions, and the im-
petuous Pedro perfectly embodies the dark-skinned, quick-tempered Latin.
After all, when Pedro challenges dictatorial authority, he does so on the
premise of violent revolution (perhaps he is even a communist) rather than
through disciplined and civic-minded due process. The Roman Catholic
Church, the power of which is established in *Magdalena*'s opening scene, has
also been blamed for Latin America's backwardness, mainly for fomenting authoritarianism, unlike "democratic" Protestantism. Absent in such arguments
is the fact that dictatorships have flourished in Anglo-Saxon, nontropical countries and that non-Catholics and nonpracticing Catholics in Latin America
have accepted authoritarian regimes.[149]

Looming over *Magdalena*'s unsavory content are the utopian premises of the genre itself. As Richard Dyer has argued, the musical's two essential features, escapism and the fantasy of wish-fulfillment, have ensured that its very identity is taken from "the stuff of utopia."[150] The same can be said for Latin America itself. Whether through colonial-period artists painting oversized fruits, intellectuals such as Waldo Frank idealizing the South, O. Henry's entrepreneurs agog for profit, or worshippers of indigenous culture, Latin America has served as a utopia for a variety of constituencies, even as others have condemned it. Some present Latin American utopia under the banner of "startling contrast," with the tourism industry especially marketing contrast to sell everything from "glaciers to beaches to rain forests," resulting in a "fetishism of difference," as Jon Beasley-Murray argues.[151] Advance publicity for *Magdalena* took that very tack. Advertisers exulted that the Magdalena River flows from "the frozen Andes to the steaming Caribbean"; the jungle too teems with contrast in that it is "peopled by native Indian tribes, some ... lowly, others ... descended from the highest pagan culture," while Europeans occupy "beautiful ranchos of the Spanish ruling class" and "decadent fishing villages" dot the tropical landscape.[152] Accordingly, critics applauded *Magdalena* as "a riot of color and excitement," as "exciting and varied," with kaleidoscopic difference ensuring that listeners felt "continuously in giddy motion" throughout.[153] Clearly this was no jungle for Caliban.

However taken with contrast, the U.S. public has historically tended uncritically to consider Latin America an *un*differentiated fantasy, one in which inhabitants are leveled so as to appear as little more than characters in what Shari Roberts calls an "ethnic masquerade."[154] Just as Anglos were cast as Indians in *H.P.*, *Magdalena* featured "blond, blue-eyed Indians who wear gaucho costumes from the Argentine, Ecuadorian hats and Peruvian ponchos, and sing Brazilian music in perfect English," as Alfred Frankenstein of the *San Francisco Examiner* described them.[155] Both difference and *loss* of identity thus clashed equally in an ill-coordinated play of caricatures and long-entrenched habits of mind, the import of which neither public nor composer was prepared to fathom and which jarred with that brief moment of Pan Americanist sameness-embracing of the prior two decades.

Magdalena's potpourri score corresponds to these fissures. Among the existing Villa-Lobos works on which Forrest and Wright drew was *Bachianas brasileiras* no. 4, now serving rather different ends than the high-flown universalism espoused in Lange's piano collection.[156] When movement 2 is introduced in the opening number ("The Jungle Chapel"), native women are peacefully weaving and grinding corn under the watchful eye of the Miracle Madonna, safely ensconced in her jungle shrine. Suddenly the fun-loving Muzos show their fondness for native amusements by playing a game of *peteca*. Shocked by their irreverence, Maria scolds them in "native" talk, strangely free of the contractions of ordinary American English. When Padre José interjects the chorale/*sertanejo*, however, proper respect for the holy place is restored, foreshadowing Pedro's eventual embrace of Christianity. The young man proves a difficult convert. Mocking the Church's emphasis on meekness, he ardently believes in the things of this world, among them the broken-down bus he drives to earn a living. His big solo number, "My Bus and I," is a hymn to individual initiative. By introducing it with pentatonic children's songs, however, Forrest and Wright ridicule his aspirations. Pedro's bus, moreover, is in far worse shape than, say, the hillbilly's little train, for unlike that spunky vehicle, the bus is both decrepit ("like the Andes, older than forever") and unreliable (passengers arrive "only twelve hours late").

A few scenes later, viewers again confront Latin America's technological backwardness, in "The Broken Pianolita." A Muzo elder sings of the river, his principal melody the solo song "Remeiro de São-Francisco" (Oarsman of the San Francisco River), from the first collection of Villa-Lobos's Modinhas e canções. During this moment of solemn contemplation, Pedro feeds coins into a rickety player piano as Muzo youths dance, kicking the instrument every time it gives up. As they continue to inflict their aggressions on the old piece of junk, a blues-inflected motive à la Gershwin with a marked backbeat and a prominent saxophone threatens to overtake the elder's song. Compelled by the frenetic rhythms of U.S. jazz, the tempo accelerates and the mechanical workings of the piano go completely awry. Just as the decrepit piano in Porgy and Bess signals indigence and diminishment, especially when juxtaposed with the full orchestra, the broken-down onstage piano in Magdalena underscores the frustrations of the young men.[157] "The Broken Pianolita" thus makes concrete the mechanical failures explicated in "My Bus and I," suggesting that Latin America is unready for the technological prowess and can-do optimism of the United States the jazzy music suggests. The Old One sings stolidly on, and Villa-Lobos's hymn to the mighty Magdalena wraps up the scene. With its breezy treatment of authoritarianism, dictatorial ineptitude, labor inequities, poverty, backwardness, and violence, the Brazilian Oklahoma! thwarts any utopian premises we might wish to read into its twisted post–Good Neighbor message.

▪ UNIVERSALISM VERSUS THE CULTURE INDUSTRY

During the cold war, Villa-Lobos continued to distance himself from nationalism. In an interview with the Cuban polymath Alejo Carpentier for the Caracas daily El Nacional (January 1953) he urged young Venezuelan composers to absorb their own folklore "but not to 'do folklore,'" a position he emphasized with the resounding admonition "No!"[158] Unless folklore could be sublimated by universalist impulses, he wanted no part of it. "Above all," he told Carpentier, composers "must always be aware of the obligation NOT TO BE EXOTICS." "Never exotics," he reiterated, lest his meaning be misunderstood.[159] Carpentier later described Villa-Lobos as "the most universal Latin American composer of the [twentieth] century."[160]

Echoes of universal folklore followed Villa-Lobos in the United States as well. In May 1936 Arthur Berger discussed Jennie Tourel's recent Columbia recording of his song cycle *Serestas* (Serenades) in a Brazilian-themed issue of the fashion magazine *Harper's Bazaar*. Between shots of leggy models posing in beach jackets against a backdrop of Rio de Janeiro's Sugarloaf, Berger remarked that "folk music the world over has its common features" and compared *Seresta* no. 5 to "a Russian peasant's lament" and a Yaqui Indian melody in Chávez's *Sinfonía India* that to him sounded "nothing so much as a British folk song."[161] In October 1963, four years after the composer's death, *Bachianas* no. 1 (now arranged for full orchestra) had pride of place under Stokowski's baton at Carnegie Hall in the first of an eight-week concert series honoring the United Nations. Musical universalism was a fitting tribute to the 111 flags that draped the stage and to the presence of some seventy-five delegates in the audience, along with First Lady Jacqueline Kennedy, U.S. Ambassador Adlai Stevenson, and Mayor Robert F. Wagner.[162] All the while, *Bachianas brasileiras* no. 5 was becoming one of Villa-Lobos's best-loved works.

Villa-Lobos also continued to negotiate with the culture industry. One project was the 1959 Mel Ferrer film *Green Mansions*, subtitled "A Romance of the Tropical Forest." Starring Anthony Perkins and Audrey Hepburn playing a child of nature, the film involves revolutions, attacks by hostile Indians, and bewitching tropical birds. To these doubtful ends the soundtrack involves extended excerpts from Villa-Lobos's concert suite *Forest of the Amazon*, music for which Bronislau Kaper is often given sole credit, since it was he who reshaped Villa-Lobos's score to fit the action, much to the composer's displeasure.[163] There was also his Symphony no. 12, performed in Washington, D.C. in 1958, in which the critic Paul Hume noted a "wide-screen, multilux color effect" and called the first movement's "big buildup not unlike that of a fine Broadway musical," adding that Broadway composers might learn a few lessons from Villa-Lobos.[164] "The Hillbilly's Little Train," labeled "vulgar" at the 1939 World's Fair, proved well suited to pops concerts.

So what was Villa-Lobos's legacy in the aftermath of Pan Americanism's golden age? In one of his Young People's Concerts, on March 8, 1961, entitled "The Latin-American Spirit," Bernstein reveled in universality. Addressing an audience of mannerly schoolchildren in white gloves and neckties, he acknowledged the "present excitement over something known as the bossa nova." But Bernstein cautions, "We mustn't begin to think that all Latin American music is only chuck-a-chuck-a-chuck-a dance music. Not by a long shot. Our Latin neighbors have produced a very impressive number of serious symphonic composers who have succeeded in preserving the folk flavor of their own countries while at the same time expanding their music into what we think of as universal art." Bernstein then explains that "certainly the most admired of all these composers was the great Brazilian, Villa-Lobos." Not surprisingly the piece that best exemplifies "what we think of as universal art" was *Bachianas brasileiras* no. 5, which Bernstein and the New York Philharmonic then performed with the soprano Netania Davrath. In an era when many elementary school music teachers drilled their students in the "three Bs," it was logical for him to ask the children:

> Now what is Bach doing in Brazil? Well, that's just the point of this piece and really the point of all the pieces Villa-Lobos composed. He wanted to bring together his native folklore elements with the great European musical tradition and unify them into a single style of his own, as he does in the very title of this piece: *Bachianas Brasileiras*. It's amazing how well he succeeded, as you will hear, especially in the first movement . . . [where] he has the soprano sing a long Bachian song.[165]

Thus youthful minds were exposed to sublimated universalism, which in their parents' day had defied German chauvinism, united the Americas, and furthered musical progress by rejecting folkloric nationalism. On none of these points does the soprano soloist offer any comment, other than to merge her song with that of the first cellist. Wordlessly her vocal line dips and arcs, inviting each listener to ascribe his or her own free-floating meaning to the Aria as it unfolds in all its suave meanderings. If much of Villa-Lobos's reception in the United States was shaped by the antinationalist appeal of universalism during the golden age of Pan Americanism, during the cold war an entirely different sort of antinationalism took hold, a phenomenon discussed in chapter 6.

6 Alberto Ginastera's *Bomarzo* in the United States

Antinationalism and the Cold War

On the evening of May 19, 1967, in Washington, D.C., the curtain fell on the world premiere of *Bomarzo*, Alberto Ginastera's second opera. The black-tie affair, attended mainly by diplomats and politicians, was not over, however.[1] No matter that the performance had started thirty minutes late, thanks to a traffic jam of chauffer-driven limousines pulling up before the Lisner Auditorium. For over ten minutes, the crowd stood to applaud the tale of sex, violence, neurosis, and other ills of contemporary anomie. None other than Vice President Hubert Humphrey led the standing ovation; also present were the historian and former advisor to President Kennedy, Arthur Schlesinger Jr.; Senator Ted Kennedy; Undersecretary of State Eugene Rostow; and the newsman Bill Moyers.[2] Among the Latin Americans in the audience were the Argentine ambassador Álvaro Alsogaray and the Colombian conductor Guillermo Espinosa, head of the Music Division of the Organization of American States (OAS), the successor organization of the Pan American Union.[3] The OAS continued to pursue cultural diplomacy with Latin America even as the Good Neighbor period was fast becoming a distant memory.[4] Likewise, its Music Division sought hemispheric bonds even as serialism, aleatory, and other avant-garde musical procedures—with which *Bomarzo* was replete—increasingly alienated the broad public that had helped to sustain the Good Neighbor Policy.

At a splendid postperformance reception at the Argentine Embassy, political figures mingled with the cast and conductor Julius Rudel. Humphrey personally congratulated Ginastera, who had traveled from Buenos Aires for the premiere along with his librettist, the Argentine novelist Manuel Mujica Láinez. According to *Time* magazine, the vice president addressed *Bomarzo*'s abstruse musical language in "good-neighborly fashion," allowing that although the opera was "difficult, discordant and different," it nonetheless had "distinction." "Everyone should go see *Bomarzo*," Humphrey added.[5] The Buenos Aires press was ecstatic. One journalist gloated that thanks to *Bomarzo*, Argentina would no longer be known merely as "the land of beef and wheat" but as a country that also distinguished itself for high culture.[6] Thus a Latin American work steeped in modernism made its mark on Washington's political circles during the cold war.

Washington's music critics were also impressed with *Bomarzo* and deemed it a brilliant successor to Ginastera's first opera, *Don Rodrigo*, which the New York City Opera had premiered the previous year to great acclaim. In a matter of weeks, however, *Bomarzo* would be banned in Buenos Aires by the Argentine military regime and, in March 1968, greeted unenthusiastically in New York, where critics found little more than clichés in its modernist idiom. Occasioning euphoria in one environment, censorship in another, and indifference in a third, *Bomarzo* obviously defies any notion of "the music itself" or a reified "work concept."[7] The opera's twisted trajectory does, however, reflect major shifts in the status of Latin American music in the United States and a new moment in musical Pan Americanism, probed in this chapter vis-à-vis Ginastera's career in the United States and the discourse of antinationalism during the cold war.

■ LATIN AMERICAN MUSIC AND THE COLD WAR

During the 1950s and 1960s the Latin American musical folklore that Copland so enthusiastically upheld was dealt a death blow, at least from the standpoint of art music. Composers now pursued objectivity and abstraction, with many, including Copland, trying their hand at serialism.[8] Other paths to high modernism, such as aleatory, converged under the rubric of experimental music. This orientation coincided with the rise of U.S. power in the postwar period and shifts in international alliances. The latter affected cultural diplomacy, which now involved "new music, new allies," as Amy C. Beal puts it.[9]

In the United States political relations with Latin America also took a new turn. As Washington policymakers anxiously watched to see whether the region would embrace U.S.-style democracy or communism, they essentially shelved Roosevelt's vision of 1933 and resumed interventionism, often in tandem with business interests or in collaboration with the newly created CIA, even when this meant supporting military juntas.[10] Guatemala is a case in point. In 1951 the left-leaning but legally elected president Jacobo Arbenz expropriated land claimed by United Fruit and, promptly tagged as a communist, was overthrown by a CIA-organized invasion force, annihilating "a stammer of freedom," as the Guatemalan poet, essayist, and diplomat Luis Cardoza y Aragón recalls.[11] In 1961 President Kennedy launched the ill-fated Bay of Pigs invasion in Cuba, and four years later President Johnson sent twenty-three thousand troops to the Dominican Republic, seen to be on the verge of a communist takeover.[12] Both Humphrey and Senator J. William Fulbright lamented this turn of events, the latter declaring in his 1966 book *The Arrogance of Power*, "Nowhere has the ambivalence in the American attitude toward revolution been more apparent and more troublesome than in the relations of the United States with Latin America."[13]

The attitudes that gave rise to such decisions were easily reduced to buzzwords. One term in the cold war lexicon for Latin America was *progress*, conspicuously showcased in Kennedy's Alliance for Progress (AFP). This set of government programs promised economic stability in Latin America; the fact that it was established a month before the Bay of Pigs invasion hints at its anticommunist agenda. *Progress* was tied to the so-called modernization theory, widely accepted in academic circles. It held that if Latin America would only modernize through economic growth, problems of resource distribution would disappear and dictatorships would be less likely to take hold. As Michael E. Latham argues, however, the modernization theory drew on long-entrenched patterns of discourse and behaviors to underscore the status of the United States as a "nation-building power."[14] Neither progress nor modernization unfolded as foreseen. During the Johnson administration, the AFP succeeded largely in strengthening U.S. business, while the modernization theory was roundly debunked by the fact that the most economically developed countries in Latin America ultimately suffered military coups, such as Argentina (1955, 1966, 1976), Brazil (1964), and Chile (1973).[15]

Another buzzword was *nationalism*, jointly equated with anti-U.S. sentiment and communism. The journalist Herbert L. Matthews, no blind supporter of U.S. policy, wrote in 1952 that the sort of nationalism taking root in Latin America was "a destructive and above all . . . 'anti-Yanqui' force."[16] In a 1953 speech, President Dwight Eisenhower proposed that those American nations that had overcome "the temptations of heedless nationalism" were the least vulnerable to the Soviets.[17] Tad Szulc, reporting for the *New York Times* on Vice President Richard Nixon's disastrous tour of Latin America in May 1958, drew on a favorite image of the era: the mob. Mobs filled with communist agitators greeted Nixon throughout Latin America, evincing a "supercharged atmosphere of extreme nationalism."[18] Standing up to the soulless, animal-like collectivity of the communist hordes, however, was the *individual*, who embodied the benefits liberal societies bestowed upon their citizens, such as free inquiry and free expression, which rested on principles of scientific objectivity.

Indeed, buzzwords such *individual* and *freedom* permeated aesthetic discourse, including music historiography. In Henry and Sidney Cowell's 1955 biography of Charles Ives, the composer is no longer an eccentric ethnographer but a cold war individualist; the authors emphasize his stature not only as an independent thinker but as one capable of representing the United States as "a bastion of autonomy . . . free of ideology," as David C. Paul has pointed out.[19] The Congress for Cultural Freedom, the CIA-backed concatenation of offices, publications, and events, promoted an anticommunist agenda in the name of freedom.[20] Scientific objectivity also became an aesthetic ideal, according to which composers, like research scientists, engaged in the presumably neutral investigation of tones, rhythms, and complex mathematical relationships. In creating ascetic, often serialist works, composers were also sheltered from the mass public, which was unready for the depth of intellectual engagement this music required, a stance articulated in Milton Babbitt's infamously titled essay "Who Cares If You Listen?"[21]

Many critics blamed the public's limitations on 1930s communism and other populist sentiments dating from that era.[22] Eric Salzman considered the "innumerable 'Hoe-Downs,' 'Hayrides,' [and] 'Square Dances'" of the 1930s and 1940s evidence of composers' willingness to gratify "the musically unwashed."[23]

Clement Greenberg railed against the baleful effects of middlebrow culture, according to which techniques of genuine avant-garde art were diluted to satisfy the newly prosperous middle class.[24] That constituency demanded "cultural goods that are up to date and yet not too hard to consume" but which nonetheless had to have "the smell of high art."[25] Some detected hypocrisy in this stance. Reporting on the 1952 Paris Festival sponsored by the Congress for Cultural Freedom (L'Oeuvre du XXième siècle), the British music critic Colin Mason noticed much "barren talk" on the part of Western artists, finding them unconcerned with actual *human* freedom, caring only that their communist brethren were free to be "cubists, surrealists, dodecaphonists and existentialists."[26] Anne C. Shreffler notes another paradox: although the abstruse serialism of cold war–era music ostensibly privileged freedom, composers willingly submitted to its musical procedures, with their strict controls. Additionally, she notes, artists were hardly "free" to be landscape painters or tonal symphonists.[27] Nor, we can add, were they free to be Latin American musical nationalists.

Certainly Latin American composers grappled with these concerns. Folkloric nationalism, once merely reactionary, could now stand for socialism or communism. The Chilean composer Juan Orrego-Salas observed that art music composers who worked with folk music were often "limited by their self-imposed nationalistic aims" and thus were captive to an ideology that "to a certain extent... fit into the patterns of 'social realism' promoted by the Communists."[28] Other Latin American composers complained of what they considered a double standard, one that essentially implied "good" and "bad" nationalism. Aurelio de la Vega, who left his native Cuba in 1959 for the United States, complained of "United States music critics accept[ing] with applause . . . the nationalism of Copland's *Billy the Kid*— gunshots and all—while sneering at the 'maracas and drums' gestures they themselves had attached as a label to every Latin American concert music piece."[29] In fact, many Latin American composers had no interest in drums and maracas. In 1958 the first electronic music studio in Latin America was established, the Estudio de Fonología of Buenos Aires.[30] The Argentine avant-garde composer Mauricio Kagel began his career, which, mainly realized in Germany, would embrace serialism, aleatory, and electroacoustic music and mixed media.[31] Since the days of Paz's solitary experiments, Latin American serialism had spread beyond Argentina. In Mexico the Spanish expatriate Rodolfo Halffter tried his hand at twelve-tone music, as did his student Jorge González Avila. The Austrian Fré Focke, a former Webern pupil, arrived in Chile in 1946, where he taught a large class that included Roberto Falabella; in Cuba, Argeliers León-Pérez followed suit.[32] The German-born Hans-Joachim Kollreuter, who emigrated to Brazil in the late 1930s, taught Cláudio Santoro and César Guerra Peixe.[33] (During his second State Department–sponsored Latin American tour, in 1947, Copland, who continued to promote folklore, met Kollreuter, whom he later tactlessly described as a "typical German twelve-toner" who "encouraged a lot of dullards to imagine they were composers.")[34] Kollreuter also led Música Viva, an aggregate of composers, critics, and artists who explored music's social role. The organization decried musical folklore, arguing that it inspired little more than "sentiments of nationalist superiority and . . . egocentric and individualist currents that separate men."[35]

Certainly some Latin American composers remained loyal to folklore. Among them was Guarnieri, over whose "profoundly Brazilian" works Copland had enthused in 1941. Guarnieri, who was put off by Kollreuter's indifference to national identity, wrote an open letter to several national newspapers in November 1950 in which he denounced the new "formalist current" and predicted that repudiating Brazilian folklore, "one of the richest in the world," portended nothing less than "the destruction of the national character."[36] Guarnieri's diatribe made waves throughout Latin America. From Mexico City, Chávez calmly noted, "In a certain South American country there is no shortage of those who say that composers who follow dodecaphony are traitors to their country"; Chávez also warned that "serial tyrannies, strictly applied horizontally and vertically . . . will never result in music of much consequence."[37] At that time, Chávez was introducing Dallapiccola's serialist works to the Mexican public, just as he had promoted Copland's music twenty years earlier.[38]

Still, in late 1954, the first Caracas Festival of Latin American Music gave little evidence of serialism, tyrannical or otherwise. Copland, however, made an abrupt about-face in reporting on the event for the New York Times. No longer was he inclined to hold forth to Latin American composers on the virtues of their own folk music; rather, he complained that "the program planners seemed . . . to overemphasize the folklore-inspired side of South American music."[39] Of course, by 1954 Copland had experimented with serialism in his Piano Quartet and reflected on the 1948 Prague declaration by Eastern bloc composers, which prompted him to link twelve-tone composition to writing "against . . . militant [communist] opposition."[40] In Caracas he resisted not only what he considered an excess of folklore but, more generally, the lack of "an experimental note" (progress), lamenting that "[of] dodecaphonic music there was not a trace." Three years later, at a second festival in the Venezuelan capital, serialism asserted itself far more robustly. The Panamanian composer and Krenek student Roque Cordero, who took second prize with his serialist Second Symphony, published the essay "¿Nacionalismo versus dodecafonismo?" in the Revista Musical Chilena.[41] A vehement exhortation to progress, the essay fairly bristles with rhetorical questions. "Should the fact that men of the present compose in the language of their time be considered illogical?" Cordero demands. "Why censure the composer of today who expresses his musical thought through the technical advances of recent decades?"[42] Unmoved by the needs of the uneducated listener, Cordero excoriates those who fail to write in accordance with their specialized training. "What has no justification," he thunders, "is that a composer who lives in the second half of the twentieth century should flaunt his ignorance, publicly admitting his lack of familiarity with the twelve-tone technique," and in doing so, denigrate "the progress achieved by the artistic disciplines over the years."[43]

Besides Copland, other critics in the United States evaluated Latin American folklore through a cold war lens. In 1961 Paul Henry Lang compared Chávez's *Sinfonía India* with the Concerto for Piano and Orchestra by Aram Khachaturian, then at the peak of his celebrity after being denounced in 1948, thanks in part to David Oistrakh's championing of his violin concerto. Lang dismissed the piano concerto as "about as modern as Chaminade after a couple of slugs of vodka," defects he believed were attributable to the communist aesthetic.[44] He also equated it with one of the culture industry's best-known products: "The commissars doubling in Marxist esthetics were right about the decadent bourgeois taint, for this concerto is the spit an' image of the music we associate with a grade B Western. I found it so miserable, cheap, and completely lacking in any musical idea that when the Cossack posse was closing in on the Kiev stage coach I fled." Lang situates the *Sinfonía India*, however, in a narrative of purposeful individualism and originality. Like the Khachaturian concerto, with its references to Armenian music, the *Sinfonía India* "suggests all manner of folk elements." Yet, Lang concludes, "Mr. Chávez's 'piracy' differs fundamentally from Khachaturian's [in that he] . . . include[es] original material." Like the autonomous Ives, Chávez had thwarted "grade B" sentiments so perilously close to "commissars" and "Marxist esthetics."

Clearly, folklore now had to go hand in hand with originality, perhaps to the point where it would be recognizable only to the cognoscenti. This ideal especially attracted Gilbert Chase, who had long mistrusted folkloric nationalism. To be sure, he had previously allowed that this orientation enabled certain "musically backward or retarded nations to achieve self-confident expression," as he declared in 1945, at the height of the Good Neighbor period.[45] Almost fifteen years later, he elaborated further on Latin American musical progress, identifying as three stages of development "Provincialism, Nationalism, and Universalism." Although the folklore-based music of "some countries" (he does not explicitly identify them) was still in thrall to provincialism, others had entered the second stage, and a few had attained the third. "Progress," Chase concludes, "eventually removes provincialism."[46] Like Weissmann and Farwell before him, Chase argued that true universalism required some "preservation of national character."[47] But whereas Villa-Lobos had sublimated Bach for "linking all peoples," Chase was less interested in the collective spirit; rather, it was the individual composer who would employ technical acumen to channel nationalist impulses toward a higher state. For Chase, the Latin American composer who best realized these ideals was Ginastera, thanks largely to his capacity to sublimate nationalism.

■ GINASTERA IN THE UNITED STATES: BECOMING A "MUSICAL ROBERT MCNAMARA"

In fact Chase's blueprint for Latin American musical progress runs loosely parallel to the tripartite division of Ginastera's works that scholars have long taken as a point of reference. The Argentine composer himself offered that scheme to his principal biographer, Pola Suárez Urtubey, in the 1960s. It comprises (1) objective nationalism, 1934–47; (2) subjective nationalism, 1947–57; and (3) neo-expressionism, 1958–63.[48] In 2001, eighteen years after the composer's death, Deborah Schwartz-Kates recognized that this model neglected twenty years of the composer's life and appropriately proposed a fourth period, "final synthesis" (1976–83); she and others caution that the style periods are far from rigid.[49] "Objective" nationalism, the first period, centered on Argentine folkloric song and dance genres, often via the persona and cultural milieu of the gaucho, the horseman of the pampas.[50] A particularly salient example is the *malambo*, a vigorous, competitive dance with alternating 3/4 and 6/8 meters and associated with gauchos. Ginastera used the *malambo* frequently, perhaps most famously in movement 4 of the ballet suite *Estancia* (1941), a favorite of the Simon de Bolívar Youth Symphony of Venezuela. Other traditional genres include the *triste* and two folk dances, the *chacarera* and the *gato*, which figure in the *Five Argentine Folk Songs* (1943). Another marker of objective nationalism is the so-called guitar chord (E-A-D-G-B-E), found in the second of the *Three Argentine Dances* (1937) for solo piano, for example.[51] In subjective nationalist works, on the other hand, Ginastera treats Argentine folklore less explicitly, either employing more daring harmonies or a rhapsodic or improvisatory style or subtly assigning it a formal role, as in *Pampeana* no. 1 for violin and piano (1947) and *Pampeana* no. 2 for cello and piano (1950).[52] Works from the neo-expressionist period can incorporate serialism, microtones, clusters, aleatory, or other avant-garde procedures.[53] Still, even in third-period works nationalist elements might insinuate themselves. Ginastera, a liberal Catholic, labeled the second movement of his Violin Concerto of 1963 a "transubstantiation" of the *triste* borrowed from the objective nationalist *Five Argentine Folk Songs*.[54] In the United States it was works such as these—true to the modernist aesthetic of the cold war but with a whiff of *argentinidad*—that established Ginastera's reputation.

Success was hardly immediate. In 1941, at the height of the Good Neighbor period, the New York press largely overlooked a broadcast of *Panambí*, which Juan José Castro conducted with the NBC Symphony during one of his several visits to the United Statets.[55] An on-air performance by Erich Kleiber five years later also went unremarked.[56] In 1946, when Ginastera visited the United States as a Guggenheim fellow, he had the pleasure of hearing his *Malambo* for solo piano in Carnegie Hall. By suggesting that it was "based on the rhythm of a primitive dance," Downes situated the work in one of the more familiar discourses in Latin American music; the song "El gato" from the *Five Argentine Folk Songs* was likewise equated with "simpler and more primitive expression."[57] Throughout the 1940s and 1950s, a handful of pianists performed selections from the *Twelve American Preludes* in New York, and singers were drawn to the wistful "Canción al árbol del olvido" (Song to the Tree of Forgetfulness) from op. 2.[58] (That song, incidentally, made a surprise appearance in a 2010 Metropolitan Opera production of Donizetti's *La fille du regiment*, when it was inserted into the beginning of act 2 so that the sixty-five-year-old Dame Kiri Te Kanawa, playing the speaking role of the Duchess of Krakenthorp, could have something to sing.)[59] Thus, during the golden age of Pan Americanism, Ginastera's objective nationalist works attracted relatively little notice, despite U.S. composers' fondness for folklore in their own representations of Latin America.

One landmark in his New York experience, however, was the February 1947 concert sponsored by the League of Composers, devoted to Ginastera and Guarnieri, two composers Copland singled out during his 1941 trip for their finesse with folklore and ability to evoke national character. Both Downes and Thomson were unimpressed by Guarnieri's music and Ginastera's subjective nationalist *Pampeana* no. 1 alike, which Downes found merely "'terre à terre' without too many clichés" and Thomson "over-ambitious."[60] Both, however, enthused over Ginastera's markedly nonfolkloric Duo for Flute and Oboe, the transparent textures and cool woodwind sonorities of which recall that monument to "pure" music divested of nationalist tics, Stravinsky's Octet. Downes praised the work (in which Carleton Sprague Smith played the flute part) as "felicitously written" and "very objective and formal, purely linear, in no sense nationalistic."[61] Thomson too approved of these qualities. Despite—perhaps even because of—its lack of regional signifiers, he proposed, "this is the kind of music that makes one believe in the New World."

As the deafening silence that greeted *Panambí* suggests, Ginastera's orchestral music fared badly, at least in New York, where reactions ranged from lukewarm to hostile. Harold C. Schonberg tagged *Pampeana* no. 3 (1954) as a "gorgeously orchestrated hunk of nothing" and Edward Downes (son of Olin Downes), hearing in it a "mildly nationalistic flavor," expressed surprise over what he considered its timid cast, which barely taxed the listener.[62] Taubman and Lang both took swipes at the *Variaciones concertantes*. Ginastera completed the work in 1953, the same year Antal Dorati and the Minneapolis Symphony Orchestra premiered it, with Walter Thalin playing the excruciatingly difficult clarinet solo in Variation 2.[63] In October 1955 Thomas Scherman and the Little Orchestra Society performed it at New York's Town Hall. Taubman acknowledged that although Ginastera gives "the instruments of the orchestra individual air to breathe," the "atmosphere created for them is so full of cloying perfume that one is quickly surfeited." Continuing in this vein he observed, "The Argentine composer is glib and slick. He knows a lot of the obvious tricks of the trade. But his opening theme is saccharine, and the variations are no improvement."[64] Lang was even more blunt. Deeming Ginastera a "musical sleight of hand man," he observed:

In [Ginastera's] case an Argentinian dabbles in French impressionism but the picture was not clear to me. I could not decide whether the pampas were transplanted to the Place Vendôme or vice versa, therefore I had to settle for the Café de la Paix which, as everyone knows, is a sort of buffer state. Mr. Ginastera is clever but he forgot one important thing: when one operates with clichés it is most dangerous to be cute and he was insufferably cute.[65]

As if charges of slick operating—not to mention cuteness—were not enough, an aura of derivativeness hung over Ginastera. On February 21, 1957, Dmitri Mitropoulos conducted the New York Philharmonic at Carnegie Hall in Ginastera's *Overture to the Criollo Faust* (Overture to the "Creole" Faust), an objective nationalist work. The *Overture* was inspired by the poem *Fausto* by the Argentine poet Estanislao del Campo and tells of a gaucho who ventures into the Argentine capital and finds himself at a performance of Gounod's *Faust*, an experience he later describes to a friend in his rustic vocabulary. According to the *New York Times*, Ginastera's overture "suggested that the gaucho had spent more time listening to Copland's *El salón México*" than to *Faust*.[66] Given Ginastera's ostensible rapport with Copland's most accessible Latin-tinged piece, it comes as no surprise that New York first heard the concert suite *Estancia* (surely the equivalent work in Ginastera's catalogue) in what amounted to a pops concert. In July 1960 in Lewisohn Stadium, the actor and cabaret singer Eartha Kitt performed songs by Kurt Weill and Duke Ellington, selections from *West Side Story*, and other miscellany such as "Beat Out Dat Rhythm on a Drum" from Oscar Hammerstein II's *Carmen Jones*. Also featured were Borodin's *Polevetsian Dances* (of *Reader's Digest's* "100 Most Beautiful Melodies" fame) and Copland's *An Outdoor Overture*. Kitt evidently dominated the evening.[67] Yet as Salzman proposed in the *New York Times*, her fans were equally "delighted with the un-stuffy, lively, rhythmic music of a couple of 'classical' moderns," even if they had not come expecting symphonic music.[68] Salzman elaborated further on *Estancia* in his review of the 1960 Everest recording, describing it as "a kind of cross between *Rodeo* and *Oklahoma!*"[69] In short, Ginastera's middlebrow credentials were secure.

Elsewhere in the United States critics reacted more favorably to these qualities. *Estancia* may have been slow to arrive in New York, but its U.S. premiere in 1954 by the Indianapolis Symphony under Fabien Sevitzky was warmly applauded, with critics responding to its pictorial qualities.[70] The indefatigable Henry Butler, who held forth in the *Indianapolis Times* not only on music but on world affairs, the Kinsey report, and the latest kitchen gadgets, was especially delighted with the *malambo*, commenting that it was "Latin Khachaturian . . . the kind of thing you want to whistle on your way out."[71] (Evidently in the Heartland, Khachaturian did not necessarily conjure up Marxist commissars and low-grade vodka.) In 1954 *Pampeana* no. 3 (Schonberg's "gorgeously orchestrated hunk of nothing") was so successful in its world premiere in Louisville, Kentucky (an important center of musical activity at midcentury) that it was repeated the following year for the third annual Music Critics Workshop. To be sure, one critic called it a "travelogue" and another claimed that it had "the earmarks of a real concert hit."[72] Reviewing the first string quartet for the *Los Angeles Times* in January 1956, Albert Goldberg suggested that although the work was not "profound," it was "stamped by a strong creative impulse and marked individuality," whereas another critic heard "loneliness and distances of Ginastera's beloved pampas" apropos a performance by the

Budapest Quartet.[73] In sum, Ginastera was seen as a friendly enough but conventional Good Neighbor.[74]

In the late 1950s, however, U.S. critics began to observe that overtly nationalistic references in Ginastera's music were receding. The backdrop for this turning point was the first of the Washington-based Inter-American Music Festivals, organized mainly by Espinosa of the OAS. Just as in earlier periods, corporate, governmental, and aesthetic constituencies collaborated to stage Pan Americanism. As John Haskins explained in the program booklet, modern festivals were "a kind of musical trade fair, a display of cultural wares for a special purpose."[75] "Trade fair" partners over the twenty-odd years of intermittent Inter-American Festivals included Allied Chemical, Merrill Lynch, Gillette, Pan American Airways, the Reader's Digest Foundation, and Standard Oil. Nearly all of the program booklets open with a greeting from the current U.S. president (the honorary Festival chair) and his wife, including that great friend of Latin America, Richard M. Nixon. Of all the cultural products displayed, international modernism was most conspicuous. Cowell, whose Symphony no. 14 was performed on the second Festival (April 22–30, 1961), commented in his program note, "Dodecaphonic internationalism eliminates everything that has been developed as a national style."[76] Practically all composers rose to the occasion. During the fourth Festival (June 19–30, 1968), when the Poor People's March on Washington required that some concerts be rescheduled, the Spanish avant-garde asserted itself, reflecting the Franco regime's campaign to refurbish Spain's international credentials and challenge the long-standing perception of the country as backward. (One surprising fruit of this project, advanced by Spanish scholars, was the notion that the 14,000-year-old cave paintings at Altamira were not primitive artifacts but rather evidence of an innately Spanish propensity for abstraction.)[77] The Washington concert of June 27, 1968, featured not folkloric *jotas* or *seguidillas* but *Objetos sonoros* (Sonorous Objects), *Geometrías* (Geometries), and *Superficie núm. 1* (Surface No. 1). It also prompted Paul Hume to declare, "In our days of instant communications, avant-garde music sounds very much the same whether it originates in Madrid, Los Angeles, Cologne, or Buenos Aires."[78] Surely the punchy headline of Alan M. Kreigsman's article in the *Washington Post*, "Composers Drop Nationalism," best sums up the Festivals' orientation (figs. 6a; 6b, 6c on website).[79]

The highlight of the first Festival, which opened on April 18, 1958, was Ginastera's String Quartet no. 2 (1958), commissioned by the Elizabeth Sprague Coolidge Foundation. It unfolds in a five-movement (fast-slow-scherzo-slow-fast) symmetrical structure that recalls Bartók's arch forms, as do some of the more rhapsodic passages in movement 4. References to sonata form in the serialist first movement situate the work in the sort of international modernism just described, with pitches from the row furnishing fifth-based harmonies. Serialist procedures are most strictly observed in movement 3, a scherzo with two trios. The row for the scherzo (trios 1 and 2 each use different rows) divides neatly

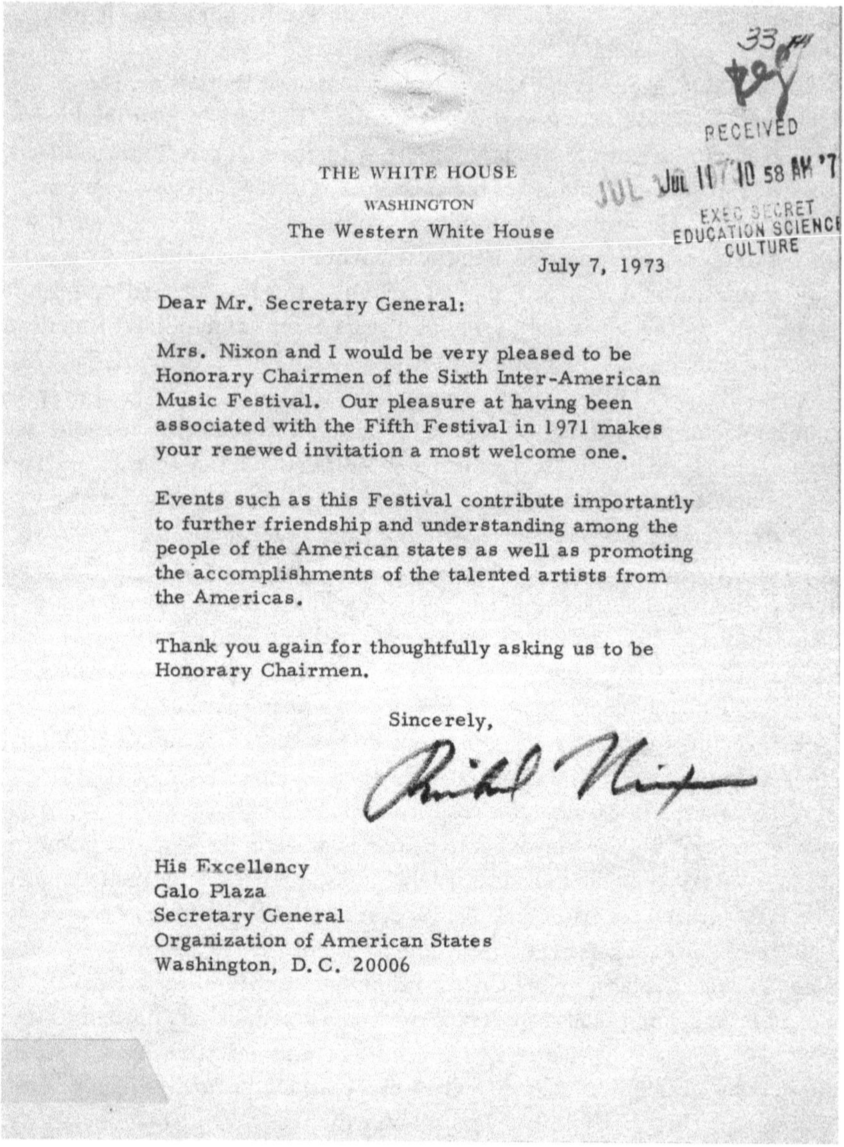

RECEIVED

EXEC SECRET
EDUCATION SCIENCE
CULTURE

THE WHITE HOUSE
WASHINGTON
The Western White House

July 7, 1973

Dear Mr. Secretary General:

Mrs. Nixon and I would be very pleased to be Honorary Chairmen of the Sixth Inter-American Music Festival. Our pleasure at having been associated with the Fifth Festival in 1971 makes your renewed invitation a most welcome one.

Events such as this Festival contribute importantly to further friendship and understanding among the people of the American states as well as promoting the accomplishments of the talented artists from the Americas.

Thank you again for thoughtfully asking us to be Honorary Chairmen.

Sincerely,

His Excellency
Galo Plaza
Secretary General
Organization of American States
Washington, D. C. 20006

Figure 6a Letter from President Richard Nixon, on the sixth Inter-American Music Festival, 1974.

into four trichords, of which two consist of a perfect fourth and a tritone (set 3–5) and two of a minor second and a minor third. Marked *Presto mágico*, the hushed, fleet scherzo is remarkable for its narrow dynamic range, within whose Webernian limits Ginastera achieves a remarkable variety of instrumental colors through harmonics (mm. 35), *glissandi* (mm. 50–59), *sul ponticello* and *col legno sul ponticello* (mm. 165–74), and several varieties of *pizzicato* (mm. 22, 228). Even in the face of all these modernist strategies, some critics connected the

3/4–6/8 meter shifts in the first movement to the *malambo*, however. Another vestige of objective nationalism was the quotation in movement 4 of "Triste" from the *Five Argentine Folk Songs*, complemented here by microtones.[80]

The quartet caused a sensation. Irving Lowens of the *Washington Evening Star* enthused, "Had these [Inter-American Music Festivals] done no more than focus the spotlight of public attention on Ginastera's brilliance, they would be memorable events in the annals of music."[81] Most praiseworthy was Ginastera's modernist bent, manifested not only in his finesse with serialism but in a quality Lowens described as "controlled turbulence." Hume, in turn, noted "superb organization," especially in the two outer movements, which "deriv[ed] much of their urgency from the strongly dissonant system [while] lacking the slightest idea of arbitrariness."[82] Even Taubman, who had taken such a dim view of *Pampeana no. 3* and the *Variaciones concertantes*, was persuaded. For him, the quartet "bespoke the seriousness and professionalism of the composer" and an "original and exciting synthesis of contemporary trends"; moreover, Taubman added, despite some references to Argentine idioms, Ginastera's quartet "reflects not a local landscape but personal vistas."[83] In other words, Ginastera was moved by the dictates of individual inspiration. The once "glib and slick" composer had arrived.

Compare these reactions to those that greeted another work performed at the first Festival, *Choro for Clarinet and Orchestra* by Guarnieri, ardent defender of national identity. Performed by Harold Wright and the National Symphony Orchestra, the piece stood out in this high-modernist company. Both Lowens and the composer-conductor Robert Evett brushed it off as little more than an example of the "rum and coca-cola" school of Latin American composers, with Lowens noting a "'south of the border' general atmosphere."[84] Guarnieri, having essentially followed the lead of Copland and Gershwin, was now reduced to a Caribbean cocktail. In alluding to the Andrews Sisters song of the same name, which had sold over 200,000 copies by 1958, Lowens and Evett overlooked the fact that "Rum and Coca-Cola" is a David and Goliath tale of victory over U.S. cultural imperialism: Morey Amsterdam, Jeri Sullavan, and Paul Baron, credited as the song's composers, were later charged with plagiarizing the work of the Trinidadian artist Lord Belasco, and a separate suit concerning the lyrics was also successful.[85]

Ginastera's career in the United States now took off. The second Festival featured his first piano concerto and the freely serialist *Cantata para América mágica* (Cantata for Magic America), commissioned by the Koussevitzky and Fromm Foundations, respectively. Although one might expect the *Cantata*'s fifty-eight percussion instruments and indigenous texts to inspire primitivist discourse, nothing of the kind ensued. Instead Hume applauded "profound intellect" and "superbly calculated" equilibrium.[86] Lowens, hearing "incredible complexity," called the *Cantata* the "logical culmination of Ginastera's evolution from militant nationalist to citizen of the Western hemisphere," a status he had achieved by eschewing "the *gauchesco* nationalism of earlier years."[87] In 1965 the third Festival featured Ginastera's *Sinfonía de Don Rodrigo* for dramatic soprano and orchestra, and the Music Advisory Panel of the State Department's Cultural Presentations program recommended his music for the Juilliard Quartet's tour of the Soviet Union.[88] For the fourth Festival, in 1968, he graciously stepped aside to allow younger composers a chance to shine.[89] During this time, Ginastera's photograph circulated in the media, his thick black glasses and serious demeanor characteristic of the cold warrior. "Cuteness" now long behind him, Ginastera even came to be tagged "a musical Robert McNamara" for his "squareness of cut . . . reverence for duty, efficiency and the middle way, alongside intellectual virtuosity and technical brilliance."[90]

New York became much friendlier to Ginastera. His violin concerto, premiered there in October 1963 by Ruggiero Ricci and the New York Philharmonic under Bernstein, was applauded as "one of the most exceptional works to come out of South America."[91] His greatest triumph in the city that had once snubbed him, however, was *Don Rodrigo*.[92] The opera inaugurated the New York State Theater in February 1966, with Plácido Domingo heading its enormous cast. Critics considered it within a narrative of antinationalist high modernism. One noted that Ginastera, "like so many others, left behind his own brand of nationalism to embrace current serial and aleatoric practices."[93] Another, praising Ginastera's "stringent dodecaphonic idiom," called *Don Rodrigo* "a twelve-tone *Otello*," recommending it to "those who may have labored under the impression that whatever originates in South America is bound to be reactionary."[94] Schonberg too, now the senior music critic at the *New York Times*, praised *Don Rodrigo*'s brilliance, observing, "Mr. Ginastera . . . knows his voice and he knows his orchestra." He detected, however, a "major flaw" in the opera, namely, its "lack of anything touching the heart."[95]

■ SUBLIMATION AND NATIONALISM DURING THE COLD WAR

Aiding Ginastera's ascent was Chase, who joined in the accolades over String Quartet no. 2, which he called the "acme of the festival."[96] But Chase had already paved the way in no fewer than three articles, all from 1957. In them he elaborated on a key feature of Ginastera's evolution: "subjective sublimation."[97] This mysterious process reconciled the asceticism and objectivity of high modernism with subtle, perhaps even imaginary traces of folk music, thus purifying and refining nationalism. For Chase, *Pampeana* no. 3 marked a turning point in Ginastera's creative development in that, despite its hints of Argentine folk music, it proceeds "along strictly formal lines," largely due to its twelve-note series, used freely.[98] Other compositions reflecting Ginastera's liberation from Argentine nationalism included String Quartet no. 1, the theme of the *Variaciones concertantes*, and the *Twelve American Preludes*, since in all these works "the national element is sublimated rather than realistic or literal."[99] In Piano Sonata no. 1, "the spirit of the malambo is . . . sublimated to the 'nth' degree"; the second movement "reaches heights of sublimation hitherto unattained by Ginastera, or by any other Argentine composer."[100]

As noted, musical sublimation was nothing new. But it achieved a special resonance during the cold war, when Freudian psychoanalysis peaked in popularity in the United States. Freud, who regarded sublimation as but one of many psychoanalytical goals, was bemused by the power his U.S. followers had assigned it, ever since the Clark College lectures, largely to justify what he called "American chastity."[101] Sublimation proved an effective lens through which to view sexual behavior; a lengthy 1932 study, *A Critique of Sublimation in Males: A Study of Forty Superior Single Men,* gauged the effects of sublimating "sex energy" (the young men deemed "superior" were, as the researchers put it, neither "'rakes . . . morons, neurotics, [nor] other abnormal personalities").[102] Not surprisingly, the authors, headed by W. S. Taylor, a professor of psychology at Smith College, concluded that sexual continence benefited society and the individual. Freud, however, cautioned that sublimation had to reckon with the reality of human drives and warned against neglecting "the original animal part of our nature," which ultimately was insusceptible to mere repression.[103] Neither could repressed drives be sublimated. "Psychoanalytic theory," Freud explained, "teaches that a drive cannot be sublimated as long as it is repressed."[104] Many in the nascent psychoanalytic community in the United States nonetheless seized on sublimation as a justification for their moral codes, which they reinforced from "dizzy, puritanical heights," as the New York psychoanalyst Monroe A. Meyer complained.[105] As phrases such as *socially acceptable* and *of value to society* came to dominate the psychoanalytic literature, sublimation's public value increased.[106] Because patients were increasingly guided to temper their drives in favor of what became known as "adjustment," the U.S. psychoanalytic community found an unexpected ally in mainstream clergy. Initially repulsed by Freud, churchmen now appropriated sublimation to reinforce religious teachings. The newfound rapport among these constituencies was celebrated in May 1956, the Freud centenary year, when psychoanalysts, psychiatrists, and clergy gathered at New York's Cathedral of St. John the Divine, an irony that would not have been lost on the atheist honoree.[107] At the same time that analysis was becoming a respectable pursuit for the middle and upper classes, terms such as *complex, Freudian slip,* and *repression* insinuated themselves into American English, and books such as *Self-Confidence through Self-Analysis* and *Be Glad You're Neurotic* became available to a wide readership.[108] When *Time* magazine featured Freud on its cover of April 23, 1956, it was clear he had arrived—in his U.S., cold war–era incarnation.[109]

The artistic community also responded to Freud, who, after all, had considered himself an artist and regarded sublimation as a necessary ingredient of artistic creation. In his essay "Leonardo da Vinci and a Memory of His Childhood," he wrote, "The sexual instinct . . . is endowed with a capacity for sublimation: that is, it has the power to replace its immediate aim by other aims which may be valued more highly and which are not sexual."[110] The concept of high-value nonsexual artistic aims finds numerous parallels in the Kantian principle of disinterest, which eschews bodily reactions while privileging form.[111] So endowed with abstract properties did form become that even pornography could be rendered as "high" art; accordingly, D. H. Lawrence's novels, Aubrey Beardsley's drawings, and James Joyce's *Ulysses* were all seen to enshrine aesthetic "autonomy, control and disinterest," as Allison Pease argues.[112] This phenomenon relates to the effort to sublimate art itself, that is, to stake out a preserve for what came to be known as "the fine arts" in an autonomous realm in which their intrinsic qualities could be contemplated free from commerce and instrumentality.[113] The essentials of this largely eighteenth-century enterprise were thus reenacted in U.S. musical circles during the cold war, when modernist art music was ensconced in a safe realm barred to the "hordes" and the "musically unwashed."

Paradoxically, even as the masses were seen as increasingly incapable of the disinterested contemplation high art required, critics extolled art's universalist aims. Kant, in distinguishing the "pleasant" (*angenehm*) from the "beautiful," argued that the latter "carries with it an *aesthetic quality* of universality," a quality that cannot be found in the merely "pleasant," which depends largely on the senses.[114] Avant-garde music, whether through its inherently edifying complexity or its ostensible separation from the market and politics, also sublimated base senses and, paradoxically, preached universalism while it reinforced the boundary between masses and elites. (This outlook was but one manifestation of the tendency to sacralize art, given special impetus in the United States since 1852, when John Sullivan Dwight of Boston founded *Dwight's Journal of Music*, which served as an arbiter of taste and moral uplift for three decades.)[115] Thus, just as Freud's U.S. followers attached moral codes to sexual sublimation, a moral dimension inhered in artistic sublimation. In *Distinction: A Social Critique of the Judgment of Taste*, Pierre Bourdieu makes this point when he argues that "pure pleasure—ascetic, empty pleasure which implies the renunciation of pleasure, pleasure purified of pleasure—is predisposed to become a symbol of moral excellence" and constitutes the process by which a work of art becomes "a test of ethical superiority, an indispensable measure of the capacity for sublimation."[116]

Adorno's reflections on sublimation are relevant here. Although no fan of Freud's artistic theory, he nonetheless proposed in *Aesthetics of Modern Music* that Freud understood better than Kant "the dynamic nature of art." Yet according to Adorno, in considering artworks largely as products of the unconscious, Freud effectively categorized them as "little more than plenipotentiaries of sensuous impulses made unrecognizable to some degree by a kind of dream-work," thus rendering the artist's advanced technique irrelevant.[117] For composers, the Freudian scheme overlooked the technical dimension of the musical form, in which its very logic is manifest.[118] Yet certain points in common between Kant and Freud resonate for Adorno. In holding that perhaps, "the most important taboo in art is the one that prohibits an animal-like attitude toward the object," Adorno argues that the strength of this taboo is "matched by the strength of the repressed urge"; doggedly pursuing disinterest, the artist creates works whose "dignity" is contingent upon "the magnitude of the interest from which they were wrested."[119] Sublimation, when properly realized, thus engages with the "dialectic of interests and disinterestedness" and, in ultimately transcending this dialectic, enables the critic to distinguish art from "cuisine and pornography."[120]

To cuisine and pornography we can add musical nationalism. Like sex, nationalism is a drive. Through native instruments and folk dances, and their unsubtle arousal of the body (and the body politic), musical nationalism arouses the impulses of the seething masses, with their animal needs, stimulating the very drives from which an elite that understands "pure" pleasure and the probity it affords will desist. As with other kinds of drives, nationalism can be repressed. But because a repressed drive cannot be sublimated, a composer must therefore work through his or her "neurosis" ("heedless nationalism," to recall Eisenhower's words) by sublimating the nationalist impulse to the higher goal of universalism, with its lofty promise of disinterest. In Ginastera's case, he was all the more remarkable for embodying Adorno's calculation of aesthetic value as proportional to the "strength of the repressed urge"; once a "militant nationalist," he had sublimated his drive toward *gauchesco* nationalism and offered "controlled turbulence" in its place.

Just as he applauded sublimation, Chase railed against the mass public. In April 1958, days before Ginastera's String Quartet no. 2 was applauded at the Inter-American Festival, he wrote a letter to the *New York Times* apropos a recent article on serial music by Taubman. Taubman, who had called dodecaphony "flayed and searing" but hardly "surprising in our Freudian age," observed that twelve-tone music awakened a wide range of reactions in the public, from "fascination and a sense of mystery to perplexity and boredom."[121] In one of his feistier utterances, Chase lashed out at the forces that compel music critics to pander to the mass audience, implicitly mourning the dearth of "moral excellence" and "ethical superiority" that a twelve-tone work might instill. Assailing listeners incapable of appreciating the art of their own time, he opined, "[A] composer, unless he is a hack or a huckster, does not write for the general public. That public is an amorphous monstrosity, corrupted by commercialism and the moronic media of mass entertainment.... He does write or paint or compose for ... a select group, capable of understanding creative thought and inventiveness in the arts. But that is not a public, it is an elite." In a final dig at the sheep-like horde, Chase concludes, in high Arnoldian dudgeon, "Art for mass consumption is trash; it always has been and always will be."[122]

Thus Chase pinpoints the essence of cold war Pan Americanist antinationalism. If nationalism had previously been transfigured by ur-classicism, dialectical indigenism, or a miraculous fusion of Bach and Brazil, it would now be so refined as to escape notice by the "amorphous monstrosity" of middlebrow culture. Thanks to sublimation, difference—and its reconciliation—could still be savored, but by an elite. Jacqueline Kennedy stated as much in the program booklet for the 1961 Inter-American Music Festival, that high-modernist event so profligate in dissonance, abstraction, and complexity that nonetheless promised to bring "into closer accord . . . accidental differences of environment, circumstance, or language" through music.[123] In *Bomarzo*, some of the ways in which Ginastera took sublimation to its logical terminus annihilated difference. The work also raised questions about Ginastera's privileged status in the United States.

■ *BOMARZO* AND THE "STRENGTH OF THE REPRESSED URGE"

Of course, Chase's scheme of sublimation overlooks those works in which no nationalist element is present, as was often the case with Ginastera's neo-expressionist works. With objective and subjective nationalism now behind him (and likely savoring his triumph at the Festivals and with *Don Rodrigo*), Ginastera was primed to fulfill his promise with *Bomarzo*, which grew out of his association with the United States; after his eponymous cantata was performed at the 1965 Coolidge Festival, Hobart Spalding, president of the Opera Society of Washington, commissioned the opera.[124] At that time, Ginastera was enjoying life in post-Perón Buenos Aires, the intellectual and artistic freedom of which some have associated with Perón's ouster and the two democratic governments that followed (Arturo Frondizi, 1958–62; Arturo Illia, 1963–66).[125] As noted in chapter 1, Ginastera also had the good fortune to direct the Rockefeller-funded Centro Latinoamericano de Altos Estudios Musicales (CLAEM), one of nine centers of the Instituto Torcuato di Tella. This mecca for avant-garde art had been founded in 1958 with support from the Ford Foundation and attracted international visitors, including Clement Greenberg.[126] A savvy administrator, Ginastera marshaled his share of these resources to invite Luigi Nono, Gian Francesco Malipiero, Iannis Xenakis, Luigi Dallapiccola, Robert M. Stevenson, Copland, Chase, and others for lectures, concerts, and classes.

Sartre, Italian neorealism, and French nouvelle vague were then the common currency of Argentine intellectuals and of the educated middle class. Julio Cortázar's *Rayuela*, a book the Argentine historian Mariano Ben Plotkin tersely describes as "not particularly easy to read," sold twenty-five thousand copies a year from 1963 until the end of the decade.[127] The Argentine government funded various cultural projects, sometimes aided by the United States. At the same time—and with an enthusiasm perhaps unequaled elsewhere—Argentines were drawn to psychoanalysis, a phenomenon Plotkin playfully dubs "Freud in the pampas." Defying the Argentine Catholic Church, members of an intellectually progressive middle class devoured frank literature on sex and other pillars of psychoanalytic theory. Psychodrama, the therapeutic acting-out of emotions and conflicts by and for patients, influenced experimental theater in Argentina, as can be seen in the works of the psychoanalyst and playwright Eduardo "Tato" Pavlovsky. The magazine *Primera Plana* covered this creative ferment and also featured Art Buchwald's columns in translation, along with reviews of films such as *¿Quién le teme a Virginia Woolf?* and *El sexo y la joven soltera* (Sex and the Single Girl). In short, cultural life in post-Perón Argentina drew on enormous reserves of pent-up intellectual and artistic energy, a high level of education among forward-looking elites, and the desires of a well-educated middle class to experience the social changes then sweeping first-world countries. Undergirding this heady moment was the explanatory power of psychoanalysis.

Bomarzo is thus a creation of its era. Partly factual and partly embellished, it recounts the life of the humpbacked sixteenth-century duke Pier Francesco Orsini, whose garden of gigantic stone monsters can still be seen in the village of Bomarzo, north of Rome. The opera unfolds in flashback, as the dying duke revisits episodes from his ignominious past, which has involved cross-dressing, parental abuse, poisoning, at least one humiliating encounter with a prostitute, various occult ceremonies, an orgy, and the hint of a homosexual relationship with a mute slave, Adul. The score teems with aleatory, atonality, serialism, microtones, clusters, extended instrumental and vocal techniques, along with parodies of medieval organum and Renaissance dances. To conventional instruments Ginastera adds harpsichord, mandolin, viola d'amore, and an enhanced percussion section.

Ginastera explained *Bomarzo*'s aesthetic principles in a lecture jointly sponsored by the Institute of Contemporary Arts and Society and the Argentine Embassy, held at the State Department Auditorium. The composer insisted that art must have "an intellectual and spiritual function that comes out of order and control" and emphasized "the problems of structure and their solution."[128] Although plot and subject matter impose certain requirements on opera, the imperative of progress had to be heeded: it was incumbent upon the composer to invent "new laws . . . new proceedings and new language . . . to remove contemporary opera from stagnant waters" (10). *Bomarzo*'s contemporaneity was manifested in the protagonist's neuroses, which, Ginastera observed, reflected the current historical moment: "an age of anxiety, an age of sex, an age of violence" (11). Accordingly, order and control lie at the heart of *Bomarzo*. Its two-act format consists of fifteen scenes separated by short interludes à la *Wozzeck*. Each scene is further divided into what Ginastera described as "three microstructures," namely, an "exposition, crisis, and conclusion," such that the form of the entire opera was replicated in each individual scene, an arrangement the composer called "very strict and severe" (12). Several self-contained numbers reinforce this uncompromising procedure, standing out against the typically asymmetrical and harmonically dense phrases. For example, Ginastera launches the opera with a fourteenth-century modal tune, the "Lamento di Tristan," sung by a shepherd boy, whose clear soprano voice is unaccompanied but for irregularly spaced flourishes in the harp.[129] The lament also acts as a framing device: when it reappears in the opera's final moments, its stark purity brings the viewer full circle while sealing the contrast between the protagonist's degradation and the boy's innocence. Other embedded numbers include the parodies of Renaissance dances in the ball scene (act 1 scene 7), in which Julia, the young woman who is supposed to marry Pier Francesco, rejects him to dance with his brother. In two *galliardas* for cello, mandolin, and harpsichord, Ginastera indicates tempi so sluggish as to mock Pier Francesco's anxieties over his masculinity, twisted renderings that amplify what some scholars have called parody's "situating" mechanism in that they comment on the presumed capacity of formal expectations to signal disinterest.[130] Likewise, the *salterello*, which accumulates tension via *squillante* cries in the brass, shrieks in the piccolo, rattling of tambourines and xylophone, and a quotation of the Dies Irae, leads not to a sustained climax but to an inconclusive fade-out that reflects the protagonist's impotence.

Another agent of control is serialism, announced in the opening Prelude. In its first notes, a pianissimo F-sharp in the string basses expands to a tritone, F-sharp–C, to launch the first of three rows, which appear with varying degrees of prominence over the course of the work. (Another theme, consisting of all twelve pitches, appears only once, at a dramatically significant moment.) The first of these rows will appear in the strings via staggered entries of the twelve pitch classes (mm. 9–14), capped off with a screech of indefinite pitch in the violins (m. 15).[131] Ginastera approaches the aggregate systematically, that is, by using the pitches of the tritone, C–F-sharp, as respective points of departure and arrival and then filling out the tritone with two chromatic hexachords, one ascending and the other descending (mm. 9–15). At mm. 34–36, row 1 is restated in smaller note values. (It will also conclude the Prelude in a vertical cluster.) Row 1 is also the all-interval row.[132] Used in Schoenberg's Serenade op. 24, Berg's *Lyric Suite*, and Nono's *Canti per 13* and *Il canto sospeso*, the all-interval row is rich in possibilities for "order and control" since its retrograde is identical to its transposition at the tritone and its inversion maintains a regular pairing of every two notes of its original form.[133] The flourish in the clarinet centered around F-sharp (m. 19) recalls the initial statement of the row while anticipating the opera's most notorious scene, the erotic ballet (act 2 scene 11).

The Prelude also anticipates ways in which control will interact with aleatory, the latter defined by Paul Griffiths as "music in which the composer has made a deliberate withdrawal of control."[134] Aleatory is embodied in the chorus, a *turba* that reacts to and comments on the action from the orchestra pit. At m. 64, sopranos and altos enter on a definite pitch (F-sharp) but almost immediately begin to moan and sigh with labial glissandi, altering the pitch and growing in intensity as the male voices enter.[135] Starting in m. 73 with the chorus's unpitched "Ahs" (against which individual voices also surface, as in mm. 72–73), the strings play the highest possible pitch *sul ponticello*. Yet in m. 75, row 2, derived from row 1 and distributed among the woodwinds, inserts itself amid the amorphous buzzing.[136] While the chorus pronounces *senza voce* the consonants L, J, G, K, P, N, the orchestra offers in a twenty-second hiatus all the transpositions of row 2 over a "free and discontinuous rhythm," as stated in the score. Row 2, which reasserts itself in a linear presentation of its I6 form (horn, m. 80), also introduces one of *Bomarzo*'s central features: frequent statements of a given row-form in unambiguous linear presentation, often emerging from a sonic haze and relying on a single instrument or instrument family.

Several such straightforward presentations of the row mark musical and dramatic structural points. The conclusion of scene 1 (Interlude 1) restates row 1 P0 (mm. 12–14) via staggered entries of pitches distributed throughout the strings, as in the Prelude. At the beginning of act 2 (mm. 9–14 of Interlude 8), we hear row 1 P10 via the now familiar staggering of the pitch class entrances in the strings. In the opera's final moments (act 2 scene 15, mm. 45–50), the dying protagonist repeats the word *immortal*, echoed by unpitched male voices. Here, row 1 P0 returns, again via gradual entrances in the strings and culminating in a shimmering cluster enhanced by labial glissandi in the chorus before melting into the shepherd boy's gentle song. Linear presentations of the row with less structural significance occur in Interlude 10, m. 10, where row 3 is heard in its prime form in the brass, in act 1 scene 2 (mm. 70–71), and in Interlude III (mm. 9–13), after the duke learns that his father has been wounded in battle, row 2 P10 emerges in the strings and horns. These linear affirmations of the row assert themselves so blatantly that one can almost imagine the listener counting to twelve. To be sure, the row also appears unordered (more typical of Ginastera's serial writing), sometimes for dramatic reasons. For example, when the astrologer Silvio encourages Pier Francesco to "have faith, have hope" (act 1 scene 1), the protagonist alludes to Paul's Epistle to the Corinthians, responding "Charity I never had," at which point, pitches 0, 1, 2, 4 of row 1 P0 follow (m. 107), with the remaining pitches sounding in the solo trumpet, all but one out of order. Immediately following the duke's response, however (m. 109), row 2 I6 (minus pitch 7) asserts itself in the horns in a linear presentation.[137] An aria sung by the prostitute Pantasilea (act 1 scene 4, mm. 144–45) concludes with an unordered set of all twelve pitches except B-flat; a complete unordered cluster heralds the offstage voice of Pier Francesco's grandmother, Diana (act 1 scene 1, m. 152). In act 1 scene 5 (mm. 52–55), Diana's conviction that the family name will endure is confirmed by her three utterances of the word *siempre*, each punctuated by tetrachords 4–5 and 4–9 against a reiterated F–G-flat in the bass (ex. 6a).

Even in the aleatoric sections a degree of control prevails. Although Ginastera specifies that "all the aleatory [*sic*] fragments must be played without strict metric duration and with great expressive freedom," he assigns each an allotted number of seconds, specifying in no small detail the technique to be employed.[138]

One representative moment is the interlude in act 1 scene 2, in which the per-cussion is grouped so that wood blocks, Chinese gongs, tam-tam, piatti, cow bells, and bongos improvise while the strings play *sul ponticello* on indetermi-nate pitches for ten- to fifteen-second increments, or "formants," to use Ginas-tera's term.

Tension between aleatory and control culminates in the erotic ballet (act 2 scene 11), which commences with Pier Francesco's fourth soliloquy. Alone on his wedding night, he has failed—not for the first time—to realize his manhood. As he begins his lament, so too do a series of chamber variations, excruciating in their concision. (None exceeds three measures, and Variations 4 and 7 are one measure each.) The theme, row 2 P6, is given in the lower strings, harp, and piano over three measures in unvarying eighth notes separated by eight rests. Variation 1 offers row 2 P4 in the solo cello; in Variation 2, row 2 RI2 is heard in the viola d'amore and Variation 3 states row 2 P2 via three tetrachords sustained in the woodwinds. In Variation 4, however, order begins to break down. Flour-ishes of sixteenth-note quintuplets present row 2 It (with pitches t and e reversed), its one-measure duration filled out with free pitches. From Variation 5, during which the duke complains of "sterile attempts" ("estériles ensayos") at erotic fulfillment, the row is conspicuous by its absence. Then, in the final varia-tion (no. 9), four trichords (3–2, 3–4, 3–5, 3–3) in the upper parts are enhanced with *pp* glissandi in the strings as Pier Francesco revisits his longing for immor-tality. After a fleeting glimpse of Pantasilea and with the dynamics at the level of "Niente!," the dancers glide onstage.

Throughout the ballet the duke thrills to a dream in which the physical repul-siveness, vulnerability, and impotence that have plagued his existence vanish. The skittish turning figure on F-sharp, introduced by the clarinet in the Prelude and colored here with the bassoon, heralds his unfolding fantasy. As seminude dancers writhe in the shadows, three groups of percussion begin improvising softly over a distant roll in the bass drum.[139] Divisi strings dissolve into glissandi and the woodwinds juxtapose sustained chords, freely improvising in "duration,

Example 6a Alberto Ginastera and Manuel Mujica Láinez. *Bomarzo*, op. 34. Act 1, scene 5. © Copyright 1967, 1977 by Boosey & Hawkes Inc. Reprinted by permission.

articulations, and timbre." Most forceful is the chorus. First sighing on indeterminate pitches, it alternates with the percussion and declaims one of its few texted utterances in the entire ballet, the word *love*, whispered "in all the languages of the world," as the score extravagantly instructs.[140] Roaming the chromatic scale, the chorus effects a gradual, unpitched crescendo as the percussion intensifies and the woodwind players dryly tap the keys of their instruments. The singers surge into the illusory climax, a sustained howl that pounds away, *ffff*. Anarchy has triumphed, the cacophony of the horde has prevailed. Yet, cutting through this spasm of imagined lust and abandon, a twelve-note theme is heard for the first and only time. Stated in the horns and strings, it authoritatively marks the falling off of the unbridled shouting, signaling the voices to collapse into indistinct sighing, to fade into noiselessness. Only a static void briefly fills the musical space. Finally, the aphoristic chamber variations that opened the scene return. However pale its reassertion, control has silenced the empty ranting of the mob.

■ *BOMARZO* AND CENSORSHIP

In Washington, critics praised *Bomarzo*, lavishing on it a range of cold war–era buzzwords: control, progress, complexity, and individual creativity. Taking *Don Rodrigo* as a point of reference, Lowens proposed that *Bomarzo*, with its more thoroughgoing dissonance and sophisticated aleatory, was "a giant advance over the earlier work"; despite the composer's borrowings from the Second Viennese School, moreover, Ginastera's serialist strategies were "distinctly sui generis."[141] Robert Jacobson applauded Ginastera's understanding of "post-Webernian serialism," hailing his manipulation of form. He also situated Ginastera well above Chase's "amorphous monstrosity," calling the composer one of the "elite" of present-day musical minds.[142] Hume, whose review appeared under the headline "*Bomarzo*: A Modern Masterpiece," celebrated the work's technical advances and identified *Bomarzo* as "an opera born of our own times."[143] Certainly no critic addressed Latin American musical nationalism or the "rum and coca-cola school." Evett even chortled that the listener expecting anything resembling Xavier Cugat was in for "the shock of his life."[144]

The Washington critics also aestheticized *Bomarzo*'s erotic elements, considering them one more element of the work's contemporaneity. For Hume, the opera "mov[ed] in a world that Sigmund Freud verbalized," whereas Lowens found the duke's problems so immediate that he rather generously confided, "I suppose all of us have Pier Francesco's fears, instincts, and appetites."[145] Another press contingent, however, saw the erotic material not through the lens of Kantian disinterest but as raw sex. "Not for Squares," admonished the headline of a piece in *Newsweek*, in which the erotic ballet was described as a "spectacular orgy in which dancers tore at each other's skimpy body stockings in frenzied licentiousness," while *Time* referred to "a sordid orgy" in which dancers appear in "nearly topless leotards."[146] Nan Robertson of the *New York Times* fairly gushed over the "embarrassment, tension, awe, excitement, astonishment" that attended the premiere and recounted, not without relish, an especially newsworthy episode. On May 12, the day of the first full rehearsal, four dancers quit to protest the movements the choreographer Jack Cole (of *Magdalena* fame) required of them in the erotic ballet. In short, "the girls" refused to "rip off their evening gowns in mid-scene and dance, seemingly nude, in body stockings."[147] Robertson is careful to note that all this depravity had a human face. Much taken with the fact that Ginastera sat through rehearsals "buttoned into his sober business suit peering over big, black-rimmed spectacles," she fretted over how someone as stolid-looking as he was even capable of writing such a work.[148] Clearly Ginastera exuded "the strength of the repressed urge."

How much Humphrey, Schlesinger, Edward Kennedy, and their Washington colleagues actually enjoyed *Bomarzo*'s sharp-edged modernism we will likely never know. But in May 1967 U.S.–Latin American relations were, as always, on the mind of official Washington. The possibility of a hemispheric common market had been recently floated at the OAS conference in Punta del Este (Uruguay), and, more significantly, Soviet influence continued to threaten the hemisphere, as the *Washington Post* headline of May 21 proclaimed: "Moscow Woos Latin Nations." Humphrey himself took a special interest in Latin America, which, as noted, sometimes put him at odds with Johnson. Evidently the vice president had digested a "difficult and discordant" work to applaud hemispheric solidarity—on his feet yet. At the time of *Bomarzo*'s premiere, however, the Argentine military regime led by Juan Carlos Onganía had been in power for a year, blatantly contradicting U.S. democratic values. Just what sort of solidarity were Humphrey and his colleagues applauding?

To consider this question, we backtrack to June 1966, when Onganía first came to power. According to some accounts, he was emboldened by the U.S.-sanctioned military coup in Brazil in March 1964.[149] In late June the Johnson administration recognized Onganía, with some elements of the U.S. press whitewashing the coup as a "transfer of power."[150] In general, press coverage of Argentina left something to be desired. Prior to the coup, when Illia's government was in its final throes, *Time* ran a column under the snappy heading "Argentina: Where the Action Is." The reporter referred to a "full Cabinet meeting last week in Argentina," adding that although this would be unremarkable "in most countries," "as [is] usual in Argentina, it was the possibility of a military coup" that had occasioned such an event; a few issues later *Time* disingenuously declared, "Washington deplores military take-overs in Latin America."[151] Later, a Fourth of July editorial in the English-language *Buenos Aires Herald* waxed effusive on the benefits of U.S.-style democracy, explaining that the North American people "answered unfailingly to demonstrate the inner strength of true democracy."[152] To celebrate the new regime, a gala concert was held at the Teatro Colón in Buenos Aires (as Esteban Buch points out, a featured work was *Estancia*), and by mid-1967 foreign companies were revising their business plans to include Argentina. As one U.S. journalist put it, all these positive changes had transpired "without the slightest interference with citizens' constitutional rights—except, of course, the right to choose a governing party."[153]

And, it seems, the right to go to the opera of one's choice. Weeks after Ginastera's triumph in Washington and just as the sixth anniversary of the Alliance for Progress was being celebrated, the production of *Bomarzo* scheduled for the Colón was throttled. The official reason was the work's sexual content: along with Antonioni's *Blow-Up* (based on a short story by Cortázar) and Pinter's *The Homecoming*, *Bomarzo* was one more casualty in Onganía's campaign for a "Christian sense of life," one he pursued in close collaboration with the Argentine Catholic Church. Onganía took as his model Franco's Spain, where similar church-state alliances enabled censors to regulate cinema, literature, the press, and education.[154] Cultural xenophobia was also common to both regimes. Onganía despised the Di Tella and its cultural project; the mere fact that Ginastera directed the CLAEM may have contributed to the banning of his opera.[155] *Bomarzo* was also seen to represent the values of the Informal Empire, which the music critic and then-director of the Colón, Enzo Valenti Ferro, identified as "sex, violence, and blood."[156] Evidently Onganía had no compunctions about cozying up to the United States for strategic and commercial support even as he demarcated his own territory in the hazier zone of culture.

The banning was widely discussed in the Argentine press. Fred Marey, music critic for the *Buenos Aires Herald*, confessed to initially thinking it was a publicity stunt and hoped, tongue-in-cheek, that the LP would not be censored too.[157] Ginastera was shaken by the decision, despite the fact that various artists and intellectuals rushed to his support.[158] Nono, recently arrived to teach at the Di Tella, issued a strongly worded statement of solidarity prohibiting the forthcoming performance of his *Varianti* at the Colón, a performance Ginastera had surely expedited.[159] In the Buenos Aires daily *La Nación*, Mujica Láinez complained that now Little Red Riding-Hood would be prohibited for depicting a sadistic wolf seducing a little girl; *Primera plana* too jumped in, with a cover story mocking new laws against public demonstrativeness.[160] Ultimately Ginastera censored himself, prohibiting performances of his works at the Colón and declaring his disappointment to the press, especially for the "arbitrariness shown in Argentina toward the fate of a work that awakened so much interest at its U.S. premiere . . . now sealed."[161] Yet the narrative of the besieged artist confronting narrow-minded officialdom is complicated by the reaction to a partial broadcast of *Bomarzo* on August 23, 1967, from Uruguay.[162] At half-past midnight, Argentine listeners could tune in to Radio Colonia to hear the Prelude, Madrigal, portions of scene 12, interlude 5, and the chorus *O Rex Gloriae* (like the Renaissance dances, a parody), along with commentary by Ginastera and Mujica Láinez. Anticipation ran high. But according to at least one reporter, listeners soon began to experience "tedium" ("comenzó a adensarse en el tedio") since the score amounted to little more than "a painstaking anthology of the most renowned procedures—aleatoric, serial, microtonal—[that] would lend themselves rather well to providing background music for an Argentine film, with its purposeful gusts of timbral artifices." In a devastating parting shot, the author observed that "the most lucrative plan would be to transform [*Bomarzo*] into a *foto-novela*."[163]

News of the "*Bomarzo* affair," as it was known in U.S. diplomatic circles in Argentina, soon began appearing in the United States.[164] A *Time* magazine article, "Sex and the Strait-Laced Strongman," addressed generally the ills of censorship and their threat to Latin America. "During his 14 months in the Casa Rosada, the mustachioed strongman has all but declared sex illegal in his already strait-laced country," the reporter declared, dismissing in a single stroke all the freedoms of the post-Perón era.[165] In invoking the "mustachioed strongman," moreover, the reporter also indulged in a stereotype familiar to the U.S. public, whether from *caudillo*-like figures in O. Henry's stories or the *buffa* version of the same, "El Exigente," the choosy coffee inspector before whom *campesinos* trembled in television commercials for Savarin throughout the 1960s. Clearly Argentina was not to be taken seriously. As for the journalist's hand-wringing over Onganía's prudishness, U.S. relations with Franco's Spain tell another story. When staunchly anticommunist Spain became attractive to U.S. cold war strategists as a site for military bases, the United States was more than willing to overlook not only Franco's prudishness and curtailment of civil liberties but his all too impressive record of politically motivated executions. In 1959, when Franco received President Eisenhower's ceremonial embrace (to the strains of "The Yellow Rose of Texas"), the Spanish dictator is said to have declared, "Now I have won the [Spanish] Civil War."[166] The sexier-than-thou tone of the *Time* report, on the other hand, essentially proposes that state-sanctioned prudishness is practiced only by repressive or undemocratic societies and that censorship is "something that others do," a phenomenon Sue Curry Jansen has explored.[167] Liberal societies habitually overlook the power of market censorship, filtered through nuclei of power such as television networks, media conglomerations, and Hollywood (as demonstrated by the Motion Picture Section of the OIAA). This habit of mind, she argues, wrongly perpetuates the idea that "free inquiry, scientific progress, and objectivity" are uniformly practiced in liberal societies.[168] Indeed, 1960s media censorship extended to entertainment, with television networks refusing to lift Pete Seeger's blacklist status and deeming the Bob Dylan song "Talkin' John Birch Paranoid Blues" unacceptable for the *Ed Sullivan Show*. Censorship also won the day when CBS muzzled Tom and Dick Smothers by pulling their politically charged *Smothers Brothers Comedy Hour* from the airwaves in 1969, at the height of its popularity.[169]

Sex nonetheless helped sell the Columbia LP of *Bomarzo*, produced shortly after the spectacular Washington premiere.[170] A widely circulated ad aestheticized the erotic elements to savvy consumers seeking the "smell of high art."

It shows Adul with two bejeweled women leaning provocatively forward, one with an exposed breast jutting forth from the shadows. (Not for nothing, in that era of topless waitresses and go-go dancers, was *Bomarzo* known as "the topless opera.") "*Bomarzo* will shock you," the copy assures the reader, adding that not only had the work been banned, but it had driven its own cast members to quit the production. Yet, Columbia Records notes, it is modernity, not salaciousness, that makes the work "sensational": with *Bomarzo*, Ginastera composed "an opera of our time." "We know," the ad confides, "that you, too, will find *Bomarzo* sensational."

The New York City Opera's performance on March 14, 1968, thus piqued a good deal of interest.[171] Advance publicity included two *New York Times* articles by Donal Henahan in which Ginastera's persona was again deemed worthy of comment. Henahan described the composer as a single-minded individual who looks "like a bank examiner and thinks like a computer," evidently an anomaly, given the intensity of his music.[172] Or, Ginastera "speaks of [*Bomarzo*] with the air of a mathematics professor elucidating an equation," sporting his thick, black-framed glasses. Upon realizing he was late for another appointment (a worry, Ginastera confessed, that was atypical of Latin Americans), the "composer of an opera obsessed with sex and violence straightened his conservative tie, put on his black raincoat, took his rolled-up umbrella and hurried out."[173] Ginastera had been forced to rise above the anarchy of contemporary Latin American society, which his native country was able to contain only through "deplorable" dictatorships. Thanks also to the image of the tightly rolled umbrella—an apt symbol of raging phallic impulse under strict control—the reader surmises that Ginastera imposes order and control not only on his music but on his own life.

Yet *Bomarzo* fell flat. Unlike their counterparts in Washington, New York's critics found it dramatically unpersuasive and musically fallow; indeed the two critical contingents might as well have been discussing different works. The modernist idiom that dazzled Washington struck New York as superficial. Robert J. Landry of *Variety* remarked that "musically *Bomarzo* is replete with orchestral devices rather than music," while Schonberg, like the Argentine critics of the broadcast from Uruguay, complained of "effects [that have been heard] ad nauseam," which "end up just that—effects."[174] Further, Schonberg added, *Bomarzo* was in fact "really very old-fashioned" in that Ginastera relies on "techniques that have been in current use for the last 15 years and, in . . . a very calculated manner, uses them in a completely derivative and external manner." Demolishing with one swift stroke Ginastera's hard-won stature as a cold war modernist in the United States, Schonberg maintained that *Bomarzo* is "the work of a man who wants to be considered a modernist rather than a man who really is a modernist."

An article entitled "*Bomarzo* Fails to Shock" was obviously a response to the ad for the Columbia LP.[175] Various critics related this failure to heightened curiosity aroused by the Argentine censors. Schonberg observed that the mayor of Buenos Aires, Eugenio Schettini, had "banned the opera without seeing it, which is customary in these matters," and speculated that many in the audience came to the opera "licking their lips." Yet such individuals were disappointed, for *Bomarzo* was "small-time compared to . . . *Lulu* or *Il Trovatore*, for that matter."[176] Critics also made short work of the erotic ballet, which Winthrop Sargeant found "no more lurid than a country square dance."[177] All in all, it was easy enough to scold third-world censors—and by extension Ginastera—even if this meant overlooking the censorship practiced in U.S. society, however conspicuous the lack of a "mustachioed strongman."

Yet Schonberg, Ginastera's most relentless critic, ultimately vacillated. "All these impressions," he mused, "could be wrong." Wrapping up his two-article screed on the opera, Schonberg speculated that Ginastera might be redeemed by history. He could well be the "Meyerbeer of atonal opera," such that *Bomarzo* would stake out new territories much as Wagner's predecessor had united "drama, excitement, and audience appeal . . . [that] deep down . . . lacked really strong, vital, and original ideas" so as to prepare the way for the true master.[178] Schonberg situates *Bomarzo* in a narrative of progress, but of progress deferred: having renounced nationalism, Ginastera was now locked in a struggle with modernism in which he was ill equipped to succeed. Yet in a limited sense he might ultimately prevail, although only if *Bomarzo* did in fact hint at future glories. Ginastera, a "militant" Latin American nationalist turned compulsively punctual mathematics professor, could participate in first-world modernism, if only from the sidelines.

With *Bomarzo*, Ginastera confronted two publics in the United States. One, enmeshed in Pan Americanist interests, identified its own values in the opera and unabashedly proclaimed them. The fact that Vice President Humphrey and his colleagues leaped to their feet to applaud *Bomarzo* suggests that Washington *needed* to hear order, progress, and perhaps even symbols of "ethical superiority." The New York public, less invested in Pan Americanism, judged the work from a comparatively depoliticized viewpoint, albeit not without a degree of hypocrisy. Ultimately the two opposing receptions canceled one another out, with the result that *Bomarzo*, like its unfortunate protagonist, has largely been judged impotent, unable to sustain the aesthetic agenda conferred on it by cold war–era Pan Americanism.[179] Of all its characteristics, the sensationalist elements have left the strongest mark, for anyone looking up the work in the *Cambridge Companion to Twentieth-Century Opera* will find it under the heading "Sexuality."[180]

Only one commentator in the United States seems to have explicitly addressed politics apropos *Bomarzo*: the conductor Julius Rudel, who described its aleatoric passages as "real democracy in action."[181] He made this claim not in indignant reaction to the ban in Buenos Aires but on the eve of the Washington premiere. That is, Rudel needed no provocation to declare that Ginastera, a figurehead of musical Pan Americanism, was such a champion of democracy that he even infused it into his most abstruse music. Despite the military regime in his native country, Ginastera was an ally in the new world order. In so idealizing aleatory, Rudel, himself an immigrant to the United States during the Nazi period, privileges the multiple, spontaneous voices and individual stirrings democracy seeks to heed. Paradoxically the aleatory Rudel exalts can just as easily represent annihilation—of the composer's individual voice, so cherished during the cold war—and which can potentially erase a composer's most characteristic traits.[182] As Shreffler notes, "If freedom is exercised too relentlessly, the human subject is annihilated or becomes invisible. . . . [And] without the subject, freedom becomes irrelevant."[183]

Rudel's remark applies especially well to the erotic ballet. In that scene, so abundant in aleatory, we are hard-pressed to detect any hint of "democracy in action," real or otherwise. More than in any other portion of the opera, the aleatoric passages pit the totality of the performing forces—chorus, orchestra, dancers—against the hapless individual. The plight of that alienated figure, huddled in isolation over his fantasized orgasm (or *amor solitario*, to use one relevant Spanish term), bespeaks "the individual's dream of the irresistible collective," as Adorno put it in a different but hardly unrelated context.[184] Nor does Pier Francesco, whose musical persona depends on all the resources of modernism, overcome the unchecked mob. In equating aleatory with democracy, Rudel unwittingly highlights the limitations of cold war triumphalism. While some feared the communist hordes and their threat to individual creativity, neo-Freudians in the United States had expanded Freud's ideas on the individual to encompass Western industrial society as a whole, of which the United Sates was the "purest" example.[185] As such, its citizens were unusually susceptible to conformity and to estrangement from the self, as a host of studies, novels, and films of the era attest. In sum, the *Angst* of the erotic ballet was truer to the reality of the cold war—the lacerating alienation of the "lonely crowd"—than to the self-congratulatory applause of official Washington. Just as Ginastera's aleatory yielded to order and control, *Bomarzo* proposes that human behavior, inhibited by agendas, biases, and long-entrenched behaviors, can never rise above the society that surrounds it. The unfortunate hunchback remains a symbol of such impotence.

7 Memory, Music, and the Latin American Cold War

Frederic Rzewski's 36 Variations on "The People United Will Never Be Defeated!"

On March 21, 1975, the *New York Times* music critic Robert Sherman found himself on a curious assignment.[1] He was sent to Hunter College to cover a concert by the Chilean folk ensemble Quilapayún, known for its performances of *nueva canción*, a genre allied with social protest. (The name means "three bearded men" in Mapuche, one of Chile's indigenous languages, and refers to the ensemble's founding members.) Quilapayún had been based in Paris and supported by various European socialist parties since the 1973 CIA-supported military coup that ended the government of Salvador Allende and brought Augusto Pinochet to power. Due to visa problems, however, the musicians landed at Kennedy International Airport twenty minutes after curtain time. Back at Hunter, it seemed there would be no concert at all. As in many artistic-political spectacles of the 1930s, a few speeches were hastily improvised, along with impromptu performances by the U.S. folksingers Barbara Dane and Mike Glick, the Argentine singer Suni Paz, and a group of Filipinos in a number called "The Masses Only Are the Makers of History."[2] As Sherman reported, these substitutions satisfied the audience only partially.[3]

Patience was rewarded when Quilapayún showed up at 11:25 p.m., each member sporting his signature black poncho. Greeted with cheers and a standing ovation, the ensemble launched into a ballad by their former collaborator, the singer and guitarist Víctor Jara, who was executed in the early days of the coup for his role in the Allende government. For Sherman, the long wait was worth it. The concert was not only a bonding experience for the primarily South American audience, but it was musically satisfying to those less immediately concerned with Chile's political fate, or indeed the Dirty War (*guerra sucia*), the rash of atrocities and "disappearances" committed throughout Latin America by military dictatorships. "With great flair," he wrote, "the ensemble fused ancient Indian and other folklore styles with contemporary protest lyrics," while Quilapayún's indigenous instruments added "a fascinating splash of exotic color." In short, folklore, "exotic color," and the music of ancient America, familiar tropes in criticism of Latin American music, were now vehicles for social protest.

Among those U.S. citizens who sympathized with Quilapayún's political stance was Frederic Rzewski, a Harvard-trained composer born in Massachusetts, who honored the victims of Pinochet's coup with his imposing *36 Variations* on *"The People United Will Never Be Defeated!"* by Sergio Ortega and Quilapayún for solo piano.[4] In comparison with other Latin-themed works by U.S. composers, *The People United* is an aberration. Unlike *El salón México* or *Cuban Overture*, with their catchy dance rhythms and vivid travel imagery, Rzewski's composition is far from celebratory, commemorating one of the bleakest chapters in U.S.–Latin American relations.[5] In rooting them in the world of *nueva canción* and social protest, the composer defies both the brand of Latin American art music taken for granted in the United States and the cold war aesthetic. Yet because Rzewski channels his materials into a time-honored musical form, abetted by an impressive array of pianistic fireworks, the Variations are firmly situated in the Western canon. This chapter explores from a Pan Americanist perspective these ostensibly conflicting agendas in *The People United*, a work, I argue, that takes a position on historical memory, a central issue in post–Dirty War Latin America.

■ MÚSICA NACIONAL IN CHILE

As the cold war dragged on, many Latin Americans came to agree with the historian Federico Gil, who declared in 1971 that "the cycles of amity and attention [on the part of the United States] toward Latin America have consistently coincided with particular crises" rather than stemming from genuine benevolence.[6] Chile, however, initially seemed immune from such conflicts, for during the 1960s the Alliance for Progress looked favorably on the centrist policies of President Eduardo Frei. In 1970, however, Chile elected Allende, a socialist who had run unsuccessfully in 1952, 1958, and 1964.[7] Attempts to "save Chile," as an internal memo by CIA Director Richard Helms put it, involved generously funding Allende's opponent, fomenting labor and transportation strikes, destabilizing the Chilean economy, and, in the strategists' strikingly Orwellian language, "neutralizing" General René Schneider, commander in chief of the Chilean Army and loyal to Allende.[8] For the Nixon administration, Allende and his party, Unidad Popular (Popular Unity), threatened U.S. business interests and embodied what Henry Kissinger, then National Security Advisor, described as the "life-and-death struggle with the Soviet Union."[9]

To the Latin American Right, a potent symbol of this struggle was *nueva canción*, which they associated with "peasants and proletarians."[10] To the Left, *nueva canción* was a music of protest but also of memory. Arising throughout Latin America during the 1950s and 1960s, it represented the communitarian values its practitioners believed to be dying.[11] One principal *nueva canción* artist, Atahualpa Yupanqui, traversed the more remote outposts of his native Argentina on horseback, absorbing local customs, just as Violeta Parra collected songs from rural Chile. There *nueva canción* was but one type of *música nacional*, an umbrella term that implied a "revalorization of folklore and rediscovery of indigenous music," as Eduardo Carrasco, a member of Quilapayún, has explained.[12] Most *nueva canción* artists sang not folk songs, however, but original, often subtly expressive compositions shaped by popular tradition.[13] Parra's "Gracias a la vida" (Thanks to Life) is emblematic. One salient aspect of her rendering is the delicate yet penetrating sound of the *cuatro*, the small, four-stringed guitar Parra called her *guitarilla*. In fact the *cuatro* is associated not so much with Chile as with Venezuela and Nicaragua, highlighting the Pan Latin American and pan-ethnic reach of *nueva canción*. The same can be said of other commonly used *nueva canción* instruments: the *tiple*, a member of the guitar family used in Colombian *bambuco* music; the *quena* (*kena* in Aymara), an Andean wooden vertical flute; Andean panpipes; and the *bombo*, a cylindrical drum. Also common is the *charango*, a ukulele-size Andean lute associated with indigenous populations and which became a potent symbol in Bolivia in 1952 after the victory of the Nationalist Revolutionary Movement.[14] Instrumental timbre was thus a defining element of *nueva canción*, and Allende's message was so closely associated with it that, according to no less an eyewitness than Jara's widow, Joan Jara, "there was no doubt that the sound of Popular Unity was that of indigenous instruments."[15]

Nueva canción artists also battled encroaching mass culture, for which they believed the Colossus of the North was largely responsible. The influence of Frank Sinatra, the Beach Boys, Diana Ross and the Supremes, Engelbert Humperdinck, and the Monkees was ubiquitous: as another Quilapayún member, Guillermo Oddo, reminisced in 1977, "Our hit parade was full of American rock"; for Joan Jara, "the mass media were filled with propaganda for the 'American Way of Life,' newspaper stands were plastered with cheap American comics; the radios swamped with American pop music."[16] In the minds of many Chileans, U.S. mass culture was linked to U.S. business, including the copper-mining companies Kennecott and Anaconda, which earned huge profits for shareholders and business elites while exploiting Chilean workers.[17] The Final Resolution of the First Protest Song Conference, held in Havana in August 1967, declared that song must be "a weapon at the service of the peoples, not a consumer product of capitalism to alienate us."[18] Ariel Dorfman and Armand Mattelart also took on U.S. corporate power, but by excoriating a quintessential symbol of the Good Neighbor period. In *How to Read Donald Duck: Imperialist Ideology in the Disney Comic* (1972) the authors reduce the protagonist of OIAA-era cartoons to an insidious "registered trademark" that spreads manufactured perkiness to subaltern populations enslaved to U.S. commerce.[19] Likewise the Víctor Jara song "Who Killed Carmencita?" ("¿Quién mató a Carmencita?") recounts the suicide of a girl from a working-class Santiago neighborhood, a victim of mindless consumerism deceived by "lies and bottled happiness."[20]

Throughout the 1960s, *nueva canción*'s symbolic power intensified and became increasingly associated with Allende. During his 1969 electoral campaign, he attended the First Festival of *Nueva Canción Chilena* in Santiago's National Stadium, where he stood under a banner that read "There can be no revolution without songs." Another festival took place in 1970, the year he became president.[21] At this time, the LP *Canto al Programa: Songs of the Popular Unity Program* was released on the government-subsidized label DICAP (Discoteca del Cantar Popular). Although *nueva canción's* actual record sales remained low, Chileans flocked to stadiums and public spaces to hear *nueva canción* artists in these massive, participatory events.[22] Allende's agenda, which included nationalizing industry and banking and defying local elites who collaborated with foreign-owned, profit-driven companies, emerged in various songs, such as the rather prosaically titled "Canción de la propiedad social y privada" (Song of Social and Private Property) and "Canción de la reforma agraria" (Song of Agrarian Reform), performed by the ensemble Inti-Illimani.[23] Such efforts corresponded to a broader campaign, detailed in Popular Unity documents, according to which film, music, theater, art, education, and the media would be recouped on behalf of the exploited Chilean people.[24]

In general, *nueva canción* artists saw the globalization of culture much as Néstor García Canclini has described it: a "mode in which the elites manage the intersection of different historical temporalities in order to incorporate them into a global project."[25] Under such circumstances local identity can become a compelling priority. Some *nueva canción* artists were nonetheless willing to compromise with global mass culture, justifying this practice as a counterhegemonic move.[26] The Cuban *nueva trova* singer Silvio Rodríguez made no secret of his admiration for the Beatles, whose music was outlawed in Cuba.[27] Twice Jara collaborated with the Chilean pop group Los Blops, recording "Abre la ventana" (Open the Window) and "El derecho de vivir en paz" (The Right to Live in Peace). The latter, which protests U.S. policy in Vietnam, incorporates electric bass and the obbligato lines of two electric guitars à la Carlos Santana, enhanced with electronic organ and a drum set; a concluding "fall," reminiscent of Jimi Hendrix's celebrated wrap-up to "The Star-Spangled Banner," comments on the rabidly anti-U.S. lyrics.[28] Jara described such compromises as "invading the cultural invasion" and argued that even commercial culture could be elevated for the greater good of spreading Popular Unity's message.[29] Here he anticipated the unlikely marriage of countercultural and commercial values soon to be consummated on Madison Avenue, thanks to which likenesses of Che Guevara came to grace the coffee mugs and tennis-racket covers of middle-class consumers in the United States.[30] Such phenomena raise the same broad questions germane to music and Pan Americanism discussed throughout this book. Is difference inevitably swallowed up by totalizing mass culture? Is rapprochement possible for those who refuse to consider "high and mass culture as objectively related and dialectically interdependent phenomena," as Jameson has proposed?[31] Who cares if you listen? Just as in prior musical testaments to Pan Americanism, Rzewski's *The People United* probes the elusive boundary between regional and universal, elites and masses, difference and sameness. Such negotiations also affected Chilean art music during the 1960s and 1970s. Challenging the cold war aesthetic, conservatory-trained composers such as Luis Advis and Sergio Ortega sought to create art music for the masses, even as some argued that elite forms were inimical to popular tastes.[32] One vehicle that fulfilled this agenda was the *cantata popular*, which combined features of the baroque cantata, loosely adapted, and folkloric genres, often with explicitly political texts based on actual events. For example, Advis's *Santa María de Iquique* recounts the 1907 massacre of nitrate workers in northern Chile by alternating *relatos* (spoken narratives), instrumental interludes, songs, choruses, and *pregones* (street cries) with trio sonata texture (no. 5). Most salient is the instrumentation. Limiting conventional instruments to cello and bass, Advis calls for two guitars, two *quenas, charango,* and *bombo,* "the sound of Popular Unity (fig. 7a, website)."

Probably the best known of these avowedly non-elitist art music composers was Sergio Ortega, who composed *cantatas populares*, operas, chamber music, and film scores and collaborated frequently with Quilapayún and Jara. His song "¡El Pueblo Unido Jamás Será Vencido!" (The People United Will Never be Defeated!) dates from a few months before the 1973 coup. He recounts that upon hearing the well-known chant during a street protest, he rushed to the piano and composed the song in a flash of inspiration.[33] Both the song and the battle cry that inspired it have endured in a parallel existence. The former served as Rzewski's theme and was also recorded by Quilapayún. The chant was shouted by Spanish-speaking protesters on the streets of London when Pinochet was arrested there in 1998. On many other occasions, it resounded in translation, as in Chicago in late 2008 during the strike by Republic Window and Door workers, when the effects of the so-called Great Recession first began creeping into public consciousness in the United States. During the 1970s it was popular in Italy, where Rzewski, then living in Rome, likely heard it.[34]

On September 11, 1973—the "other September 11," as Dorfman has called it—the presidential palace in Santiago was attacked by Hawk Hunter fire bombers and Allende shot himself through the chin with a submachine gun.[35] Another casualty was *nueva canción*. So keenly did Pinochet and his forces fear its influence that just days after the coup, Jara was taken to the National Stadium and shot. The emblematic timbres of *nueva canción* were silenced as well. Carrasco recalls, "In the first weeks of the [coup] . . . all the best-known folklorists were called to a meeting to be informed that certain folkloric instruments such as the *quena* and the *charango* were [now] prohibited."[36] Performance venues (*peñas*) were closed, and DICAP was ordered to erase all of its master tapes; the company itself was then shut down and its archives destroyed.[37] Classically trained musicians with no particular connection to *nueva canción* were also vulnerable. According to Orrego-Salas, the conductor Jorge Peña was put to death for touring with a children's orchestra in Cuba.[38] Nor was film music exempt: movies seen to foment communism—sometimes by evincing too great an interest in Russia, as was the case with that dangerous statement of Marxist values, *Fiddler on the Roof*—were prohibited.[39] Like the Ministry of Truth in

George Orwell's *1984*, Pinochet's cultural blackout (*apagón cultural*) sought to obliterate any memory—of the Allende era.

Indeed, according to Orwell's Ministry of Truth, "control of the past depends above all on the training of memory," just as memory's flip side, forgetting, was also fundamental: "If it is necessary to rearrange one's memories or to tamper with written records, then it is necessary to forget *why* one has done so." Orwell's fictionalized account of memory's vagaries is scientifically grounded.[40] As the psychologist Daniel L. Schachter observes, an individual habitually reformulates his or her memories to accommodate the demands of the present, always conditioned by the needs of self and society in the face of changing circumstances.[41] In Pinochet's Chile, the vanquished Left realized these needs by venerating *nueva canción* in the aftermath of Jara's execution. Thanks to the international careers of Quilapayún and Inti-Illimani, a global audience also paid homage to its values. Musical memory on the Right was also reshaped. Months after the coup, the indigenous instruments of "peasants and proletarians" began easing their way back into Chilean musical life, now, however, enhancing works by Telemann, Vivaldi, Geminiani, and other baroque composers thanks to the ensemble Barroco Andino (Andean Baroque).[42] The guitar and *charango* furnished the continuo of movement 2 of the "Winter" concerto in Vivaldi's *Four Seasons*, for example, with the *quena* taking the melody. Whereas these instruments had once reinforced lyrics of change and resistance at stadium sing-alongs, they advanced no overt political agenda in Barroco Andino's textless repertory, which was frequently presented to relatively restricted audiences, often in churches.

This phenomenon dovetails with the unusual status worldwide of baroque music in the 1960s and 1970s, which Robert Fink has explored in relation to the late-capitalist cultural practice of repetition.[43] The urge to repeat ourselves, he argues, manifests itself not only in mass production and advertising but in various forms of musical expression, such as minimalism (minimal music), techno, and the Suzuki method of music instruction, the Japanese system transplanted to the United States in the 1960s according to which children listen to recordings of their pieces several hours a day and repeat them many hundreds of times in practice.[44] Another vehicle for repetition is the music of Vivaldi, Telemann, and Geminiani, with its reiterative patterns, slow harmonic rhythm, and predictable structures. The vogue for this repertory coincided with the development of the LP and the record changer, enabling listeners to play one concerto grosso after another and immerse themselves in hours of "continuous and uninterrupted listening pleasure," as marketers claimed.[45] *Immerse* is the key word. Critics of this music, dubbed "barococo," doubted that it was actually listened to; rather, barococo music might accompany a cocktail party at which the clinking of glasses and hum of urbane conversation ensured that the Vivaldi concerto whirring in the background functioned as little more than patterned noise confirming the guests' sense of their secure place in the world. Accordingly critics of barococo music inveighed against its lack of "depth" and "organicism," finding its "bright, brittle, fast-moving, surface glitter" bereft of artistic integrity.[46] Of course, similar charges have been leveled at minimalism. Just as the repeated patterns in Geminiani encourage hypnosis (immersion) rather than thoughtful analysis, minimalism has been attacked as "regressive and infantile," reflecting, like barococo music, the conformity of late capitalist society.[47] In eschewing complexity in favor of antiteleological repetitiveness, often by repeating a single melodic fragment, minimalist composers also repudiated the cold war aesthetic.[48]

In Barroco Andino, the *quena, charango,* and *tiple,* rendered neutral by the cultural blackout, could be perceived as "glitter," little more than colorful timbres piggybacking onto an elitist expression wholly divorced from the status of the instruments themselves. Riding the surface of this repetitive repertory, the indigenous instruments lulled Pinochet's censors and obscured collective memory.[49] This relationship, between repeating and remembering, is also essential to *The People United.* In that work, Rzewski pits a carefully crafted teleological structure against the compulsion to repeat, a phenomenon intimately related to memory and forgetting.

■ *"THE PEOPLE UNITED WILL NEVER BE DEFEATED!"*
THROUGH A PAN AMERICANIST LENS

In 1975 Rzewski discussed the cold war aesthetic in an interview with Walter Zimmerman, the German composer and enthusiast for U.S. experimental music.[50] Because "the most advanced music was abstract, serial, formalistic . . . [with] a kind of universal validity," Rzewski explained, composers of his generation concluded that the audience was negligible.[51] He sensed, however, that new approaches were in the offing: "Now I think the new question we're coming up with . . . is precisely . . . *who* is the audience, who am I trying to speak to, and what am I trying to say. Am I working for the bourgeois public? Am I working for Rockefeller . . . or the banks or the students?"[52] Making no secret of his Marxist sympathies, Rzewski composed not only *The People United* but *Attica* (1971), which takes as its subject matter the brutal suppression of a riot at Attica Prison in New York State, and *Four North American Ballads* (1978–79), solo-piano arrangements of U.S. labor songs.[53] On account of such works, he was dubbed a "political composer."[54]

Ironically, *The People United* grew out of the 1976 Bicentennial of the United States. Several organizations, including the National Endowment for the Arts, the New York State Council on the Arts, the Washington Performing Arts Society, and several major symphony orchestras, made available $40,000 for twelve pianists to commission and perform works by U.S. composers, establishing the Bicentennial Piano Series.[55] Ursula Oppens commissioned *The People United* and premiered it in Washington on February 7, 1976. Scholars have commented on the incongruousness of musically showcasing one of the most dismal episodes in U.S.–Latin American relations in Bicentennial-happy Washington.[56] Yet Rzewski intended no such meaning. Much the way the U.S. Communist Party leader Earl Browder declared in the 1930s that "communism [was] twentieth-century Americanism," Rzewski considered the Bicentennial "the celebration of our own ongoing revolutionary ideals in the United States."[57] Thanks to the work of Senator Frank Church of Idaho and the journalist Seymour Hersh, moreover, the public of 1976 was becoming increasingly aware of the CIA's involvement in bringing Pinochet to power, of cover-ups by the Nixon administration, and of the regime's atrocities.[58] In some circles, there was deep and sustained soul-searching, along with cynicism and shame, over the true nature of U.S.-style democracy in the post-Vietnam, post-Watergate era. If the fireworks and omnipresent red-white-and-blue bunting of the Bicentennial were staged to awaken one version of historical memory, The People United rudely challenged it.

Critics have taken a variety of positions on the work over the years. Some have circumvented its political intent, marveling instead at its virtuosity.[59] Others have applauded the work's political message. Paul Driver described The People United as "a clenched fist of protest" and even claimed that the Variations "had a significant consciousness-raising effect at the time of their first performance" despite the absence of any corroborating accounts.[60] Recalling Waldo Frank's praise for "wholeness"—and with near Rosenfeldian enthusiasm—Driver concluded that in The People United, "Rzewski has been remarkably able to express the musical and the political connotations of his thinking . . . at the same time."[61] Reviewing Oppens's 1978 performance at Carnegie Hall, Ainslee Cox, however, complained of long-windedness, observing that like many another political statement, "[The People United] is filled with rhetoric and lasts half the night."[62] John Rockwell was far more vehement on Rzewski's attempt to blend the musical and the political. Proposing that the composer's concern for his audience was little more than quaint, Rockwell acknowledged that politically committed music had once enjoyed a certain status in the history of music in the United States, largely in relation to late nineteenth- and early twentieth-century immigration, with its "initial squalor."[63] But by the time Rzewski came of age, composers in the United States had repudiated political art, a shift that, in part, reflected the liberal society in which they lived and, Rockwell "innocently" suggested, the fact that "people were just happier in . . . capitalist democracies than they were elsewhere."[64] Rzewski also erred in his choice of idiom. In indulging in the romantic virtuosic piano variations, Rockwell maintained, he "subvert[ed] his esthetic inclinations to his political opinions," trying to "slip his audience a political pill in the sugar coating of a musical style they will find palatable."[65] In contrast to the authentic political music of artists better qualified to represent the oppressed (Rockwell cites rock, reggae, and ska groups), Rzewski and other so-called political composers both sabotage their message and retard the progress of art:

Rzewski's political art is an art of condescension. And of folly. . . . Neither [Cornelius Cardew] nor Rzewski nor Christian Wolff has . . . made much of an impact on the working classes, or on the third-world masses, or on China, or whomever it is they are ostensibly celebrating in their music. . . . And despite an occasional flurry of press attention, they haven't done much to sway the petty bourgeoisie in any perceivable direction.[66]

Not surprisingly, Wolff—one of Rockwell's politically minded composers—admired the Variations. In his liner notes for Oppens's recording (Vanguard, 1979), he argued that far from pandering to the public, Rzewski synthesized political and musical objectives in a completely new way. So effective is this synthesis that Wolff even hears Allende's party as a unifying concept: "The movement of the whole piece is towards a new unity—an image of popular unity—made up of related but diverse, developing elements . . . coordinated and achieved by a blend of irresistible logic and spontaneous expression."[67]

To test these contrasting assertions, we consider Rzewski's choice of form. As Elaine Sisman has noted, variation form is often stigmatized.[68] For one thing, it depends upon repetition, and its overall structure may involve little more than the stringing together of short, strophic forms, all resting on the same harmonic progression. As such, it presumably lacks the narrative depth or formal integrity of teleological, end-oriented schemes such as sonata and rondo. Likewise the often arbitrary ordering of variations suggests that developmental complexity may be absent. Since some composers choose popular tunes as themes (and proceed to treat them as little more than a pretext for virtuosic display), variation form has often gratified a less than savvy public, one competent only to follow the most basic of cues. Yet, Sisman notes, composers throughout history have been stimulated by the rhetorical challenge of achieving diversity within all these restrictions.

In shaping this potentially unsatisfactory form, Rzewski marshals a tremendous range of compositional devices, including manipulations of the all-combinatorial hexachord, tone clusters, Webernian textures, minimalism, registral displacements, shades of jazz, improvisation, and aleatory. (In several passages, the pianist is asked to whistle, shout, or sing.)[69] Showing requisite solidarity for Pinochet's victims is no mean feat for the performer. Throughout this grueling work, Rzewski not only requires the pianist to be something of a quick-change artist to accommodate this stylistic variety but also demands a level of endurance and technical polish comparable to that required for virtuosic works by Liszt or Rachmaninoff. From the rapid shifts required in Variation 4 to the wide leaps and *glissandi* of Variation 10, the relentless toccata-like Variation 20, or the rapid repeated notes of Variation 23, the pianist must sustain this high level of energy for nearly an hour. To be sure, Rzewski urges the interpreter on with spirited instructions ("confidently," "struggling," "with determination," "expansive, with a victorious feeling," "in a militant manner," "relentless, uncompromising"), coaxing out of the performer the very athleticism he so amply demonstrates in his most recent recording.[70]

Other compositional strategies awaken memory. One is musical quotation, which may conjure up a composer's personal associations (these may or not be intelligible to listeners) or serve as a synecdoche for an era or for a previous musical work.[71] Although Rzewski intended the Variations primarily as an homage to the "struggle in Chile and similar struggles worldwide," he also commented that "parallels to present threats exist in the past and . . . it is important to learn from them."[72] In quoting Hanns Eisler's "Solidarity Song," composed for a Berlin-based agitprop troupe and used in a 1932 film, Rzewski transports listeners to what Seeger called "proletarian music" of the 1930s, the workers' choruses composed by art music composers and dotted with meter shifts, accented dissonances, and angular, sometimes unpredictable melodic turns that did not necessarily come naturally to singing workers.[73] (Seeger, for example, wondered if Copland's workers' song "Into the Streets May First!" would ever be sung "on the picket line.")[74] In The People United, Rzewski bridges the rift between masses and elites by counterbalancing Eisler's idealized musical utterance with a "real" workers' song, "Bandiera rossa," which was widely sung in Italy in the beginning of the twentieth century and is considered a classic of the genre.[75] By showcasing it, especially in the written-out cadenza to Variation 13, Rzewski expressed his personal gratitude to the many Italians who sheltered Chilean refugees during the 1970s.[76] Of course, Rzewski quotes Ortega's theme, redolent of the more recent past, at the outset. But he also gives it pride of place throughout The People United, ensuring that its presence is felt in nearly all the variations and that it weaves a unifying thread through the eclectic display of musical styles. Another memory charged strategy Rzewski employs is allusion. Less unambiguous than quotation, allusion can depend not only on motives but on similarities of formal structure, intervallic patterns, rhythm, metrical structure, placement of agogic accents, texture, or register between two musical works.[77] Given its less than straightforward nature, the memory awakened by music allusion is likelier to be open to multiple readings.[78]

Rzewski also builds memory into the Variations' overall structure. Defying the limitations of the form, he arranges the work in broadly proportioned units that confer "organic inevitability" on the whole while confirming the listener's sense of musical time, thus recalling the monumental sets of keyboard variations from the Western canon. For example, in Bach's "Goldberg" Variations (a work to which The People United is often loosely compared) the listener senses a regularly paced unfolding of time thanks to the canons that occur every three variations. In Thirty-three Variations on a Waltz by Diabelli, op. 120, Beethoven forges a narrative of "consolidation and transfiguration," especially from Variation 25, as William Kinderman notes.[79] Given the weight of the magnificent concluding fugue in Brahms's Variations on a Theme of Handel, op. 24, that work is also end-oriented; movement-like groupings of variations that accumulate weight and tension as the work progresses also contribute to its teleological momentum.[80]

In *The People United* the listener encounters far more than a mere "stringing to-gether" of harmonically similar substructures. Rather, Rzewski divides the work into six sets of six variations, the individual variations of which comprise twenty-four measures each. With one exception, the sixth variation of every set recalls through consecutive four-measure snippets that set's previous five variations in their original order. Set 6 (Variations 31–36) sums up *all* the previous variations: in Variation 31, Rzewski refers to Variations 1, 7, 13, 19, and 25 via four-measure units; in Variation 32 he refers to Variations 2, 8, 20, and 26, for example. In con-cluding these compendium variations, he sometimes telescopes the material re-collected at the beginning of the variation; in the last four measures of Variation 31, for instance, we find one-measure references to Variations 1, 7, 13, 19. At the end of set 6, an optional cadenza precedes a restatement of the theme. Thus *The People United* consistently prods the listener not only to remember past musical events but to digest them in the ongoing present as they filter through time. Such filtering is a necessary ingredient in apprehending and constructing the past. As the historian Donald A. Ritchie states, "Only the passage of time enables people to make sense out of earlier events in their lives."[81] The rhetorical force of *The People United* depends largely on the desire to "make sense" in this way (fig. 7b, website).

By strewing our path to the final set with so many musical reminiscences, Rzewski ensures that by the time the listener arrives at set 6, linear, forward-moving time will find itself in tension with the past of the work, mirroring the tension between the memory of past events and linear time.[82] Jonathan Kramer, who has explored musical memory in relation to our perceptions of musical time, observes that "the perceptual present stretches out in both directions [past and present] from the instant of now." The "instant of now" is finite, however, because it ultimately "blends into the past as [musical] information moves into memory."[83] Throughout *The People United*, the listener senses this uncertainty over "the instant of now," especially in the climactic set 6, which, in forcing repe-tition to a degree unprecedented in the rest of the work, invites us to look back at the Variations' entire history—a term sometimes used interchangeably with memory.[84] To be sure, many musical works recall earlier ideas for coherence or intelligibility. The degree to which *The People United* insists on past musical events is exceptional, however. Whereas Rockwell found Rzewski's variation form and its romantic flourishes a cheap shot, Wolff essentially credits set 6, the "extraordinary intensification, ... clarification and unification" of which depend on the overall formal design, for the work's narrative power.[85]

The one significant departure from the otherwise strict structure of *The People United* is set 5 (Variations 25–30). Among its distinguishing features is length: each of its variations breaks the bonds of the twenty-four-measure scheme, with the summarizing variation, no. 30, running at seventy-two measures, the longest in the entire work. Set 5 also encompasses greater diversity of quotation and allusion than any previous set and boasts the greatest stylistic variety; Robert Wason registers "extreme stylistic dichotomies" and proposes that Rzewski arranges these so as to provoke conflict.[86] It would seem that critical praise for the work's "clarification and unification" should thus take into account the peculiarities of set 5. Its first variation, Variation 25, begins with subtle shifts in tempo that culminate at m. 7 in a melodic open fifth that Rzewski asks be played "like a question." A four-bar, thickly voiced sequence (Variation 25, mm. 41–43) leads to the "answer," namely, the B section of Eisler's "Solidarity Song," which dominates Variation 26, to be played "in a militant manner." The A section appears only in m. 21, with a tonal center of D; an all-combinatorial hexachord, 6–20, then figures, embedding both D-minor and A-minor triads (a procedure introduced in Variation 2).[87] The rare listener acquainted with the text of "Solidarity Song" may recall the injunction at this point, "Go forward and do not forget" ("Vorwärts! Und nicht vergessen die Solidarität!"), which Rzewski highlights with a gradual thinning of texture such that the largely unembellished melodic line surfaces over a resonant, arpeggiated bass (mm. 21ff.); the boisterous climax coinciding with Eisler's setting of the word "Solidarity!"[88] Following this outburst is Variation 27, in which a fifth-based melody is swapped off between the pianist's hands, leading to a cadenza in which "repetitions (or omissions) . . . may be varied ad lib." The cadenza then launches an extended section dominated by melodic fragments of narrow intervallic range, repeated in steady eighth-note values and enhanced with parallel triads over a drone accompaniment, all the while absorbing several meter changes.

This is the first of four minimalist passages in the work, all of which are concentrated in set 5. The unceasing pulsations and reiterative patterns of minimalism, as in barococo music, presumably lack teleological thrust, or a sense of "climax and directionality," as the minimalist composer La Monte Young noted.[89] In Variation 27, moreover, the goal-less minimalist passage interrupts the end-driven structure imposed on the variation form that has prevailed throughout the entire work to that point. Holding sway for over two pages, it risks plunging the memory-consciousness of the first four sets, along with the forward motion of time, into shapeless stasis. The listener lacks teleological moorings and becomes immersed in waves of time-bending repetitions over a slow-moving surface. To be sure, a series of chords in triple meter (marked "fierce") interrupts, followed by a nine-measure restatement of the opening material of Variation 27. But the interruption makes barely a dent; an even longer minimalist passage promptly ensues, now a scalar pattern centering around B that gradually expands registrally such that a two-bar fragment is repeated for over two and a half pages. In Variation 28, Rzewski begins by recalling the march character of "Solidarity Song" with repeated chords (or single notes) in the left hand and triadic harmonies in the right. He then inserts a fragment of Ortega's theme at mm. 23–26, which he treats sequentially. Beginning in m. 27, he isolates an even briefer rhythmic fragment of the same, ultimately spinning it out into steady waves of eighth notes, another minimalist passage from which a contextually surprising quotation surfaces. A fugitive yet unmistakable glimpse of the C-major Prelude of Book I of Bach's *Well-Tempered Clavier* arises out of the motoric spinning, only

Example 7a Frederic Rzewski. *36 Variations on "The People United Will Never Be Defeated!" by Sergio Ortega and Quilapayún.* Variation 27, mm. 23–38. Reprinted by kind permission of Seesma (Sociedad Española de Ediciones Musicales, S.A.).

to be liquidated via repeated broken triads. Unlike "Bandiera rossa" or "Solidarity Song," the *Well-Tempered Clavier* exists apart from the rough-and-tumble of politics and the struggles of the masses. It does, however, comment on minimalism; one critic called the C-major Prelude one of minimalism's "old and honorable antecedents" given its unvarying rhythm and repeated patterns.[90] This emblematic status even served as fodder for "joke minimalism," as in Peter Schickele's *Einstein on the Fritz,* in which the pianist repeats the first bars eight times each.[91] (The C-major Prelude, minus the fugue, also appears in book 5 of the Suzuki piano method so that young students may repeat it "100,000 times," as Shinichi Suzuki, the originator of the method, advocated.)[92] (exs. 7a, 7b).

In Variation 29, Rzewski introduces a new melodic fragment with prominent perfect fourths, insistent repetition, and agogic displacements, an allusion to Steve Reich's *Violin Phase* of 1967. Scored for either a single violinist and three-track tape or for four violins (Reich's preference), *Violin Phase* is an emblematic example of "gradual phase-shifting," as Reich himself called this process.[93] As in Reich's *Piano Phase* of the same year, *Violin Phase* plays with our notions of

Example 7b Frederic Rzewski. *36 Variations on "The People United Will Never Be Defeated!" by Sergio Ortega and Quilapayún.* Variation 28, mm. 45–48. Reprinted by kind permission of Seesma (Sociedad Española de Ediciones Musicales, S.A.).

"ahead" and "behind," ultimately rendering these familiar musical concepts meaningless.[94] He was hardly out to create a trancelike state in his audience. Rather, Reich hoped listeners would focus on details made more prominent through repetition or on unexpected relationships taking shape over the course of the musical process. (Rzewski himself tested this idea in his *Les Moutons de Panurge* of 1969.)[95] Given the lack of distinction between "ahead" and behind," the "instant of now" is also hard to pin down. Many who listen to this music lose awareness of time; paradoxically, despite minimalism's almost rabidly tonal language, listeners' tonal expectations are thwarted so as to engender what K. Robert Schwartz has called "a transitory aural illusion to the realm of reality."[96] By quoting a fragment of Ortega's theme (mm. 7 and 14) and weaving it into the musical process, Rzewski interjects "the realm of reality," mingling quotation with allusion, both charged with memory and both obscuring further the carefully arranged referents to past musical events earlier in the piece (exs. 7c, 7d).

In injecting stasis into the Variations' forward momentum, the minimalist variations of Set 5 also arrest memory. As David Schwartz has pointed out, minimalism's rejection of formal designs rooted in progression and development thwarts the ways of memory.[97] Philip Glass discussed minimalism and memory apropos his own *Music in Twelve Parts* (1974), four hours long and rarely performed but considered an icon of musical minimalism.[98] As Glass explains, the music occurs outside of ordinary time, in a repetitive realm in which "neither memory nor anticipation . . . have a place in sustaining the reality of the musical experience."[99] Repetition has long been considered the antithesis of true memory. In his essay "Remembering, Repeating, and Working-Through," Freud considers it but a substitute for memory, and a poor one at that. A neurotic patient, he notes, "repeats instead of remembering"; under the weight of repressed experiences or fantasies, he or she is afflicted with the "compulsion to repeat, which now replaces the impulse to remember."[100] Such patients are unable to situate their past behavior in anything other than a repetition-dominated present; that is, they are capable only of "repeating a still-present past," as Dominick LaCapra calls this syndrome.[101] Freud also addresses patients' inability to discriminate between repeating and remembering in "Beyond the Pleasure Principle," wherein he describes patients who "*repeat* the repressed material as a

Example 7c Frederic Rzewski, *36 Variations on "The People United Will Never Be Defeated!" by Sergio Ortega and Quilapayún*. Variation 29, mm. 1–3. Reprinted by kind permission of Seesma (Sociedad Española de Ediciones Musicales, S.A.).

Example 7d Steve Reich. *Violin Phase* (Reich VIOLIN PHASE). © 1979 Universal Edition (London) Ltd. All rights reserved. Used by permission of European American Music Distributors Company, U.S. and Canadian agent for Universal Edition (London) Ltd.

contemporary experience instead of, as the physician would prefer to see, *remembering* it as something belonging to the past."[102] Paul Ricoeur, in his magisterial study *Memory, History, Forgetting*, simply states, "Repetition amounts to forgetting."[103] For these reasons, torture victims undergoing therapy are treated in such a way as to make them stop mentally repeating their grotesque experiences. Once they can do more than merely relive—repeat—their trauma, they will have achieved the ability to *remember*, with its enabling capacity to distinguish past from present. Therapists may even ask patients to speak their stories into a tape recorder as if making a documentary, thereby containing the trauma in the past and investing it with the trappings of historical record keeping.[104]

To what extent do these concerns inform set 5? With Variation 29 concluded, we might wonder how the minimalist variations will be treated in Variation 30, the summarizing variation of the set. All are recalled (with eight rather than four measures per reminiscence) except Variation 29. Yet, as Platonic theory has it, memory is "the presence of the absent thing."[105] By suppressing Variation 29, Rzewski invites us to *remember* the blurring of "ahead" and "behind" it introduced, now suddenly assigned the status of "the absent thing"—of memory. In apprehending this absence, we register the waves of minimalism in set 5, dropped, as if by chance, into a grand-narrative, memory-studded formal strategy perhaps unprecedented in its cumulative thrust. Unaware of the passage of time and with the regularly timed account of "earlier events" suddenly held in abeyance, we grope for the "absent thing."

In set 5, we question the very mechanisms of memory and forgetting, critical today to Latin Americans confronting the Dirty War. Some look backward, combing the past for accountability and seeking punishment for government officials, the military, the clergy, and the ordinary citizens involved in the grisly agendas of the various regimes. Others advocate "moving forward." These debates shape legislation, public display, scholarship, and art. In Argentina a museum was established in 2004 at the Navy Mechanics School, a center of torture during the dictatorship of 1976–83. Photographs of those "disappeared" still gaze at readers from the pages of the Buenos Aires daily *Página 12*, usually on the anniversary of the day these individuals were last seen. Films such as *The Official Story* (1985) and *Hermanas* (2005), along with novels by José Rodríguez Elizondo, José Leandro Urbina, and Alberto Fuguet, grapple with the quirks, omissions, and concealments of memory.[106] Composers address these themes, as in Rafael Aponte-Ledée's *En memoria a Salvador Allende* and Hilda Dianda's . . . *después el silencio*.[107] Also urgently debated is the relationship between memory and discourse. However problematic the status of the Argentine author Jorge Luis Borges vis-à-vis the Dirty War, his explorations of memory and discourse in the short story "The Night of the Gifts" ("La noche de los dones") remain compelling; its narrator concludes a tale of love, death, and revelation by remarking, "The years pass and I've told this story so many times that I no longer know whether I remember it as it was or whether it's only my words I'm remembering."[108] Another Borges character, often cited in memory studies, is Funes el Memorioso (literally, "Funes the Prodigious Rememberer"), who is cursed with remembering everything, from the shapes of clouds to the leaves on every tree. In short, Funes is incapacitated: unable to synthesize or generalize, he can neither refer to general concepts nor synthesize the events of the past in a coherent narrative, despite his consummate command of its details. The dilemma of Borges's protagonist thus poses a fundamental question: How much can we stand to remember? It is difficult to imagine any post–Dirty War artistic treatment of memory that does not somehow grapple with this conundrum.

In *The People United* the notoriously close-mouthed Rzewski provides his own answer in the sixth and final set. Just as the patient "working through" neurosis must be helped to distinguish memory from mere repetition, the patient must also come to acknowledge that his neurosis is not "contemptible but . . . an enemy worthy of his mettle."[109] Accordingly, set 6 takes on the lacunae in memory evoked in set 5. The delicate interplay among the past of the piece, our memory of it, and the future-oriented, ongoing sweep of the form, once interrupted but now on track again, burst forth in a final message of formal coherence and searing inevitability. In sum, the minimalist passages of *The People United* declare that memory is fragile. The sixth and final set proclaims that it is also essential.

Epilogue

This book has asked: What do we in the United States know about Latin American art music, and how do we know it? I have approached this question in several ways. For one thing, I have connected it to the broader pursuit of defining "America" and, by extension, American music. To that end, I have compared criticism of familiar and less familiar works by Latin American composers (along with works about Latin America by U.S. composers) with the discourse of Pan Americanism at different points in that project. I have also taken into account musical trends in Latin America and opinions of Latin Americans. As such, broad outlines of sameness-embracing have emerged, a phenomenon not previously probed in depth in relation to this repertory. It inspired, often fancifully, tributes to a shared classicism, to the unity of the machine and the indigenous heritage, to a common American rhythm, to antinationalist universalism, and to sublimation. By the 1970s the rhetoric of difference, however, came to inform U.S. scholarship of Latin American music, responding in part to north-south conflicts during the cold war, when Latin Americans resisted the hegemonic power of the United States by asserting nationalism. Some U.S. scholars, surely in sympathy, followed suit.

Comparing these contrasting epistemologies leaves no doubt that representations are created rather than intrinsic.[1] In formulating future representations, we can ask if a given work will be served by exoticizing or essentializing adjectives and whether claims of "national effect" or "national character" should be privileged. At the same time, we can acknowledge the structures of hierarchy and privilege that have sustained many a universalist project throughout history, along with the crimes that have been committed in universalism's name. There is no reason why sameness-embracing universalism aware of its often sorry past cannot be open to new points of reference, including difference-generating relationships as they have unfolded within larger historical processes. Perhaps most important, such an endeavor will disclose new identities for musical works previously marginalized by scholars of American music.

Where does the repertory discussed in this book stand today? Although Chávez's sonatas and sonatinas inspired some of Rosenfeld's most effusive prose, nowadays they are rarely heard. But echoes of the discursive world they inhabited in the 1920s reverberate. Just as Rosenfeld expounded upon Chávez's "austerity" in relation to the qualities of ur-classicism, critics today characterize his music as "austere" or as inhabiting an "austere sonic realm."[2] Yet "austerity" has also served Copland's Piano Variations: as Arthur Berger remarked in 1953, references to the work seldom went "unaccompanied by the epithet 'austere.'"[3] It has also been marshaled to distinguish the Variations from contemporaneous

European music, with one critic deeming them "leaner and more austere" than "works from around the same time" by Schoenberg.[4] Like Rosenfeld invoking physical prowess and the solitude of "high deserts," recent critics hear Copland's Variations as "muscular and hard-hitting," a result of Copland's "compress[ing] every ounce of possible power into a single tone," with "hard-edged grandeur," a "thorny" quality, a "spacious use of register," and the "authoritative, broad-sweeping sense of grandeur."[5] In short, our current understanding of Copland's Piano Variations rests on images of raw energy and vast spaces, perhaps to be conquered by a solitary individual not unlike Rosenfeld's masculine primitive, who embodied the power of the vast American continent decades ago.[6]

With the choreographed version of *H.P.*, listeners encountered a tango that is really a ragtime-flavored *danzón*, a *sandunga* with echoes of Bach inventions, and a mechanical-human hybrid who doubles as a Yaqui Indian. With its esoteric references and production problems, the ballet was essentially dead on arrival in 1932, despite its well-advertised message of Pan Americanist bonding. The work has lived on in a concert suite, however, and has been recorded. Still, Chávez eliminated the music for the final tableau, the accompaniment to the depiction onstage of the workers' riot, which occasioned a hasty attempt at damage control by the Pan American Union. Certainly the reception of Chávez's music in the United States confirms the elasticity of primitivist discourse during his time. The allure of the primitive sparks classicist yearnings, inspires cultural envy for a more authentic existence, conflates mechanistic prowess with primeval forces, and awakens nostalgia for lost masculinity. Whatever the shifting reception of his works in the United States, Chávez himself sought to embrace sameness, arguing in 1953 that "Mexico, like the United States, is an American branch of occidental culture" with its "own characteristics . . . but essentially it is not different."[7] But by the cold war, exoticism had won out. Whereas in 1936 McPhee found the *Sinfonía India* to have "nothing of the exotic," in the late 1970s it was deemed "exotic-primitivistic" with "primitivistic elements in [a] unique style"; discussing more generally the handful of Indianist works Chávez composed, Béhague notes their "evident exoticism," compatible with "the prevailing nationalism of [their] time."[8] As suggested here, such criticism echoes *its* own time.

Villa-Lobos continues to be appreciated in terms of some of the themes introduced during the Good Neighbor period, with the Aria of *Bachianas brasileiras* no. 5 perhaps his best-loved work. As for *Magdalena*, it has been revived only seldom, once in a concert version to mark the Villa-Lobos centenary. On that occasion, only one commentator, Andrew Porter of the *New Yorker*, seems to have noticed the parade of stereotypes therein, commenting that many aspects of the book were "actually unpleasant."[9] Other critics either fall silent on the work or disregard its unfortunate content, with one referring in 1992 to a "light-hearted South American fantasy" and another going so far as to praise it as "an authentic cross-cultural" work.[10] The irony is that had *Magdalena* been produced as a Hollywood movie during the Good Neighbor period, it would likely have been nixed (or substantively modified) by Addison Durland of the Production Code Administration. Certainly jungle rhetoric has followed Villa-Lobos, even if unsublimated primitivism largely failed him in the United States. Some more recent language is as rhapsodic as that of the 1930s. In 1996 one critic sensed in Villa-Lobos's music the "inhospitable wildness of the virgin forest, the feeling of solitude, the noise of frightened animals, the yells and screams of monkeys and other jungle animals attacked by boa constrictors."[11] Likewise, the rhythmically tame *Characteristic African Dances*—surely a repository of *branqueamento* if there ever was one—have effectively been placed in the same league as Caliban, with recent critics fascinated by "rhythmic intensity" and "rhythmic invention" and one even hearing the "uncompromisingly violent" dances to rely on "driving, intricate cross rhythms . . . constant and primitive repetition of rhythm."[12] In the face of all of this excitement one wonders what chance sameness-embracing can have.

With regard to Ginastera, scholars continue to consider sublimation and its potential to transform nationalist elements.[13] Malena Kuss has addressed nationalism in Ginastera reception at greatest length, taking the composer as a test case for what she considers prejudices concerning Latin American musical nationalism. In 1998 she argued that when Ginastera formulated the tripartite periodization of his music he acted unthinkingly, inadvertently privileging the folkloric. "He wasn't as astute [as Stravinsky]," Kuss declares, alluding to the Russian composer's attempts to cover his folkloric tracks in *The Rite of Spring*, which Pierre Boulez, Pieter Van den Toorn, and others have upheld as an abstract work.[14] For Kuss, Ginastera's strategies in the piano sonatas are "just as 'abstract' as Stravinsky's procedures in the *Rite*" given that both composers distill folklore to arrive at "a purely sonorous construction."[15] She even hears "abstract musical language" in *Estancia*, Ginastera's most nationalist work.[16] Perhaps it is no surprise to find Ginastera himself expressing relief in April 1983, roughly two months before he died, that "nobody is left today to think that Latinamerican [*sic*] music takes refuge with an obsolete folklore, but that it represents the sound and alive expression of a continent whose wealth is appreciated allover [*sic*] the contemporary world through its works."[17] Of course, the extent to which Ginastera's observation is valid, either today or in the past, has been the subject of this book.

As for recent criticism of Good Neighborly works by U.S. composers looking southward, some surprising trends emerge. Whereas early critics of *Cuban Overture* tended to look down their noses at the work's popular aura, today's commentators take it more seriously by highlighting its intellectual dimensions. These include Gershwin's copious sketches, the contrapuntal forays in the work itself (such as the three-part contrapuntal episode leading to the second theme), and manipulations of the basic rhumba rhythm $(3 + 3 + 2)$ in prime and retrograde form.[18] Thus in the recent reception of the *Cuban Overture*, the work's learned characteristics figure prominently, a curious anomaly in the literature of travel music. *El salón México* has also shed the taint of travel music, despite its creator's intentions. Insisting that Copland was more than "a compiler of musical Baedekers," in 1953 Arthur Berger argued that *El salón México* abounds with "complex" strategies such as "displacement." Like Kuss, he also privileged "abstraction," as in the G-major triad in the opening fanfare "abstracted from its context" in the folk tune "El Palo Verde."[19] Elizabeth B. Crist's analysis is especially bold. She relates *El salón México* to Pan Americanism's presumably leftist outlook and to Kenneth Burke's concept of the "proletarian grotesque." Discrepancy, discordance, deformation, and fragmentation are the hallmarks of Burke's aesthetic, which reflect "the social tensions of industrial capitalism as the traditional tunes are exploited and distorted" in *El salón México* through "unruly" accompaniments, "errant dissonances," "staggering" rhythms, and "drunken harmonies."[20] However striking such adjectivization, it fails to account for *El salón México*'s rootedness in tonality and functional harmony, manifested in several long stretches of harmonic stability, that is, the "surprisingly decorous" score noted by at least one early critic. Nor does the political reality add up: as shown here, the Mexican vogue and Pan Americanism in general were by no means solely leftist preoccupations, and Pan Americanism itself was often a tool of U.S. imperialism. Moreover, at least some Latin Americans have taken a dim view of *El salón México* and of the branding of Latin American music by U.S. composers in general. Just as de la Vega complained of a double standard in musical nationalism with regard to Copland's music, Juan Carlos Paz found *El salón México* "merely picturesque," corresponding to "an aesthetic of opportunism ... [with] more vulgarity than intrinsic merit."[21] The Argentine composer Daniel Devoto once sniped that Copland expressed admiration for Chávez to "atone for having composed *El salon méxico*."[22] Copland's *Three Latin-American Sketches*, finished in 1971 and in essentially the same vein as *El salón México*, have earned similar critiques; in 1972 Raymond Ericson predicted "wide circulation" and anticipated that the *Three Latin-American Sketches* would "augment Copland's royalties if not his artistic stature."[23] Until we establish stronger criteria to distinguish music that responds to the call of the culture industry and music that serves as "the voice of the people," works such as *El salón México* will simply be whatever we want them to be.

As for Rzewski's *The People United*, it has received mixed reviews in Latin America, and despite its sympathetic stance does not seem to be that widely known in Chile.[24] The prominent composer Graciela Paraskevaídis, based in Montevideo, has allowed that Rzewski "expresses his solidarity and pays homage to the tortured and the disappeared." Still, just as Caliban is captive to Prospero's language, Rzewski relies on "the language of the oppressor, imposed in Latin America in the name of the cross and the sword during centuries of physical, spiritual, and cultural annihilation," letting himself be "seduced by a musical model that is hardly of revolutionary character."[25] Orrego-Salas, on the other hand, disinclined to link variation form to the implements of the conquest, hears *The People United* "as a musical expression and not as a political statement," adding that "it becomes eloquent in its association with Ortega's song because [it] is a good composition."[26] Clearly absolute music remains an attractive concept even as memory, the great equalizer, must thrive north and south. Only then can we in the United States hope to put into perspective the nearly two centuries that have elapsed since the era of the Monroe Doctrine, the precepts and polemics of which have insinuated themselves into so many discourses. Music, as one of those discourses, must also remember.

Have we made progress in the United States? If historians such as William Warren Sweet wrote off Latin Americans as "half-breeds" in 1919, virtually no recent U.S. critic of *The People United* neglects to mention the CIA's role in bringing Pinochet to power. Pan Americanism and its sameness-embracing spirit, more than a quirk of history, can potentially enhance our work as music scholars. As to whether such a premise is utopian, even Copland, the figurehead of musical Pan Americanism in the United States, came to wonder if the idea of a north-south historiography of American music was "perhaps naïve."[27] Naïveté, an epithet often brandished in debates over utopianism, may well have informed constructions such as Chávez's ur-classicism, Villa-Lobos's universalism, and Ginastera's sublimation. Yet even if all were fashioned within the narrative of musical Pan Americanism, with its hopeful—some would say utopian—agenda of hemispheric union, that is no reason to overlook the historiographical and practical ramifications of this ideal.[28]

How do these matters affect the teaching of music history and literature in the twenty-first century? A brief overview of more general trends will put the question in context. Besides the interventions in Latin America described earlier, anti-Hispanic sentiment reared its head in the United States immediately after World War II. Some 500,000 Hispanics, mainly Mexican Americans, fought in Europe and the Pacific. Unlike African Americans, they were not segregated in the service. But Hispanic members of the Greatest Generation returned home to a country that, from their perspective, seemed to repudiate the ideals for which they had fought and for which so many of their brethren died. Separate schools for Latinos and whites were the norm in many states until the landmark court case *Méndez v. Westminster School District* declared this practice inherently unequal in 1947, setting the precedent for *Brown v. Board of Education* in 1954.[29] Ultimately, Bolton's concept of "Greater America" was largely forgotten. In the 1920s, the Berkeley professor had passionately argued that taking the thirteen English colonies as a point of origin for U.S. history would "raise a nation of chauvinists" and ensure that many a general historian would have difficulty "spelling Ecuador correctly or be quite sound on the question of whether Chihuahua is north or south of Tierra del Fuego."[30] In the cold war, Black Legend stereotyping thrived. A 1964 sixth-grade textbook, for example, informed students that "most

Spaniards and Portuguese came to the New World to get rich," whereas "most settlers in the English colonies came to build permanent homes and a better way of life"; these gold-crazed Spaniards, moreover, "left women behind," whereas the upstanding English, imbued with the values of home and hearth, "brought families along."[31] High school students read that while "Europeans" in the United States "established democratic governments... [through] hard work, vast natural resources, and the use of smart business methods," their counterparts in Latin America were "not much interested in farming" and had the misfortune to be the descendants of "a backward people who were unwilling to learn new ways."[32]

Music history pedagogy often reflects the musical world around us. Between 1987 and 1997, the more than five hundred concerts given by the Chicago Symphony Orchestra included exactly one work by a Latin American composer.[33] Although the recording industry markets a handful of Latin American "standards," it often does so through incongruous representational strategies, such as the palm trees, conga drums, and Mexican sombreros that grace the cover of a 2002 recording of *Estancia*, Ginastera's evocation of the windswept Argentine pampas. With some happy exceptions, Latin American art music is barely a presence in most college and university music departments, even as Latin American studies programs have been a fixture of academic life since the 1960s. (Some specialists in Latin American studies do address music, although some of their efforts are strangely free of musical analysis or even basic terminology. One author, in a widely cited book, manages to compare at length Copland's "inspired" *El salón México* with Gershwin's "mediocre" *Cuban Overture* without once referring to a musical score.)[34] Despite enthusiasm in the 1990s for cultural diversity, some Ph.D. programs in musicology were slow to accept Spanish for the foreign-language requirement, having done so only in the past ten years. This history is worth considering in light of the fact that the Hispanic population in the United States reached 16 percent in 2010 and is projected to be 29 percent by 2050.[35]

Compare the hard-won disciplinary legitimacy of music of the United States. Since the 1970s specialists in this area have succeeded in reshaping many musicological priorities, resulting in revamped curricula, previously unimaginable areas of specializations, a learned society, two journals, and new orientations for college and university graduate programs. By the 1990s, a decade of fast-paced change for musicology, it seemed that the question Edward Lowinsky had posed in the heat of disciplinary battle three decades earlier—"How did American music become what it is?"—had caught fire.[36] Yet throughout most of the years since, that question has tended to exclude Hispanic music-making in the United States along with the concept of greater America. As J. Peter Burkholder observes, the first edition of Donald Jay Grout's *A History of Western Music* (1960) contained exactly one paragraph on Latin America.[37] Scholars of music in the United States were so prone to take the thirteen New England colonies as a point of origin that for decades Owen da Silva's *Mission Music of California* of

1941 was the only single-volume study dedicated to early Catholic musical practices.[38] In 2009 Craig H. Russell published a study of mission music in which he noted a "general lack of intellectual curiosity" toward this repertory, an institutionalized indifference that "repeats itself in blissful laxity and inattention" despite ample reason to go beyond the New England colonies.[39] To be sure, in the twenty-first century, Anglocentric narratives have lost ground, as a survey of recent textbooks shows.[40] Yet congratulations are not entirely in order. The most recent edition of a widely used history of music in the United States, whose author acknowledges the presence of a variety of these competing traditions, nonetheless asserts that "we must still recognize" the preeminence of New England in our heritage, musical and otherwise.[41]

Why must we? And why, given the longevity of the Hispanic presence in music of the United States—and indeed in the Western canon—have we taken so long to give it its due?[42] Over the course of writing this book I have frequently found myself recalling a question posed by an Argentine student in the doctoral seminar I taught at the University of Buenos Aires. Having read the chapter in Howard Pollack's biography of Copland titled "South of the Border," she wondered aloud, "What border?" Her question was purely a matter of orientation; she had no idea that for U.S. readers the Rio Grande is a north-south dividing point and that speakers of American English often use the term *south of the border* as a metonym for Latin America. Yet how succinctly her query encapsulated Martí's wrestling with the concept of "our America," with all its political and cultural vicissitudes!

We could cultivate a Pan Americanist lens for any number of reasons. Demographics in the United States, as well as the need to redress past omissions and existing prejudices, would seem compelling enough. There is also that inching toward cosmopolitan habits of mind, summarized earlier, which encourage us to eschew crude, deterministic models of hegemon and subaltern and recognize that beyond mawkish pleas for "harmony," the actual and ongoing interpenetration of cultures—What border?—is now part of daily life, of new "imagined communities" that go beyond the nation-state. On a typical day in my former university in East Lansing, Michigan, I would look around the classroom and see a young man from Colombia and another from the Basque country. Down the hall a Venezuelan colleague would study scores in his office; elsewhere students from Brazil, Argentina, Mexico, Venezuela, Bolivia, and Panama congregated. For whatever reason, they came to mid-Michigan rather than California, Texas, or Florida. Can we in the United States really take seriously the notion of a Latin American Other? Of course we will continue to wrangle over identity, history, and memory; the day that debate stops is the day we embrace not sameness but complacency. But we of the United States can no longer write our musical history from the standpoint of an unproblematic American "we." There is simply no point in overlooking the presence of one continent in the history of the other.

■ NOTES

■ Introduction

1. Whitaker, *The Western Hemisphere Idea*, 3.

2. See Ninkovitch, *The Diplomacy of Ideas*, 30.

3. In mid-1940 Smith traveled to Latin America on behalf of the Committee on Inter-American Relations in the Field of Music (a counterpart of that of the OIAA), resulting in a 355-page mimeographed report of his findings in fifteen countries. See Shepard, "The Legacy of Carleton Sprague Smith," 633–47. Smith's writings on Latin America range from reportage ("Music Libraries in South America") to criticism ("The Composers of Chile") to the delightful etiquette guide "What Not to Expect in South America."

4. See, for example, *Music in Latin America: A Brief Survey*, vol. 3 (Washington, D.C.: Pan American Union, 1942) and numerous studies of individual Latin American composers or countries published by the Union.

5. Oja, *Making Music Modern*, 279. Several musicologists have addressed Latin American art music composers in the United States, although not explicitly in the context of Pan Americanism. See, for example, Saavedra, "Of Selves and Others"; Parker, *Carlos Chávez*; Appleby, *Heitor Villa-Lobos*. Two studies that do consider Pan Americanism and art music are Payne, "Creating Music of the Americas During the Cold War," and Campbell, "Shaping Solidarity." See also Prutsch, *Creating Good Neighbors?*

6. Ruth A. Solie, "Introduction: On 'Difference,'" in *Musicology and Difference*, 1.

7. Agawu, *Representing African Music*.

8. Crist, *Music for the Common Man*, 69.

9. Blackwood, *Music of the World*, 99.

10. Salvatore, *Imágenes de un imperio*, 27.

11. Barthes, who made this comment in a 1972 interview, is cited in Jacques Attali, *Noise: The Political Economy of Music*, trans. Brian Massumi (Minneapolis: University of Minnesota Press, 1985), 18–19.

12. Béhague, *Music in Latin America*, 126, 168.

13. Agawu, *Representing African Music*, 59–61. Agawu notes that in parts of Africa the lyre and the *mbira* are the main instruments, whereas in other African traditions, bows rather than drums predominate.

14. Béhague, *Music in Latin America*, 101. On Villanueva, see Lorenz, "Voices in Limbo."

15. In light of such declarations we might even find ourselves wondering about hemiolas in Brahms. Are they, too, "rhythmic-nationalist," as Lorenz queries (see n14)? Perhaps only Johannes's less-famous brother Fritz grasped the true essence of the hemiola, given that he spent part of his career in Caracas.

16. Nicolas Slonimsky's "South American fishing trip" of 1941 resulted in *Music of Latin America*. On the composers mentioned above, see 247–48, 131, 184. Lorenz compares these passages in Slonimsky with parallel descriptions in Béhague's *Music in Latin America* (145, 205–7, 149–51). See Lorenz, "Voices in Limbo," appendix 4. Emilio Ros-Fábregas discusses Slonimsky's project in "Nicolas Slonimsky (1894–1995) y sus escritos sobre música en Latinoamérica." Another Russian émigré drawn to Latin America was Lazare Saminsky, cofounder of *Modern Music*, who, after undertaking his own "fishing

trip" in 1940, also recorded his impressions. See Saminsky, "South American Report," "In the Argentine," and "Ibero-Indian America" in his *Living Music of the Americas*, 195–254.

17. Mayer-Serra, *Panorama de la música mexicana*, 96.

18. On organicism's explanatory power, see Solie, "The Living Work." In "Edward Mac-Dowell," Richard Crawford discusses the appeal of organicist and universalist discourse in the United States at the turn of the twentieth century.

19. Hess, *Questions and Answers in Chemistry*, 58; Coriat, *What Is Psychoanalysis?*, 73. Few scholars address music in relation to sublimation. See, however, Puri, "Dandy Interrupted"; Huebner, *French Opera at the Fin de Siècle*, 157–58; Lee, "A Minstrel in a World without Minstrels"; Chowrimootoo, "Bourgeois Opera."

20. Lange, "Prefacio," vii.

21. This well-known dichotomy is set forth in Dahlhaus, "Nationalism and Music," in *Between Romanticism and Modernism*, 89. On the "dialectics of nationalism and universality," see Dahlhaus, *Nineteenth-Century Music*, 37.

22. Mari Carmen Ramíriez and Héctor Olea, prologue, in Mari Carmen Ramírez and Héctor Olea, eds., *Inverted Utopias: Avant-Garde Art in Latin America* (New Haven: Yale University Press, 2004), xv. Of the vast literature on exoticism and music, much of it sparked by Edward Said's *Orientalism* of 1978, see Ralph P. Locke, *Musical Exoticism: Images and Reflections* (Cambridge: Cambridge University Press, 2009); McClary, *Georges Bizet*; Jonathan Bellman, ed., *The Exotic in Western Music* (Boston: Northeastern University Press, 1998); Born and Hesmondhalgh, *Western Music and Its Others*. On the extent to which the musicological concept of exoticism may "cover up, gloss over, the varieties of treatment of otherness," see Timothy D. Taylor's discussion of colonialism, imperialism, and globalization in music in *Beyond Exoticism*, 9–14. A Latin Americanist offshoot of orientalism, applied mainly to literature, is "tropicalization." Developed by Frances R. Aparicio and Susana Chávez-Silverman, the concept involves the tendency to view Latin America as an undifferentiated tropical fantasy. See Aparicio and Chávez-Silverman, *Tropicalizations*.

23. See, for example, the views of the Venezuelan composer (and a beneficiary of Good Neighbor cultural diplomacy) Juan Bautista Plaza in Labonville, *Juan Bautista Plaza and Musical Nationalism in Venezuela*, 143.

24. On "tourist nationalism," see Taruskin, "Colonialist Nationalism."

25. Hess, *Manuel de Falla and Modernism in Spain*, especially 289–91.

26. Crist, *Music for the Common Man*, 45.

27. Saavedra, "Los escritos periodísticos de Carlos Chávez," 83–87. Similar treatment of Ginastera has also provoked complaints. See Kuss, "Nacionalismo, identificación y Latinoamérica."

28. See Sandoval Sánchez, "*West Side Story*," 170. On *El salón México*, see Devoto, "Panorama de la musicología latinoamericana," 92. More insistently than his U.S. colleagues, Copland envisioned a Latin American art music based on folklore. See Copland, "The Composers of South America." See also San Juan, *Beyond Postcolonial Theory*, 22–23.

29. Miller, "The Historiography of Nationalism and National Identity in Latin America." See also Turino, "Nationalism and Latin American Music."

30. Bhabha, "Of Mimicry and Man."

31. Attali, *Noise*, 92. Along similar lines, Saavedra notes that a "universal" discourse that "claims to be complete, logical, rational, objective, and explanatory . . . rests on certain widely held assumptions . . . (1) that Western music enjoys a uniform and progressive development, logical and autonomous . . . and (2) that there exists a patrimony of masterpieces . . . recognized as universal and indisputably valuable" . . . ("Of Selves and Others," 5).

32. See Kimsey, "'One Parchman Farm or Another,'" 112.

33. Adorno, *Aesthetic Theory*, 17.

34. Magaldi, "Cosmopolitanism and World Music in Rio de Janeiro at the Turn of the Twentieth Century," 333. See also Madrid and Corona, *Postnational Musical Identities*.

35. Robbins, "Introduction," 2, italics in original. See also Fojas, *Cosmopolitanism in the Americas*; Gupta and Ferguson, "Beyond Culture"; Gidal, "Contemporary 'Latin American' Composers of Art Music in the United States."

36. Foucault, *The History of Sexuality*, 11.

37. There is at present no comprehensive study of Copland and Latin America, although his activities there are summarized in Crist, *Music for the Common Man*, 43–69; Pollack, *Aaron Copland*, 216–33; Abrams Ansari, "'Masters of the President's Music,'" 129–33; and Campbell, "Shaping Solidarity," 79–92. See also Hess, "Copland in Argentina."

38. Salvatore, *Imágenes de un imperio*, 15.

39. García Canclini, *Hybrid Cultures*.

40. Alejandro Madrid usefully distinguishes among modernism, modernity, and modernization in relation to Latin America. See Madrid, *Sounds of the Modern Nation*, 5–7. On musical modernism in the United States, see Oja, *Making Music Modern*; Broyles and von Glahn, *Leo Ornstein*.

41. Radano and Bohlman, *Music and the Racial Imagination*, 1. See also Brown, *Western Music and Race*.

42. Enloe, *Bananas, Beaches and Bases*. See also Stam, *Tropical Multiculturalism*, 1–2.

43. Torgovnick, *Gone Primitive*.

44. To say that comprehensive biographies of all three composers already exist would be an exaggeration. Interested readers, however, will be able to easily fill in much biographical information not given here.

45. Crawford, *The American Musical Landscape*, 4. This lack of accord is fertile ground for study. Charles Hiroshi Garrett has compellingly argued that the concept of an American music is best explored as "a terrain of conflict," thus joining a host of scholars who explore a phenomenon Sacvan Bercovitch aptly terms "dissensus," that is, the effects of difference and divisiveness in the historiography of the United States. See Garrett, *Struggling to Define a Nation*, 16; Bercovitch, *The Rites of Assent*.

46. For a nuanced discussion of the meaning of "America," see Radway, "What's in a Name?"

47. Belnap, "Diego Rivera's Greater America." My discussion of *H.P.* extends Saavedra's observation on the ballet's hybrid character, the "mestizo" dances of which, she notes, reflect "a new taste for [musical] hybridizations . . . that had come to public attention during the [Mexican] Revolution" ("Of Selves and Others," 132).

48. Roberts, *The Latin Tinge*, 84.

49. Fredric Jameson, preface to Fernández Retamar, *Caliban and Other Essays*, xii.

■ **Chapter 1. The Roots of Musical Pan Americanism**

1. "Tu has entendido la palabra 'americana' tal como nosotros entendemos la palabra 'estadounidense.' Al hablar yo de una estética americana, abarcaba a todo el continente desde Alaska hasta Tierra del Fuego. . . . Tienes que agregar el 50 percent latinoamericano y poner en evidencia desde las ruinas de los Mayas y Aztecas hasta las actuales generaciones musicales de Norte y Sud América." Letter, March 16, 1964, Alberto Ginastera to Gilbert Chase, Correspondence file, Box 11, Instituto Torcuato di Tella, Buenos Aires.

2. In the introduction to the first edition (1955), a study of "the music made or continuously used by the people of the United States," Chase notes that the term *America* is "more

properly applicable to the Western Hemisphere as a whole," serving as a "symbolic name that binds us all to common ideals of peace, friendship, and cooperation." With regard to his own restricted use of the term, he pleads "euphony and convenience, supported by a literary tradition that has ample precedent." Chase, *America's Music from the Pilgrims to the Present*, xxi–xxii. This passage is removed from the introduction to the second edition (1966). In the third edition (1987), a foreword by Richard Crawford replaces Chase's introduction.

3. "No somos 'norteamericanos,' porque lo son también los mexicanos y los canadienses. De modo que si no nos llamamos 'americanos' en el sentido nacional nos quedamos sin nombre alguno. ¡Triste suerte para un gran país!" Letter, April 2, 1964, Gilbert Chase to Alberto Ginastera, Box 11, Instituto Torcuato di Tella, Buenos Aires. In 1942 Chase issued a related caution, namely that pre-Conquest culture, often subsumed under the rubric "Latin American," is "in no sense Latin American but 'Indo-American.'" Chase, *A Guide to the Music of Latin America* (1942), ii; see also the second edition (1972).

4. Martí, *Nuestra América*.

5. On Martí's experience of "unequal modernization" in the Americas, see Ramos, *Divergent Modernities*, 151–279.

6. Alfred Thayer Mahan argued in favor of this practice in his widely read *The Influence of Sea Power upon History* (Boston: Little, Brown, 1890).

7. Martí, "The Truth about the United States," 49–50.

8. José Martí, "Carta a Manuel Mercado (May 18, 1895)," in *Obras completas* (Caracas 1964), in Holden and Zolov, *Latin America and the United States*, 63.

9. "The Hispanicisation of America," 35.

10. Jack Delano, for example, roundly asserts that "no one in Puerto Rico ever refers to the United States as 'America' and no Puerto Rican ever did" (*Puerto Rico Mío*, 4).

11. The Yale historian Samuel Flagg Bemis, for example, who refers exactly once to Bolívar in his 470-page study, *The Latin American Policy of the United States*, privileges U.S. influence in inculcating Pan American unity, calling the "persistent revolutionary movement in Hispanic America [of the first decades of the nineteenth century]" not "a reflex spasm of the Napoleonic conflict but rather an heroic and magnificent climax of the Anglo-American Revolution itself: the achievement of that American System for which the North American Revolution had pointed the way" (39–40).

12. Langley, *America and the Americas*, 49–54.

13. A still useful discussion of Latin American views of the Monroe Doctrine is Gordon Connell-Smith, "Latin America in the Foreign Relations of the United States."

14. Cited in Holden and Zolov, *Latin America and the United States*, 13–14. See also Hodgson, *The Myth of American Exceptionalism*.

15. Cited in Rodríguez, *Changing Race*, 75.

16. Hanke, introduction to *Do the Americas Have a Common History?*, 12. See also Berger, *Under Northern Eyes*, 35–36. The label *Hispanic* is much debated in light of its failure to distinguish one Latin American nation from another, especially in terms of their respective ethnicities and postindependence legacy. See Oboler, "'So Far from God, So Close to the United States.'"

17. Cited in Holden and Zolov, *Latin America and the United States*, 101.

18. Although many in the United States seized upon "Spanish treachery" as the reason the U.S. battleship *Maine* exploded in Havana Harbor and killed 266 in February 1898, a study decades later by the U.S. Department of the Navy strongly suggests that spontaneous combustion of coal fuel ignited the ship's ammunition magazines. See Rickover, *How the "Maine" Was Destroyed*.

19. See Bermann, *Under the Big Stick*.

20. William Eleroy Curtis, *The Capitals of Spanish America* (New York: Harper, 1888), 472.

21. Powell, *Tree of Hate*; see also Maltby, *The Black Legend in England*.

22. Cited in Powell, *Tree of Hate*, 123.

23. Cited in Espinosa, *Inter-American Beginnings of U.S. Cultural Diplomacy*, 11.

24. Cited in Espinosa, *Inter-American Beginnings of U.S. Cultural Diplomacy*, 10.

25. Carnegie, "Distant Possessions," 244.

26. Cited in Holden and Zolov, *Latin American and the United States*, 119.

27. Rosenberg, *Financial Missionaries to the World*, 207.

28. See photographs of the 1893 Chicago World's Columbian Exposition in Salvatore, *Imágenes de un imperio*, 51. See also Munro, "Investigating World's Fairs."

29. Warren Susman explores the "culture of abundance" (introduced on xx) in *Culture as History*.

30. Williams, *Empire as a Way of Life*.

31. Said, *Culture and Imperialism*, 11, italics in original.

32. Cited in Haring, *South America Looks at the United States*, 43.

33. Haring, *South America Looks at the United States*, 48–57; Espinosa, *Inter-American Beginnings of U.S. Cultural Diplomacy*, 7–63.

34. Roa Bárcena, *The View from Chapultepec*, 44.

35. Darío, *Selected Poems of Rubén Darío*, 169–70.

36. Cited in Holden and Zolov, *Latin America and the United States*, 123. On Argentina's status in the early twentieth century, see Shumway, *The Invention of Argentina*, x.

37. Rodó, *Ariel*, 79.

38. Reid, "The Rise and Decline of the Ariel-Caliban Antithesis in Spanish America."

39. Carlos Fuentes, prologue to Rodó, *Ariel*, 13.

40. Bradford, cited in Marx, *The Machine in the Garden*, 41.

41. Cheyfitz, *The Poetics of Imperialism*, 23.

42. Ezra Pound, "Hugh Selwyn Mauberly: E. P. Ode Pour l'Election de son Sepulchre," in *Personae*, 191.

43. Stearns, *Civilization in the United States*, iii–iv.

44. Deems Taylor, "Music," in Stearns, *Civilization in the United States*, 203.

45. Stearns, preface to *Civilization in the United States*, vii.

46. Taruskin, "Colonialist Nationalism," part 11.

47. Among the numerous studies on the reception of the "New World," see Crawford, "Dvorak and the Historiography of American Music." See also Charles Hamm, "Dvorak, Nationalism, Myth, and Racism," 275–80; Beckerman, *Dvorak and His World*, 157–91.

48. Cited in Horowitz, "Dvorak and Boston," 8.

49. Domínguez and de los Santos, *The Bronze Screen*.

50. See Woll, *The Latin Image in American Film*, 6–28.

51. A catalogue of Hispanic film stereotypes is found in Ramirez Berg, "Stereotyping and Resistance." See also Noriega, "Citizen Chicano." On press cartoons, see Johnson, *Latin America in Caricature*.

52. Cited in Koegel, "*Canciones del país*," 164.

53. Koegel, "Crossing Borders"; see also Koegel and Tablada, "Compositores Cubanos y Mexicanos en Nueva York."

54. Koegel, "Crossing Borders," 101–3.

55. Magdanz, "'Sobre las olas.'" The waltz made a fortune for Rosas's publishers but earned the composer next to nothing, as he was paid only an initial fee, a common practice of the day.

56. Koegel, "Crossing Borders," 105.

57. See Taylor Gibson, "The Music of Manuel M. Ponce, Julián Carrillo, and Carlos Chávez in New York," 68–72. On 65–68 Taylor Gibson discusses an important interpreter of Ponce's music, the Mexican singer Clara Sánchez, who gave nine New York recitals between 1925 and 1932. The Mexican singer Carmen García Cornejo recorded "Estrellita" in 1917 (Koegel, "Crossing Borders," 103).

58. On the significance of this work, see Stein, *Songs of Mortals, Dialogues of the Gods*, 254n131; see also Robert M. Stevenson's edition (Lima: Instituto Nacional de Cultura, 1976).

59. Stevenson, "Opera Beginnings in the New World"; Catalyne, "Manuel de Zumaya."

60. Sturman, *Zarzuela*, 55–58. See also Kanellos, *A History of Hispanic Theatre in the United States*.

61. On Los Angeles, see Koegel, "Mexican Musicians in California and the United States."

62. Sturman, *Zarzuela*, 58; see also Koegel, "*Canciones del país*," 178.

63. Also in 1916, Enrique Granados's opera *Goyesca*, which some critics called a zarzuela, premiered at the Metropolitan Opera. See Clark, *Enrique Granados*, 152–60; Hess, *Enrique Granados*, 30–31.

64. Sturman, *Zarzuela*, 59–64.

65. Garrett points out that Morton identified not as black or white but as a Creole, thus posing a challenge to much of jazz history, which has tended to posit a black versus white racial model. Garrett, *Struggling to Define a Nation*, 50.

66. Garrett, *Struggling to Define a Nation*, 57.

67. *Rhumba* is the name of the ballroom dance popular in the United States, whereas *rumba* signifies an Afro-Cuban ritual.

68. See Roberts, *The Latin Tinge*, 44–60. The tango's origins in brothels has perhaps been unduly mythologized. See Baim, *Tango*, 13–42.

69. On the urgency of such debates in the aftermath of World War I, see Watkins, *Proof through the Night*, 333–54.

70. See Crawford, *The American Musical Landscape*, 3–37.

71. Copland, *Music and Imagination*, 104.

72. Brooks, "On Creating a Usable Past."

73. Stevenson, "Nino Marcelli, Founder of the San Diego Symphony Orchestra."

74. Kolb and Wolffer, *Silvestre Revueltas*.

75. Taylor Gibson, "The Music of Manuel M. Ponce, Julián Carrillo, and Carlos Chávez in New York," 81–126. See also Madrid, *Sounds of the Modern Nation*, 18–48.

76. Taylor Gibson, "The Music of Manuel M. Ponce, Julián Carrillo, and Carlos Chávez in New York," 72–76.

77. Haring, *South America Looks at the United States*, 7.

78. Haring, *South America Looks at the United States*, 42.

79. Fagg, *Pan Americanism*, 3.

80. On an anti-hookworm campaign in Costa Rica, see Palmer, "Central American Encounters with Rockefeller." On economic experiments such as "people's capitalism" and "progressive capitalism" in Brazil and Venezuela, see Rivas, *Missionary Capitalist*.

■ **Chapter 2. Carlos Chávez and Ur-Classicism**

1. On the origins and significance of the series, see Oja, "The Copland-Sessions Concerts and Their Reception in the Contemporary Press."

2. "Young Composers [*sic*] Work Opens Concert Series."

3. Works performed, along with personnel, are listed in Oja, "The Copland-Sessions Concerts and Their Reception in the Contemporary Press," 227. Among them was Thomson's "Five Phrases from The Song of Solomon," for which Copland ventured to play percussion. See Olmstead, *The Correspondence of Roger Sessions*, 107.

4. Olmstead, "The Copland-Sessions Letters," 4.

5. "Young Composers [*sic*] Work Opens Concert Series."

6. Stokes, "Realm of Music."

7. Henderson, "Present American Composers." Neither the *New York World* nor the *New York Evening Post* appear to have covered the concert.

8. Tyron, "Two American Modernists."

9. Oja, *Making Music Modern*, 231–82.

10. Saavedra, "Of Selves and Others," 158–62.

11. Downes, "Music: Presenting American Composers."

12. Copland, "Carlos Chávez—Mexican Composer" (1928). See also Copland's essay of the same title (1933), in which he elaborates on many of the points made in 1928.

13. Saavedra, "Of Selves and Others," 139–48, 150–56. The critic cited (156) is Manuel Casares.

14. Saavedra, "Los escritos periodísticos de Carlos Chávez."

15. Saavedra, "Of Selves and Others," 139; on Ponce, modernism, and Mexican musical nationalism, see 17–50.

16. Their actual presence is another matter. Daniel K. L. Chua acknowledges "the musicological myth that the mixed style [of the mid-eighteenth century] somehow transmuted into the 'Classical style' . . . to form the language of absolute music." Chua, *Absolute Music and the Construction of Meaning*, 71.

17. This outlook had its precedents. For example, the work of the nineteenth-century U.S. painter George Caleb Bingham has been seen to embody "the idea of an American classicism arising naturally out of native attitudes." E. Maurice Block, cited in Novak, *American Painting of the Nineteenth Century*, 156.

18. On creation myths in the United States, see Albanese, *Sons of the Fathers*, 9. See also Rozwenc, "Edmundo O'Gorman and the Idea of America," 115.

19. Gombrich, *The Ideas of Progress and Their Impact on Art*, 30.

20. Messing, *Neoclassicism in Music from the Genesis of the Concept through the Schoenberg/Stravinsky Polemic*; see also Hess, *Manuel de Falla and Modernism in Spain*, 199–275; Taruskin, "Back to Whom?" Stravinsky set forth some of neoclassicism's basic premises in the famous essay "Some Ideas about my Octuor," cited in White, *Stravinsky and His Works*, 574–77.

21. Stravinsky, Boulanger, Fauré, and others referred to *la musique pure*; that the concept differed in certain respects from the German idea of absolute music (some program music, for example, could be considered pure music) lent it largely French connotations. See Stravinsky and Craft, *Conversations with Igor Stravinsky*, 40–41. Prior uses of the term in France by Vincent d'Indy, Jean Marnold, Gaston Carraud, Déodat de Sévérac, and Émile Vuillermoz are treated in Hart, "The Symphony in Theory and Practice in France, 1900–1914," 150–51.

22. Richard Taruskin discusses this phenomenon, along with Stravinsky's political motives, in "Russian Folk Melodies in *The Rite of Spring*."

23. Cited in Hess, *Manuel de Falla and Modernism in Spain*, 190. See also "Une Lettre de Stravinsky sur Tchaikovsky," *Figaro*, May 18, 1922, cited and translated in Taruskin, *Stravinsky and the Russian Traditions*, 2: 1533–34.

24. Cited in Oja, *Making Music Modern*, 232–33.

25. Cowell, "Towards Neo-Primitivism," 150.

26. Farwell, "Roy Harris," 23–24.

27. Downes, "Young Composer's 'Anti-Impressionism' Need of New Orchestral Programs."

28. Lourie, "Neogothic and Neoclassic," 8.

29. See Root, "The Pan American Association of Composers." On Chávez's relationship to the organization, see Taylor Gibson, "The Music of Manuel M. Ponce, Julián Carrillo, and Carlos Chávez in New York," 156–58. For a trenchant discussion of Varèse's legacy in the United States and "the myth of unjust neglect" of his works, see Oja, *Making Music Modern*, 26–44.

30. Root, "The Pan American Association of Composers," 52.

31. Root, "The Pan American Association of Composers," 54. As Stephanie N. Stallings observes, Slonimsky's memories of the organization have largely shaped its legacy, given that he outlived other participants by several decades ("Collective Difference," 61; see also 61–132).

32. Cited in Root, "The Pan American Association of Composers," 58, 56.

33. Cited in Root, "The Pan American Association of Composers," 58.

34. Cited in Root, "The Pan American Association of Composers," 54.

35. S., "Works of Latin Americans Heard," 29.

36. Silet, *The Writings of Paul Rosenfeld*, xix–xxx. See also Leibowitz, *Musical Impressions*. On the *Dial*, see Joost and Sullivan, *D. H. Lawrence and The Dial*.

37. Wilson, "Imaginary Conversation," 179, 180.

38. Schumann, *On Music and Musicians*.

39. Rosenfeld, "Cowell," in *Discoveries of a Music Critic*, 280.

40. Rosenfeld, *An Hour with American Music*, 14, 12.

41. Rosenfeld, *An Hour with American Music*, 29–31. In the wake of folksong research by the Works Progress Administration during the 1930s, Rosenfeld came to recognize an American folk music. See his "Folksong and Cultural Politics." Ideologies surrounding folk music in the 1930s are summarized in Hess, "Competing Utopias?"

42. Rosenfeld, *An Hour with American Music*, 44.

43. Not just academia but the broader public reacted to Bergson, with books such as *Bergson for Beginners* (which today would surely be called *Bergson for Dummies*). See Quirk, *Bergson and American Culture*, 26.

44. Peter Demetz, introduction to Benjamin, *Reflections*, xvii, xl.

45. The essay appeared in Rosenfeld, *By Way of Art*, 273–83. Subsequent citations are in parentheses in the text.

46. Rosenfeld evidently saw the score of *Los cuatro soles*, one of Chávez's few explicitly Indianist works, which premiered July 22, 1930, by the Orquesta Sinfónica de México in a concert version (Saavedra, "Of Selves and Others," 288–89). A staged version was not mounted until 1951. See also Parker, "Carlos Chávez's Aztec Ballets."

47. Rosenfeld, *By Way of Art*, 274, 276, 278–79. To be sure, this landscape (which Saavedra aptly terms "Tex-Mex") is highly selective. Saavedra, "Of Selves and Others," 160.

48. Rosenfeld subsequently declared that Chávez's works contain no European influence: "They recall no . . . echoes of Bach and Händel, Rameau or Clementi" ("The New American Music," 629).

49. It should be clear that I question Oja's contention that "Rosenfeld located Chávez securely within the neoclassical spectrum" (*Making Music Modern*, 276). As shown below, more than once Rosenfeld expressed his distaste for neoclassicism, a stance incompatible with his enthusiasm for Chávez. To take just two examples: in 1930 he complained that

neoclassicism lacked "the authority of a large spirit" and that it had "made objectivity an end in itself," thus ensuring the absence of both "the fresh and the necessary"; a year later he acknowledged that while some might well label Chávez's music neoclassical, unlike the recent "classicizing pieces of Strawinsky, Hindemith, Casella, and the rest," Chávez's works bear no "stigmata of intellectualism and theory in the shape of staleness and archaicism." See Rosenfeld, "Neo-Classicism and Paul Hindemith," 194; Rosenfeld, "The New American Music," 629. Rosenfeld's views on Stravinsky's neoclassicism are discussed below.

50. Kenworthy, *America/Américas*, 18.

51. The speechwriter was Peggy Noonan. Cited in Kenworthy, *America/Américas*, 135.

52. Discussed in Smith, *Virgin Land*, 250–60; Marx, *The Machine in the Garden*, especially 66–72.

53. Moulard, *Tabula Rasa*.

54. Letter representing view of an Indian cacique (chief) Potirava, cited in McNapsy, "Conquest or Inculturation," 91.

55. Davies, "The Italianized Frontier," 3; see also Whitaker, *The Western Hemisphere Idea*, 7. Nonviolent religious advocated a policy of adaptation, according to which friars learned native languages such as Guaraní or Quechua and integrated into the community.

56. Ramírez, "A Highly Topical Utopia," 3.

57. Discussed in Young, "The West and American Cultural Identity," 139.

58. Young, "The West and American Cultural Identity," 138; see also Rozwenc, "Edmundo O'Gorman and the Idea of America."

59. Cited in Winterer, *The Culture of Classicism*, 163.

60. Cited in Winterer, *The Culture of Classicism*, 159. The so-called Aryan model of Greek culture wrongly denies the mixing of Europeans, Africans, and Semites. See Bernal, *Black Athena*.

61. Tomlinson, *The Singing of the New World*, 7.

62. Frank, *Our America*, 231; see also Frank, *America Hispana*, 317–20.

63. Frank, *Virgin Spain*.

64. Frank, *The Re-Discovery of America*, 216, 65. See also Williams, *Radical Journalists*, 105–28.

65. Delpar, *The Enormous Vogue of Things Mexican*.

66. The article, "Topics of the Times," was retrospective, appearing on April 15, 1933.

67. Cited in Delpar, *The Enormous Vogue of Things Mexican*, 17.

68. Lucie-Smith, *Latin American Art of the 20th Century*, 13.

69. Mayer-Serra, *Panorama de la música Mexicana*, 95. See also Miranda, *Ecos, Alientos y Sonidos*, 11.

70. Pach, "The Art of the American Indian."

71. Pach, "The Greatest American Artists."

72. *Los Angeles Daily Times*, November 12, 1922, cited in Delpar, *The Enormous Vogue of Things Mexican*, 136.

73. "Mexican Art Show in Exhibition Here." Statistics are given in Delpar, *The Enormous Vogue of Things Mexican*, 144–45.

74. Jewell, "Deep Well of Culture." On a similar premise, in 1929 Senator Simon Guggenheim established the Latin American program of the Guggenheim Foundation on the premise that the United States had much to learn from "those countries that are our elder sisters in the civilization of America," enabling several Latin American composers to visit the United States. "Latin American and Caribbean Competition," John Simon Guggenheim Memorial Foundation, 2012, http://www.gf.org/applicants/the-latin-american-caribbean-competition/.

75. Lois Wilcox (Orozco's former assistant), cited in Jewell, "About Orozco's New Frescoes." See also "Charlot's Frescoes Shown"; Mumford, "Orozco in New England." Mumford largely overlooked Orozco's attack on U.S. higher education and capitalism in general. See Delpar, *The Enormous Vogue of Things Mexican*, 149; Bass, "*The Epic of American Civilization*," 161.

76. Reiman, "Prometheus Unraveled."

77. Boas, *The Mind of Primitive Man*, 98. See especially Boas's final chapter, "Race Problems in the United States."

78. Stocking, "The Ethnographical Sensibility of the 1920s and the Dualism of the Anthropological Tradition," 212–13.

79. Stocking, "The Ethnographic Sensibilities of the 1920s and the Dualism of the Anthropological Tradition," 216. In 1924 Sapir's essay "Culture Genuine and Spurious" appeared in full in the *American Journal of Sociology*. See Sapir, *Selected Writings of Edward Sapir in Language, Culture, and Personality*, 308–31.

80. Sapir, "Culture Genuine and Spurious," 316.

81. On the influence of *Patterns of Culture*, see Susman, *Culture as History*, 153–54.

82. Benedict, *Patterns of Culture*, 129. Benedict was careful to note that she did not equate ancient Greece with indigenous America but used the term *Apollonian* to distinguish the Zuni from other native communities (79).

83. Redfield, *Tepotzlan*, 83.

84. Cited in Stocking, "The Ethnographic Sensibility of the 1920s and the Dualism of the Anthropological Tradition," 224.

85. Cited in Stocking, "The Ethnographic Sensibilities of the 1920s and the Dualism of the Anthropological Tradition," 220.

86. Although he admired Mexico, Carleton Beals later criticized Roosevelt's Good Neighbor Policy. See *The Coming Struggle for Latin America*, especially 310.

87. Cited in McLuhan, *Dream Tracks*, 156.

88. Brenner, *Idols behind Altars*, 32.

89. Bynner, "While the Train Pauses at Torreon [*sic*]," 2.

90. Ingle, *Mayan Revival Style*, 24–25.

91. Ingle, *Mayan Revival Style*, 15.

92. Hampton, "Rebirth of Prehistoric American Art," 633; "Reviving Mayan Architecture."

93. Cited in Ingle, *Mayan Revival Style*, 81–83.

94. Hauser cited in Delpar, *The Enormous Vogue of Things Mexican*, 193; Hampton, "Rebirth of Prehistoric American Art," 632.

95. Torgovnick, *Gone Primitive*, 8–9.

96. Redfield, *Tepotzlan*, 83.

97. Chase, *Mexico*, 1933, 83, 168.

98. Letter from Copland to Mary Lescase, January 13, 1933, cited in Copland and Perlis, *Copland, 1900–1942*, 216. Self-identifying is of course one way for artists and intellectuals to show solidarity with marginalized groups. On the eve of the premiere of his "gypsy ballet" *El amor brujo*, Manuel de Falla announced to the Madrid press that he had lived the work "as if a gypsy [him]self" (cited in Hess, *Manuel de Falla and Modernism in Spain*, 56). Frank claimed that he lived in the South "among the Negroes as if [he] were a Negro" (cited in Williams, *Radical Journalists*, 113).

99. Although Rosenfeld found but few "pieces of [Lawrence's], novels or poems or essays, that are entirely successful things in themselves," he conceded that Lawrence was "an original mind giving itself in an easily original idiom" ("D. H. Lawrence," 126).

100. The *Dial* published an unenthusiastic, unsigned review in June 1926 (vol. 80, p. 520), probably by Alyse Gregory. See Joost and Sullivan, *D. H. Lawrence and The Dial*, 190.

101. Discussed in Torgovnick, *Gone Primitive*, 164. For a less utopian view of the novel, see Keen, *The Aztec Image in Western Thought*, 553–56.

102. See Fitz-Gerald, "The Opportunity and the Responsibility of the Teacher of Spanish," 11–12.

103. Fitz-Gerald, "The Opportunity and the Responsibility of the Teacher of Spanish," 12.

104. Herbert Eugene Bolton, "The Epic of Greater American," in Hanke, *Do the Americas Have a Common History?*, 67–100.

105. Cited in Hanke, *Do the Americas Have a Common History?*, 11.

106. Bolton and Marshall, *The Colonization of North America*. Bolton's class at Berkeley, which he fondly dubbed a "Seven Ring Circus," was one of the most popular on campus, enrolling over a thousand students in a given semester. See Bolton, "Confessions of a Wayward Professor," 362. An early account of the difficulties in establishing courses on Latin American history in U.S. universities is "Report on the Teaching of Latin American History" by the Pan American Union.

107. Sweet, *A History of Latin America*, 222.

108. See Mariátegui, *La realidad peruana*, 7–11.

109. Dos Passos, "Paint the Revolution!," 15. See also the 1925 essay "Destruction of Tenochtitlan" by William Carlos Williams in *In the American Grain*, 27–38.

110. "Organize to Foster Artistry in Mexico"; Kert, *Abby Aldrich Rockefeller*, 106.

111. Stocking, "The Ethnographic Sensibility of the 1920s and the Dualism of the Anthropological Tradition," 219.

112. "Dazzling Pageant Is Aztec Gold," *New York Times*, May 3, 1929. See also Delpar, *The Enormous Vogue of Things Mexican*, vii.

113. On Shawn's experimental choreography, see *Los Angeles Times*, October 10, 1920, cited in Ingle, *Mayan Revival Style*, 10.

114. Ziegfeld also entered the world of the Indian in Samuel Goldwyn's 1930 film adaptation *Whoopee!* See Pisani, *Imagining Native America in Music*, 1, 282–85.

115. "Gorgeous Pageant 'Aztec Gold' Marks Charity Carnival."

116. "Gorgeous Pageant 'Aztec Gold' Marks Charity Carnival."

117. Levy, *Frontier Figures*, 16. The Indian presence endured in the musical and in film music. See also Pisani, *Imagining Native America in Music*, 277–329.

118. Farwell cited in Levy, *Frontier Figures*, 38.

119. Rosenfeld, *By Way of Art*, 283; Copland, "Carlos Chávez—Mexican Composer" (1928), 323. Copland reiterated this idea in *Music and Imagination*, 90. See also Pollack, *George Gershwin*, 148.

120. Leonard Bernstein, "The Absorption of Race Elements into American Music" (B.A. thesis, Harvard University, 1939), in *Findings*, 48.

121. See Taylor Gibson, "The Music of Manuel M. Ponce, Julián Carrillo, and Carlos Chávez in New York," 132–39.

122. Tablada, cited in Saborit, "Mexican Gaieties," 141.

123. Saavedra, "Of Selves and Others," 146, 167–69. Saavedra discusses other early performances of Chávez's music on 157.

124. Levin, "From the New York Avant-Garde to Mexican Modernists," 107. See also Parker, "Copland and Chávez," 434. In September 1932 in Mexico City, Chávez presented the first all-Copland concert to be given anywhere, the program for which is given in Copland and Perlis, *Copland, 1900–1942*, 215.

125. Eventually he became frustrated with the organization, however. Taylor Gibson, "The Music of Manuel M. Ponce, Julián Carrillo, and Carlos Chávez in New York," 157–58.

126. Rosenfeld, "The New American Music," 629.

127. Rosenfeld, "The New American Music," 629.

128. Copland, "Carlos Chávez—Mexican Composer" (1928), 323. To be sure, Copland added that Chávez's immersion in the "ritualistic music of the Mexican Indian" had not always served him well. (Copland found *El fuego nuevo*, for example, "too literal.") But such setbacks were simply part of artistic growth. Chávez quoted Indian themes in only a few works, including *Los cuatro soles* and *Sinfonía India*. See Saavedra, "Of Selves and Others," 136.

129. Copland, "Carlos Chávez—Mexican Composer" (1928), 322.

130. Copland, "Carlos Chávez—Mexican Composer" (1928), 322. Copland does not elaborate on his understanding of absolute music. In seeing absolute music "as a manifestation of life," however, he approximates Wagner (rather than Hanslick), as in, say, *The Artwork of the Future*. See Wagner, *Richard Wagner's Prose Works*, 120–40.

131. Weissmann, "The Tyranny of the Absolute," 19.

132. Weissmann, "Race and Modernity," 4, 3, 6. Weissmann was pilloried by the Nazis in their campaign against "degenerate music." Potter, *Most German of the Arts*, 18.

133. Henry Cowell, cited in Taylor Gibson, "The Music of Manuel M. Ponce, Julián Carrillo, and Carlos Chávez in New York," 159. Taylor Gibson discusses Chávez's association with Cowell on 155–60.

134. Rosenfeld, *By Way of Art*, 275.

135. For additional commentary on the piano sonata, see Citkowitz, "Forecast and Review," 155–56; García Morillo, *Carlos Chávez*, 63–66; Parker, *Carlos Chávez*, 35; Oja, *Making Music Modern*, 275–78.

136. Rosenfeld, *By Way of Art*, 276.

137. Rosenfeld, *By Way of Art*, 280.

138. Rosenfeld, *An Hour with American Music*, 19–20.

139. Rosenfeld, *By Way of Art*, 273.

140. Berger, "Time's Arrow and the Advent of Musical Modernity," 7. See also Rumpf, "A Kingdom Not of This World."

141. Rosenfeld, *An Hour with American Music*, 18.

142. Chua, *Absolute Music and the Construction of Meaning*, 3.

143. Lourie, "Neogothic and Neoclassic," 8.

144. Citkowitz, "American Composers, XII," 4, 10.

145. Cited in Oja, *Making Music Modern*, 234.

146. Levy, "'The White Hope of American Music,'" 142.

147. Levy, *Frontier Figures*, 24.

148. Farwell, "Roy Harris," 21. All page numbers cited in this paragraph are from this article.

149. Levy, "'The White Hope of American Music,'" 136.

150. Oja, *Making Music Modern*, 286. When the *Rite* premiered in Paris in 1913, Jacques Rivière wrote of the work's "absolute purity," adding that never had there been "a music so magnificently limited" (*Stravinsky and the Russian Traditions*, 2: 990–95).

151. Downes, "*Sacre du Printemps* Played."

152. Henderson, "Boston Orchestra Plays Stravinsky's Impressive Ballet."

153. Sanborn, "Honors of the Season," 5.

154. Chávez, "Technique and Inner Form," 28. The article first appeared in Mexico as "Interior y exterior" in *La Antorcha*, December 6, 1924 (Saavedra, "Of Selves and Others,"

157n27). Taylor Gibson notes that Minna Ledermann initially asked Chávez to discuss classical and popular music. The fact that Chávez avoided any discussion of Mexican popular music, offering instead an article on formal-technical matters, Taylor Gibson speculates, may reflect his ambivalence over being labeled a nationalist ("The Music of Manuel M. Ponce, Julián Carrillo, and Carlos Chávez in New York," 161).

155. Chávez, "Technique and Inner Form," 28. Chávez also discussed organicism in art in "The Two Persons," 153, in which he declares that art is "a conception—idea or emotion in the act of possessing some organic form," expounding upon "the organic material that conditions art."

156. Revilla, *El arte en México*, 19; Tablada, cited in Fernández, *Estética del arte mexicano*, 50.

157. Belnap, "Diego Rivera's Greater America," 78. See also Hernández Campos, "The Influence of the Classical Tradition, Cézanne, and Cubism on Rivera's Artistic Development," 119; Rodríguez, *Guia de los murales de Diego Rivera en la Secretaría de Educación Pública*, 133.

158. Revilla, *El arte en México*, 19.

159. Knight, "Racism, Revolution, and *Indigenismo*," 77.

160. Cited and translated in Knight "Racism, Revolution, and *Indigenismo*," 77.

161. Saavedra, "Of Selves and Others," 56. On Vasconcelos's pragmatism, see 62–64.

162. Chávez conducted the orchestra until 1948. See Carmona, *Carlos Chávez*, 153. Saavedra discusses *El fuego nuevo* (which, as she notes, was not well received) and *Sinfonía de la Patria*, another canceled work of Chávez that has fallen into obscurity, in "Of Selves and Others," 288–95, 122–27.

163. Vasconcelos, "Indología." On 1121 Vasconcelos defines *indología*, a coined term, as "the entire ensemble of reflections [he seeks] to present apropos contemporary life, origins, and future . . . of what we know as the Ibero-American race."

164. Vasconcelos, "Indología," 1260. As director of the Orquesta Sinfónica de México, Chávez took on a similar project, performing the Western classics in the open air or other informal environments, often for working-class audiences. Carlos Chávez, "Music in a Mexican Test Tube," *New York Times*, July 2, 1939, cited in Hess, "Miguel Ángel Estrella."

165. Saavedra, "Of Selves and Others," 92.

166. Vasconcelos, "Indología," 1185.

167. Cited and translated in Saavedra, "Of Selves and Others," 66.

168. Vasconcelos, "Indología," 1228–29.

169. Saavedra, "Of Selves and Others," 68.

170. Cited and translated in Saavedra, "Of Selves and Others," 70.

171. Cited and translated in Saavedra, "Of Selves and Others," 77.

172. Saavedra, "Of Selves and Others," 100–105.

173. Vasconcelos, "El monismo estético," 9, 15.

174. Rosenfeld, "Beethoven," in *Discoveries of a Music Critic*, 67–82. Subsequent page references refer to this essay.

175. Rosenfeld may have had in mind Schopenhauer, whose works he knew and who declared that "the will turns away from life. . . . Man now attains to the state of voluntary renunciation, resignation, and true indifference" (*The World as Will and Representation*, 1: 379).

176. Rosenfeld, "Igor, Tu N'est Qu'un Villain," part 5 of the larger essay "Thanks to the International Guild," in *By Way of Art*, 41.

177. Rosenfeld, "Igor, Tu N'est Qu'un Villain," 42.

178. Rosenfeld, "Igor, Tu N'est Qu'un Villain," 36, 40, 41.

179. Rosenfeld, *By Way of Art*, 274.

180. Rosenfeld, *By Way of Art*, 281.

181. Rosenfeld, *By Way of Art*, 281, 274.

182. Rosenfeld, *By Way of Art*, 283.

183. Fles, "Chavez Lights New Music with Old Fires," 1.

184. Torgovnick, *Gone Primitive*, 9.

■ Chapter 3. The Good Neighbor Onstage: Carlos Chávez's *H.P.* and Dialectical Indigenism

1. Harry L. Hewes, "Brilliant Throng Defies Rain for *H.P.* Premiere," *Philadelphia Morning Public Ledger*, April 1, 1932, cited in Taylor Gibson, "The Music of Manuel M. Ponce, Julián Carrillo, and Carlos Chávez in New York," appendix F.

2. Henry, "*H.P.* Makes Premiere Here with a Bang as Sparkplugs Go into a Song and Dance." Here Beck was having a little fun with his public: he wrote two reviews of the ballet (neither very flattering), one signed by the "lowbrow" Beck C. Henry and the other by the "more dignified" Henry C. Beck (his real name).

3. Martin, quoting program in "The Dance: A Mexican Ballet." Later critics would take a similar tack. Robert L. Parker, for example, writes that the work "contrasts the naturalness and sensuality of the tropics" with "northern industrialization" (*Carlos Chávez*, 109).

4. Watkins, "Chávez's Ballet 'H.P.' Has Debut in Philadelphia."

5. Stokowski offered his impressions of Mexico to the *Philadelphia Evening Bulletin* of January 18, 1932, cited in Daniel, *Stokowski*, 283.

6. Reiss, "'H.P.' Presentation Is Swell Occasion but Lacks Timely Proletarian Touch."

7. Martin, "The Dance: A Handicap Event."

8. Elsie Finn, "Composer of *H.P.* Arrives in Philadelphia," *Philadelphia Record*, March 5, 1932, cited in Taylor Gibson, "The Music of Manuel M. Ponce, Julián Carrillo, and Carlos Chávez in New York," appendix F. See also "Philadelphia Hears Premieres of Works by Antheil and Chávez."

9. Smith, interview with Alexis Dolinoff, 113. Press reports, with their detailed lists of attendees, suggest that the only ambassador present was Causaranc.

10. Geist and Monleón, introduction to *Modernism and Its Margins*, xxiii.

11. "Stokowski to Give Chávez Ballet," 6.

12. Belnap, "Diego Rivera's Greater America."

13. García Morillo, *Carlos Chávez*, 47. See also Parker, "Carlos Chávez and the Ballet."

14. Coady, "American Art" (part 2), 54–55.

15. Coady, "American Art" (part 2), 55.

16. Coady, "American Art" (part 1), 3–4.

17. Seldes, "Thompson's Panorama, the Woolworth Building, and Do It Now."

18. See Oja, *Making Music Modern*, 238.

19. On early performances of *Pacific 231* in the United States, see n87 below. On April 10, 1931, Stokowski conducted the U.S. premiere of *Pas d'acier* at Philadelphia's Metropolitan Opera House under the auspices of the League of Composers and the Philadelphia Orchestra Association; the work then traveled to New York, where it was performed on April 21 and 22. Lee Simonson reformulated Diaghilev's 1927 production as a satire on "the rhythm of machine industry and its large-scale 'efficiency.'" Now known as *The Age of Steel*, the ballet incorporated a workers' rebellion. See "*Oedipus Rex* Gets American Premiere." On Simonson's departures from the Diaghilev production, see Martin, "The Dance: Social Satire." *The Iron Foundry* was performed in July 1931 at the Hollywood Bowl under the title *The Spirit of the Factory*, with some sixty dancers choreographed by Adolph Bolm. See Schallert, "Huge Ovation for Rodzinski."

20. Tristan Tzara, "Dadaist Manifesto," excerpted in Kolocotroni et al., *Modernism*, 279. Oja discusses links between Antheil's music and Dada in *Making Music Modern*, 71–94. Antheil, however, allied himself with surrealism, citing his interest in Luis Buñuel's *Le chien andalou* and remarking that "the surrealist movement had, from the very beginning, been [his] friend." Antheil, *Bad Boy of Music*, 300.

21. Quoted in Downes, "Kussevitsky [*sic*] as a Magnetic Personality."

22. Sometimes real factory equipment was used, as in another Soviet project, the Concert of Factory Sirens of 1920. See Albright, *Modernism and Music*, 183. Downes reacted to Arseny Avramoff's "symphony for factory whistles" in "Music," *New York Times*, December 3, 1930.

23. Thompson, "Fly-Wheel Opera," 39. See also Felber, "Step-Children of Music"; Stuckenschmidt, "Machines."

24. Tashjian, *Skyscraper Primitives*, 3.

25. Gershwin, "The Composer in the Machine Age," 264. On European futurism, see Radice, "'Futurismo,'" 1–2; Venn, "Rethinking Russolo"; Filippo Tommaso Marinetti, "The Founding and Manifesto of Futurism," in Kolocotroni et al., *Modernism*, 249–56.

26. The term appears in a 1925 article for the *Guardian* and is discussed in Tashjian, *Skyscraper Primitives*, 132, and Oja, *Making Music Modern*, 91. See also Munson, *Waldo Frank*, 24.

27. Munson, *Waldo Frank*, 25.

28. Antheil, "The Negro on the Spiral, or a Method of Negro Music," in Albright, *Modernism and Music*, 389.

29. Novo, "Nueva York (Continente vacío)."

30. Ponce, "S.M. el Fox."

31. Schmidt, *The Roots of "Lo Mexicano,"* 98.

32. See Madrid, *Sounds of the Modern Nation*, 58–59 and (on Chávez) 62–63.

33. Siqueiros's statements appeared in the single issue of the magazine *Vida Americana*, published in Barcelona in 1921, cited in Hurlburt, *The Mexican Muralists in the United States*, 196.

34. Siqueiros, cited in Hurlburt, *The Mexican Muralists in the United States*, 197. Siqueiros also cautioned against "lamentable reconstructions so fashionable among us," that is, "the seemingly inescapable need of critics of primitive art to explain it in terms of scientific positivism while shortchanging their original meanings." On this point, see García Canclini, *Hybrid Cultures*, 28–29.

35. Charlot, *The Mexican Mural Renaissance*, 9.

36. Cited and translated in Helm, *Mexican Painters*, 84.

37. My remarks on the murals are largely indebted to Belnap, "Diego Rivera's Greater America," 77–82.

38. See, for example, "Dance in Tehuantepec" of 1928.

39. Covarrubias, *Mexico South*, xxv, xxvii.

40. Rodríguez, *Guia de los murales de Diego Rivera en la Secretaría de Educación Pública*, 24.

41. Rodríguez, *Guia de los murales de Diego Rivera en la Secretaría de Educación Pública*, 42. See also Weinstock, *Mexican Music*, 24.

42. Yellis, "Prosperity's Child," 55–56.

43. Elsewhere in the Secretariat murals, Rivera cites "Las esperanzas de la Patria por la rendición de [Pancho] Villa." See Mendoza, *Lírica narrativa de México*, 116–17, 41.

43. Belnap, "Diego Rivera's Greater America," 78.

44. Evans, "If I Should Go Back to Mexico."

45. Downs, *Diego Rivera*. Rivera discusses the project in his essay "Dynamic Detroit," 293.

46. Vasconcelos, "La raza cósmica," in *Obras completas*, 2: 903–1067. Portions of "La raza cósmica" appear in English translation in Burns, *Latin America*, 125–29.

47. Rodríguez, *Changing Race*, 106–8. See also Guterl, *The Color of Race in America*, 27–51. Some scholars link this mutability to the colonial period, when Spaniards accustomed to contact with North Africa brought a so-called Mediterranean perception of race to the Americas. See Forbes, *Black Africans and Native Americans*, 100–106.

48. Rodríguez, *Changing Race*, 112–20. Further, as Jack D. Forbes notes, many of these terms did not necessarily "imply interracial mixture nor . . . make any assertion about ancestry" (*Black Africans and Native Americans*, 101). The *casta* paintings of the colonial period, which depict this complex mixing, are a compelling document of this terminological plenty—and the desire to enshrine it in art. See Katzew, *Casta Painting*, 4–5. On musical ramifications of mestizaje, see Pérez-Torres, "Mestizaje in the Mix," 209.

49. Knight, "Racism, Revolution, and *Indigenismo*," 85.

50. Vasconcelos addressed these points in a 1926 lecture for the Harris Foundation in Chicago (published in Vasconcelos and Gamio, *Aspects of Mexican Civilization*). He remarked that "North America has developed in accordance with a law of similarity of races," whereas Latin America had habitually "struggl[ed] along according to a sort of varying rhythm of radical changes and contrasts" (41). Spencer's status in Mexico is discussed in Knight, "Racismo, Revolution and *Indigenismo*," 86.

51. Grant, *The Passing of the Great Race or The Racial Basis of European History*, 18. Vasconcelos critiques Grant in "Indología," 1198–205.

52. O'Brien, *The Racial Middle*, 3–4. See also Rodríguez, *Changing Race*, 78–79, 154. Popular culture addressed these matters as well. In *Tarzan of the Apes* (1912), the first of twenty-four novels on Tarzan, readers might be "titillated by the threat of racial, species, or class miscegenation" without actually confronting it in ordinary life. Cheyfitz, *The Poetics of Imperialism*, 13–4. See also Torgovnick, *Gone Primitive*, 42–72.

53. Honour, *The European Vision of America*, 11; Roberts, "'The Lady in the Tutti-Frutti Hat,'" 147–48.

54. The term *banana republic* appears in "The Admiral." For an account of how the media and commerce appropriated it (most notably in the fashionable clothing chain), see Safire, *Safire's Political Dictionary*, 41–42.

55. Salvatore, *Imágenes de un imperio*, 46–47. LeGrand cautions against "dualistic assumptions" in "Living in Macondo."

56. Cardoso and Faletto, *Dependency and Development in Latin America*, x–xi. See also Raúl Prebisch, "A New Economic Model for Latin America," in Holden and Zolov, *Latin America and the United States*, 198–200; Packenham, *The Dependency Movement*, 15; Joseph, "Close Encounters," especially 12; Vasconcelos, "Indología," 1075; Vasconcelos warned against "soft Pan Americanism" with its potential for "invading imperialism" (1124–28). See also 1272–80 ("The Conflict") and his essay "Bolivarismo y Monroismo."

57. Vasconcelos, "Indología," 1127, 1124–28; see also 1107, 1127; Elsewhere he took a more conciliatory tone. In his Harris Foundation talks, he declared, "It is possible to build a strong, powerful civilization of the New World, without trying to impose one type of civilization upon the other, without even trying to argue which is the better . . . the Latin or the Anglo-Saxon, for both are useful and perhaps both are indispensable for the present and future power and glory of the continent" (Vasconcelos and Gamio, *Aspects of Mexican Civilization*, 20).

58. Skidmore and Smith, *Modern Latin America*, 6. See also Aparicio and Chávez-Silverman, *Tropicalizations*.

59. Aparicio, "Ethnifying Rhythms, Feminizing Cultures," 106–12.

60. Enloe, *Bananas, Beaches and Bases*, 129–30.

61. Poovey, "Accommodating Merchants," 12.

62. Rivera was expelled from the Party in 1929 for perceived coziness with the right-leaning government of Plutarco Elías Calles (Siqueiros, "Rivera's Counter-Revolutionary Road," 17–18). For his self-defense, see Diego Rivera, "Raíces políticas y motivos personales de la controversia Siqueiros-Rivera: Stalinismo vs. bolchevismo leninista," in *Política y arte*, 111–25.

63. Belnap, "Diego Rivera's Greater America," 75; see also Kert, *Abby Aldrich Rockefeller*, 348.

64. Blanksten, *Perón's Argentina*, 7.

65. Carpenter, *Skyscrapers*, prefatory note in score (New York: Schirmers, 1926).

66. Hampton, "Rebirth of Prehistoric American Art," 634; see also Mujica, *History of the Skyscraper*, 19.

67. Unidentified clipping of April 17, 1930, cited in Daniel, *Stokowski*, 280.

68. Mujica, *History of the Skyscraper*, 67.

69. Letter, Barreda to Chávez, February 8, 1925, in Carmona, *Epistolario selecto de Carlos Chávez*, 54.

70. Letter, Gorostiza to Chávez, October 11, 1926, in Carmona, *Epistolario selecto de Carlos Chávez*, 70.

71. Letter, Varèse to Chávez, February 8, 1926, in Carmona, *Epistolario selecto de Carlos Chávez*, 66–67.

72. In an article for *Eolus* published shortly thereafter, he paid homage to Varèse. See Chávez, "Antecedents and Consequents," 13. Other works on the program included Colin McPhee's Pastorale and Rondino for two flutes, clarinet, trumpet, and piano; a piano trio by Ildebrando Pizetti; Anton Webern's *Fünf geistliche Lieder* op. 15; William Grant Still's *Darker America*; and *Three Pagan Hymns* by Goossens himself. R.C.B.B., "Modernists Evoke Laughter and Applause," *Musical America*, December 4, 1926, 7.

73. Program note (V. I, c. 2, exp. 2, Escritos, Archivo Chávez, Archivo General de la Nación), cited in Taylor Gibson, "The Music of Manuel M. Ponce, Julián Carrillo, and Carlos Chávez in New York," 142.

74. Program note (V. I, c. 2, exp. 2, Escritos, Archivo Chávez, Archivo General de la Nación), cited in Taylor Gibson, "The Music of Manuel M. Ponce, Julián Carrillo, and Carlos Chávez in New York," 142.

75. The archaic *mariache* (rather than *mariachi*) is a form of pronunciation that appears in rural communities. Sheehy, *Mariachi Music in America*, 96–97.

76. Cited in Taylor Gibson, "The Music of Manuel M. Ponce, Julián Carrillo, and Carlos Chávez in New York," 142. See also introduction, n28.

77. The manuscripts are JOB 84–11, 97 a–k. The chamber version is JOB 84–11, 97k, is unbound and dated 1926. It is scored for piccolo, flute, E-flat and B-flat clarinets, oboe (the player doubles on English horn), two bassoons, horn, trumpet, trombone, strings, and various percussion instruments, including timpani, suspended and crash cymbals, *güiro*, and tambourine. Some percussion parts lack instrumentation and, with several penciled-in deletions, prompts to the conductor, and performance indications in English and French, make for a rather rough manuscript. JOB 84–11, 97j, a bound and more finished manuscript, is for full orchestra and is sixteen measures longer than the chamber version. The last page (155) is marked "C.Ch México 1926–27." Measure numbers here refer to the version for full orchestra, in which the chamber setting is fleshed out.

78. The Mexican conductor Eduardo Mata, who died in 1995, planned to reconstruct and record the entire work with the London Symphony Orchestra, but never realized

this project. Robert L. Parker, interview with Mata, August 1980, cited in Parker, *Carlos Chávez*, 110n5.

79. On pentatonicism in the Indianist music of Farwell, Frederick Burton, Charles Wakefield Cadman, and many other composers, see Pisani, *Imagining Native America in Music*.

80. Pollack, *Aaron Copland*, 129. For a discussion of "Sidewalks of New York" in Copland's *Statements* (1935), see Crist, *Music for the Common Man*, 34–40.

81. The fragment appears in JOB 84–11, folder 97i, the orchestral version of movement 4, dated 1926. It also appears in its sounding (rather than transposed) format in JOB 84–11, folder 97f, a conductor's cue sheet for the Philadelphia production used to coordinate the interludes with changes in lighting and the raising and lowering of several drop curtains.

82. After assuming the directorship of the Orquesta Sinfónica de México in 1928, Chávez performed the concert version of John Alden Carpenter's *Skyscrapers* (Agea, *21 años de la Orquesta Sinfónica de México*, 73). Just as Chávez juxtaposes popular-style melodies against ostinato-driven modernist machine music in "Dance of Men and Machines," Carpenter treats quotations of actual popular melodies much the same way. Carpenter's "Song of the Skyscraper" has been described as a "primal pseudo–Native American (Indian) theme." See Judith Tick, "Program Note," American Symphony Orchestra, http://www.americansymphony.org/concert_notes/skyscrapers (accessed January 15, 2013). Upon hearing a concert version of *H.P.* in 1937, Francis D. Perkins wrote, "There were times when a listener could remember Carpenter's *Skyscrapers*" ("Carlos Chávez Directs First of 6 Concerts").

83. Cited in Taylor Gibson, "The Music of Manuel M. Ponce, Julián Carrillo, and Carlos Chávez in New York," 142.

84. R.C.B.B., "Modernists Evoke Laughter and Applause," 7.

85. Cited in Saborit, "Mexican Gaieties," 141.

86. Henderson, "Modern Works Given in Concert." See also Samaroff, "Music" (signed W.H.S.). Lawrence Gilman of the *Herald Tribune* and Leonard Liebling of the *New York American* left before the concert was over (Taylor Gibson, "The Music of Manuel M. Ponce, Julián Carrillo, and Carlos Chávez in New York," 144).

87. Downes, "Music: More of the Ultra-Modern." For Downes's enthusiastic reaction to *Pacific 231*, see "Koussevitzky Gets Ovation in Boston." See also his remarks apropos Walter Damrosch's performance a few weeks later in "Music." A performance in February 1928 by Toscanini attracted a large public. See "Throng Hears Concert."

88. Rosenfeld, "Musical Chronicle," 177.

89. Rosenfeld, *By Way of Art*, 274–75.

90. Letter, Cowell to Chávez, October 3, 1929, in Carmona, *Epistolario selecto de Carlos Chávez*, 101. The work does not appear in Root's catalogue of PAAC concerts (Root, "The Pan-American Association of Composers," 62–69). For the exchange between Chávez and Harris, see Carmona, *Epistolario selecto de Carlos Chávez*, 153–54. Pro Musica turned down *H.P.* in early 1933 because at that time, the organization was planning an all-U.S. program. On Pro Musica, see Oja, *Making Music Modern*, 179–81.

91. See Saavedra, "Los escritos periodísticos de Carlos Chávez," 78. Saavedra compares Chávez's social-political thinking with that of Charles Seeger, associated with the leftist Composers Collective in "The American Composer in the 1930s." In a 1942 retrospective, Otto Mayer-Serra sums up Chávez's advocacy of art for all levels of society and opposition to the "so-called 'elite' art of intellectual aristocracy." See "Carlos Chávez: Una monografía crítica."

92. Taylor Gibson, "The Music of Manuel M. Ponce, Julián Carrillo, and Carlos Chávez in New York," 144–47. On the *Corrido de "El Sol,"* see Waseen, "Carlos Chávez and the Corrido."

93. Schmitz, "A Profile of Catherine Littlefield," 50.

94. Visitor statistics are given in Hurlburt, *Mexican Muralists in the United States*, 123. See also "Diego Rivera Exhibits in New York," 48.

95. Belnap, "Diego Rivera's Greater America," 87–88.

96. For example, *New York Herald Tribune*, November 14, 1931, cited in Hurlburt, Mexican Muralists in the United States, 123.

97. Martin, "Ballet or Ballyhoo?"

98. Grand Opera Program, 6.

99. Unidentified critic, cited in Stevenson, "Carlos Chávez's United States Press Coverage," 126.

100. Stevenson, "Carlos Chávez's United States Press Coverage," 126.

101. Smith, interview with Alexis Dolinoff, 112. My thanks to Bill Engelke of Ace Hardware in Bowling Green, Ohio, for clarification on the various components of H.P.'s costume.

102. References are to the Boosey & Hawkes score, published in 1959.

103. Grand Opera Program, 6.

104. Despite these incongruities, García Morillo contends that the composer "hit upon the exact spirit of this Buenos Aires dance" (*Carlos Chávez*, 52). Nor was Otto Mayer-Serra impressed; he accused Chávez of reproducing "an atmosphere of vulgar dancing" ("un ambiente de dancing vulgar") in lieu of shaping his material into "sonic combinations ruled by internal and exclusively musical logic" (*Panorama de la música mexicana*, 160).

105. I am indebted to the composer Ricardo Lorenz for this observation, as well as for insights on the *danzón*'s essential characteristics.

106. Crist, *Music for the Common Man*, 65–66.

107. The English-language version by Carol Raven, titled "Farewell Boys," is quite close to César Vedani's Spanish's lyrics. In the 1940s a version by Anne Shelton called "Pablo the Dreamer" and having nothing to do with the original Spanish was recorded. For an exploration of the "latune," a popular-song genre with various trappings of "Latin" music but with English lyrics often at odds with the original Spanish texts, see Pérez Firmat, "Latunes." Pérez Firmat discusses "Adios muchachos" on 191–92n13. I would add here only that the tango was also featured in the 1939 movie *Another Thin Man* and was perhaps best known in the United States as "I Get Ideas" from Louis Armstrong's 1951 recording, the text of which, again, has nothing to do with the Spanish lyrics.

108. Grand Opera Program, 6.

109. See Baqueiro Fóster, "El Huapango."

110. See Parker, "A Recurring Melodic Cell in the Music of Carlos Chávez."

111. Bowles, "On Mexico's Popular Music," 225.

112. T. M. Scruggs, "Marimba and Other Musics of Guatemala and Nicaragua," in Schechter, *Music in Latin American Culture*, 81.

113. Chávez simply asks for "one large marimba." Orchestral marimbas in Mexico at this time did not necessarily follow the standard five-octave size common today. I wish to thank Gwen Burgett for clarification on this point.

114. With too few variants to be considered a complex, the *sandunga* consists of several melodies that are interchanged in performance. Several are given in Orozco, *Tradiciones y leyendas del Istmo de Tehuantepec*, 215–23. I wish to thank John Koegel for clarification on classifying the *sandunga*.

115. For example, Amalia Batista, the protagonist of the eponymous 1936 *zarzuela* by the Cuban composer Rodrigo Prats, is described as "la mulata sandunguera" who "makes men

crazy" (Thomas, *Cuban Zarzuela*, 71). Some have argued that the word has Zapotec origins. See Orozco, *Tradiciones y leyendas del Istmo de Tehuantepec*, 59–60.

116. Unidentified and uncatalogued program note from 1941 on a *sandunga* that was probably arranged by Mauricio Muñoz, Biblioteca Nacional (Buenos Aires). I wish to thank Silvia Glocer for calling this source to my attention. See also Vásquez, *Música popular y costumbres regionales del estado de Oaxaca*, 26.

117. Eisenstein's "Introduction to the Scenario of the Film *Que viva México!*," cited in Seton, *Sergei Eisenstein*, 508; Podalsky, "Patterns of the Primitive," 31.

118. Compare, for example, the *sandungas* cited in Orozco, *Tradiciones y leyendas del Istmo de Tehuantepec* (217, 221) and Vásquez, *Música popular y costumbres regionales del estado de Oaxaca* (29) with Chávez's score. See also Orbón, "Las Sinfonías de Carlos Chávez," 155.

119. See the two-part article by Andrés Henestrosa, "Música Mestiza de Tehuantepec."

120. An analogous section of Carpenter's *Skyscrapers* involves a "a sudden 'black-out' of the lights," followed by a "stiff and relentless process of workmen, lock-stepping" (Carpenter, *Skyscrapers*, prefatory note). The manuscript copy of *H.P.* reads, "Black out, curtain down." Chávez's indication is in JOB 97 j.

121. Grand Opera Program, 6.

122. Souvenir program, cited in Hewes, "The Mexican Ballet-Symphony *H.P.*," 423. It is not clear that Hewes is the author.

123. See Rivas, *Missionary Capitalist*, especially 10–34.

124. "Stokowski Directs *H.P.* in First Dress Rehearsal as Stock Attacks Moderns."

125. Martin, "The Dance: A Handicap Event"; Martin, "Mexican Ballet in World Premiere."

126. Thompson, "Philadelphia Gives Chávez Ballet, *H.P.*, in World Premiere," 7.

127. Henry, "*H.P.* Makes Premiere Here with a Bang as Sparkplugs Go into a Song and Dance." See n2 above on this critic's use of two names.

128. Reiss, "'H.P.' Presentation Is Swell Occasion but Lacks Timely Proletarian Touch."

129. Belnap, "Diego Rivera's Greater America," 89.

130. See Oja's illuminating discussion on Ballet Mécanique in *Making Music Modern*, 71–94. In his autobiography, Antheil complains of the extent to which the manager, Donald Friede, played up the work's potential for controversy, presumably against his intentions. See Antheil, *Bad Boy of Music*, 190–91.

131. Beck C. Henry (Henry C. Beck's "lowbrow" alter ego), in Henry, "*H.P.* Makes Premiere Here with a Bang as Sparkplugs Go into a Song and Dance."

132. Watkins, "Chávez's Ballet 'H.P.' Has Debut in Philadelphia."

133. Martin, "*H.P.* New Ballet Fantastic Affair."

134. Thompson, "Philadelphia Gives Chávez Ballet, *H.P.*, in World Premiere," 7.

135. Thompson, "Philadelphia Gives Chávez Ballet, *H.P.*, in World Premiere," 7.

136. Blitzstein, "Forecast and Review," 165.

137. Blitzstein, "Forecast and Review," 165.

138. Blitzstein, "Forecast and Review," 166. In fact, Chávez's compatriots applauded his evocation of the "seductive, dancing South" when movements 2 and 3 were performed in Mexico, although they were less taken with the modernist "machine" music of the outer movements (Saavedra, "Of Selves and Others," 164n49).

139. Blitzstein, "Forecast and Review," 166.

140. A literal translation would be "like a pig sty." Herrera, *Frida*, 132.

141. Rosenfeld, "American Premieres."

142. Rosenfeld, "American Composers, VIII: Carlos Chávez," 158.

143. Rosenfeld, "American Composers, VIII: Carlos Chávez," 153.

144. See, for example, Smith, "'A Distinguishing Virility.'" Levy has explored the extent to which the western frontier and the image of the unabashedly masculine cowboy informed the reception of Roy Harris's music ("'The White Hope of American Music,'" 165n43).

145. Rosenfeld, "American Composers, VIII: Carlos Chávez," 155, 158.

146. Cited in Tick, "Charles Ives and Gender Ideology," 95; Rosenfeld, *An Hour with American Music*, 40.

147. Hubbs, *The Queer Composition of America's Sound*, 75.

148. Seldes, *The Seven Lively Arts*, 58–59. See Barbara Melosh, *Engendering Culture: Manhood and Womanhood in New Deal Public Art and Theater* (Washington, D.C.: Smithsonian Institution Press, 1991), 30; Kimmel, *Manhood in America*, 192–94, 199–200.

149. Thompson, "Philadelphia Gives Chávez Ballet, *H.P.*, in World Premiere," 7.

150. Martin, "The Dance: A Handicap Event"; Martin, "Mexican Ballet in World Premiere."

151. Adorno, *Philosophy of Modern Music*, 144. On the mechanical presence in early twentieth-century theater, see Edward Gordon Craig's "From the Actor and the Über-Marionette" (1907), in Kolocotroni et al., *Modernism*, 150–54. See also Watkins, *Pyramids at the Louvre*, 310–14.

152. Chávez's ballet on the Medea legend, *La hija de Cóliquide* (Daughter of Colchis), renamed *Dark Meadow* by Martha Graham, is discussed in Bannerman, "A Dance of Transition," 6. On the relationship between the incidental music for Cocteau's adaptation and the *Sinfonía Antígona*, see Parker, "De música incidental a sinfonía."

153. Taubman, "Mexican Novelty Offered by Iturbi."

154. Taubman, "Mexican Novelty Offered by Iturbi." On Taubman's career, see Robinson, "'A Ping, Qualified by a Thud,'" 86n29.

155. Warren Storey Smith, "Composer as Guest Conductor" and "Chávez Tells of Efforts to Create Music Variety," cited in Weinstock, *Carlos Chávez*, 12 and 13, respectively.

156. Martin, "Chávez Conducts Phila. Orchestra," cited in Weinstock, *Carlos Chávez*, 8.

157. Irving Kolodin, "Five Key Men," *Vogue*, October 1936, reproduced in Weinstock, *Carlos Chávez*, 14.

158. Smith, "Composer as Guest Conductor," cited in Weinstock, *Carlos Chávez*, 12.

159. Downes, "Chávez Conducts Boston Orchestra."

160. Perkins, "Carlos Chávez Directs First of 6 Concerts"; Philip Klein, "Mexican Maestro Presides over Weekly Concert," *Philadelphia Daily News*, cited in Weinstock, *Carlos Chávez*, 8. See also Downes, "Chávez Presents Opening Program."

161. Rosenfeld, "Chávez," *Discoveries of a Music Critic*, 337–43.

162. See, for example, Saavedra, "Of Selves and Others," 302–16; Parker, *Carlos Chávez*, 70–72; Stevenson, *Music in Mexico*, 243; García Morillo, *Carlos Chávez*, 88–95. Béhague's comments are discussed in the epilogue.

163. As Saavedra notes, some of Chávez's identifications of these melodies are not entirely accurate.

164. A formal diagram (endorsed by Chávez) appears in García Morillo, *Carlos Chávez*, 94.

165. Saavedra, "Of Selves and Others," 316.

166. Taubman, "Mexican Composers."

167. Chávez, "Revolt in Mexico," 39.

168. Weinstock, "Carlos Chávez," 436. See also "Chávez Tells of Efforts to Create Music Variety," cited in Weinstock, *Carlos Chávez*, 13.

169. Weinstock, "Carlos Chávez," 438.

170. Quoted in Kaufmann, "Carlos Chávez," 11.

171. "Chávez Tells of Efforts to Create Music Variety," in Weinstock, *Carlos Chávez*, 13.

172. McPhee, "Forecast and Review," 42.

173. McPhee, "Forecast and Review," 42.

174. Cuney-Hare, *Negro Musicians and Their Music*, 178.

175. Cage, "Chávez and the Chicago Drought," 186.

176. Delpar, *The Enormous Vogue of Things Mexican*, 203–8.

177. Knight surveys various positions on the Cárdenas years in "Cardenismo."

178. Hurlburt, *The Mexican Muralists in the United States*, 9; Rivas, *Missionary Capitalist*, 25–26.

179. Mayer-Serra commented in 1942 that the preludes had failed to spark the "curiosity" of Mexican pianists ("Bibliografía," 208).

180. Stevenson, *Music in Mexico*, 2.

181. Weinstock, *Mexican Music*, 11.

182. Saavedra, "Of Selves and Others," 322.

183. Weinstock, *Mexican Music*, 11.

■ **Chapter 4. Caliban and Unsublimated Primitivism: Villa-Lobos at the 1939 World's Fair**

1. Santomasso, "The Design of Reason," 34.

2. *The New York World's Fair Illustrated by Camera*, n.p.

3. Segal, "Utopian Fairs."

4. See Pollack, *George Gershwin*, 691–92.

5. William Grant Still, cited in Smith, *William Grant Still*, 64; *Guidebook*, cited in Rydell, *World of Fairs*, 131–32.

6. Pollack, *Aaron Copland*, 332–33; Schebera, *Kurt Weill*, 270.

7. Carter, "Forecast and Review," 243, 238.

8. Carter, "Forecast and Review," 243.

9. Thompson, "Burle Marx Conducts with Soprano and Two Pianists as Soloists."

10. Rosenfeld, "Current Chronicle"; Perkins, "Philharmonic Plays Brazilian Music at Fair"; Chotzinoff, "Brazilian Music Heard on Philharmonic Program"; O'Gorman, "Philharmonic in Brazilian Program at World's Fair"; Kolodin, "Marx Leads Music by Brazilians"; Bohm, "Philharmonic Heard under Brazil Auspices." See also Gates, "Brazilian Music," 132–33.

11. Downes: "Brazilian Music Is Played at the Fair"; "Brazilian Music on Fair Program"; "Art of Villa Lobos."

12. Rosenfeld, "Current Chronicle," 515. Performances of Villa-Lobos's music in the United States are detailed in Lopes, "The Evolution of Heitor Villa-Lobos's Music." Selected reviews are also cited in Appleby, *Heitor Villa-Lobos*.

13. Downes, "Schola Cantorum Gives Novelties."

14. Citkowitz, "Spring Concerts in New York," 169.

15. Martin, "Martha Graham in Hectic Recital"; see also Graham, "Seeking an American Art of Dance"; Helpern, "The Technique of Martha Graham," 40, 41.

16. Schwerké, "A Brazilian Rabelais."

17. Downes, "Brazilian Music Is Played at the Fair"; Downes, "Art of Villa Lobos."

18. Williams, *Culture Wars in Brazil*, 201–27.

19. Cristina Magaldi discusses the historiographical ramifications of this concept, including the backlash from twentieth-century critics, who refused to consider the possibility that European music mediated in the "various local subcultures." See *Music in Imperial Rio de Janeiro*, ix–xv; see also the same author's "Cosmopolitanism and World Music in Rio de Janeiro at the Turn of the Twentieth Century."

20. Discussed in Magaldi, *Music in Imperial Rio de Janeiro*, 137–38.

21. Cited, along with other Italian press sources, in Magaldi, *Music in Imperial Rio de Janeiro*, 138.

22. See Mário de Andrade, *Ensaio sobre a música brasileira*, 14.

23. Villa-Lobos probably made three significant trips early in his career: to Espirito Santo, Bahía, Pernambuco in 1905, to the southern provinces in 1906, and to the Amazon and northern Brazil in 1911 or 1912. See Béhague, *Heitor Villa-Lobos*, 5–6. Guérios discusses the difficulties in documenting these trips in "Heitor Villa-Lobos e o Ambiente Artístico Parisiense," 86–87.

24. Béhague summarizes criticism of the 1915 concert in *Heitor Villa-Lobos*, 8–9.

25. John P. Murphy notes that the verb *chorar*, which means "to weep" or "to lament," was sometimes applied to the mournful style of phrasing among some Brazilian musicians (*Music in Brazil*, 31). Presumably Villa-Lobos's use of the term in its plural form was intended to "denote the plurality of his sources." See Marx, introduction, Programs 1 and 2, p. 4.

26. Livingston-Isenhour and Caracas García, *Choro*, 2–3, 43.

27. Livingston-Isenhour and Caracas García, *Choro*, 17.

28. Graça Aranha, "A emoção estética na arte moderna," 27.

29. Andrade, *Hallucinated City*. On Andrade's stature in Brazilian musical scholarship, see Béhague, "Ecuadorian, Peruvian, and Brazilian Ethnomusicology," 23–24.

30. Lucie-Smith, *Latin American Art of the 20th Century*, 38–40.

31. The programs are given in Tarasti, *Heitor Villa-Lobos*, 67.

32. Wisnik, *O coro dos contrários*, 72.

33. Museu Villa-Lobos, *Villa-Lobos, Sua Obra*, 169–70.

34. Ronald de Carvahlo, "A música de Villa-Lobos," cited and translated in Béhague, *Heitor Villa-Lobos*, 13.

35. *Heitor Villa-Lobos Piano Music* (Mineola, N.Y.: Dover, 1996). There is no such designation in the edition published by Casa Arthur Napoleõ in Rio de Janeiro, 1900.

36. Martin, "Stokowski Bids His Audience 'Good-by.'"

37. On this period, which involved an influx of immigrants after 1870, see Burns, *A History of Brazil*, 197–257.

38. Davis, *White Face, Black Mask*, 1–19.

39. Skinner, *Black into White*, 64–77.

40. Skinner, *Black into White*, 68. On Roosevelt's racism and its impact on U.S. foreign policy, see Bradley, *The Imperial Cruise*.

41. For a discussion of Villa-Lobos's two suites for solo piano, *O prole do Bebe* (The Baby's Family) nos. 1 and 2 in terms of racial theory, see Dasilva, "Misleading Discourse and the Message of Silence."

42. Skinner, *Black into White*, 173–92.

43. Livingston-Isenhour and Caracas García, *Choro*, 13–14.

44. "The Aesthetic of Life" ("A estética da vida"), cited and translated in Nunes, "Anthropophagic Utopia, Barbarian Metaphysics," 60.

45. Lucie-Smith, *Latin American Art of the 20th Century*, 44. Parakilas explores the concept of auto-exoticism in "How Spain Got a Soul," 189–93.

46. Dunn, *Brutality Garden*, 15–17.

47. An English translation of the manifesto, which Oswald published in his own São Paulo–based journal *Revista de Antropofagia* (Cannibal Magazine), is in Bary, "Oswald de Andrade's Cannibalist Manifesto." See also Jackson, "Three Glad Races."

48. See Castro-Klarén, "A Genealogy for the 'Manifesto antropófago,'" 298.

49. Castro-Klarén, "A Genealogy for the 'Manifesto antropófago,'" 297.

50. Budasz, "Of Cannibals and the Recycling of Otherness," 2–3.

51. Williams, *Culture Wars in Brazil*, 44–48.

52. Wright, *Villa-Lobos*, 39.

53. Mariz, *Heitor Villa-Lobos*, 51.

54. Discussed in Mariz, *Heitor Villa-Lobos*, 52–53.

55. On charges of epigonism leveled against Villa-Lobos (especially by Jean Cocteau), see Guérios, "Heitor Villa-Lobos e o Ambiente Artístico Parisiense," 81–108.

56. Museu Villa-Lobos, *Villa-Lobos, Sua Obra*, 154.

57. Chevalier, "Oeuvres de Villa-Lobos," 450.

58. Prunières, "Les Concerts," 258.

59. See Fry, "Rethinking the *Revue nègre.*"

60. Alexander Benois, cited and translated in Taruskin, *Stravinsky and the Russian Traditions*, 1: 965.

61. Cited and translated in Appleby, *Heitor Villa-Lobos*, 86.

62. Cited and translated in Appleby, *Heitor Villa-Lobos*, 86.

63. Wright, *Villa-Lobos*, 78.

64. During 1934–37 Vargas served as president under constitutional rule. Williams, *Culture Wars in Brazil*, 6–9.

65. Good Neighborliness also affected historical memory; Bemis, for example, argued in 1943 that although the United States had "been an imperialistic power since 1898," it had exercised only a "comparatively mild imperialism" (*The Latin American Policy of the United States*, 385).

66. Cited in Holden and Zolov, *Latin America and the United States*, 141.

67. Fagg, *Pan Americanism*, 49–50.

68. Cited in Holden and Zolov, *Latin America and the United States*, 142.

69. The Endowment was established in 1910. See Ninkovitch, *The Diplomacy of Ideas*, 8.

70. Gellman, *Good Neighbor Diplomacy*, 146; Ninkovitch, *The Diplomacy of Ideas*, 29–30.

71. As Haring noted in 1928, "One of the oddities of Pan-Americanism is that it does not yet include the Dominion of Canada" (*South America Looks at the United States*, 54n30).

72. Ninkovitch, *Diplomacy of Ideas*, 30.

73. Gellman, *Good Neighbor Diplomacy*, 1.

74. Schwartz, *Flying Down to Rio*, 249, 313.

75. Letter, Vincent G. Hart, assistant to the director of the Production Code Administration, to Sidney Kramer (RKO Distributing Corporation), July 19, 1935, Margaret Herrick Library at the Academy of Motion Picture Arts and Sciences, Special Collections Correspondence File.

76. Cited in Schwartz, *Flying Down to Rio*, 309–10.

77. Translated and cited in Williams, *Culture Wars in Brazil*, 13.

78. Dávila, "Myth and Memory," 262–63.

79. In September 1922 arias from Gomes's opera were heard in Brazil's first-ever radio program. See McCann, *Hello, Hello Brazil*, 22.

80. Magaldi, "Two Musical Representations of Brazil," 205. As Magaldi points out (205n1), the name of the program was changed in 1962 to *A voz do Brazil* (The Voice of Brazil).

81. Cited in Skinner, *Black into White*, 199.

82. Bakota, "Getúlio Vargas and the Estado Novo," 209.

83. The 1993 documentary *It's All True: Based on an Unfinished Film by Orson Welles*, incorporates original footage. See also Stam, *Tropical Multiculturalism*, 107–32.

84. Campos Hazan, "Raça, Nação e Jose Mauricio Nunes Garcia."

85. Rowe and Schelling, *Memory and Modernity*, 122–38.

86. Cited in Clark, "Doing the Samba on Sunset Boulevard," 265. On popular music during the Vargas years, see Shaw, *The Social History of Brazilian Samba*, 26–43.

87. Shaw, "Vargas on Film," 212.

88. Shaw, "Vargas on Film," 212.

89. Cavalcanti, *When Brazil Was Modern*, 12.

90. On Costa and anti-Semitism, see Williams, *Culture Wars in Brazil*, 57.

91. Graeff, *Cidade Utopia*. Brasilia was neither completed nor designated the capital until after the Vargas years, however. In 1945 Vargas was forced from office but, like Perón in Argentina, was called back by popular acclaim. Beginning in 1951 he again served as president, committing suicide in 1954.

92. Williams, *Culture Wars in Brazil*, 69–82.

93. Squeff and Wisnik, "Villa-Lobos e o estado novo," 150.

94. Wright, *Villa-Lobos*, 107–9.

95. Villa-Lobos, *A música nacionalista*, cited and translated in Wright, *Villa-Lobos*, 108.

96. Villa-Lobos, *A música nacionalista*, cited and translated in Vassberg, "Villa-Lobos," 56.

97. An explanation of this pedagogy is found in Villa-Lobos, *O ensino popular de música no Brasil*, 19–45.

98. Villa-Lobos, *O ensino popular de música no Brasil*, 11–12.

99. See Peppercorn, "Some Aspects of Villa-Lobos' Principles of Composition," 29. For an overview of Villa-Lobos's experience with film music, see Wright, "Villa-Lobos and the Cinema."

100. Museu Villa-Lobos, *Villa-Lobos, Sua Obra*, 143.

101. The African American composer R. Nathaniel Dett, for example, found pentatonicism in spirituals, music of "Old China," and the songs of North American Indians (Dett, "Negro Music," 1245).

102. Weber, "Value Judgments in Social Science," in Runciman, *Max Weber*, 94–95. For additional views of Weber on music and European notions of progress, see "The History of the Piano" in the same volume (378–82).

103. Nettl, *The Study of Ethnomusicology*, 36–37.

104. Lévi-Strauss, for example, was said to speak "in one breath" of "Wagner and Chabrier, symphony and fugue" and the music of South American Indians (Nettl, *The Study of Ethnomusicology*, 37).

105. Béhague, *Heitor Villa-Lobos*, 1. See Paula C. Barros, *O romance de Villa-Lobos*, cited and translated in Béhague, *Heitor Villa-Lobos*, 5–6.

106. McKenna, *Myra Hess*, 90–91.

107. Rosenfeld, "Bach Conquers Musical America," 315.

108. Daniel, *Stokowski*, 1051–52.

109. Rosenfeld, "Bach Conquers Musical America," 314–19.

110. Williams discusses the various stages of planning for the Fair in *Culture Wars in Brazil*, 205–8.

111. Williams, *Culture Wars in Brazil*, 208.

112. Thompson, "Brazilian Music Given at Museum."

113. Appelbaum, *The New York World's Fair 1939/1940*, xii.

114. Appelbaum, *The New York World's Fair 1939/1940*, 123.

115. Cited in Holden and Zolov, *Latin America and the United States*, 17.

116. O'Connor, "The Usable Future."

117. Rydell, *World of Fairs*, 111.

118. Cited in Rydell, *World of Fairs*, 10.

119. Williams, *Empire as a Way of Life*, 31.

120. Walter Benjamin, "Paris, Capital of the Nineteenth Century," in *Reflections*, 152.

121. The National Cash Register Building was eventually transferred to the amusement zone for lack of "decorum." Santomasso, "The Design of Reason," 36.

122. "Review of 1939 New York World's Fair," 55, 64.

123. Gutheim, "Buildings at the Fair," 286.

124. Gutheim, "Buildings at the Fair," 316.

125. "Review of 1939 New York World's Fair," 64.

126. Goodwin, *Brazil Builds*, 92.

127. Goodwin, *Brazil Builds*, 84.

128. The first movement of no. 8 (for orchestra) is simply marked "Preludio." The two movements of no. 9, composed in 1945 in two versions (chorus, orchestra), are marked "Preludio" and "Fuga," respectively. On the recycled pieces in *Bachianas* no. 2, see Peppercorn, "Villa-Lobos 'Ben Trovato,'" 33.

129. See Hall, "Americans in Venice."

130. The translation "The Smallholder's Little Train" (in the sense of landholder) is often given for the title of the fourth movement. A *caipira* (hillbilly), however, would never have owned land.

131. Wright, *Villa-Lobos*, 89.

132. Marx, "Brazilian Portrait," 15.

133. Béhague, *Heitor Villa-Lobos*, 107.

134. Perkins, "Philharmonic Plays Brazilian Music at Fair."

135. Thompson, "Burle Marx Conducts with Soprano and Two Pianists as Soloists."

136. Downes, "Art of Villa Lobos."

137. Rosenfeld, "Current Chronicle," 517.

138. The term is Guy Debord's in *The Society of the Spectacle*.

139. Rosenfeld, "Current Chronicle," 517.

140. Slonimsky, "A Visit with Villa-Lobos," 7.

141. Another Villa-Lobos work heard at the Fair, the orchestral composition *Caixinha de Boas-Festes* (Box of Surprises), was also dismissed as "light," with Jerome Bohm comparing it to Victor Herbert's *Babes in Toyland*. Bohm, "Philharmonic Heard under Brazil Auspices."

142. Rosenfeld, "Current Chronicle," 517.

143. Marx, "Brazilian Portrait," 16; Downes, "Brazilian Music Is Played at the Fair." See also Carter, "Forecast and Review," 243.

144. Marx, "Brazilian Portrait," 14.

145. O'Gorman, "Philharmonic in Brazilian Program at World's Fair"; Marx, "Brazilian Portrait," 14.

146. Perkins, "Philharmonic Plays Brazilian Music at Fair"; Thompson, "Burle Marx Conducts with Soprano and Two Pianists as Soloists."

147. Rosenfeld, "Current Chronicle," 515.

148. Perkins, "Philharmonic Plays Brazilian Music at Fair."

149. Downes, "Brazilian Music Is Played at the Fair."

150. Hornbostel, "African Negro Music," 52.

151. Wallaschek, *Primitive Music*, 232.

152. Gray, *A Survey of Contemporary Music*, 142–45.

153. Faulkner, "Does Jazz Put the Sin in Syncopation?"

154. Thomson, "On Being American," in *A Virgil Thomson Reader*, 305. See also Thomson's "Aaron Copland," 70.

155. Harris, cited in Copland, *Music and Imagination*, 83.

156. Brody, "Founding Sons," 30.

157. Copland, *Music and Imagination*, 84–85.

158. "Las obras de música escritas en los Estados Unidos en estos últimos tiempos tienen una estructura rítmica particular. Es una influencia perceptible en todos nosotros. . . . La complejidad de ritmos es una de las caracteristicas principales de nuestra música." Leopoldo Hurtado, "Aaron Copland habla de la música norteamericana," *Argentina Libre*, October 9, 1941, Aaron Copland Collection, Box 358, Folder 24, Library of Congress.

159. Brody, "Founding Sons," 22.

160. Dett, "Negro Music," 1246, 1243.

161. Cuney-Hare, *Negro Musicians and Their Music*, 132.

162. Discussed in Block, "Bernstein's Senior Thesis at Harvard." The thesis is in Bernstein, *Findings*, 36–99.

163. Leonard Bernstein, "The Absorption of Race Elements into American Music." See Block, "Bernstein's Senior Thesis at Harvard," 57–58.

164. Bernstein, "The Absorption of Race Elements into American Music," in *Findings*, 95.

165. Bernstein, "The Absorption of Race Elements into American Music," in *Findings*, 97, italics in original.

166. Bernstein, "Jazz in Serious Music," 64, discussed in Block, "Bernstein's Senior Thesis at Harvard," 64–65.

167. Oja, "Bernstein Meets Broadway."

168. Coriat, *Repressed Emotions*, 40.

169. Freud, *Totem and Taboo*, 6.

170. Cowell, "Towards Neo-Primitivism," 149.

171. Kramer, *Classical Music and Postmodern Knowledge*, xiii.

172. Fredric Jameson, foreword to Fernández Retamar, *Caliban and Other Essays*, viii.

173. Fernández Retamar, *Caliban and Other Essays*, 16, 3–4.

174. Downes, "Brazilian Music on Fair Program."

175. Retamar, *Caliban and Other Essays*, 6.

176. In 1945 Villa-Lobos added a second movement, "Dance/Martelo." On transcriptions for voice and guitar, voice and piano, viola or cello, piano (by Villa-Lobos) or for organ and band by arrangers, see Béhague, *Heitor Villa-Lobos*, 105.

177. Béhague, *Heitor Villa-Lobos*, 118.

178. Thompson, "Burle Marx Conducts with Soprano and Two Pianists as Soloists"; Perkins, "Philharmonic Plays Brazilian Music at Fair."

179. Downes, "Art of Villa Lobos."

▪ Chapter 5. The Golden Age: Pan Americanist Culture, War, and the Triumph of Universalism

1. Disney made a total of three such trips between 1941 and 1943, resulting in cartoons, shorts, and educational films. See Cartwright and Goldfarb, "Cultural Contagion," 169.

2. Unidentified official from the Office of the Coordinator of Inter-American Affairs (OIAA), cited in Woll, *The Latin Image in American Film*, 55–57.

3. Strauss, "Donald Duck's Disney." See also Lavine and Wechsler, *War Propaganda and the United States.*

4. Statement issued by Robert Spencer Carr, "Ideas for More Walt Disney Films for South American Release," cited in Burton-Carvajal, "'Surprise Package,'" 133. See also Burton-Carvajal's "Don (Juanito) Duck and the Imperial-Patriarchal Unconscious."

5. Growther, "The Screen."

6. Discussed more fully in chapter 7. Shale, *Donald Duck Joins Up*, 48. A general view of Disney in Latin America is found in Smoodin, *Animating Culture*, 138–56. On Disney's brush with left-wing labor groups in Latin America, see Denning, *The Cultural Front*, 411.

7. Burton-Carvajal, "'Surprise Package,'" 135–36.

8. See Barreda Laos, *Hispano-América en guerra?* Drawing on archives opened in the 1970s, Ronald C. Newton argues that U.S. officials' fears of Nazi infiltration into Argentina were exaggerated. See *The "Nazi Menace" in Argentina*, especially xiv–xv.

9. I wish to thank Milton Azevedo for identifying the uniforms.

10. See Granja Tachuchian, "Panamericanismo, propaganda e musica erudite."

11. Gellman, *Good Neighbor Diplomacy*, 148–50.

12. The body created in 1940 was the Office for the Coordination of Commercial and Cultural Relations between the American Republics. The name was later shorted to the Office of the Coordinator of Inter-American Affairs, which appears in the literature as either OCIAA, CIAA, or OIAA, used here. See also Rowland, *History of the Office of the Coordinator of Inter-American Affairs.*

13. See Ninkovitch, *The Diplomacy of Ideas*, 37n4. See also Wertenbaker, *A New Doctrine for the Americas*, 160–65.

14. Rivas, *Missionary Capitalist*, 46; Minutes, OIAA Music Committee, February 6, 1941, Aaron Copland Collection, Box 355, Folder 10, p. 9, Library of Congress.

15. See, for example, reactions in Buenos Aires to *Argentine Nights* (Universal, 1940) with the Andrews Sisters in "Argentine Rioters End U.S. Movie," unidentified newspaper dated May 5, 1941, Margaret Herrick Library at the Academy of Motion Picture Arts and Sciences, Special Collections Clippings File.

16. Cited in O'Neil, "The Demands of Authenticity," 372.

17. Cited in O'Neil, "The Demands of Authenticity," 369–70.

18. Rowland, *History of the Office of the Coordinator of Inter-American Affairs*, 72.

19. Arthur Freed in *Variety*, cited in Woll, *The Latin Image in American Film*, 58.

20. See Smoodin, *Animating Culture*, 138–56; Faber, "Learning from the Latins," 270–72. Evidently Douglas Fairbanks Jr.'s trip was less than successful; he offended so many Latin Americans that plans for similar trips by other stars (Alice Faye, Wallace Beery, and Ann Sheridan) were scrapped. Woll, *The Latin Image in American Film*, 57.

21. On the structure of the OIAA, see Cramer and Prutsch, "Nelson A. Rockefeller's Office of Inter-American Affairs," 787–88. Other committee members included Evans Clark, executive director of the Twentieth Century Fund; Marshall Bartholomew (Yale University); and William Berrien, advisor on Latin American studies to the American Council of Learned Societies. Others came and went, such as Philip Barbour of the National Broadcasting Company and Davidson Taylor, assistant to the vice president of CBS. There was also the Spanish expatriate Gustavo Durán. See Hess, "Anti-Fascism by Another Name."

22. Hess, "Leopold Stokowski, 'Latin' Music, and Pan Americanism"; Meyer, "Toscanini and the Good Neighbor Policy."

23. See Chase, "Music of the New World," 49; Lawler, "Latin Americans See Our Musical Life." Musicological initiatives are summed up in Hess, "'De aspecto inglés pero de alma española.'"

24. Letter, Arthur Loesser to Carleton Sprague Smith, April 14, 1941, Aaron Copland Collection, Box 355, Folder 10, Library of Congress.

25. Copland, "The Composers of South America," 76. Also, as Abrams Ansari points out, when Copland made a list of recordings of works by U.S. composers to be distributed in Latin America, he favored works of "a more conservative nature" ("'Masters of the President's Music,'" 131–32). On folk music's role in cultural diplomacy, see Pernet, "For the Genuine Culture of the Americas."

26. Copland, "The Composers of South America," 80, 78. "Mozart" is not an unusual first name in Brazil, where surnames of famous foreign individuals, along with their variants—Edison (Edson), Robinson (Robson)—are common. Camargo Guarnieri eventually dropped "Mozart," signing his name "M. Camargo Guarnieri" so as "not to offend a master," as he explained. Cited in Verhaalen, *Camargo Guarnieri*, 2. See also Tyrrell, "M. Camargo Guarnieri and the Influence of Mário de Andrade's Modernism." Paz is discussed in greater detail below.

27. Copland's oft-cited words are found in Aaron Copland, "Composer from Brooklyn," in *Our New Music*, 229.

28. Seeger, "Grass Roots for American Composers," 146–48. See also Zuck, *A History of Musical Americanism*, 139–46; Crist, *Music for the Common Man*.

29. Roberts, *The Latin Tinge*, 77.

30. Daniel, *Dance and Social Change in Contemporary Cuba*, 13–17.

31. Cugat, *Rumba Is My Life*. As a native speaker of Spanish, Cugat would avoid the American English spelling, a point on which purists such as Gilbert Chase also weighed in. He once complained, "I have no idea how the 'h' got into [rhumba] but it does not belong there, any more than the 'ñ' belongs in 'habanera.'" Letter, Chase to Gladys E. Chamberlain, March 25, 1942, Chase Collection, Box 1, Folder 3 (New York Public Library).

32. Goldberg, *George Gershwin*, 362; Schwartz, *Gershwin*, 220.

33. Pollack, *George Gershwin*, 535–36.

34. Sanborn, "Gershwin Sets Mark in Stadium."

35. Taubman, "Music: 17,000 Hear Gershwin Program."

36. J.D.B., "Stadium Filled as 17,000 Hear Gershwin Play."

37. Beckett, "In the World of Music."

38. Downes, "Musicians' Group Opens New Season." See also "New Orchestra Opens Series at Popular Prices."

39. Thompson, "Music: Musicians' Symphony Begins New Series of Concerts with George Gershwin in Triple Role."

40. Steinberg, *Nights in the Gardens of Spain*, 19.

41. Pollack notes that the dates of study are "fuzzy" but that Gershwin probably worked with Cowell intermittently over a two-year period between 1927 and 1931 (*George Gershwin*, 127–28). See also Nicholls, "Transethnicism and the American Experimental Tradition."

42. Cowell, "Improving Pan-American Music Relations," 264.

43. Cowell also composed *Tango* for piano (1914), *The Exuberant Mexican: Danza Latina* for band (1939), *Grandma's Rhumba* for band (1946), *O'Higgins of Chile: An Opera in Three Acts* (begun in 1949), *Zapados* [*sic*] *sonidos* for mixed chorus and tap dancer (1964), and *Última actio* for mixed chorus (1965). See Lichtenwanger, *The Music of Henry Cowell*.

44. See Downes, "Women's Orchestrette Classique."

45. R.L. (Robert Lawrence?), "Novelties Played by Orchestrette." Robinson notes that Lawrence was employed at the *Herald Tribune* until some point in 1943 ("'A Ping, Qualified by a Thud,'" 86). Lichtenwanger, *The Music of Henry Cowell*, 175–76. On 213 Lichtenwanger discusses "Grandma's Rhumba," which Cowell composed in 1946 for the All-State Band of Michigan.

46. See Broyles and von Glahn, *Leo Ornstein*.

47. Hess, "Jean Berger."

48. Kirkpatrick, "Aaron Copland's Piano Sonata," 246. Rosenfeld feared (in private) that Copland had "sold out." Pollack, *Aaron Copland*, 99.

49. Toor, *Cancionero Mexicano*; Campos, *El folklore y la música Mexicana*. On *El salón México*, see Pollack, *Aaron Copland*, 298–303; Crist, *Music for the Common Man*, 48–59; Butterworth, *The Music of Aaron Copland*, 68–72; Smith, *Aaron Copland*, 174–77.

50. Blitzstein, "Composers as Lecturers and in Concerts," 49.

51. Chase, *America's Music from the Pilgrims to the Present* (1955), 498–99. In the third edition of this book (1987), Chase seems to have softened, commenting that "the audience is always happy" with *El salón México* (481).

52. Downes, "Copland Novelty in Premiere Here." See also I.K., "Music of the Week End"; Chotzinoff, "Words and Music."

53. Sanborn [P.S.], "Boston Orchestra Honors Composer."

54. Bagar, "Boult Conducts N.B.C. Symphony Orchestra"; Perkins, "NBC Symphony Concert Led by Boult, of BBC"; "Words and Music: Sir Adrian Boult Conducts N.B.C. Orchestra Expertly."

55. Adorno, "The Radio Symphony," 262–63. On "atomized listening" versus its polar opposite, "structural listening," and various related polemics, see Leppert, "Music 'Pushed to the Edge of Existence.'"

56. Bohm, "Boston Symphony Heard Again in Carnegie Hall."

57. Copland, *"El salón México,"* 17.

58. Copland, "The Story behind My *El salón México,*" 3.

59. See Downes, "Choral Works, New and Old"; Perkins, "Music."

60. Villa-Lobos, cited in Smith, "Song of Brazil," 43–44.

61. Wright discusses the lawsuit that ultimately ensued on account of Villa-Lobos having used Cearense's text without permission (*Villa-Lobos*, 72-77).

62. Downes, "Music Presented of South America"; Perkins, "Music."

63. McPhee, "South American Once More," 245. McPhee admired the "naïve and pleasant noisiness" of *Maracuta de Chico Rei* but found Castro's *Sinfonía Bíblica* a "slavish" illustration of the text. Marx's Pater noster, on the other hand, was "better organized."

64. McPhee, "South America Once More," 245–46.

65. McPhee, "South America Once More," 246.

66. Despite substantive differences in their styles, Portinari is often compared to Rivera for his communist leanings and interest in mural painting, which included a series for the Ministry of Education in Rio de Janeiro. Lucie-Smith, *Latin American Art of the 20th Century*, 72.

67. Shaw, *The Social History of Brazilian Samba*, 38–39.

68. Dávila, "Myth and Memory," 270–71.

69. Marx, introduction to *Festival of Brazilian Music*, 3.

70. Grant, *Maestros of the Pen*, 226–55.

71. See, for example, Lederman, "Composer Tells All."

72. Thomson, *A Virgil Thomson Reader*, 182.

73. As for the program booklet, which Thomson asserted was rife with "clumsinesses," written in an "English style ... just within the limits of literacy," he indulges in some rather imaginative explanations. In explaining *choros* as "an exact equivalent of our word 'chorus' as that is used in swing jargon," however, he confirms his own admission that he was "no whiz" at Portuguese. Neither did he clarify the Portuguese translation of the word *butterfly* apropos Villa-Lobos's piece for solo violin, *A Mariposa Na Luz*. He states that to judge from the music, the title should have been translated as "The Moth in the Flame" (rather than "butterfly"). In fact, *mariposa* does mean "moth" in Brazilian Portuguese ("butterfly" is *borboleta*). See "Music: More Brazil."

74. Thomson, "Music: Heavy Hands across Caribbean."

75. Thomson, "Music: Heavy Hands across Caribbean."

76. Thomson, "Music: Heavy Hands across Caribbean." Thomson would revise his view of Bartók, writing in 1949 of the Hungarian composer's "nobility of soul." See Thomson, *A Virgil Thomson Reader*, 324.

77. Thomson, "On Being American," in *A Virgil Thomson Reader*, 305.

78. Thomson found in *American Creed*'s final pages some "unexpected, original . . . and beautiful" passages; moreover they had "exactly as much to do with America as mountains or mosquitoes or childbirth have, none of which has any ethnic significance whatsoever" (*A Virgil Thomson Reader*, 198–99).

79. Thomson, "Music: More Brazil."

80. Thomson, "Music: More Brazil."

81. Robinson, "'A Ping, Qualified by a Thud,'" 114–17. See also Hubbs, "Frenchness as American Queerness," in *The Queer Composition of America's Sound*, 140–45.

82. Tarasti, *Heitor Villa-Lobos*, 324–34.

83. Thomson, cited in Robinson, "'A Ping, Qualified by a Thud,'" 80.

84. Thomson, "Music: Heavy Hands across Caribbean."

85. Thomson, "Music: More Brazil."

86. Downes, "Brazilian Series of Concerts Ends."

87. Downes, "Brazilian Series of Concerts Ends."

88. Perkins, "Brazil's Music Is Interpreted by Rubinstein."

89. McPhee, "Jungles of Brazil," 42.

90. McPhee, "Jungles of Brazil," 42.

91. McPhee, "Jungles of Brazil," 41–42.

92. Thomson, "Music: More Brazil"; Thompson, "Brazilian Music Given at Museum"; Downes, "Brazilian Music Heard in Concert." See also Downes, "From Brazil."

93. See Potter, "From Jewish Exile in Germany to German Scholar in America." While employed at Smith, Einstein was welcomed at Hartt by its (Jewish) founder, Moshe Paranov, and taught there part time into the 1950s. University Archives, Hartt School, Mortensen Library, University of Hartford, Box 5A.

94. Einstein, "War, Nationalism, Tolerance," 4, 3. See also Einstein's "National and Universal Music," in which he complains that "the smallest national unit ... strives to convert its musical dialect into a national art," including "Paraguayan and even Tierra del Fuegan symphonies announced and exploited alongside those of Schönberg and Mahler."

95. Sessions, "Music and Nationalism," 11.

96. Sessions, "On the American Future," 71–72. See also Manfred Bukofzer's postwar piece, "The New Nationalism."

97. Farwell, "Nationalism in Music."

98. Farwell, "Nationalism in Music," 1234. All parenthetical citations in this paragraph refer to this article.

99. Franco discusses postwar movements in literature in *The Modern Culture of Latin America*, 103–32. On motivations for neoclassicism in Latin America, see Béhague, *Music in Latin America*, 245–46.

100. Miranda discusses the extent of Ponce's engagement with neoclassicism in *Ecos, Alientos y Sonidos*, 205–6.

101. Labonville, *Juan Bautista Plaza and Musical Nationalism in Venezuela*, 170, 166.

102. Ardévol, *Introducción a Cuba*, 5.

103. Ardévol, *Introducción a Cuba*, 91.

104. *New Music* 7, no. 4 (1934): 3–5.

105. Slonimsky, *Music of Latin America*, 163.

106. Saminsky, "In the Argentine," 33. On Castro and folklore, see García Muñoz, "Juan José Castro," 21. Numerous other neoclassical works by Argentine composers are discussed in Omar Corrado, "Neoclasicism y objetividad en la música argentina de la década de 1930," in *Música y modernidad en Buenos Aires*, 75–223.

107. On the role of children's pieces in shaping Stravinsky's neoclassical style, see Messing, *Neoclassicism in Music from the Genesis of the Concept through the Schoenberg/Stravinsky Polemic*, 95–99. Siccardi's children's pieces include *Preludios para Yoyito* and Ginastera's *Piezas infantiles* and the *Rondo sobre temas infantiles argentinos*.

108. Paz, "Bach y la música de hoy," 80.

109. Corrado, "Viena en Buenos Aires," 8. Corrado catalogues other international performances of Paz's music, including a performance of three of his dodecaphonic works by the pianist Rita Kurzmann in Vienna in 1938. On serialism in Latin America, see also Paraskevaídis, "Música dodecafónica y serialismo en America Latina." A problematic English translation is "An Introduction to Twelve-Tone Music and Serialism in Latin America."

110. Paraphrased in Saminsky, "In the Argentine," 32. See also Hess, "Copland in Argentina."

111. Cortesi, "Brazil at War Stirs Latins."

112. Schirmer catalogue, cited in Hess, "Jean Berger," 43.

113. Lange, "Americanismo musical," 117. A review of the *Boletín latino-americano de música*, the journal Lange founded and in which this essay appeared, is found in Chase, "Recent Books."

114. Perhaps imbued with antinationalist zeal, Schirmer's translators were less than accurate. The Spanish reads, "El nacionalismo en música nació, sin excepción, por reflejo" (Nationalism in music was born, without exception, as a reflection [of "local, regional, national, and universal influences"]). Lange, "Prefacio," vii.

115. Lange, "Prefacio," xxiv.

116. Museu Villa-Lobos, *Villa-Lobos, Sua Obra*, 145.

117. Wright, *Villa-Lobos*, 92.

118. Museu Villa-Lobos, *Villa-Lobos, Sua Obra*, 145–46.

119. Museu Villa-Lobos, *Villa-Lobos, Sua Obra*, 146.

120. On Villa-Lobos's visit, see Appleby, *Heitor Villa-Lobos*, 137–54; Napp, *Personal Representatives in Musikverlegerischerin Kulturbeziehungen*.

121. This autonomous committee disbursed funds for the OIAA. On bringing Villa-Lobos to the United States, see letter, Henry Allen Moe to Copland, August 14, 1941, Aaron Copland Collection, Box 358, Folder 25, Library of Congress; see also the letter from Charles Seeger to Henry Allen Moe, 27 August 191, Aaron Copland Collection, Box 355, Folder 11.

122. Copy of a letter, Lincoln Kirstein to Carleton Sprague Smith, July 10, 1941 (Buenos Aires), received by Aaron Copland on July 17, 1941, Aaron Copland Collection, Box 355, Folder 25, Library of Congress.

123. Aaron Copland, "Report of South American Trip, August 19–December 13, 1941," Aaron Copland Collection, Box 358, Folder 28, p. 34, Library of Congress.

124. Letter, Charles Seeger (citing John W. Beattie) to Henry Allen Moe, September 8, 1941, Aaron Copland Collection, Box 355, Folder 11, Library of Congress.

125. Stevenson, "Heitor Villa-Lobos's Los Angeles Connection," 2.

126. Stevenson, "Brazilian Report of Villa-Lobos's First Los Angeles Visit," 10.

127. Stevenson, "Brazilian Report of Villa-Lobos's First Los Angeles Visit," 10.

128. Stevenson, "Brazilian Report of Villa-Lobos's First Los Angeles Visit," 9. In his 1956 book *A Volta do Gato Prêto*, Veríssimo paints an extremely unflattering picture of Villa-Lobos's behavior during this visit. Taking into account Veríssimo's prodigious novelistic gifts and suspicious of various factual errors he commits, Stevenson questions the Brazilian author's veracity.

129. Events on all these dates were reviewed except for that on January 28, sponsored by the League of Composers at the MoMA, which appears to have been announced but not reviewed. See Abresch, "Events in the World of Music." Copland, who later remarked that as the organizer of the MoMA concert, he did not have access to many of Villa-Lobos's scores and therefore had "settled for music that was not the best Villa-Lobos," recalls the date as February 1945. Copland and Perlis, *Copland Since 1943*, 80.

130. "Talk of the Town: Villa-Lobos," 16. In the same piece, Villa-Lobos refers to working on a harmonica concerto for the virtuoso Larry Adler, a commission that was eventually passed on to Jean Berger, who completed the work. See Hess, "Jean Berger," 47–48.

131. Downes, "Hector Villa-Lobos."

132. Sabin, "Villa-Lobos, Man of Action, Pays First Visit to U.S.," 7.

133. Fine, "Boston Hears Villa-Lobos," 189. Villa-Lobos also confessed to the *Boston Herald* that he was unfamiliar with the music of Piston, Schuman, Barber, and Harris. See Elie, "Heitor Villa-Lobos."

134. The most complete reference to the Bach transcription in the reviews is that of Paul Bowles, who identifies the work as "J. S. Bach's Sonata in E-flat Major for Pedal-Clavier composed for Friedemann Bach" (Bowles, "Villa-Lobos Directs Own Works in Concert with City Symphony"). It does not appear in Daniel's catalogue of Stokowski's Bach transcriptions (*Stokowski*, 1051–52).

135. Downes, "Villa-Lobos Guest at the City Center."

136. Bowles, "Villa-Lobos Directs Own Works in Concert with City Symphony." See also Bagar, "City Symphony Concert."

137. Downes, "Villa-Lobos Guest at the City Center."

138. Bowles, "Villa-Lobos Conducts Own Works in Concert with City Symphony."

139. Thompson, "Own Works Led by Villa-Lobos."

140. Thompson, "Two Choros Led by Villa-Lobos." See also Bagar, "Music: Villa-Lobos Conducts Own Two Brilliant Choros"; Johnson, "Words and Music: A Surprise 'Toy' Symphony."

141. Thomson, "Music: Children's Day." The title of Thomson's review refers to the performance of the "Toy" Symphony, then thought to be by Franz Joseph Haydn.

142. Knapp, *The American Musical and the Formation of National Identity*, 3–18. Villa-Lobos himself called *Magdalena* "a musical adventure" (Museu Villa-Lobos, *Villa-Lobos, Sua Obra*, 177). Howard Barnes described it as "a conventional light opera," while Brooks Atkinson vacillated between "musical drama" and "musical play." Barnes, "The Theaters: *Magdalena*"; Atkinson, "At the Theatre."

143. Louis Biancolli (critic for the *New York World-Telegram*), *New York Times* advertisement for the New York run, September 26, 1948, cited in Stevenson, "Heitor Villa-Lobos's Los Angeles Connection," 7.

144. Publicity is discussed in Stevenson, "Heitor Villa-Lobos's Los Angeles Connection."

145. Porter, "Musical Events Most Select and Generous," 163. See also Peppercorn, *The World of Villa-Lobos in Pictures and Documents*, 228.

146. Roosevelt, *Theodor Roosevelt*, 514, 520.

147. Cited in Bradley, *Imperial Cruise*, 204.

148. Brecht, *Brecht On Theatre*, 150–51.

149. Skidmore and Smith, *Modern Latin America*, 6.

150. Dyer, "Entertainment and Utopia," 177.

151. Beasley-Murray, translator's introduction, xii–xiii; see also Skidmore and Smith, *Modern Latin America*, 3–5.

152. Cited in Peppercorn, *The World of Villa-Lobos in Pictures and Documents*, 228.

153. Soames, "*Magdalena* Superb Opera by Top Cast"; Hobart, "*Magdalena* Is Exciting Theater." See also Taubman, "Musical Theatre"; Fisher, "Villa-Lobos Music Makes Light Opera Grand"; Holden, "A Lush Musical by Villa-Lobos."

154. Roberts, "'The Lady in the Tutti-Frutti Hat,'" 143–53.

155. Frankenstein, "Villa-Lobos at Large."

156. These existing works include selections from the *Guia Práctico* (an extensive collection of folk songs arranged for piano), the piano work *Ibericaribe*, the opera *Izaht*, "Impressões seresteiras" (from the piano set *Ciclo brasileiro*), various selections from *Modinhas e canções* for solo voice, and *Choros* no. 11 for piano and orchestra. Tarasti, *Heitor Villa-Lobos*, 403–6. Caracas García discusses some of the same sources in "American Views of Brazilian Musical Culture," 641.

157. Reynolds, "*Porgy and Bess*," 3.

158. Cited in Carpentier, *Ese músico que llevo dentro*, 14.

159. Carpentier, *Ese músico que llevo dentro*, 14.

160. Carpentier, "El Ángel de las Maracas," 191.

161. Berger, "Heitor Villa-Lobos," 222–23.

162. See Johnson, "Words and Music."

163. Appleby, *Heitor Villa-Lobos*, 162.

164. Hume, "Villa-Lobos's New No. 12 Is Festival Hit."

165. Bernstein, *Young People's Concerts*, vol. 13.

■ **Chapter 6. Alberto Ginastera's *Bomarzo* in the United States: Antinationalism and the Cold War**

1. "*Bomarzo* Scores in Washington Premiere."

2. Two of Rostow's assistants, Lucius Battle and William Bundy; White House chief of protocol James Symington; cultural chief of the Johnson administration Roger Stevens; and president of George Washington University, Lloyd H. Elliot also attended. "*Bomarzo* Spell Gripping."

3. "*Bomarzo*, de A. Ginastera Fue Ovacionada en Washington."

4. In 1945 the Governing Board of the Pan American Union drafted a charter for the "improvement and strengthening of the pan-American system," which resulted in the OAS charter, approved in 1948. It was actually the replacement organization for the Union of American Republics, the staff organization for which was the Pan American Union (Holden and Zolov, *Latin America and the United States*, 190). It was established on the premise of reinstating the "unilateral character of the Monroe Doctrine" such that the United States would not be "at the mercy of getting the assent of the [United Nations] Security Council," as Truman's secretary of war, Henry L. Stimson, put it. Cited in Rabe, *Eisenhower and Latin America*, 13.

5. "Sex and the Strait-Laced Strongman," 33. See also "At *Bomarzo* World Premiere."

6. "Argentina," 24; "Música argentina en clave internacional," *Panorama*, July 1967, cited in Buch, *The Bomarzo Affair*, 86. One exception was Jorge D'Urbano, who objected to *Bomarzo* on aesthetic grounds and for its sexual content. See D'Urbano, "Calculada audacia."

7. See Goehr, *The Imaginary Museum of Musical Works*, especially 89–119; see also Strohm, "Looking Back at Ourselves."

8. On Copland, see DeLapp, "Copland in the Fifties"; DeLapp-Birkett, "Aaron Copland and the Politics of Twelve-Tone Composition in the Early Cold War United States." Broader discussions of serialism in the cold war include Shreffler, "Ideologies of Serialism"; Straus, "The Myth of Serial 'Tyranny' in the 1950s and 1960s"; Shreffler, "The Myth of Empirical Historiography"; Straus, "A Response to Anne C. Shreffler"; Straus, "A Revisionist History of Twelve-Tone Serialism in American Music"; Straus, *Twelve-Tone Music in America*.

9. Beal defines experimental composers as "those who had adopted neither neoclassical nor serial styles or techniques" (*New Music, New Allies*, 3). Her book discusses West German patronage of experimental music. Among numerous recent studies on cultural diplomacy during the cold war, see Fosler-Lussier, *Music Divided*. See also Saunders, *The Cultural Cold War*, especially 347–51, which treats Latin America; Guilbaut, *How New York Stole the Idea of Modern Art*. On initial opposition in the U.S. Congress to the use of avant-garde music in cultural diplomacy, see Fosler-Lussier, "American Cultural Diplomacy and the Mediation of Avant-garde Music."

10. Skidmore and Smith, *Modern Latin America*, 373–83.

11. Cited in Holden and Zolov, *Latin America and the United States*, 205. See also Schlesinger, *Bitter Fruit*.

12. See Solberg, *Hubert Humphrey*, 275–77.

13. Fulbright, *The Arrogance of Power*, 82.

14. Latham, *Modernization as Ideology*, 70.

15. Discussed in Skidmore and Smith, *Modern Latin America*, 7.

16. Matthews, cited in Payne, "Creating Music of the Americas During the Cold War," 61. Matthews's acquaintance with Fidel Castro earned him the epithet of communist sympathizer in some circles. See DePalma, *The Man Who Invented Fidel*.

17. "Text of Address by President Eisenhower at Pan American Union."

18. Szulc, "Beneath the Boiling-Up in South America."

19. Paul, "From American Ethnographer to Cold War Icon," 446.

20. See Wellens, *Music on the Frontline*.

21. Babbitt, "Who Cares if You Listen?" Martin Brody notes that the title was an "editorial substitution for Babbitt's own, less inflammatory heading, 'The Composer as Specialist,'" and argues that it has been bandied about by Babbitt's detractors. See Brody, "'Music for the Masses,'" 162–63.

22. Warshow, "The Legacy of the 1930s."

23. Salzman, "Modern Music in Retrospect."

24. Greenberg, "Avant-Garde and Kitsch." See also Macdonald, "A Theory of Mass Culture."

25. Greenberg, "Art," 241.

26. Mason, "The Paris Festival," 19.

27. Shreffler, "Ideologies of Serialism," 222, 255.

28. Orrego-Salas, "The Young Generation of Latin American Composers," 8. Composers Orrego-Salas cites include Harold Gramatges, Edgardo Martín, Evencio Castellanos, César Guerra Peixe, Cláudio Santoro, and José Pablo Moncayo.

29. Vega, "Latin American Composers in the United States," 164.

30. In 1959 another studio was established in Córdoba (Argentina). See Viñao, "An Old Tradition We Have Just Invented."

31. Heile, *The Music of Mauricio Kagel.*

32. Other Focke pupils are listed in Paraskevaídis, "An Introduction to Twelve-Tone Music and Serialism in Latin America," 143.

33. Mariz, *Cláudio Santoro,* 17, 23–28; Mariz, "César Guerra-Peixe." See also Orrego-Salas, "The Young Generation of Latin American Composers."

34. Copland and Perlis, *Copland Since 1943,* 79–80.

35. "Manifesto 1946," cited in Neves, *Música contemporânea brasileira,* 95.

36. Cited in Neves, *Música contemporânea brasileira,* 121–24.

37. "En algún país sudamericano, no ha faltado quien diga que los compositores que siguen el dodecafonismo son traidores a la patria. Las tiranías serials, estrictamente aplicadas horizontal y verticalmente . . . no puede preverse que vayan a dar lugar a manifestaciones musicales de mucha altura" (Chávez, "El dodcafonismo en México," 69, 72). This document is evidently an off-print of a preconcert talk scheduled for Mexico's City's Colegio Nacional on November 5, 1954, Aaron Copland Collection, Box 227, Folder 2, Library of Congress.

38. Munoz, "Dallapiccola Program Stirs Controversy in Mexico City."

39. Copland, "Festival in Caracas."

40. Copland, *Music and Imagination,* 75, emphasis in original. DeLapp has explored Copland's adaption of serialism in relation to his brush with McCarthyism. See "Copland in the Fifties."

41. Although the first prize was divided between Blas Galindo and Camargo Guarnieri (for Symphony in Four Movements and Choro for Piano and Orchestra, respectively) Chase claimed that Cordero's symphony "received the greatest public ovation." Chase, "Caracas Host to Second Latin American Festival," 11.

42. Cordero, "¿Nacionalism versus dodecafonismo?," 28.

43. Cordero, "¿Nacionalism versus dodecafonismo?," 34.

44. Lang, "Music: New York Philharmonic."

45. Chase, "The Foundations of Musical Culture in Latin America," 42.

46. Chase, "Creative Trends in Latin American Music: II," 28. Chase concludes his study of music in the United States with the same argument, that "Ives's outlook was local but never provincial" (*America's Music from the Pilgrims to the Present,* 678).

47. Chase, "Creative Trends in Latin American Music," 28.

48. Ginastera himself labeled these periods "objetivo," "nacionalismo subjetivo," and "neo-expresionista." See Suárez Urtubey, *Alberto Ginastera,* 68–69. Given the label for the second category, Malena Kuss's contention that "Ginastera never uttered the word 'nationalism' in the context of this—widely cited—remark" is difficult to interpret. See Kuss, "Nacionalismo, identificación y Latinoamérica," 137.

49. Schwartz-Kates, "Ginastera, Alberto (Evaristo)." She summarizes debates on periodization of Ginastera's music in *Alberto Ginastera,* 23–24. See also Suárez Urtubey, *Alberto Ginastera en cinco movimientos,* 28, and the same author's *Ginastera: Veinte años después,* 15–27, which covers the works from Ginastera's years in Switzerland, where he settled in 1971.

50. On the gaucho tradition in Argentine art music, see Schwartz-Kates, "The *Gauchesco* Tradition as a Source of National Identity in Argentine Art Music." See also the same author's "Alberto Ginastera, Argentine Cultural Construction, and the Gauchesco Tradition."

51. The guitar chord is also found in several subjective nationalist works, such as *Pampeana* no. 3 (1954), String Quartet no. 1 (1948), Piano Sonata no. 1 (1952), and the *Variaciones concertantes* (1953). See Scarabino, *Alberto Ginastera,* 75. It can also emerge in serialist

contexts in neoexpressionist works, such as *Don Rodrigo*. Kuss, "Nacionalismo, identificación y Latinoamérica," 143. For a broad study of Ginastera's harmonic language in his early works, see Carballo, "De la Pampa al cielo."

52. Schwartz-Kates, "Ginastera, Alberto (Evaristo)."

53. One of the first scholars to address Ginastera's twelve-tone music (as part of a broader study) was David Edward Wallace in "Alberto Ginastera." See also Tabor, "Alberto Ginastera's Late Instrumental Style," especially 7–17, 25–26; Fobes, "A Theoretical Investigation of Twelve-Tone Rows, Harmonic Aggregates, and Non–Twelve Tone Materials in the Late Music of Alberto Ginastera."

54. See Suárez-Urtubey, *Alberto Ginastera*, 69.

55. "Music in the Air." See also Manso, *Juan José Castro*, 81–85.

56. "Radio Concerts."

57. Downes, "Argentine Pianist Scores in Program." On "El gato," see C.H., "Gareth Anderson Heard." On Jenny Tourel's performance of the *Five Argentine Folk Songs*, see "The Programs of the Week."

58. The U.S. premiere of the *American Preludes* (composed 1944) seems to have taken place in Washington (September 8, 1946), albeit a partial one: Simon Sadoff performed "Tribute to Aaron Copland" and "Tribute to Juan José Castro" at the National Gallery. My thanks to Jean Henry of the Gallery Archives for this information. See also Eversman, "Simon Sadoff Gives Pleasing Performance."

59. Schweitzer, "Donizetti Returns, Offering Plenty of Chemistry and Nine High C's."

60. Downes, "2 South American Composers Guests"; Thomson, "Music."

61. See also the essay by Smith, "Alberto Ginastera's 'Duo for Flute and Oboe.'"

62. Schonberg, "7 Modern Works Heard in South"; Downes, "Barnett Directs Orchestral Unit."

63. The work was recorded in 1955 on the Mercury label. See Foreman, "Ginastera: A Discography"; Schwartz-Kates, *Alberto Ginastera*, 176–79.

64. Taubman, "Music: Little Orchestra Society."

65. Lang, "Music: Little Orchestra Society."

66. R.P. [Ross Parmenter], "Work by Berlioz Heard at Concert."

67. Harrison, "Eartha Kitt Heard in Song Program at the Stadium."

68. Salzman, "Eartha Kitt Sings Stadium Program."

69. Salzman, "Records: Chávez." Chávez conducts the Stadium Symphony Orchestra of New York.

70. Patrick, "Sevitzky's Current Bill Features Crisp Playing." The premiere took place on January 24 (the work was repeated the next day) in 1954, not 1945, as is often stated. I thank Tom Akins, former director of Archives of the Indianapolis Symphony Orchestra, for this clarification.

71. Butler, "Henry Butler Says." See also Butler's "Concert Best, Week Is Quiet"; Whitworth, "Symphony and Guest Pianist in Top Form."

72. See Owsley Brown III and Jerome Hiller, directors, *Music Makes a City* (DVD, 2010). Reviews include Anderson, "Louisville Orchestra's Opening Concert Called Best Yet"; Beirfield, "Strengthened Orchestra Displays Skill at Opening"; Lees, "Critics Laud Symphony after Concert Here"; Mootz, "Critics Hear Orchestra and Open Workshop."

73. Goldberg, "Ginastera Quartet Lively, Novel Work"; Anderson, "Ginastera Ranked High for His Musical Creativeness."

74. In fact, critics of Ginastera's Piano Sonata no. 1, solicited for the first Pittsburgh International Contemporary Music Festival and premiered by Joanna Harris in November 1952,

revived the familiar Pan Americanist trope of "freshness." See Lissfelt, "Music Festival Ends with Piano, Organ Selections"; Lissfelt, "Pittsburgh Holds Contemporary Music Festival;" Steinfirst, "Final Festival Concerts Draw Fair Attendance".

75. Haskins, preface in program booklet for First Inter-American Music Festival, 7, Guillermo Espinosa Collection, Latin American Music Center, Indiana University. See also Evett, "New Music of the Americas."

76. Cowell, program booklet, Second Inter-American Music Festival, 48.

77. On the so-called Altamira School, see Díaz Sánchez, "Al servicio del espíritu," 273–76. The "superseding of purely folkloric data" in current music was applauded in *Índice*, a Madrid-based magazine that published articles on Rothko, Beckett, and other avant-garde figures. See, for example, "No deseamos lanzar un manifiesto." See also Custer, "Contemporary Music in Spain." An updated version of the same article appeared under the same title in *Musical Quarterly* 51, no. 1 (1965): 44–60.

78. Hume, "Music of Spain's Avant-garde Heard Here."

79. Kriegsman, "Composers Drop Nationalism."

80. In the 1959 edition, the words "Triste es el día sin sol, triste es la noche sin luna" (Sad is the day without sun, sad is the night without the moon) appear over the appropriate pitches in the viola part (mvt. 4, mm. 51–54). In the 1968 edition of the quartet, Ginastera removed the "Triste" quotation, which Kuss considers a reference to the woman who would eventually be his second wife, Aurora Nátola. On this point, however, see Schwartz-Kates, *Alberto Ginastera*, 39.

81. Lowens, "Ginastera Harp Work Superbly Performed." See also Lowens, "Current Chronicle" (1958). On Lowens's career, including his role in the first Inter-American Conference of Music Critics (Washington, 1973), see Holly, "Irving Lowens and *The Washington Star*." The conference is discussed on 60–62.

82. Hume, "Postlude"; see also Lowens, "Current Chronicle" (1958), 379.

83. Taubman, "Three New Works Heard in Capital."

84. Evett, "New Music of the Americas," 23; Lowens, "Current Chronicle" (1958), 378, 381.

85. Holden and Zolov, *Latin America and the United States*, 170–73.

86. Hume, "Ginastera Emerges as Giant in Music Festival's Finale."

87. Lowens, "Ginastera's Cantata Enchanting, Exciting"; Lowens, "Current Chronicle" (1961), 532. On the serialist elements in the work, see Suárez Urtubey, "La *Cantata para América mágica*."

88. Fosler-Lussier, "American Cultural Diplomacy and the Mediation of Avant-Garde Music," 236.

89. See Ginastera, "Why the Inter-American Must Be a Festival of Youth." The same article appeared in *Inter-American Music Bulletin* 66 (1968): 6–9.

90. Henahan, "(1) 'Why Not?'"

91. Salzman, "Peripatetic Philharmonic."

92. See Vincent, "New Opera in Buenos Aires."

93. Klein, "Ginastera: A Most Happy Composer."

94. F.M. (Frank Merkling), "Reports: United States," 30. See also Kuss, "Type, Derivation, and Use of Folk Idioms in Ginastera's *Don Rodrigo*."

95. Schonberg, "Music: City Opera Company Sparkles in Its Rich, New Setting."

96. Chase, "New World Music," 12.

97. Chase, "Alberto Ginastera: Argentine Composer," 447. Since Chase addressed "subjective sublimation" before Ginastera demarcated his style periods, it may be that Ginastera

borrowed the term from Chase, with whom he was acquainted, especially during Chase's tenure as a cultural attaché in Buenos Aires during 1953–55.

98. Chase, "Alberto Ginastera: Argentine Composer," 447.

99. Chase, "Current Musical Trends in South America," 177.

100. Chase, "Alberto Ginastera: Portrait of an Argentine Composer," 14, 15. On 13 of the same article, Chase addresses Ginastera's "sublimation of national elements" via "contemporary compositional procedures." He also praised other Latin American composers along these lines. Of Cordero's Symphony no. 2, he remarked, "Whatever national elements this music may embody have been sublimated in the composer's creative consciousness and emerge as aspects of his total personality" ("Caracas to Host Second Latin American Festival," 11).

101. Cited in Hale, *Freud and the Americans*, 341.

102. Taylor, "A Critique of Sublimation in Males," 16–17, 115.

103. Lecture 5, cited in Ruitenbeek, *Varieties of Personality Theory*, 42. As Peter Gay points out, *instinct* and *drive* can be treated interchangeably in translating the German *Trieb* (*The Freud Reader*, 564n1). See also Sigmund Freud, "Instincts and Their Vicissitudes," in *The Standard Edition of the Complete Psychological Works of Sigmund Freud*, vol. 14.

104. Freud wrote, "One must remove the repression by overcoming the resistances before achieving partial or complete sublimation." Letter to Jackson Putnam, May 14, 1911, cited in Hale, *Freud and the Americans*, 340–41.

105. Cited in Hale, *Freud and the Americans*, 341.

106. See, for example, Coleman (1950), Brown (1940), Orgel (1946), and Symonds (1946), cited in Laughlin, *Mental Mechanisms*, 80.

107. Ruitenbeek, *Freud and America*, 145, 150–56.

108. Engel, *American Therapy*, 1–42.

109. Freud had appeared on the cover of *Time* previously (October 27, 1924, and June 26, 1939).

110. Sigmund Freud, "Leonardo da Vinci and a Memory of His Childhood," in *The Standard Edition of the Complete Psychological Works of Sigmund Freud*, 11: 78.

111. Pease, *Modernism, Mass Culture, and the Aesthetics of Obscenity*, 22.

112. Pease, *Modernism, Mass Culture, and the Aesthetics of Obscenity*, 75.

113. Woodmansee, *The Author, Art, and the Market*; see especially 11–12.

114. Kant, *Critique of Judgment*, 50, italics in original.

115. See Chmaj, "Fry versus Dwight." On the sacralization of art, see also Levine, *Highbrow/Lowbrow*, 83–168.

116. Bourdieu, *Distinction*, 491.

117. Adorno, *Aesthetic Theory*, 15.

118. Discussed in Lee, "A Minstrel in a World without Minstrels," 658.

119. Adorno, *Aesthetic Theory*, 16.

120. Adorno, *Aesthetic Theory*, 17, 18.

121. Chase does not identify the article, but it must have been Taubman's "In Time to Come?"

122. Chase, "The Mail Pouch."

123. Program booklet, 2nd Inter-American Music Festival.

124. Margrave, "Current Chronicle," 411–13.

125. Pellettieri, *Cien años de teatro argentino*, 129. On Ginastera's tangles with the Perón government, see Schwartz-Kates, *Alberto Ginastera*, 8.

126. See King, *El Di Tella y el desarrollo cultural argentino en la década del sesenta*, 31, 81–100, 157–63. Important background on the Argentine avant-garde is discussed in Giunta, *Vanguardia, internacionalismo y política*. Giunta gives details of Greenberg's 1964 visit on 21.

In addition to Rockefeller money, the Centro Latinoamericano de Altos Estudios Musicales was aided by internal funds. See Neiburg and Plotkin, *Intelectuales y expertos*, 248. On the CLAEM, see Herrera, "Politics of Creation / Creation of Politics"; Rubio et al., *La música en el Di Tella*.

127. Plotkin, *Freud in the Pampas*, 81.

128. Later reprinted as Ginastera, "How and Why I Wrote *Bomarzo*." Page numbers cited in the text refer to this edition.

129. Kuss notes the melody's presence in Arnold Schering's *Geschichte der Musik in Beispielen* of 1931; see "Symbol und Phantasie in Ginasteras *Bomarzo*," n24. Another borrowing is the chorus "O Rex Gloriae," a Gregorian melody in parallel fifths against atonal and erratically spaced harmonies, which Esteban Buch has identified as an antiphon for the Ascension of the Virgin (*Antiphonale Monasticum pro Diurnis Horis*). See Buch, *The Bomarzo Affair*, 13. A third melody, supposedly Babylonian-Hebrew, remains undocumented. See Suárez Urtubey, "Ginastera's *Bomarzo*," 16.

130. See Hutcheon, *A Theory of Parody*, 53.

131. Measure numbers are taken from the Boosey & Hawkes perusal score.

132. See Buch, "Ginastera y Nono"; Kuss, "Symbol und Phantasie in Ginasteras *Bomarzo*," 93–95.

133. See Buch, "Ginastera y Nono," 63–69.

134. Griffiths, "Aleatory."

135. Kuss notes its derivations from row 1 ("Symbol und Phantasie in Ginasteras *Bomarzo*," 94).

136. Additional details on the choral writing are given in Suárez Urtubey, *Alberto Ginastera en cinco movimientos*, 89–91.

137. Similar examples include act 1 scene 3, where the pitches of row 1 Ie are scrambled as Pier Francesco longs for immortality (mm. 122–23); later in that scene (m. 150), row 2 I4 is presented in linear fashion, albeit with pitches reordered.

138. "Notes to the Conductor," Boosey & Hawkes perusal score.

139. Ginastera instructed the choreographer Jack Cole to "create the steps without music" so that "only when dancers and orchestra rehearse together, the conductor will adjust [the timing of] the formants to the . . . action of the ballet." "Notes to the Conductor," Boosey & Hawkes perusal score.

140. Here Ginastera prevailed upon the chief of the Music Division of the Library of Congress, Harold Spivacke, who in a research marathon lasting an entire weekend undertook the daunting assignment to find equivalents for the word *love* in as many foreign languages as possible. Schwartz-Kates, "The Correspondence of Alberto Ginastera," 300.

141. Lowens, "Current Chronicle" (1967), 555–57.

142. Jacobson, "Capital Ginastera in Washington."

143. Hume, "*Bomarzo*." See also by the same author "An Opera Is Born."

144. Evett, "*Bomarzo*, Si, *Rigoletto*, No," 29.

145. Hume, "*Bomarzo*"; Lowens, "Current Chronicle" (1967), 555.

146. "Music: Not for Squares," 90; "In a Gloomy Garden," 77.

147. Robertson, "*Bomarzo*."

148. Robertson, "*Bomarzo*."

149. La Feber, "Latin American Policy," 78.

150. Eight Latin American countries recognized Onganía as well. Plotkin argues that the coup "initially had the approval of broad sectors of [Argentine] society," although its "long-lasting traumatic effects" became apparent soon enough (*Freud in the Pampas*, 77).

151. "Argentina," 24.

152. "An American and Inter-American Anniversary."

153. Cited in La Feber, "Latin American Policy," 79.

154. Abellán, *Censura y creación literaria en España.*

155. Biglia and Lifschitz, "*Bomarzo*," 241.

156. Quoted in Biglia and Lifschitz, "*Bomarzo*," 244.

157. F.M. (Fred Marey), "Beware the Ides of *Bomarzo.*"

158. Interview, Graciela Paraskevaídis and author, June 28, 2009, Buenos Aires.

159. Buch, *The Bomarzo Affair*, 124; covered also in F.M., "Beware the Ides of *Bomarzo*," 13.

160. "Argentina: Prohibida para adolescentes." On the shutdown of *Primera Plana* in August 1969, see Pellettieri, *Cien años de teatro argentino*, 130.

161. "Ginastera prohíbe que se den sus obras en el Colón," *La Prensa*, August 6, 1967, cited in Buch, *The Bomarzo Affair*, 125.

162. "El cuento de la buena pipa." On Uruguayan radio during this time, see Estrella, *Música para la esperanza*, 199.

163. "Una cuidadosa antología de los procedimientos más notorios—aleatorios, serials y microtonales—, y más bien se prestaría para fondo musical de un film argentino, con sus industriosas ráfagas de artificios tímbricos. . . . El gran negocio sería transformar la opera en foto-novela" ("El cuento de la buena pipa"). A *foto-novela* is a booklet or pamphlet in comic book format with photographs.

164. Discussed in Buch, *The Bomarzo Affair*, 17–22.

165. "Sex and the Strait-Laced Strongman," 33.

166. Carr, *Spain*, 715.

167. Jansen, *Censorship, the Knot That Binds Power and Knowledge*, 4.

168. Jansen, *Censorship, the Knot That Binds Power and Knowledge*, 4.

169. Bianculli, *Dangerously Funny*. Bob Dylan is discussed on 41.

170. Lowens "Current Chronicle" (1967), 562.

171. The New York performance was to benefit the City Center of Music and Drama with proceeds matched by the Ford Foundation. "*Bomarzo* Premiere to Aid City Center."

172. Henahan, "(1) 'Why Not?'"

173. Henahan, "Sex and Violence in His Opera?"

174. Landry, "*Bomarzo* Not So Good on Melody," 70; Schonberg, "The Opera."

175. Weinstock, "America."

176. Schonberg, "The Opera."

177. Sargeant, "Musical Events," 126.

178. Schonberg, "*Bomarzo.*"

179. *Bomarzo* returned to New York City Opera in October 1969 and was followed by performances in Los Angeles, Kiel and Zurich (1970) and London (1976). After Onganía's fall in 1970, *Bomarzo* was played on Argentine radio, followed by a performance at the Colón on April 29, 1972, and again in 2003. Buch, *The Bomarzo Affair*, 166–69.

180. Cooke, *Cambridge Companion to Twentieth-Century Opera*, 51.

181. Cited in Robertson, "*Bomarzo.*"

182. Simms, *Music of the Twentieth Century*, 357.

183. Shreffler, "Ideologies of Serialism," 221. On the subject-material risks inherent in serialism, see Adorno, *Philosophy of Modern Music*, 68.

184. Adorno, *Mahler*, 33.

185. Ruitenbeek, *Freud and America*, 108–11.

■ **Chapter 7. Memory, Music, and the Latin American Cold War: Frederic Rzewski's *36 Variations on "The People United Will Never Be Defeated!"***

1. Sherman, "Politics and Music by Chilean Group."

2. On these spectacles, see, for example, Rey García, *Stars for Spain*, 414–19.

3. Sherman, "Politics and Music by Chilean Group."

4. When the score was published (Tokyo: Zen-On, 1979), Rzewski changed the title (previously *36 Variations on "The People United Will Never Be Defeated!"*) to acknowledge his sources. See Madsen, "Music as Metaphor," 9.

5. Frederic Rzewski, liner notes to *The People United Will Never Be Defeated!*, Hat Art CD, 1994.

6. Gil, *Latin American–United States Relations*, 284.

7. Sigmund, *The Overthrow of Allende and Politics of Chile*, 131–32.

8. Peter Kornbluh observes that these notes constitute "the first record of an American president ordering the overthrow of a democratically elected government" (*The Pinochet File*, 1–2). Allende's defeat in the election of 1964 is discussed in the CIA's *Chilean Election Operation of 1964: A Case History 1961–1964*, a "two-volume internal history of clandestine support for the Christian Democrats," cited by Kornbluh on 3–4. Kornbluh discusses Nixon's business ties in Chile on 6–7, 18–19. On the strikes, see Boorstein, *Allende's Chile*, 87–88. See also Chavkin, *The Murder of Chile*, 39–80.

9. Cited in Madsen, "Music as Metaphor," 23.

10. Gonzáles, "Hegemony and Counter-Hegemony of Music in Latin America," 73. On *nueva canción*'s links to Marxism, see Reyes Matta, "The 'New Song' and Its Confrontation in Latin America."

11. See John M. Schechter, "Beyond Region: Transnational and Transcultural Traditions," in Schecter, *Music in Latin American Culture*, 425–37.

12. Eduardo Carrasco, cited in Bianchi et al., "Discusión sobre la música chilena," 115.

13. Orrego-Salas, "La nueva canción chilena," 2.

14. See Rios, "Bolero Trios, Mestizo Panpipe Ensembles, and Bolivia's 1952 Revolution," 304–7.

15. Jara, *An Unfinished Song*, 145.

16. Cited in Rockwell, "The Pop Life"; Jara, *An Unfinished Song*, 120.

17. A list of other companies with operations in Chile is given in Sigmund, *The Overthrow of Allende and Politics of Chile*, 132. See also Kornbluh, *The Pinochet File*, xv–xix.

18. "Resolución Final del Encuentro de la Canción Protesta."

19. Dorfman and Mattelart, *How to Read Donald Duck*, 28.

20. Taffet, "'My Guitar Is Not for the Rich,'" 91.

21. According to Joan Jara, it was the second festival that sealed the affiliation between *nueva canción* and Allende, as in 1969 some traditionalist and/or politically uncommitted groups also participated. Jara, *An Unfinished Song*, 145.

22. Party, "Beyond 'Protest Song.'"

23. Gordon, "Inti-Illimani," 41. See also Gonzáles, "Inti-Illimani and the Artistic Treatment of Folklore."

24. Gonzalez, "Ideology and Culture under Popular Unity." See also Sigmund, *The Overthrow of Allende and the Politics of Chile*, 94–95; Raymond, *Salvador Allende and the Peaceful Road to Socialism.*

25. García Canclini, "Memory and Innovation in the Theory of Art," 428.

26. González, "Hegemony and Counter-Hegemony of Music in Latin America," 67–68.

27. On Argentine *rock nacional*, influenced by rock and roll, blues, heavy metal, rockabilly, Argentine folk music, and a variety of other genres, especially popular during the military

dictatorship of 1976–83, see Vila, "Argentina's 'Rock nacional,'" 3; see also the same author's "Rock nacional and Dictatorship in Argentina."

28. See Torres, *Victor Jara Obra Musical Completa*, 192–95. My thanks to Ken Prouty for his insights on this song.

29. Jara and Mitchell, *Victor Jara*, 64–67.

30. Frank, *The Conquest of Cool*. On the commercial appropriation of Che Guevara's image, see Casey, *Che's Afterlife*.

31. Jameson, "Reification and Utopia in Mass Culture," 133.

32. Jara, *An Unfinished Song*, 196; see also Gonzáles, "Inti-Illimani and the Artistic Treatment of Folklore," 269.

33. Sergio Ortega, liner notes for Frederic Rzewski's *The People United Will Never Be Defeated!*, Stephen Drury, piano (New Albion NA 063, 1994).

34. As of this writing, Rzewski is no longer giving interviews on his music.

35. After the terrorist attacks on New York's Twin Towers in 2001, Dorfman commented widely in the media on the coincidence of the dates. On Allende's suicide, see Sigmund, *The Overthrow of Allende and Politics of Chile*, 4–5.

36. Carrasco, quoted in Bianchi et al., "Discusión sobre la música chilena," 115. See also Gordon, "Inti-Illimani," 41.

37. Jara, *An Unfinished Song*, 257.

38. Interview, Madsen and Orrego-Salas, in Madsen, "Music as Metaphor," 203–4. Orrego-Salas served Allende (and also Frei) as honorary consul. When Pinochet came to power Orrego-Salas, in residence in the United States since 1961, resigned his position. His *Biografía mínima de Salvador Allende* for voice, guitar, "distant trumpet," and percussion on a text by the Chilean poet David Valjalo (1983) pays homage to the Allende years (Madsen, "Music as Metaphor," 204–5). On Peña, see Olsen and Sheehy, *South America, Mexico, Central America, and the Caribbean*, 90.

39. Coad, "Rebirth of Chilean Cinema," 42.

40. Douglass and Vogler, *Witness and Memory*, 16.

41. Schacter, *The Seven Sins of Memory*, 138.

42. Morris, "'Canto porque es necesario cantar,'" 123–24.

43. Fink, *Repeating Ourselves*, 169–207.

44. On minimalism in advertising, see Frank, *The Conquest of Cool*, especially 68 and 105. Several composers grouped under the rubric "minimalist" have found the term restrictive and reject it, despite its common usage. See, for example, Schwartz, "Steve Reich," 376.

45. Cited in Fink, *Repeating Ourselves*, 180.

46. See H. C. Robbins Landon's description of a cocktail party enhanced by the music of "Albinoni, Geminiani, Corelli, Locatelli, and of course, the father-figure of barococo music, Antonio Vivaldi" in "A Pox on Manfredini," which Fink dissects at some length in *Repeating Ourselves*, 187–90.

47. Fink, *Repeating Ourselves*, 5–19.

48. On the "repetitive, static surface" and its perceived "underlying affinity with meditation, drugs, and body over mind" in the music of Philip Glass, see Swan, "The Spell of Philip Glass," 28.

49. Perhaps emboldened by Barroco Andino, in the mid-1970s Chilean folk musicians who remained in Chile resumed using indigenous instruments, now accompanying innocuous or metaphorical lyrics. Because the resulting genre, known as *canto nuevo*, sought to recapture some of the values of *nueva canción*, it suffered at the hands of the government, which often made permits for concert halls and radio appearances difficult to obtain and kept

a blacklist of performers banned from television or radio. Morris, "'Canto porque es necesario cantar,'" 124–27. See also Neustadt, "Music as Memory and Torture."

50. On Zimmerman and his role in American experimentalism, see Beal, *New Music, New Allies*, 218–24.

51. Zimmerman, *Desert Plants*, 307.

52. Cited in Zimmerman, *Desert Plants*, 307. Zimmerman's editorial practice of using literal transcriptions was not completely congenial to Rzewski. See Beal, *New Music, New Allies*, 221.

53. On Rzewski's Marxism, see Asplund, "Frederic Rzewski and Spontaneous Political Music."

54. Rockwell, *All American Music*, 84–95.

55. "Bicentennial Bonanza."

56. See, for example, Pollack, *Harvard Composers*, 383.

57. See Ryan, *Earl Browder*, especially 103–7. Rzewski is cited in Schonberg, "Music: Some Moderns." See also Margles, "Rzewski's Music Has Moral Message," 13.

58. On September 8, 1974, for example, the *Times* ran a front-page story by Seymour Hersh with the headline "CIA Chief Tells House of 8 Million Campaign against Allende in '70–'73." Discussed in Kornbluh, *The Pinochet File*, 225–30.

59. See, for example, Joseph McLellan, "Brilliant Pianist," *Washington Post*, February 9, 1976; Schonberg, "Music: Some Moderns."

60. See Driver, "Recordings," 25. Oppens, for example, believed that "the piece was received primarily as a work of music." Quoted in Madsen, "Music as Metaphor," 201. Leighton Kerner of the *Village Voice* also supported the work's political stance. See his "Composers Defiant Will Never Be Refuted."

61. Driver, "Recordings," 25, italics in original.

62. Cox, "New York," 39.

63. Rockwell, *All American Music*, 91.

64. Rockwell, *All American Music*, 91.

65. Rockwell, *All American Music*, 93, 89.

66. Rockwell, *All American Music*, 93–94.

67. Wolff, *The People United Will Never Be Defeated!* The recording was named Record of the Year by Record World. Wolff's program notes have been uniformly praised. See Wason, "Tonality and Atonality in Frederic Rzewski's *Variations on 'The People United Will Never Be Defeated!,'"* 111; Burge, "About Pianists," 46.

68. Sisman, "Variations."

69. Analyses of *The People United* include Wason, "Tonality and Atonality in Frederic Rzewski's *Variations on 'The People United Will Never Be Defeated!'"*; Melton, "Frederic Rzewski's *The People United Will Never Be Defeated!*" See also Pollack, *Harvard Composers*, 383–89.

70. *Rzewski Plays Rzewski: Piano Works 1975–1999* (Nonesuch, 2002).

71. Burkholder, "Quotation." Of the extensive musicological literature on quotation, see Rosen's classic "Influence."

72. Rzewski, liner notes to *The People United Will Never Be Defeated!*

73. Blake, "Eisler, Hanns." On workers' choruses, see Zuck, *A History of Musical Americanism*, 121–38; Reuss and Reuss, *American Folk Music and Left-Wing Politics*, 44–47. See also Seeger, "On Proletarian Music."

74. Cited in Crist, *Music for the Common Man*, 29.

75. Schobeß, "Review," 206.

76. Rzewski, liner notes to *The People United Will Never Be Defeated!*

77. An authoritative study of allusion is Reynolds, *Motives for Allusion*; see especially 1–23.

78. The music of Brahms, especially, has focused attention on the interpretive potential of allusion. See Brodbeck, *Brahms/Symphony no. 1*; Knapp, "Utopian Agendas."

79. Kinderman, *Beethoven's Diabelli Variations*, 111–30. See also Driver, "Recordings," 25–26.

80. Rink, "Opposition and Integration in the Piano Music."

81. Donald A. Ritchie, "A Foreword," in Jeffrey, *Memory and History*, viii.

82. See Berger, "Time's Arrow and the Advent of Musical Modernity," 8. See also Trippett, "Composing Time."

83. Kramer, *The Time of Music*, 370.

84. Douglass and Vogler, *Witness and Memory*, 18–19.

85. Wolff, liner notes for *The People United Will Never Be Defeated!*

86. Wason, "Tonality and Atonality in Frederic Rzewski's *Variations on 'The People United Will Never Be Defeated!,'*" 112.

87. Wason, "Tonality and Atonality in Frederic Rzewski's *Variations on 'The People United Will Never Be Defeated!,'*" 133. As Wason proposes, Rzewski's exploitation of this hexachord constitutes "one of the very few instances of a twelve-tone vernacular," generating neither tonality or atonality but "music in the middle" (109–10).

88. Wason, "Tonality and Atonality in Frederic Rzewski's *Variations on 'The People United Will Never Be Defeated!,'*" 133.

89. La Monte Young, cited in Kostelanetz, *A Theatre of Mixed Means*, 186–87. In the same interview, Young states that the "main influence upon [his] actual writing style was Dr. Robert Stevenson," who taught him baroque music and sixteenth-century counterpoint and to whose memory this book is dedicated.

90. Walsh, "The Heart Is Back in the Game," 61.

91. Fink, *Repeating Ourselves*, 169–70.

92. Suzuki, *Nurtured by Love*.

93. Reich, *Writings about Music*, 50–54.

94. Fink, *Repeating Ourselves*, 106.

95. Kramer, *The Time of Music*, 388–94.

96. Schwartz, "Steve Reich," 387.

97. Schwartz, "Postmodernism, the Subject, and the Real in John Adams's *Nixon in China*," 134.

98. Clements, "Music in 12 Parts" (writing of the 2010 Brighton Festival).

99. Philip Glass, cited in Mertens, *American Minimal Music*, 79.

100. Sigmund Freud, "Remembering, Repeating, and Working-Through," in *The Standard Edition of the Complete Psychological Works of Sigmund Freud*, 12: 151.

101. LaCapra, *Representing the Holocaust*, xii.

102. Freud, *Beyond the Pleasure Principle*, in *The Standard Edition of the Complete Psychological Works of Sigmund Freud*, 18:19.

103. Ricoeur, *Memory, History, Forgetting*, 445.

104. Weine, *Testimony after Catastrophe*, 11. Weine discusses work with Chilean torture victims on 5–17.

105. Ricoeur, *Memory, History, Forgetting*, 6. See also Sisman, "Memory and Invention at the Threshold of Beethoven's Late Style," 55–57.

106. See O'Connell, "Narrating History through Memory in Three Novels of Post-Pinochet Chile."

107. These musical works and others are discussed in an important essay by Paraskevaídis, "Algunas reflexiones sobre música y dictadura en América Latina."

108. Borges, *The Book of Sand* (*El Libro de arena*), 73.

109. Freud, "Remembering, Repeating, and Working-Through," in *The Standard Edition of the Complete Psychological Works of Sigmund Freud*, 152.

■ Epilogue

1. Akhil Gupta and James Ferguson, "Culture, Power, Place: Ethnography at the End of an Era," in Gupta and Ferguson, *Culture, Power, and Place*, 2.

2. Pollack, *Aaron Copland*, 219; Oja, *Making Music Modern*, 275. See also Béhague, *Music in Latin America*, 131; Chase, "Creative Trends in Latin American Music," 27.

3. Berger, *Aaron Copland*, 25.

4. Oja, *Making Music Modern*, 246. One assumes the Schoenberg works in question are op. 33a and 33b, from 1929 and 1931, respectively.

5. Oja, *Making Music Modern*, 243; Levin and Tick, *Aaron Copland's America*, 146; Hitchcock, *Music in the United States*, 206; Howard Pollack, "Copland, Aaron," Grove Music Online, ed. L. Macy, http://www.grovemusic.com (accessed October 24, 2010); Oja, *Making Music Modern*, 251, 248.

6. Pollack is one of few commentators to refer to what we might call the "Other" Piano Variations, that this, those Copland marked "naively" or "warmly." Pollack also reminds us of Copland's wish—not satisfied—that Walter Gieseking, known for his refinement of tone color in Debussy and Mozart, perform the work. See Pollack, *Aaron Copland*, 151. Rosenfeld himself described the Variations as "all iron, all metal, all stone" and in which "some painful mobilization of energies is under way, gathering intensity, finally through much wrestling and travail bringing themselves into harmony and union with things as they are," noting "austere grandeur" ("Aaron Copland's Growth," 46, 47).

7. *New York Times*, March 22, 1953, cited in Stevenson, "Carlos Chávez's United States Press Coverage," 128.

8. Béhague, *Music in Latin America*, 135, 131. Saavedra discusses a scant number of Chávez's Indianist works and the extent to which the *Sinfonía India* dwarfs the rest of his production ("Of Selves and Others," 2).

9. Porter, "Musical Events Most Select and Generous," 163.

10. Wright, *Villa-Lobos*, 128; Evans Haile, producer and conductor of the 1987 performance, is quoted in Holden, "A Lush Musical by Villa-Lobos." Béhague mentions *Magdalena* in passing, and Peppercorn simply notes that it "had a mixed reception." See Béhague, *Heitor Villa-Lobos*, 28; Peppercorn, *The World of Villa-Lobos in Pictures and Documents*, 228–29.

11. Peppercorn, *The World of Villa-Lobos in Pictures and Documents*, 48–49. On 51 Peppercorn includes photos of "an Indian of the Amazon region such as Villa-Lobos must have seen during his travels," "a pretty Indian of the Amazon region attired in feathers," and "Bahia women in their attractive dresses and headgear" à la *National Geographic*.

12. Appleby, *Heitor Villa-Lobos*, 30; Wright, *Villa-Lobos*, 9–10.

13. Robert P. Morgan refers (in quotation marks) to Ginastera's "sublimation" of "ethnic attributes" (*Twentieth-Century Music*, 320). Schwartz-Kates follows Chase in referring to Ginastera as having "integrated sublimated symbols in forging an original Argentine style" and "sublimated malambo rhythms." Schwartz-Kates, "Ginastera, Alberto (Evaristo)." See also references to the "highly sublimated Argentine imagery" of the Second String Quartet (Schwartz-Kates, "The *Gauchesco* Tradition as a Source of National Identity in Argentine Art

Music," 892). Béhague also refers to "subjective sublimation," noting that it was Chase who "appropriately termed" it as such. Béhague, *Music in Latin America*, 218.

14. Kuss, "Nacionalismo, identificación, y Latinoamérica," 137. On Stravinsky's "astuteness," see chapter 2. Taruskin discusses some of the more influential approaches to analysis of the work in "Russian Folk Music in *The Rite of Spring*," 505; see also Van den Toorn, *Stravinsky and the Rite of Spring*, 9.

15. Kuss, "Nacionalismo, identificación, y Latinoamérica," 136. It is difficult to interpret Kuss's assessment (135) of Willi Apel's discussion of nationalism in the 1969 edition of the *Harvard Dictionary of Music*. She claims, for example, that Apel associates nationalism with peripheral countries but fails to mention his scare quotes around the word *peripheral*. She also maintains that Apel "of course omits mention" of Latin America; however much Kuss may disapprove of Apel's description of Villa-Lobos and Chávez as "outstanding nationalist composers of Latin America," such a remark can hardly be considered an omission. See Apel, "Nationalism," 565.

16. Kuss, "Nacionalismo, identificación, y Latinoamérica," 139.

17. Letter, Ginastera to Guillermo Espinosa, April 16, 1983, "Alberto Ginastera, Dr. H.C.," Espinosa Collection: Correspondence Ginastera Folder (no. 4 8.4), Latin American Music Center, Indiana University.

18. Gilbert, *The Music of Gershwin*, 34–35. On Gershwin's approach, including manipulation of the "Échale salsita" theme, see Pollack, *George Gershwin*, 178, 537. See also Schwartz, *Gershwin*, 225; Peyser, *The Memory of All That*, 198.

19. Berger, *Aaron Copland*, 63–65.

20. Crist, *Music for the Common Man*, 59, 56, 54.

21. Paz, *La Música en los Estados Unidos*, 111.

22. Devoto, "Panorama de la musicología latinoamericana," 92.

23. Ericson, "Lilit Gampel, 12, Violinist Plays Like Mature Artist."

24. This observation is by no means definitive but is rather an impression based on informal conversations with Chilean colleagues, some of whom were unaware of the work before coming to the United States. A former Barroco Andino member, Patricio Wang, recalls Rzewski performing the work in the Conservatory of The Hague and asking that a group of Chileans sing Ortega's song before the performance. Email with author, February 3, 2011, and facilitated by Jan Fairley, whom I thank for this information.

25. Paraskevaídis, "Algunas reflexiones sobre música y dictadura en América Latina," 7.

26. Quoted in Madsen, "Music as Metaphor," 102.

27. Copland and Perlis, *Copland Since 1943*, 78.

28. A summary of the extensive literature on music and utopia is given in Hess, "Competing Utopias?," 325n34. See also Moricz, *Jewish Identities*, 203–5; Taruskin, *The Danger of Music and Other Anti-Utopian Essays*.

29. See García, *Mexican Americans*. Felix Longoria, a Texas serviceman killed in action in the Pacific and denied burial in his own town, found his final resting place in Arlington National Cemetery only after Senator Lyndon Johnson took up the matter. A particularly grotesque affront to hemispheric harmony, revealed in late 2010 by Susan M. Reverby and much in the news at that time, involved U.S. government researchers deliberately infecting nearly seven hundred Guatemalans with syphilis between 1946 and 1948—when penicillin was widely available—under the banner of public health, another version of the Tuskegee "experiment" perpetrated against African Americans.

30. Hanke, introduction to *Do the Americas Have a Common History?*, 68, 20.

31. Cited in Powell, *Tree of Hate*, 139.

32. Cited in Powell, *Tree of Hate*, 141–42.

33. Statistics compiled in Lorenz, "Voices in Limbo," 3. To be sure, in October 2010 the Chicago Symphony marked Mexico's independence from Spain by performing Carlos Chávez's *Sinfonía India*. See also Robert D. King's self-published manuscript, "Primary Study for Boston Symphony Orchestra: Personnel and Repertoire" (Boston, 1994). With some exceptions, the situation for Spanish-language opera is similar. See *Annals of the Metropolitan Opera, 1883–2000: The Complete Chronicle of Performances and Artists* (CD-ROM, Metropolitan Opera Guild, 2001).

34. Pike, *The United States and Latin America*, 281–83.

35. These statistics, from the Pew Research Center, are cited in "The Hispanicisation of America," 35. Historically such statistics have been less than straightforward, as the 1930 and 1940 censuses show. In the former, "persons of Mexican birth or parentage who were not definitely reported as white or Indian were designated Mexican" and counted with "other races" (that is, not white). In 1940, however, the policy was reversed, such that "persons of Mexican birth or ancestry who were not definitely Indian or of other nonwhite race" were classified as white. U.S. Bureau of the Census, 1932 and 1943, cited in Rodríguez, *Changing Race*, 83–84. Thus, for a brief moment in the United States, the Mexican "race" enjoyed a special category. But only a decade later it was subsumed by "white"—unless, that is, individual Mexicans struck the census taker as "definitely Indian or of other nonwhite race." In 1971 the U.S. Census Bureau began using the category Hispanic, generally considered an ethnic group and thus fraught with that categorization's complexities and lack of consistency. In the 2010 census question 8 asked, "Is person of Hispanic, Latino, or Spanish origin?" Possible answers are "no," "yes, Mexican, Mexican Am., Chicano," "yes, Puerto Rican," "yes, Cuban," "yes, another Hispanic, Latino, or Spanish origin." Alternatively one can designate one's origin by printing in a box "Argentinean, Colombian, Dominican, Nicaraguan, Salvadoran, Spaniard, and so on." The difference between "Spaniard" and "Spanish origin" remains unclear. Question 9, which relates to race, states, "For this census, Hispanic origins are not races."

36. Edward Lowinsky's "Character and Purposes of American Musicology," 230, responded to Kerman's "A Profile for American Musicology" in the same publication, in which Kerman expressed his reservations on American music; additional commentary from Kerman is in "Letter from Joseph Kerman."

37. Grout, *A History of Western Music*, cited in Burkholder, "Music of the Americas and Historical Narratives," 402.

38. da Silva, *Mission Music of California*.

39. Russell, *From Serra to Sancho*, 4. See also Summers, "Spanish Music in California"; Summers, "New and Little Known Sources of Hispanic Music from California"; studies by Koegel and Lemmon cited in Russell.

40. See, for example, Crawford, *An Introduction to America's Music*; Candelaria and Kingman, *American Music*. Burkholder et al., *A History of Western Music*, integrate Ibero-America to a far greater degree than previous editions of this widely used text. Burkholder elucidates some of his own valuable contributions in "Music of the Americas and Historical Narratives." It should be noted, however, that in light of Crawford's treatment of early Catholic music-making in the Americas (*An Introduction to America's Music*, 2001) it is misleading to assert that early Catholic music-making had been "virtually ignored" in music history surveys prior to Burkholder's seventh edition (2006), as suggested on 421n15. In addition, Burkholder's discussion of the sarabande's supposed "Central American provenience" is confusing, given his situating it, following Stevenson, in Mexico (that is, in North America). See Burkholder,

"Music of the Americas and Historical Narratives," 422n27. On music in Florida and in the California missions, see, respectively, Housewright, *A History of Music and Dance in Florida* and Russell, *From Serra to Sancho*.

41. Hitchcock, *Music in the United States*, 1.

42. Many have expressed surprise that Latin America is barely a gasp in Richard Taruskin's monumental *The Oxford History of Western Music*.

■ BIBLIOGRAPHY

Abellán, Manuel L. *Censura y creación literaria en España (1939–1976)*. Badalona: Ediciones Península, 1980.

Abrams Ansari, Emily. "'Masters of the President's Music': Cold War Composers and the United States Government." Ph.D. diss., Harvard University, 2009.

Abresch, James. "Events in the World of Music." *New York Times*, January 28, 1945.

Adorno, Theodor. *Aesthetic Theory*. Trans. C. Lenhardt. London: Routledge & Kegan Paul, 1984.

———. *Mahler: A Musical Physiognomy*. Trans. Edmund Jephcott. Chicago: University of Chicago Press, 1992.

———. *Philosophy of Modern Music*. Trans. Anne G. Mitchell and Wesley V. Blomster. New York: Seabury Press, 1973.

———. "The Radio Symphony." 1941. In Richard Leppert, ed., *Essays on Music: Theodor W. Adorno*. Trans. Susan H. Gillespie. Berkeley: University of California Press, 2002, 251–70.

Agawu, Kofi. *Representing African Music: Postcolonial Notes, Queries, Positions*. New York: Routledge, 2003.

Agea, Francisco, ed. *21 años de la Orquesta Sinfónica de México, 1928–1948*. Mexico City: OSM, 1948.

Albanese, Catherine L. *Sons of the Fathers: The Civil Religion of the American Revolution*. Philadelphia: Temple University Press, 1976.

Albright, Daniel, ed. *Modernism and Music: An Anthology of Sources*. Chicago: University of Chicago Press, 2004.

"An American and Inter-American Anniversary." *Buenos Aires Herald*, July 4, 1967.

Anderson, Dwight. "Ginastera Ranked High for His Musical Creativeness." *Courier-Journal* (Louisville, Ky.), February 3, 1957.

———. "Louisville Orchestra's Opening Concert Called Best Yet." *Courier-Journal* (Louisville, Ky.), October 21, 1954.

Andrade, Mário de. *Ensaio sôbre a música brasileira*. São Paulo: Livraria Martins Editora, 1962.

———. *Hallucinated City*. Trans. Jack E. Tomlins. Kingsport, Tenn.: Vanderbilt University Press, 1968.

Ansermet, Ernest. "Los problemas del compositor American: El problema formal." *Sur* 2 (Fall 1931): 170–80.

———. "Los problemas del compositor americano: El compositor y su tierra." *Sur* 1 (Summer 1931): 118–28.

Antheil, George. *Bad Boy of Music*. Garden City, N.Y.: Doubleday, Doran, 1945.

Aparicio, Frances R. "Ethnifying Rhythms, Feminizing Cultures." In Ronald Radano and Philip V. Bohlman, eds., *Music and the Racial Imagination*. Chicago: University of Chicago Press, 2000, 95–112.

Aparicio, Frances R., and Susana Chávez-Silverman. *Tropicalizations: Transcultural Representations of Latinidad*. Hanover, N.H.: University Press of New England, 1997.

Apel, Willi. "Nationalism." In *Harvard Dictionary of Music.* 2nd ed., revised and enlarged. Cambridge: Belknap Press of Harvard University Press, 1969, 564–65.

Appelbaum, Stanley. *The New York World's Fair 1939/1940.* New York: Dover, 1977.

Appleby, David P. *Heitor Villa-Lobos: A Life (1887–1959).* Lanham, Md.: Scarecrow Press, 2002.

Ardévol, José. *Introducción a Cuba: La Música.* Havana: Instituto del Libro, 1969.

"Argentina." *Time,* July 8, 1967, 24.

"Argentina: Prohibida para adolescentes." *Primera Plana* 5, no. 243 (1967): 22–28.

Arizaga, Rodolfo. *Juan José Castro.* Buenos Aires: Editoriales Culturales Argentinas, 1963.

Asplund, Christian. "Frederic Rzewski and Spontaneous Political Music." *Perspectives of New Music* 33, nos. 1/2 (1995): 418–41.

"At *Bomarzo* World Premiere." *Washington Post,* May 22, 1967.

Atkinson, Brooks. "At the Theatre: Heitor Villa-Lobos, Brazilian Composer, Has Written the Musical Score for *Magdalena.*" *New York Times,* September 21, 1948.

Babbitt, Milton. "Who Cares if You Listen?" *High Fidelity* 8, no. 2 (1958): 38–40, 126–27.

Bagar, Robert. C. "Boult Conducts N.B.C. Symphony Orchestra." *New York World-Telegram,* May 16, 1938.

——. "City Symphony Concert." *New York-World Telegram,* February 13, 1945.

——. "Music: Villa-Lobos Conducts Own Two Brilliant Choros." *New York World-Telegram,* February 9, 1945.

Baim, Jo. *Tango: Creation of a Cultural Icon.* Bloomington: Indiana University Press, 2007.

Bakota, Carlos Steven. "Getúlio Vargas and the Estado Novo: An Inquiry into Ideology and Opportunism." *Latin American Research Review* 14, no. 1 (1979): 205–10.

"Bali Ha'i-by-the-River." *Time,* June 15, 1953, 43.

Bannerman, Henrietta. "A Dance of Transition: Martha Graham's *Heriodiade* (1944)." *Dance Research* 24, no. 1 (2006): 1–20.

Barnes, Howard. "The Theaters: *Magdalena.*" *New York Herald Tribune,* n.d. New York Public Library clippings file.

Baqueiro Fóster, Gerónimo. "El Huapango." *Revista Musical Mexicana* 8 (April 21, 1942): 174–83.

Barreda Laos, Felipe. *Hispano-América en guerra?* Buenos Aires: Linari, 1941.

Bary, Leslie. "Oswald de Andrade's Cannibalist Manifesto." *Latin American Literary Review* 19, no. 38 (1991): 35–47.

Bass, Jacquelynn. "*The Epic of American Civilization*: The Mural at Dartmouth College (1932–34)." In Renato González Mello and Diane Miliotes, eds., *José Clemente Orozco in the United States, 1927–1934.* Hanover, N.H.: Hood Museum of Art, 2002, 142–85.

Beal, Amy. *New Music, New Allies: American Experimental Music in West Germany from the Zero Hour to Reunification.* Berkeley: University of California Press, 2006.

Beals, Carleton. *The Coming Struggle for Latin America.* New York: Halcyon House, 1938.

Beasley-Murray, Jon. Translator's introduction to Beatriz Sarlo, *Scenes from Postmodern Life.* Cultural Studies of the Americas, vol. 7. Minneapolis: University of Minnesota Press, 2001.

Beckerman, Michael ed. *Dvorak and His World.* Princeton: Princeton University Press, 1993.

Beckett, Henry. "In the World of Music: Gershwin Program Brings Record Audience to Stadium Concert by Philharmonic-Symphony Orchestra." *New York Evening Post,* August 17, 1932.

Béhague, Gerard. "Ecuadorian, Peruvian, and Brazilian Ethnomusicology: A General View." *Latin American Music Review* 3, no. 1 (1982): 17–35.

————. *Heitor Villa-Lobos: The Search for Brazil's Musical Soul.* Austin: Institute of Latin American Studies, University of Texas at Austin, 1994.

————. *Music in Latin America: An Introduction.* Englewood Cliffs, N.J.: Prentice Hall, 1978.

Beirfield, Abby. "Strengthened Orchestra Displays Skill at Opening." *Louisville (Ky.) Times,* October 21, 1954.

Belnap, Jeffrey "Diego Rivera's Greater America: Pan-American Patronage, Indigenism, and H.P." *Cultural Critique* 63 (2008): 61–98.

Bemis, Samuel Flagg. *The Latin American Policy of the United States.* New York: Harcourt, Brace & World, 1943.

Benedict, Ruth. *Patterns of Culture.* New York: Houghton Mifflin, 1934.

Benjamin, Walter. *Reflections: Essays, Aphorisms, Autobiographical Writings.* Ed. Peter Demetz. Trans. Edmund Jephcott. New York: Harcourt Brace Jovanovich, 1978.

Bercovitch, Sacvan. *The Rites of Assent: Transformations in the Symbolic Construction of America.* New York: Routledge, 1993.

Berger, Arthur. *Aaron Copland.* New York: Oxford University Press, 1953.

————. "Heitor Villa-Lobos." *Harper's Bazaar* 80, no. 5 (1946): 115, 222–24.

Berger, Karol. "Time's Arrow and the Advent of Musical Modernity." In Karol Berger and Anthony Newcomb, eds., *Music and the Aesthetics of Modernity.* Isham Library Papers 6, Harvard Publications in Music 21. Cambridge: Harvard University Press, 2005, 3–22.

Berger, Mark T. *Under Northern Eyes: Latin American Studies and U.S. Hegemony in the Americas, 1898–1990.* Bloomington: Indiana University Press, 1995.

Bermann, Karl. *Under the Big Stick: Nicaragua and the United States Since 1848.* Boston: South End Press, 1986.

Bernal, Martin. *Black Athena: The Afroasiatic Roots of Classical Civilization.* Vol. 1: *The Fabrication of Ancient Greece, 1785–1985.* 3 vols. New Brunswick, N.J.: Rutgers University Press, 1987.

Bernstein, Leonard. *Findings.* New York: Simon and Schuster, 1982.

————. "Jazz in Serious Music." In *The Infinite Variety of Music.* New York: Simon and Schuster, 1962.

————. *Young People's Concerts.* New York: Sony Classical Video Music Education, 1993, vol. 13.

Beveridge, David. *Rethinking Dvorak: Views from Five Countries.* Oxford: Clarendon Press, 1996.

Bhabha, Homi. "Of Mimicry and Man: The Ambivalence of Colonial Discourse." In Frederick Cooper and Ann Laura Stoler, eds., *Tensions of Empire: Colonial Cultures in a Bourgeois World.* Berkeley: University of California Press, 1997, 152–60.

Bianchi, Soledad, Luis Bocaz, and Carlos Orellana. "Discusión sobre la música chilena." *Araucaria de Chile* 2 (1978): 111–73.

Bianculli, David. *Dangerously Funny: The Uncensored Story of the Smothers Brothers Comedy Hour.* New York: Simon & Schuster, 2010.

"Bicentennial Bonanza." *Time,* March 24, 1975, 69.

Biglia, Juan Carlos, and David Lifschitz. "*Bomarzo*: La prohibición." *Revista Argentina de Musicología* 3, no. 4 (2002–3): 235–87.

Blackwood, Alan. *Music of the World.* Englewood Cliffs, N.J.: Prentice-Hall, 1991.

Blake, David. "Eisler, Hanns." Oxford Music Online, http://www.oxfordmusiconline.com/subscriber/article/grove/music/08667 (accessed October 11, 2009).

Blanco Aguinagua, Carlos. "On Modernism from the Periphery." In Anthony L. Geist and José B. Monleón, eds., *Modernism and Its Margins: Reinscribing Cultural Modernity from Spain and Latin America.* New York: Garland, 1999, 3–16.

Blanksten, George I. *Perón's Argentina.* Chicago: University of Chicago Press, 1953.

Blitzstein, Marc. "Composers as Lecturers and in Concerts." *Modern Music* 13, no. 1 (1935): 47–50.

———. "Forecast and Review: Music and Theatre—1932." *Modern Music* 9, no. 4 (1932): 164–66.

Block, Geoffrey. "Bernstein's Senior Thesis at Harvard: The Roots of a Lifelong Search to Discover an American Identity." *College Music Symposium* 48 (2008): 52–68.

Boas, Franz. *The Mind of Primitive Man.* New York: Macmillan, 1911.

Bohm, Jerome D. [J.D.B.] "Boston Symphony Heard Again in Carnegie Hall: Aaron Copland's Mexican Piece Warmly Received." *New York Herald Tribune,* November 20, 1938.

———. "Philharmonic Heard under Brazil Auspices." *New York Herald Tribune,* May 10, 1939.

Bolton, Herbert Eugene. "Confessions of a Wayward Professor." *Americas* 6, no. 3 (1950): 359–62.

Bolton, Herbert Eugene, and Thomas Maitland Marshall. *The Colonization of North America, 1492–1783.* New York: Macmillan, 1920.

"*Bomarzo,* de A. Ginastera Fue Ovacionada en Washington." *El Mundo,* May 21, 1967.

"*Bomarzo* Premiere to Aid City Center." *New York Times,* May 3, 1968.

"*Bomarzo* Scores in Washington Premiere." *Buenos Aires Herald,* May 22, 1967.

"*Bomarzo* Spell Gripping." *Washington Evening Star,* May 20, 1967.

Boorstein, Edward. *Allende's Chile: An Inside View.* New York: International Publishers, 1977.

Borges, Jorge Luis. *The Book of Sand (El Libro de arena).* Trans. Norman Thomas Di Giovanni. New York: E. P. Dutton, 1977.

Born, Georgina, and David Hesmondhalgh, eds. *Western Music and Its Others: Difference, Representation, and Appropriation in Music.* Berkeley: University of California Press, 2000.

Bossom, Alfred. *Building to the Sky: The Romance of the Skyscraper.* London: Studio, 1934.

Bourdieu, Pierre. *Distinction: A Social Critique of the Judgement of Taste.* Trans. Richard Nice. Cambridge: Harvard University Press, 1984.

Bowles, Paul. "On Mexico's Popular Music." *Modern Music* 28, no. 4 (1941): 225–30.

———. "Villa-Lobos Directs Own Works in Concert with City Symphony." *New York Herald Tribune,* February 14, 1945.

Bradley, James. *The Imperial Cruise: A Secret History of Empire and War.* Boston: Little, Brown, 2009.

Brecht, Bertolt. *Brecht On Theatre: The Development of an Aesthetic.* Trans. John Willet. London: Methuen, 1978.

Brenner, Anita. *Idols behind Altars.* New York: Harcourt Brace, 1929.

Brodbeck, David. *Brahms/Symphony no. 1.* Cambridge: Cambridge University Press, 1997.

Brody, Martin. "Founding Sons: Copland, Sessions, and Berger on Genealogy and Hybridity." In Carol J. Oja and Judith Tick, eds., *Aaron Copland and His World.* Princeton: Princeton University Press, 2005, 15–43.

———. "'Music for the Masses': Milton Babbitt's Cold War Music Theory." *Musical Quarterly* 77, no. 2 (1993): 161–92.

Brooks, Van Wyck. "On Creating a Usable Past." *Dial,* April 11, 1918, 337–41.

Brown, Julie, ed. Western *Music and Race*. Cambridge: Cambridge University Press, 2007.

Broyles, Michael, and Denise von Glahn. *Leo Ornstein: Modernist Dilemmas, Personal Choices*. Bloomington: Indiana University Press, 2007.

Buch, Esteban. *The Bomarzo Affair: Ópera, perversión y dictadura*. Buenos Aires: Adriana Hidalgo editora, 2003.

———. "Ginastera y Nono: Encuentros y variantes." *Revista del Instituto Superior de Música* 9 (2002): 62–85.

Budasz, Rogério. "Of Cannibals and the Recycling of Otherness." *Music and Letters* 87, no. 1 (2005): 1–15.

Bukofzer, Manfred. "The New Nationalism." *Modern Music* 23, no. 4 (1946): 243–47.

Burge, David. "About Pianists." *Clavier* 27, no. 1 (1988): 46–47.

Burkholder, J. Peter. *All Made of Tunes: Charles Ives and the Uses of Musical Borrowing*. New Haven: Yale University Press, 1995.

———. "Music of the Americas and Historical Narratives." *American Music* 27, no. 4 (2009): 399–423.

———. "Quotation." Oxford Music Online, http://www.oxfordmusiconline.com/subscriber/article/grove/music/52854 (accessed July 12, 2010).

Burkholder, J. Peter, Donald Jay Grout, and Claude Palisca. *A History of Western Music*, 8th ed. New York: Norton, 2010.

Burns, E. Bradford *A History of Brazil*. 3rd ed. New York: Columbia University Press, 1993.

———. *Latin America: Conflict and Creation. A Historical Reader*. Englewood Cliffs, N.J.: Prentice Hall, 1993.

Burton-Carvajal, Julianne. "Don (Juanito) Duck and the Imperial-Patriarchal Unconscious: Disney Studios, the Good Neighbor Policy, and the Packaging of Latin America." In Andrew Parker, Mary Russo, Doris Sommer, and Patricia Yaeger, eds., *Nationalism and Sexualities*. New York: Routledge, 1992, 21–41.

———. "'Surprise Package': Looking Southward with Disney." In Eric Smoodin, ed., *Disney Discourse: Producing the Magic Kingdom*. New York: Routledge, 1994, 131–47.

Butler, Henry. "Concert Best, Week Is Quiet." *Indianapolis Times*, January 24, 1954.

———. "Henry Butler Says." *Indianapolis Times*, January 25, 1954.

Butterworth, Neil. *The Music of Aaron Copland*. London: Toccata, 1985.

Bynner, Witter. "While the Train Pauses at Torreon [*sic*]." *Laughing Horse*, no. 14 (Autumn 1927): 1–6.

Cage, John. "Chávez and the Chicago Drought." *Modern Music* 19, no. 2 (1942): 185–86.

Calinescu, Matei. *Five Faces of Modernity*. Durham, N.C.: Duke University Press, 1987.

Campbell, Jennifer. "Shaping Solidarity: Music, Diplomacy, and Inter-American Relations, 1936–1946." Ph.D. diss., University of Connecticut, 2010.

Campos, Rubén M. *El folklore y la música Mexicana*. Mexico City: Publicaciones de la Secretaria de Educación Pública, 1928.

Campos Hazan, Marcelo. "Raça, Nação e Jose Mauricio Nunes Garcia." *Resonancias* 24 (2009): 23–40.

Candelaria, Lorenzo, and Daniel Kingman. *American Music: A Panorama*. 4th ed. New York: Schirmer Books, 2012.

Caracas Garcia, Thomas George. "American Views of Brazilian Musical Culture: Villa-Lobos's Magdalena and Brazilian Popular Music." *Journal of Popular Culture* 37, no. 4 (2004): 634–47.

Carballo, Erick. "De la Pampa al cielo: The Development of Tonality in the Compositional Language of Alberto Ginastera." Ph.D. diss., Indiana University, 2006.

Cardoso, Fernando Enrique, and Enzo Faletto. *Dependency and Development in Latin America. Dependencia y desarrollo en América Latina (1971),* expanded and emended. Trans. Marjory Mattingly Urquidi. Berkeley: University of California Press, 1979.

Carmona, Gloria. *Carlos Chávez, 1899–1978: Iconografía.* Mexico City: Consejo Nacional Para la Cultura y las Artes, Instituto Nacional de Bellas Artes, 1994.

———, ed. *Epistolario selecto de Carlos Chávez.* Mexico City: Fondo de Cultura Económica, 1989.

Carnegie, Andrew. "Distant Possessions: The Parting of Ways." *North American Review* 167, no. 501 (1898): 239–49.

Carpentier, Alejo. "El Ángel de las Maracas." In *Obras Completas de Alejo Carpentier,* vol. 12. Madrid: Siglo Veintiuno Editores, 1987, 185–92.

———. *Ese músico que llevo dentro.* Madrid: Alianza Editorial, 1987.

Carr, Raymond. *Spain: 1808–1975.* 2nd ed. Oxford: Clarendon Press, 1982.

Carter, Elliott. "Forecast and Review: O Fair World of Music!" *Modern Music* 16, no. 4 (1939): 238–43.

———. "Late Winter, New York, 1937." *Modern Music,* March–April 1937, 147–54.

Cartwright, Lisa, and Brian Goldfarb. "Cultural Contagion: On Disney's Health Education Films for Latin America." In Eric Smoodin, ed., *Disney Discourse: Producing the Magic Kingdom.* New York: Routledge, 1994, 169–80.

Casey, Michael. *Che's Afterlife: The Legacy of an Image.* New York: Vintage Books, 2009.

Castro-Klarén, Sara. "A Genealogy for the 'Manifesto antropófago,' or the Struggle between Socrates and the Caraïbe." *Nepantla: Views from South* 1, no. 2 (2000): 295–322.

Catalyne, Alice Ray. "Manuel de Zumaya (ca. 1678–1756): Mexican Composer for Church and Theater." In Burton L. Karson, ed., *Festival Essays for Pauline Alderman.* Provo, Utah: Brigham Young University Press, 1976, 101–24.

Cavalcanti, Lauro. *When Brazil Was Modern: Guide to Architecture 1928–1960.* Trans. Jon Tolman. New York: Princeton Architectural Press, 2003.

C.H. "Gareth Anderson Heard." *New York Times,* April 12, 1948.

Charlot, Jean. *The Mexican Mural Renaissance, 1920–1925.* New Haven: Yale University Press, 1963.

"Charlot's Frescoes Shown." *New York Times,* May 8, 1931.

Chase, Gilbert. "Alberto Ginastera: Argentine Composer." *Musical Quarterly* 43, no. 4 (1957): 439–60.

———. "Alberto Ginastera: Portrait of an Argentine Composer." *Tempo* 44 (1957): 11–17.

———. *America's Music from the Pilgrims to the Present.* New York: McGraw-Hill, 1955.

———. "Caracas Host to Second Latin American Festival." *Musical America* 77, no. 6 (1957): 11–12.

———. "Creative Trends in Latin American Music: II." *Tempo* 50 (1959): 25–28.

———. "Current Musical Trends in South America." *Musical America* 77, no. 3 (1957): 31, 176–79.

———. "The Foundations of Musical Culture in Latin America." In *Intellectual Trends in Latin America.* Papers Read at a Conference on Intellectual Trends in Latin America Sponsored by Institute of Latin-American Studies of the University of Texas, Austin, April 13–14, 1945. Austin: University of Texas Press, 1945, 35–43.

———. *A Guide to the Music of Latin America.* New York: AMS Press, 1942.

———. *A Guide to the Music of Latin America.* 2nd ed., revised and enlarged. Washington, D.C.: Pan American Union and Library of Congress, 1972.

———. "The Mail Pouch: Twelve Tones Fall on Deaf Ears." *New York Times,* April 13, 1958.

———. "Music of the New World." *Music Educators Journal* 30, no. 2 (1943): 17–18, 49.

———. "New World Music: Inter-American Festival in Washington. D.C." *Americas* 10, no. 7 (1958): 10–13.

———. "Recent Books: Americanismo Musical." *Modern Music* 20, no. 3 (1943): 214–15.

Chase, Stuart. *Mexico: A Study of Two Americas.* 1931. New York: Macmillan, 1933.

Chávez, Carlos. "Antecedents and Consequents." *Eolus* 6, no. 1 (1927): 12–15.

———. "El dodecafonismo en México." Lecture text. Mexico City: Memoria de El Colegio Nacional, 1954.

———. "Revolt in Mexico." *Modern Music* 13, no. 3 (1936): 35–40.

———. "Technique and Inner Form." *Modern Music* 5, no. 4 (1928): 28–31.

———. "The Two Persons." *Musical Quarterly* 15, no. 2 (1929): 153–59.

Chavkin, Samuel. *The Murder of Chile: Eyewitness Accounts of the Coup, the Terror, and the Resistance Today.* New York: Everest House, 1982.

Chevalier, Lucien. "Oeuvres de Villa-Lobos." *Le Monde Musical* 38, no. 12 (1927): 450.

Cheyfitz, Eric. *The Poetics of Imperialism: Translation and Colonization from* The Tempest *to* Tarzan. New York: Oxford University Press, 1991.

Chmaj, Betty E. "Fry versus Dwight: American Music's Debate over Nationality." *American Music* 3 no. 1 (1985): 63–84.

Chotzinoff, Samuel. "Brazilian Music Heard on Philharmonic Program." *New York Post,* May 10, 1939.

———. "Words and Music: Boston Symphony Draws Throng to Carnegie Hall." *New York Post,* November 21, 1938.

Chowrimootoo, Christopher. "Bourgeois Opera: *Death in Venice* and the Aesthetics of Sublimation." *Cambridge Opera Journal* 22, no. 2 (2011): 177–218.

Chua, Daniel K. L. *Absolute Music and the Construction of Meaning.* Cambridge: Cambridge University Press, 1999.

Citkowitz, Israel. "American Composers, XII: Walter Piston—Classicist." *Modern Music* 13, no. 2 (1936): 3–10.

———. "Forecast and Review: Winter Music, New York, 1933." *Modern Music* 10, no. 3 (1933): 154–57.

———. "Spring Concerts in New York." *Modern Music* 9, no. 4 (1932): 168–72.

Clark, Walter Aaron. "Doing the Samba on Sunset Boulevard: Carmen Miranda and the Hollywoodization of Latin American Music." In Walter Aaron Clark, ed., *From Tejano to Tango: Latin American Popular Music.* New York: Routledge, 2002, 252–76.

———. *Enrique Granados: Poet of the Piano.* New York: Oxford University Press, 2006.

Clements, Andrew. "Music in 12 Parts." *Guardian,* May 14, 2010, http://www.guardian.co.uk/music/2010/may/14/music-in-12-parts-review (accessed May 4, 2011).

Coad, Malcolm. "Rebirth of Chilean Cinema." In Ruth Petries, ed., *Film and Censorship: The Index Reader.* London: Cassel, 1997, 39–47.

Coady, R. J. "American Art" (part 1). *The Soil* 1, no. 1 (1916): 3–4.

———. "American Art" (part 2). *The Soil* 1, no. 2 (1917): 54–56.

Connell-Smith, Gordon. "Latin America in the Foreign Relations of the United States." *Journal of Latin American Studies* 8, no. 1 (1976): 137–50.

Cooke, Mervyn, ed. *Cambridge Companion to Twentieth-Century Opera.* Cambridge: Cambridge University Press, 2005.

Copland, Aaron. "Carlos Chávez—Mexican Composer." *New Republic* 54 (May 2, 1928): 322–23.

———. "Carlos Chávez—Mexican Composer." In Henry Cowell, ed., *American Composers on American Music.* Stanford: Stanford University Press, 1933, 102–6.

———. "The Composers of South America." *Modern Music* 19, no. 2 (1942): 75–82.

———. "Festival in Caracas." *New York Times,* December 26, 1954.

———. *Music and Imagination.* 1952. Cambridge: Harvard University Press, 1966.

———. *Our New Music: Leading Composers in Europe and America.* New York: McGraw-Hill, 1941.

———. "*El Salón México.*" Program booklet. Boston Symphony Orchestra, Fifty-eighth Season, 1938–39, 16–17.

———. "The Story behind My *El salón México.*" *Tempo* no. 4 (July 1939): 2–4.

Copland, Aaron, and Vivian Perlis. *Copland, 1900–1942.* New York: St. Martin's Press, 1984.

Copland, Aaron, and Vivian Perlis. *Copland Since 1943.* New York: St. Martin's Press, 1989.

Cordero, Roque. "¿Nacionalism versus dodecafonismo?" *Revista Musical Chilena* 13 (1959): 28–38.

Coriat, Isador H. *Repressed Emotions.* New York: Brentano's, 1920.

———. *What Is Psychoanalysis?* New York: Moffat, Yard, 1919.

Corrado, Omar. "Música culta y política en Argentina entre 1930 y 1945." *Música e Investigación* 9 (2001): 1–11.

———. *Música y modernidad en Buenos Aires, 1920–1940.* Buenos Aires: Gourmet Musical Ediciones, 2010.

———. "Viena en Buenos Aires: Notas sobre la primera recepción de la Escuela de Viena en Argentina." *Pauta* (Mexico) 108 (October–December 2008): 8–41.

Cortesi, Arnaldo. "Brazil at War Stirs Latins." *New York Times,* August 23, 1942.

Covarrubias, Miguel. *Mexico South.* New York: Knopf, 1947.

Cowell, Henry. "Improving Pan American Music Relations." *Modern Music* 19, no. 4 (1942): 263–65.

———. Program booklet, Second Inter-American Music Festival, April 22–30, 1961.

———. "Towards Neo-Primitivism." *Modern Music* 10, no. 3 (1932–33): 149–53.

Cox, Ainslee. "New York." *Music Journal,* January 1979, 39.

Cramer, Gisela, and Ursula Prutsch. "Nelson A. Rockefeller's Office of Inter-American Affairs (1940–1946) and Record Group 229." *Hispanic American Historical Review* 86, no. 4 (2006): 785–806.

Crawford, Richard. *The American Musical Landscape.* Berkeley: University of California Press, 1993.

———. "Dvorak and the Historiography of American Music." In David Beveridge, ed., *Rethinking Dvorak: Views from Five Countries.* Oxford: Clarendon Press, 1996, 257–63.

———. "Edward MacDowell: Musical Nationalism and an American Tone Poet." *Journal of the American Musicological Society* 49, no. 3 (1996): 528–60.

———. *An Introduction to America's Music.* New York: Norton, 2001.

Crist, Elizabeth B. *Music for the Common Man: Aaron Copland During the Depression and War.* Oxford: Oxford University Press, 2005.

"El cuento de la buena pipa." *Primera plana* 5, no. 243 (1967): 68.

Cugat, Xavier. *Rumba Is My Life.* New York: Didier, 1948.

Cuney-Hare, Maud. *Negro Musicians and Their Music.* Washington, D.C.: Associated Publishes, 1936.

Custer, Arthur. "Contemporary Music in Spain." *Musical Quarterly* 48, no. 1 (1962): 1–18.

Dahlhaus, Carl. *Between Romanticism and Modernism.* Trans. Mary Whittall. Berkeley: University of California Press, 1980.

———. *Nineteenth-Century Music.* Trans. J. Bradford Robinson. Berkeley: University of California Press, 1989.

Daniel, Oliver. *Stokowski: A Counterpoint of View*. New York: Dodd, Mead, 1982.

Daniel, Yvonne. *Dance and Social Change in Contemporary Cuba*. Bloomington: Indiana University Press, 1995.

Darío, Rubén. *Selected Poems of Rubén Darío: A Bilingual Anthology*. Ed. Alberto Acereda. Trans. Will Derusha. Lewisburg, Pa.: Bucknell University Press, Associated University Presses, 1993.

da Silva, Owen. *Mission Music of California*. Los Angeles: Warren F. Lewis, 1941.

Dasilva, Fabio. "Misleading Discourse and the Message of Silence: An Adornian Introduction to Villa-Lobos's Music." *International Review of the Aesthetics and Sociology of Music* 10, no. 2 (1979): 167–80.

Davies, Drew Edward. "The Italianized Frontier: Music of the Durango Cathedral, *Español* Culture, and the Aesthetics of Devotion in Eighteenth-Century New Spain." Ph.D. diss., University of Chicago, 2006.

Dávila, Jerry. "Myth and Memory: Getúlio Vargas's Long Shadow over Brazilian History." In Jens R. Hentschke, ed., *Vargas and Brazil: New Perspectives*. New York: Palgrave Macmillan, 2006, 257–82.

Davis, Darién J. *White Face, Black Mask*. East Lansing: Michigan State University Press, 2009.

Debord, Guy. *The Society of the Spectacle*. Trans. Donald Nicholson-Smith. New York: Zone Books, 1994.

Delano, Jack. *Puerto Rico Mío: Four Decades of Change*. Washington, D.C.: Smithsonian Institution Press, 1990.

DeLapp, Jennifer. "Copland in the Fifties: Music and Ideology in the McCarthy Era." Ph.D. diss., University of Michigan, Ann Arbor, 1997.

DeLapp-Birkett, Jennifer. "Aaron Copland and the Politics of Twelve-Tone Composition in the Early Cold War United States." *Journal of Musicological Research* 27, no. 1 (2008): 31–62.

Delpar, Helen. *The Enormous Vogue of Things Mexican: Cultural Relations between the United States and Mexico, 1920–1935*. Tuscaloosa: University of Alabama Press, 1992.

Denning, Michael. *The Cultural Front: The Laboring of American Culture in the Twentieth Century*. London: Verso, 1998.

DePalma, Anthony. *The Man Who Invented Fidel: Cuba, Castro, and Herbert L. Matthews of the New York Times*. New York: Public-Affairs, 2006.

Dett, R. Nathaniel. "Negro Music." In Oscar Thompson, ed., *The International Cyclopedia of Music and Musicians*. New York: Dodd, Mead, 1939, 1243–46.

Devoto, Daniel. "Panorama de la musicología latinoamericana." *Acta musicologica* 31, nos. 3–4 (1959): 91–109.

Díaz Sánchez, Julián. "Al servicio del espíritu: La redefinición de la vanguardia artística en el franquismo." In Ignacio Henares Cuellar, María Isabel Cabrera García, Gemma Pérez Zalduondo, and José Castillo Ruíz, eds., *Dos décadas de cultura artística en el franquismo*. 2 vols. Granada: University of Granada, 2001, 1: 269–85.

"Diego Rivera Exhibits in New York." *Bulletin of the Pan American Union* 66, no. 1 (1932): 48–52.

Domínguez, Alberto, and Nancy de los Santos, directors. *The Bronze Screen: One Hundred Years of the Latino Image in Hollywood*. Questar, 2002.

Dorfman, Ariel, and Armand Mattelart. *How to Read Donald Duck: Imperialist Ideology in the Disney Comic*. Trans. David Kunzle. New York: International General, 1975.

Dos Passos, John. "Paint the Revolution!" *New Masses* 2, no. 5 (1927): 15–17.

Douglass, Ana, and Thomas A. Vogler, eds. *Witness and Memory: The Discourse of Trauma*. New York: Routledge, 2003.

Downes, Edward. "Barnett Directs Orchestral Unit." *New York Times*, November 12, 1958.

Downes, Olin. "Argentine Pianist Scores in Program." *New York Times*, March 12, 1946.

———. "Art of Villa Lobos: Works of Brazilian Composer Show Blend of Genius and Naivete." *New York Times*, May 14, 1939.

———. "Brazilian Music Heard in Concert." *New York Times*, October 17, 1940.

———. "Brazilian Music Is Played at the Fair." *New York Times*, May 5, 1939.

———. "Brazilian Music on Fair Program." *New York Times*, May 10, 1939.

———. "Brazilian Series of Concerts Ends." *New York Times*, October 21, 1940.

———. "Chávez Conducts Boston Orchestra." *New York Times*, April 11, 1936.

———. "Chávez Presents Opening Program." *New York Times*, February 12, 1937.

———. "Choral Works, New and Old." *New York Times*, April 14, 1940.

———. "Copland Novelty in Premiere Here." *New York Times*, November 20, 1938.

———. "From Brazil." *New York Times*, October 13, 1940.

———. "Hector Villa-Lobos: Visiting Composer Discusses Sources of Nationalism in Art." *New York Times*, December 17, 1944.

———. "Koussevitzky Gets Ovation in Boston." *New York Times*, October 11, 1924.

———. "Kussevitsky [*sic*] as a Magnetic Personality—Prokofiev and the Powers of Evil." *New York Times*, June 15, 1924.

———. "Music." *New York Times*, November 3, 1924.

———. "Music: More of the Ultra-Modern." *New York Times*, November 29, 1926.

———. "Music: Presenting American Composers." *New York Times*, April 23, 1928.

———. "Music Presented of South America." *New York Times*, April 18, 1940.

———. "Musicians' Group Opens New Season." *New York Times*, November 2, 1932.

———. "*Sacre du Printemps* Played." *New York Times*, February 1, 1924.

———. "Schola Cantorum Gives Novelties." *New York Times*, January 15, 1930.

———. "2 South American Composers Guests." *New York Times*, February 24, 1947.

———. "Villa-Lobos Guest at the City Center." *New York Times*, February 13, 1945.

———. "Women's Orchestrette Classique." *New York Times*, December 1, 1936.

———. "Young Composer's 'Anti-Impressionism' Need of New Orchestral Programs." *New York Times*, March 29, 1925.

Downs, Linda Bank. *Diego Rivera: The Detroit Industry Murals*. New York: Detroit Institute of Arts, Norton, 1999.

Driver, Paul. "Recordings: Rzewski *The People United Will Never Be Defeated!*" *Tempo* 136 (1981): 24–27.

Dunn, Christopher. *Brutality Garden: Tropicália and the Emergence of a Brazilian Counterculture*. Chapel Hill: University of North Carolina Press, 2001.

D'Urbano, Jorge. "Calculada audacia." *Panorama* 50 (1967): 56–57.

———. *Música en Buenos Aires*. Buenos Aires: Editorial Sudamericana, 1966.

Dyer, Richard. "Entertainment and Utopia." In Rick Altman, ed., *Genre: The Musical*. London: Routledge and Kegan Paul, 1981, 175–89.

Einstein, Alfred. "National and Universal Music." *Modern Music* 14, no. 1 (1936): 3–11.

———. "War, Nationalism, Tolerance." *Modern Music*, November–December 1939, 3–9.

Elie, Rudolph, Jr. "Heitor Villa-Lobos: Genius, South American Department." *Boston Herald*, February 25, 1946.

Engel, Jonathan. *American Therapy: The Rise of Psychotherapy in the United States*. New York: Gotham Books, 2008.

Enloe, Cynthia. *Bananas, Beaches and Bases: Making Feminist Sense of International Politics*. Berkeley: University of California Press, 1990.

Ericson, Raymond. "Lilit Gampel, 12, Violinist Plays Like Mature Artist." *New York Times,* June 9, 1972.

Espinosa, J. Manuel. *Inter-American Beginnings of U.S. Cultural Diplomacy, 1936–1948.* Washington, D.C.: Department of State Publications, 1976.

Estrella, Miguel Ángel. *Música para la esperanza: Conversaciones con Jean Lacouture.* Buenos Aires: Ediciones de la Flor, 1985.

Evans, Ernestine. "If I Should Go Back to Mexico." *Century Magazine* 111 (February 1926): 459–60.

Eversman, Alice. "Simon Sadoff Gives Pleasing Performance." *Washington Evening Star,* September 9, 1946.

Evett, Robert. "*Bomarzo, Si, Rigoletto,* No." *New Republic* 156 (June 10, 1967): 28–29.

———. "New Music of the Americas." *New Republic* 138 (April 28, 1958): 23.

Faber, Sebastiaan. "Learning from the Latins: Waldo Frank's Progressive Pan-Americanism." *New Centennial Review* 3, no. 1 (2003): 257–95.

Fagg, John Edwin. *Pan Americanism.* Malabar, Fla.: Robert E. Krieger, 1982.

Farwell, Arthur. "Nationalism in Music." In Oscar Thompson, ed., *The International Cyclopedia of Music and Musicians.* New York: Dodd, Mead, 1939, 1234–39.

———. "Roy Harris." *Musical Quarterly* 18, no. 1 (1932): 18–32.

Faulkner, Anne Shaw. "Does Jazz Put the Sin in Syncopation?" In Robert Walser, ed., *Keeping Time: Readings in Jazz History.* New York: Oxford University Press, 1999, 32–36.

Felber, Erwin. "Step-Children of Music." *Modern Music* 4, no. 4 (1926): 31–33.

Fernández, Justino. *Estética del arte mexicano.* Mexico City: Universidad Nacional Autónoma de México, 1972.

Fernández Retamar, Roberto. *Caliban and Other Essays.* Trans. Edward Baker. Minneapolis: University of Minnesota Press, 1989.

Fine, Irving Gifford. "Boston Hears Villa-Lobos; Attends Theatre." *Modern Music* 22, no. 3 (1945): 188–90.

Fink, Robert. *Repeating Ourselves: American Minimalism as Cultural Practice.* Berkeley: University of California Press, 2005.

Fisher, Marjorie M. "Villa-Lobos Music Makes Light Opera Grand." *San Francisco News,* n.d., New York Public Library clippings file.

Fitz-Gerald, John D. "The Opportunity and the Responsibility of the Teacher of Spanish." *Hispania* 1 (November 1917): 11–18.

Fles, Barthold. "Chavez Lights New Music with Old Fires." *Musical America* 48, no. 22 (1928): 1, 21.

F.M. [Fred Marey]. "Beware the Ides of *Bomarzo*: Hue and Cry about Ban of Ginastera's Opera as Local Censors Are Overstepping Their Faculties." *Buenos Aires Herald,* July 24, 1967.

F.M. [Frank Merkling]. "Reports: United States." *Opera News* 30 (March 26, 1966): 30.

Fobes, Christopher A. "A Theoretical Investigation of Twelve-Tone Rows, Harmonic Aggregates, and Non–Twelve Tone Materials in the Late Music of Alberto Ginastera." Ph.D. diss., State University of New York at Buffalo, 2006.

Fojas, Camilla. *Cosmopolitanism in the Americas.* West Lafayette, Ind.: Purdue University Press, 2005.

Forbes, Jack D. *Black Africans and Native Americans: Color, Race and Caste in the Evolution of Red-Black Peoples.* Oxford: Basil Blackwell, 1988.

Foreman, Lewis. "Ginastera: A Discography." *Tempo* no. 118 (September 1976): 17–22.

Fosler-Lussier, Danielle. "American Cultural Diplomacy and the Mediation of Avant-garde Music." In Robert Adlington, ed., *Sound Commitments: Avant garde Music and the Sixties.* Oxford: Oxford University Press, 2009, 232–53.

———. *Music Divided: Bartók's Legacy in Cold War Culture.* Berkeley: University of California Press, 2007.

Foucault, Michel. *The History of Sexuality.* Vol. 1. Trans. Robert Hurley. New York: Vintage Books, 1978.

Franco, Jean. *The Modern Culture of Latin America: Society and Artist.* London: Pall Mall Press, 1967.

Frank, Thomas C. *The Conquest of Cool: Business Culture, Counterculture, and the Rise of Hip Consumerism.* Chicago: University of Chicago Press, 1997.

Frank, Waldo. *America Hispana: A Portrait and a Prospect.* New York: Charles Scribner's Sons, 1931.

———. *Our America.* New York: Boni and Liveright, 1919.

———. *The Re-Discovery of America.* New York: Charles Scribner's Sons, 1929.

———. *Virgin Spain.* New York: Boni and Liveright, 1926.

Frankenstein, Alfred. "Villa-Lobos at Large: Afloat with a Note on the Magdalena." *San Francisco Examiner,* n.d., New York Public Library clippings file.

Freud, Sigmund. *The Standard Edition of the Complete Psychological Works of Sigmund Freud.* Trans. James Strachey. 1957. New York: Hogarth Press and the Institute of Psycho-Analysis, 1961.

———. *Totem and Taboo: Resemblances between the Psychic Lives of Savages and Neurotics.* Trans. James Strachey. 1913; rpt. New York: Norton, 1950.

Fry, Andy. "Rethinking the *Revue nègre*: Black Musical Theatre in Inter-War Paris." In Julie Brown, ed., *Western Music and Race.* Cambridge: Cambridge University Press, 2007, 258–75.

Fulbright, J. William. *The Arrogance of Power.* New York: Random House, 1966.

Gamio, Manuel. *Forjando Patria.* Trans. Fernando Armstrong-Fumero. Boulder: University Press of Colorado, 2010.

García, Mario T. *Mexican Americans: Leadership, Ideology, and Identity, 1930–1960.* New Haven: Yale University Press, 1989.

García Canclini, Néstor. *Cultura y comunicación entre lo global y lo local.* La Plata, Argentina: Facultad de Periodismo y Comunicación Social de la Plata, 1997.

———. *Hybrid Cultures: Strategies for Entering and Leaving Modernity.* 1989. Trans. Christopher L. Chiappari and Silvia L. López. Minneapolis: University of Minnesota Press, 1995.

———. "Memory and Innovation in the Theory of Art." *South Atlantic Quarterly* 92, no. 3 (1993): 423–43.

García Morillo, Roberto. *Carlos Chávez: Vida y obra.* Mexico City: Fondo de Cultura Económica, 1960.

García Muñoz, Carmen. "Juan José Castro (1895–1968)." *Cuadernos de música iberoamericana* 1 (1996): 3–24.

Garrett, Charles Hiroshi. *Struggling to Define a Nation: American Music and the Twentieth Century.* Berkeley: University of California Press, 2008.

Gates, Eunice Joiner. "Brazilian Music." *Hispania* 22, no. 2 (1939): 129–34.

Gay, Peter, ed. *The Freud Reader.* New York: Norton, 1989.

Geist, Anthony L., and José B. Monleón, eds. *Modernism and Its Margins: Reinscribing Cultural Modernity from Spain and Latin America.* New York: Garland, 1999.

Gellman, Irwin F. *Good Neighbor Diplomacy: United States Policies in Latin America, 1933–1945*. Baltimore: Johns Hopkins University Press, 1979.

Gershwin, George. "The Composer in the Machine Age." In Oliver M. Sayler, ed., *Revolt in the Arts: A Survey of the Creation, Distribution and Appreciation of Art in America*. New York: Brentano's, 1930, 264–69.

Gidal, Marc. "Contemporary 'Latin American' Composers of Art Music in the United States: Cosmopolitans Navigating Multiculturalism and Universalism." *Latin American Music Review* 31, no. 1 (2010): 40–78.

Gil, Federico. *Latin American–United States Relations*. New York: Harcourt Brace Jovanovich, 1971.

Gilbert, Steven E. *The Music of Gershwin*. New Haven: Yale University Press, 1995.

Ginastera, Alberto. "How and Why I Wrote *Bomarzo*." *Central Opera Service Bulletin*, 9, no. 5 (1967): 10–13.

———. "Why the Inter-American Must Be a Festival of Youth." *Sunday Star* (Washington, D.C.), June 23, 1968. Latin American Music Center, Indiana University.

Giunta, Andrea. *Vanguardia, internacionalismo y política: Arte argentino en los años sesenta*. Buenos Aires: Paidós, 2001.

Goehr, Lydia. *The Imaginary Museum of Musical Works: An Essay in the Philosophy of Music*. Oxford: Clarendon Press, 1992.

Goldberg, Albert. "Ginastera Quartet Lively, Novel Work." *Los Angeles Times*, January 5, 1956.

Goldberg, Isaac. *George Gershwin: A Study in American Music*. New York: F. Ungar, 1958.

Gombrich, E. H. *The Ideas of Progress and Their Impact on Art*. New York: Cooper Union School of Art and Architecture, 1971.

González, Juan Pablo. "Chilean Musicians' Discourse of the 1980s: A Collective Poetics, Pedagogy and Socio-Aesthetics of Art and Popular Music." Ph.D. diss., University of California at Los Angeles, 1990.

———. "Hegemony and Counter-Hegemony of Music in Latin America: The Chilean Pop." *Popular Music and Society* 15 (1991): 63–78.

———. "Inti-Illimani and the Artistic Treatment of Folklore." *Latin American Music Review* 10, no. 2 (1989): 267–86.

Gonzalez, Mike. "Ideology and Culture under Popular Unity." In Philip O'Brien, ed., *Allende's Chile*. New York: Praeger, 1976, 106–27.

Goodwin, Philip L. *Brazil Builds: Architecture New and Old, 1652–1942 / Construção Brazil: Arquitetura moderna e antiga*. New York: Museum of Modern Art, 1943.

Gordon, Diane. "Inti-Illimani: Chile's Masters of the 'New Song.'" *Guitar Player* 31 (October 1997): 41–42.

"Gorgeous Pageant 'Aztec Gold' Marks Charity Carnival." *New York Herald Tribune*, May 3, 1929.

Gottlieb, Jack, ed. *Leonard Bernstein's Young Peoples Concerts*. New York: Doubleday, 1992.

Graça Aranha, José Pereira de. "A emoção estética na arte moderna." In *Espírito Moderno*. 2nd ed. São Paulo: Companhia Editora Nacional, 1932.

Graeff, Edward A. *Cidade Utopia*. Belo Horizonte, Brazil: Editora Vega, 1979.

Graham, Martha. "Seeking an American Art of Dance." In Oliver M. Sayler, ed., *Revolt in the Arts: A Survey of the Creation, Distribution and Appreciation of Art in America*. New York: Brentano's, 1930, 249–55.

Granja Tachuchian, Maria de Fátima. "Panamericanismo, propaganda e musica erudite: Estados Unidos e Brasil (1939–1948)." 2 vols. Ph.D. diss., University of São Paulo, 1998.

Grant, Madison. *The Passing of the Great Race or The Racial Basis of European History*. 4th revised ed. New York: Charles Scribner's Sons, 1921.

Grant, Mark N. *Maestros of the Pen: A History of Classical Music Criticism in America*. Boston: Northeastern University Press, 1998.

Gray, Cecil. *A Survey of Contemporary Music*. 2nd ed. Oxford: Oxford University Press, 1927.

Greenberg, Clement. "Art." *Nation* 162, no. 8 (1946): 241–42.

———. "Avant-Garde and Kitsch." In Francis Frascina, ed., *Pollock and After: The Critical Debate*. 2nd ed. London: Routledge, 2000, 21–33.

Greenblatt, Stephen. "Resonance and Wonder." In Ivan Karp and Steven D. Lavine, eds., *Exhibiting Cultures: The Poetics and Politics of Museum Display*. Washington, D.C.: Smithsonian Institution, 1991, 42–56.

Griffiths, Paul. "Aleatory." Oxford Music Online, http://www.oxfordmusiconline.com/subscriber/article/grove/music/00509 (accessed July 11, 2010).

Grout, Donald Jay. *A History of Western Music*. New York: Norton, 1960.

Growther, Bosley. "The Screen." *New York Times*, February 13, 1943.

Guérios, Paulo Renato. "Heitor Villa-Lobos e o Ambiente Artístico Parisiense: Convertendo-se em un Músico Brasileiro." *Mana* 9, no. 1 (2003): 81–108.

Guilbaut, Serge. *How New York Stole the Idea of Modern Art: Abstract Expressionism, Freedom, and the Cold War*. Trans. Arthur Goldhammer. Chicago: University of Chicago Press, 1983.

Gupta, Akhil, and James Ferguson. "Beyond Culture: Space, Identity, and the Politics of Difference." In Akhil Gupta and James Ferguson, eds., *Culture, Power, and Place: Explorations in Critical Anthropology*. Durham, N.C.: Duke University Press, 1997, 33–51.

Gupta, Akhil, and James Ferguson, eds. *Culture, Power, and Place: Explorations in Critical Anthropology*. Durham, N.C.: Duke University Press, 1997.

Guterl, Matthew Pratt. *The Color of Race in America, 1900–1940*. Cambridge: Harvard University Press, 2001.

Gutheim, Frederick A. "Buildings at the Fair." *Magazine of Art* 32, no. 5 (1939): 286–89, 316.

Hale, Nathan G., Jr. *Freud and the Americans: The Beginnings of Psychoanalysis in the United States, 1876–1917*. New York: Oxford University Press, 1971.

Hall, Raymond. "Americans in Venice." *New York Times*, October 16, 1938.

Hamm, Charles. "Dvorak, Nationalism, Myth, and Racism." In David Beveridge, ed., *Rethinking Dvorak: Views from Five Countries*. Oxford: Clarendon Press, 1996, 275–80.

Hampton, Edgar Lloyd. "Rebirth of Prehistoric American Art." *Current History* 25, no. 5 (1925): 625–34.

Hanke, Lewis, ed. *Do the Americas Have a Common History? A Critique of the Bolton Theory*. New York: Knopf, 1964.

Haring, Clarence H. *South America Looks at the United States*. 1928. New York: Arno Press and the *New York Times*, 1970.

Harrison, Jay S. "Eartha Kitt Heard in Song Program at the Stadium." *New York Herald Tribune*, July 11, 1960.

Hart, Brian. "The Symphony in Theory and Practice in France, 1900–1914." Ph.D. diss., Indiana University, 1993.

Haskins, John. Preface in program booklet for First Inter-American Music Festival, April 18–20, 1958, 7. Guillermo Espinosa Collection, Latin American Music Center, Indiana University.

Heile, Björn. *The Music of Mauricio Kagel*. Aldershot, U.K.: Ashgate, 2006.

Helm, McKinley. *Mexican Painters*. 1941. New York: Dover, 1989.

Helpern, Alice. "The Technique of Martha Graham." *Studies in Dance History* 2, no 2 (1991): 36–49.

Henahan, Donal. "Sex and Violence in His Opera? Ginastera Agrees with Censors." *New York Times*, February 14, 1968.

———. "(1) 'Why Not?' (2) 'One Step Forward.'" *New York Times*, May 10, 1968.

Henderson, W. H. "Boston Orchestra Plays Stravinsky's Impressive Ballet." *New York Herald*, February 1, 1924.

Henderson, W. J. "Modern Works Given in Concert." *New York Sun*, November 29, 1926.

———. "Present American Composers." *New York Sun*, April 23, 1928.

Henestrosa, Andrés. "Música Mestiza de Tehuantepec." *Revista Musical Mexicana*, nos. 5 and 7 (March 7 and April 7, 1942): 107–9, 151–54.

Henry, Beck C. "*H.P.* Makes Premiere Here with a Bang as Sparkplugs Go into a Song and Dance." *Philadelphia Record*, April 1, 1932.

Hernández Campos, Jorge. "The Influence of the Classical Tradition, Cézanne, and Cubism on Rivera's Artistic Development." In Linda Downs and Ellen Sharp, eds., *Diego Rivera: A Retrospective*. New York: Founders Society Detroit Institute of Arts and Norton, 1986, 119–29.

Herrera, Luis Eduardo. "Politics of Creation / Creation of Politics, or Composing Peripheries: Musical Creation, Political Repression, and Cold-War Strategies in Dictatorial Argentina." Ph.D. diss., University of Illinois at Urbana-Champaign, forthcoming.

Herrera, Hayden. *Frida: A Biography of Frida Kahlo*. New York: Harper & Row, 1983.

Hess, Carol A. "Anti-Fascism by Another Name: Gustavo Durán, the Good Neighbor Policy, and *franquismo* in the United States." In Gemma Pérez-Zalduondo, ed., *Música, ideología y política en la cultura artística durante el franquismo (1938–1975)*. Madrid: Ministerio de España y Fundación Brepols, forthcoming.

———. "Competing Utopias? Musical Ideologies in the 1930s and Two Spanish Civil War Films." *Journal of the Society for American Music* 2, no. 3 (2008): 319–54.

———. "Copland in Argentina: Pan Americanist Politics, Folklore, and the Crisis of Modernism." *Journal of the American Musicological Society* 66, no. 1 (2013): 191–250.

———. "'De aspecto inglés pero de alma española': Gilbert Chase, Spain, and Musicology in the United States." *Revista de Musicología*, forthcoming.

———. *Enrique Granados: A Bio-Bibliography*. Westport, Conn.: Greenwood Press, 1991.

———. "Jean Berger: A 'Good Neighbor' in the United States." *American Music Research Center Journal* 18 (2010): 39–52.

———. "Leopold Stokowski, 'Latin' Music, and Pan Americanism." *Inter-American Music Review* 18, nos. 1–2 (2008): 395–401.

———. *Manuel de Falla and Modernism in Spain, 1989–1936*. Chicago: University of Chicago Press, 2001.

———. "Miguel Ángel Estrella: (Classical) Music for the People, Dictatorship, and Memory." In Patricia Hall, ed., *The Oxford Handbook of Music Censorship*. New York: Oxford University Press, forthcoming.

Hess, John A. *Questions and Answers in Chemistry*. Revised ed. New York: College Entrance Book Company, 1934.

Hewes, Harry L. "The Mexican Ballet-Symphony *H.P.*" *Bulletin of the Pan American Union* 66, no. 6 (1932): 421–24.

"The Hispanicisation of America: The Law of Large Numbers." *Economist* 396, no. 8699 (2010): 35–36.

Hitchcock, H. Wiley. *Music in the United States: A Historical Introduction*. 4th ed. Upper Saddle River, N.J.: Prentice-Hall, 2000.

Hobart, John. "*Magdalena* Is Exciting Theater." *San Francisco Chronicle*, n.d. New York Public Library clippings file.

Hodgson, Godfrey. *The Myth of American Exceptionalism.* New Haven: Yale University Press, 2009.

Holden, Robert H., and Eric Zolov, eds. *Latin America and the United States: A Documentary History.* New York: Oxford University Press, 2000.

Holden, Stephen. "A Lush Musical by Villa-Lobos." *New York Times,* November 19, 1987.

Holly, Janice E. "Irving Lowens and *The Washington Star:* The Vision, the Demise." Ph.D. diss., University of Maryland, 2007.

Honour, Hugh. *The European Vision of America.* Cleveland: Cleveland Museum of Art, 1975.

Hornbostel, Erich von. "African Negro Music." *Africa: Journal of the International African Institute* 1 (1928): 30–62.

Horowitz, Joseph. "Dvorak and Boston." *American Music* 19, no. 1 (2001): 3–17.

Housewright, Wiley L. *A History of Music and Dance in Florida, 1565–1865.* Tuscaloosa: University of Alabama Press, 1991.

Howard, John Tasker. *This Modern Music: A Guide for the Bewildered Listener.* New York: Thomas Y. Crowell, 1942.

Hubbs, Nadine. *The Queer Composition of America's Sound: Gay Modernists, American Music, and National Identity.* Berkeley: University of California Press, 2004.

Huebner, Steven. *French Opera at the Fin de Siècle: Wagnerism, Nationalism, and Style.* New York: Oxford University Press, 1999.

Hume, Paul. "*Bomarzo:* A Modern Masterpiece." *Washington Post,* May 20, 1967.

———. "Ginastera Emerges as Giant in Music Festival's Finale." *Washington Post,* May 1, 1961.

———. "Music of Spain's Avant-garde Heard Here." *Washington Post,* June 28, 1968. Latin American Music Center, Indiana University.

———. "An Opera Is Born." *Américas* 19, no. 7 (1967): 34–37.

———. "Postlude: Three Quartets Have World Premieres." *Washington Post and Times Herald,* April 20, 1958.

———. "Villa-Lobos's New No. 12 Is Festival Hit." *Washington Post and Times Herald,* April 21, 1958.

Hurlburt, Laurance P. *The Mexican Muralists in the United States.* Albuquerque: University of New Mexico Press, 1989.

Hurtado, Leopoldo. "Aaron Copland habla de la música norteamericana." *Argentina Libre,* October 9, 1941. Aaron Copland Collection, Library of Congress, Box 358, Folder 24.

Hutcheon, Linda. *A Theory of Parody.* 1985. Urbana: University of Illinois Press, 2000.

I.K. "Music of the Week End: Boston Symphony Matinee." *New York Sun,* November 21, 1938.

"In a Gloomy Garden." *Time,* May 26, 1967, 77.

Ingle, Marjorie. *Mayan Revival Style: Art Deco Maya Fantasy.* Salt Lake City, Utah: Peregrine Smith, 1984.

Jackson, K. David. "Three Glad Races: Primitivism and Ethnicity in Brazilian Modernist Literature." *Modernism/Modernity* 1, no. 2 (1994): 89–112.

Jacobson, Robert. "Capital Ginastera in Washington." *Saturday Review,* June 24, 1967, 59, 64.

Jameson, Fredric. "Reification and Utopia in Mass Culture." *Social Text* 1, no. 1 (1979): 130–48.

Jansen, Sue Curry. *Censorship, the Knot That Binds Power and Knowledge.* New York: Oxford University Press, 1988.

Jara, Joan. *An Unfinished Song: The Life of Victor Jara.* New York: Ticknor & Fields, 1984.

Jara, Joan, and Adrian Mitchell. *Victor Jara: His Life and Songs.* Ottawa: Elm Tree Books, 1976.

J.D.B. [Jerome D. Bohm]. "Stadium Filled as 17,000 Hear Gershwin Play." *New York Herald Tribune*, August 17, 1932.

Jeffrey, Jaclyn, ed. *Memory and History: Essays on Recalling and Interpreting*. Lanham, Md.: University Press of America, 1994.

Jewell, Edward Alden. "About Orozco's New Frescoes." *New York Times*, February 1, 1931.

———. "Deep Well of Culture." *New York Times*, October 19, 1930.

Johnson, Harriett. "Words and Music: A Surprise 'Toy' Symphony—Villa Lobos and Francescatti." *New York Post*, February 9, 1945.

———. "Words and Music: UN Shares in Stokowski Opening." *New York Post*, October 8, 1963.

Johnson, John J. *Latin America in Caricature*. Austin: University of Texas Press, 1980.

Joost, Nicholas, and Alvin Sullivan, *D. H. Lawrence and The Dial*. Carbondale: Southern Illinois University Press, 1970.

Joseph, Gilbert M. "Close Encounters: Toward a New History of U.S.–Latin American Relations." In Gilbert M. Joseph, Catherine C. LeGrand, and Ricardo Salvatore, eds., *Close Encounters of Empire: Writing the Cultural History of U.S.–Latin American Relations*. Durham, N.C.: Duke University Press, 1998, 3–46.

Kanellos, Nicolás. *A History of Hispanic Theatre in the United States: Origins to 1940*. Austin: University of Texas Press, 1990.

Kant, Immanuel. *Critique of Judgment*. Trans. J. H. Bernard. New York: Hafner, 1951.

Katzew, Ilona. *Casta Painting: Images of Race in Eighteenth-Century Mexico*. New Haven: Yale University Press, 2004.

Kaufmann, Helen L. "Carlos Chávez: Decidedly No Mañana Mexican." *Musical America* 61, no. 14 (1936): 11, 36.

Keen, Benjamin. *The Aztec Image in Western Thought*. New Brunswick, N.J.: Rutgers University Press, 1971.

Kenworthy, Eldon. *America/Américas: Myth in the Making of U.S. Policy toward Latin America*. University Park: Pennsylvania State University Press, 1995.

Kerman, Joseph. "Letter from Joseph Kerman." *Journal of the American Musicological Society* 18, no. 3 (1965): 426–27.

———. "A Profile for American Musicology." *Journal of the American Musicological Society* 18, no. 1 (1965): 61–69.

Kerner, Leighton. "Composers Defiant Will Never Be Refuted." *Village Voice* 24, no. 65 (1979): 66.

Kert, Bernice. *Abby Aldrich Rockefeller: The Woman in the Family*. New York: Random House, 1993.

Kimmel, Michael. *Manhood in America: A Cultural History*. New York: Free Press, 1996.

Kimsey, John. "'One Parchman Farm or Another': Mose Allison, Irony and Racial Formation." *Journal of Popular Music Studies* 17, no. 2 (2005): 105–32.

Kindermann, William. *Beethoven's Diabelli Variations*. Oxford: Clarendon Press, 1987.

King, John. *El Di Tella y el desarrollo cultural argentino en la década del sesenta*. Buenos Aires: Arte Gaglianone, 1985.

———. *Sur: A Study of the Argentine Literary Journal and Its Role in the Development of a Culture, 1931–1970*. Cambridge: Cambridge University Press, 1986.

Kirkpatrick, John. "Aaron Copland's Piano Sonata." *Modern Music* 10, no. 4 (1942): 246–50.

Klein, Howard. "Ginastera: A Most Happy Composer." *New York Times*, February 20, 1966.

Knapp, Raymond. *The American Musical and the Formation of National Identity*. Princeton: Princeton University Press, 2005.

————. "Utopian Agendas: Variation, Allusion, and Referential Meaning in Brahms's Symphonies." In David Brodbeck, ed., *Brahms Studies 3*. Lincoln: University of Nebraska Press, 2001, 129–89.

Knight, Alan. "Cardenismo: Juggernaut or Jalopy?" *Journal of Latin American Studies* 26, no. 1 (1994): 73–107.

————. "Racism, Revolution, and *Indigenismo*: Mexico, 1910–1940." In Richard Graham, ed., *The Idea of Race in Latin America, 1870–1940*. Austin: University of Texas Press, 1990, 71–113.

Koegel, John. "*Canciones del país*: Mexican Musical Life in California after the Gold Rush." *California History* 78, no. 3 (1999): 160–87.

————. "Crossing Borders: Mexicana, Tejana, and Chicana Musicians in the United States and Mexico." In Walter Aaron Clark, ed., *From Tejano to Tango: Latin American Popular Music*. New York: Routledge, 2002, 99–101.

————. "Mexican Musicians in California and the United States, 1910–1950." *California History* 84, no. 1 (2006): 7–29, 64–69.

Koegel, John, and José Juan Tablada. "Compositores Cubanos y Mexicanos en Nueva York: 1880–1920." *Historia Mexicana* 56, no. 2 (2006): 533–612.

Kolb, Roberto, and José Wolffer, eds. *Silvestre Revueltas: Sonidos en rebellion*. Mexico City: Universidad Nacional Autónoma de México, Escuela Nacional de Música, Dirección General de Apoyo al Personal Académico, 2007.

Kolocotroni, Vassiliki, Jane Goldman, and Olga Taxidou, eds. *Modernism: An Anthology of Sources and Documents*. Chicago: University of Chicago Press, 1998.

Kolodin, Irving. "Marx Leads Music by Brazilians." *New York Sun*, May 10, 1939.

Kornbluh, Peter. *The Pinochet File: A Declassified Dossier on Atrocity and Accountability*. New York: New Press, 2003.

Kostelanetz, Richard. *A Theatre of Mixed Means*. New York: Dial Press, 1968.

Kramer, Jonathan. *The Time of Music: New Meanings, New Temporalities, New Listening Strategies*. New York: Schirmer Books, 1988.

Kramer, Lawrence. *Classical Music and Postmodern Knowledge*. Berkeley: University of California Press, 1995.

Kriegsman, Alan M. "Composers Drop Nationalism." *Washington Post*, July 7, 1968. Latin American Music Center, Indiana University.

Kuss, Malena. "Nacionalismo, identificación y Latinoamérica." *Cuadernos de música iberoamericana* 6 (1998): 133–49.

————. "Symbol und Phantasie in Ginasteras *Bomarzo*." In Friedrich Spangemacher, ed., *Alberto Ginastera*. Bonn: Boosey & Hawkes, 1984, 88–102.

————. "Type, Derivation, and Use of Folk Idioms in Ginastera's *Don Rodrigo* (1964)." *Latin American Music Review* 1, no. 2 (1980): 176–95.

Labonville, Marie Elizabeth. *Juan Bautista Plaza and Musical Nationalism in Venezuela*. Bloomington: Indiana University Press, 2007.

LaCapra, Dominick. *Representing the Holocaust: History, Theory, Trauma*. Ithaca, N.Y.: Cornell University Press, 1994.

LaFeber, Walter. "Latin American Policy." In Robert A. Divine, ed., *Exploring the Johnson Years*. Austin: University of Texas Press, 1981, 64–90.

Landon, H. C. Robbins. "A Pox on Manfredini." *High Fidelity* 11, no. 6 (1961): 38–39, 86–87.

Landry, Robert J. "*Bomarzo* Not So Good on Melody: Major Production but Minor Score." *Variety*, March 20, 1968, 70.

Lang, Paul Henry. "Music: Little Orchestra Society." *New York Herald Tribune*, October 18, 1955.

———. "Music: New York Philharmonic." *New York Herald Tribune*, April 8, 1961.

Lange, Francisco Curt. "Americanismo musical." *Boletín latino-americano de música* 2 (1936): 117–30.

———. "Prefacio." In *Latin-American Art Music for the Piano by Twelve Contemporary Composers*. New York: G. Schirmer, 1942.

Langley, Lester D. *America and the Americas: The United States in the Western Hemisphere*. Athens: University of Georgia Press, 1989.

Latham, Michael E. *Modernization as Ideology: American Social Sciences and "Nation Building" in the Kennedy Era*. Chapel Hill: University of North Carolina Press, 2000.

Laughlin, Henry P. *Mental Mechanisms*. Washington, D.C.: Butterworths, 1963.

Lavine, Harold, and James Wechsler. *War Propaganda and the United States*. New Haven: Yale University Press, 1940.

Lawler, Vanett. "Latin Americans See Our Musical Life." *Bulletin of the Pan American Union* 76, no. 7 (1942): 368–73.

Lederman, Minna. "Composer Tells All." *New Republic*, 102 (March 25, 1940): 416.

———. *The Life and Death of a Small Magazine*. ISAM Monographs, no. 18. Brooklyn: Institute for Studies in American Music, 1983.

Lee, Sherry D. "A Minstrel in a World without Minstrels: Adorno and the Case of Schreker." *Journal of the American Musicological Society* 58, no. 3 (2005): 639–96.

Lees, Eugene. "Critics Laud Symphony after Concert Here." *Louisville (Ky.) Times*, October 8, 1955.

LeGrand, Catherine C. "Living in Macondo: Economy and Culture in a United Fruit Company." In Gilbert M. Joseph, Catherine C. LeGrand, and Ricardo Salvatore, eds., *Close Encounters of Empire*. Durham, N.C.: Duke University Press, 1998, 333–68.

Leibowitz, Herbert A. ed. *Musical Impressions: Selections from Paul Rosenfeld's Criticism*. London: George Allen & Unwin, 1969.

Leppert, Richard. "Music 'Pushed to the Edge of Existence' (Adorno, Listening, and the Question of Hope)." *Cultural Critique* 60 (2005): 92–133.

Levin, Gail. "From the New York Avant-Garde to Mexican Modernists: Copland and the Visual Arts." In Carol J. Oja and Judith Tick, eds., *Aaron Copland and His World*. Princeton: Princeton University Press, 2005, 101–19.

Levin, Gail, and Judith Tick. *Aaron Copland's America: A Cultural Perspective*. New York: Watson-Guptil, 2000.

Levine, Lawrence W. *Highbrow/Lowbrow: The Emergence of Cultural Hierarchy in America*. Cambridge: Harvard University Press, 1988.

Lévi-Strauss, Claude. *Structural Anthropology*. Trans. Claire Jacobson and Brooke Grundfest Schoepf. New York: Basic Books, 1963.

Levy, Beth E. *Frontier Figures: American Music and the Mythology of the American West*. Berkeley: University of California Press, 2012.

———. "'The White Hope of American Music': Or, How Roy Harris Became Western." *American Music* 10, no. 2 (2001): 131–67.

Lichtenwanger, William. *The Music of Henry Cowell: A Descriptive Catalogue*. ISAM Monographs no. 23. Brooklyn: Institute for Studies in American Music, 1985.

Lissfelt, J. Fred. "Music Festival Ends with Piano, Organ Selections." *Pittsburgh Sun-Telegraph*, November 30, 1952.

———. "Pittsburgh Holds Contemporary Music Festival." *Musical America* 72, no. 16 (1952): 3, 28.

Livingston-Isenhour, Tamara Elena, and Thomas George Caracas García. *Choro: A Social History of a Brazilian Popular Music*. Bloomington: Indiana University Press, 2005.

Locke, Ralph P. "Constructing the Oriental 'Other': Saint-Saëns's *Samson et Dalila.*" *Cambridge Opera Journal* 3, no. 3 (1991): 261–302.

———. "Exoticism and Orientalism in Music: Problems for the Worldly Critic." In Paul Bové, ed., *Edward Said and the Work of the Critic: Speaking Truth to Power.* Durham, N.C.: Duke University Press, 2000, 257–82.

———. "Reflections on Orientalism in Opera and Musical Theatre." *Opera Quarterly* 10, no. 1 (1993): 49–73.

Lopes, Luiz Fernando. "The Evolution of Heitor Villa-Lobos's Music: Sources, Style, and Reception." Ph.D. diss., Indiana University, forthcoming.

Lorenz, Ricardo. "Voices in Limbo: Identity, Representation, and Realities of the Latin American Composer." Unpublished paper, University of Chicago, 1999.

Lourie, Arthur. "Neogothic and Neoclassic." *Modern Music* 5, no. 3 (1928): 3–8.

Lowens, Irving. "Current Chronicle." *Musical Quarterly* 44, no. 3 (1958): 378–82.

———. "Current Chronicle." *Musical Quarterly* 47, no. 4 (1961): 530–34.

———. "Current Chronicle." *Musical Quarterly* 53, no. 4 (1967): 551–62.

———. "Ginastera Harp Work Superbly Performed." *Evening Star* (Washington, D.C.), January 10, 1968.

———. "Ginastera's *Bomarzo* Spectacular Triumph." *Washington Evening Star*, May 20, 1967.

———. "Ginastera's *Cantata* Enchanting, Exciting." *Evening Star* (Washington, D.C.), May 1, 1961.

Lowinsky, Edward. "Character and Purposes of American Musicology: A Reply to Joseph Kerman." *Journal of the American Musicological Society* 18, no. 2 (1965): 222–34.

Lucie-Smith, Edward. *Latin American Art of the 20th Century.* 2nd ed. London: Thames & Hudson, 2004.

Macdonald, Dwight. "A Theory of Mass Culture." In John Storey, ed., *Cultural Theory and Popular Culture: A Reader.* 2nd ed. Harlow, U.K.: Pearson Prentice Hall, 1994, 22–36.

Madrid, Alejandro L. *Sounds of the Modern Nation: Music, Culture, and Ideas in Post-Revolutionary Mexico.* Philadelphia: Temple University Press, 2009.

Madrid, Alejandro L., and Ignacio Corona, eds. *Postnational Musical Identities: Cultural Production, Distribution, and Consumption in a Globalized Scenario.* Lanham, Md.: Lexington Books, 2008.

Madsen, Jessica. "Music as Metaphor: A Study of the Political Inspiration behind Frederic Rzewski's *36 Variations on 'El Pueblo Unido Jamás Será Vencido!'* (The People United Will Never Be Defeated!), a Chilean Nueva Canción by Sergio Ortega and Quliapa-yún." Doctor of Musical Arts document, University of Cincinnati, 2003.

Magaldi, Cristina. "Cosmopolitanism and World Music in Rio de Janeiro at the Turn of the Twentieth Century." *Musical Quarterly* 92, nos. 3–4 (2009): 329–64.

———. *Music in Imperial Rio de Janeiro: European Culture in a Tropical Milieu.* Lanham, Md.: Scarecrow Press, 2004.

———. "Two Musical Representations of Brazil: Carlos Gomes and Villa-Lobos." In Carmen Nava and Ludwig Lauerhass Jr., eds., *Brazil in the Making: Facets of National Identity.* Lanham, Md.: Rowman & Littlefield, 2006, 205–27.

Magdanz, Teresa. "'Sobre las olas': Cultural Synecdoche of the Past." *Journal of the Society for American Music* 1, no. 3 (2007): 301–40.

Maltby, William S. *The Black Legend in England: The Development of Anti-Spanish Sentiment, 1558–1660.* Durham, N.C.: Duke University Press, 1971.

Manso, Carlos. *Juan José Castro.* Buenos Aires: De los Cuatro Vientos Editorial, 2006.

Margles, Pamela. "Rzewski's Music Has Moral Message." *Music Magazine* 8, no. 1 (1985): 11–13.

Margrave, Wendell. "Current Chronicle." *Musical Quarterly* 51, no. 2 (1965): 409–13.

Mariátegui, José Carlos. *7 Ensayos de interpretación de la realidad peruana.* Montevideo: Ejido, 1928.

Mariz, Vasco. "César Guerra-Peixe (1914–1993)." *Inter-American Music Review* 14, no. 1 (1994–95): 169–70.

———. *Cláudio Santoro.* Rio de Janeiro: Civilização Brasileira, 1994.

———. *Heitor Villa-Lobos.* Rio de Janeiro: Zahar Editores, 1981.

Martí, José. *Nuestra América.* Nuestra mayúscula America series. Buenos Aires: Nuestra América Editorial, 2005.

———. "The Truth about the United States." In Philip S. Foner, ed., *Inside the Monster by José Martí: Writings on the United States and American Imperialism.* Trans. Elinor Randall, Luis A. Baralt, Held Foner, and Juan de Onís. New York: Monthly Review Press, 1975, 49–54.

Martin, John. "The Dance: A Handicap Event." *New York Times,* April 10, 1932.

———. "The Dance: A Mexican Ballet." *New York Times,* March 27, 1932.

———. "The Dance: Social Satire." *New York Times,* April 19, 1931.

———. "Mexican Ballet in World Premiere." *New York Times,* April 1, 1932.

———. "Martha Graham in Hectic Recital." *New York Times,* April 22, 1934.

Martin, Linton. "Ballet or Ballyhoo?" *Philadelphia Inquirer,* March 27, 1932.

———. "H.P. New Ballet Fantastic Affair." *Philadelphia Inquirer,* April 1, 1932.

———. "Stokowski Bids His Audience 'Good-by.'" *Philadelphia Inquirer,* November 24, 1928.

Marx, Burle. "Brazilian Portrait—Villa Lobos." *Modern Music* 17, no. 1 (1939): 10–17.

———. Introduction to *Festival of Brazilian Music.* Program booklet. New York: MoMA, October 16–20, 1940, Programs 1–2, Program 3.

Marx, Leo. *The Machine in the Garden: Technology and the Pastoral Ideal in America.* New York: Oxford University Press, 1964.

Mason, Colin. "The Paris Festival." *Tempo* 24 (Summer 1952): 12–13, 15–19.

Mayer-Serra, Otto. "Bibliografía." *Revista Musical Mexicana* 9 (May 7, 1942): 208.

———. "Carlos Chávez: Una monografía crítica." *Revista Musical Mexicana* 3 (February 7, 1942): 62–63.

———. *Panorama de la música mexicana.* Mexico City: El Colegio de México, 1942.

McCann, Bryan. *Hello, Hello Brazil: Popular Music in the Making of Modern Brazil.* Durham, N.C.: Duke University Press, 2004.

McClary, Susan. *Georges Bizet: Carmen.* Cambridge: Cambridge University Press, 1992.

McKenna, Marian. *Myra Hess: A Portrait.* London: Hamish Hamilton, 1976.

McLuhan, T. C. *Dream Tracks: The Railroad and the American Indian, 1890–1930.* New York: Harry N. Abrams, 1985.

McNapsy, Clement J. "Conquest or Inculturation: Ways of Ministry in Early Jesuit Missions." In Kenneth Keulman, ed., *Critical Moments in Religious History.* Macon, Ga.: Mercer University Press, 1993, 77–94.

McPhee, Colin. "Forecast and Review." *Modern Music* 13, no. 3 (1936): 41–46.

———. "Jungles of Brazil." *Modern Music* 18, no. 1 (1940): 41–43.

———. "South American Once More." *Modern Music* 17, no. 4 (1940): 245–46.

Mendoza, Vicente T. *Lírica narrativa de México: El Corrido.* Estudios de Folklore 2. Mexico City: Instituto de Investigaciones Estéticas and Universidad Nacional Autónoma, 1964.

Melton, Laura. "Frederic Rzewski's *The People United Will Never Be Defeated!*: An Analysis and Historical Perspective." Doctor of Musical Arts document. Rice University, 1997.

Mertens, Wim. *American Minimal Music*. Trans. J. Hautekiet. London: Kahn & Averill, 1983.

Messing, Scott. *Neoclassicism in Music from the Genesis of the Concept through the Schoenberg/Stravinsky Polemic*. 1988. Rochester, N.Y.: University of Rochester Press, 1996.

"Mexican Art Show in Exhibition Here." *New York Times*, October 14, 1930.

Meyer, Donald C. "Toscanini and the Good Neighbor Policy: The NBC Symphony Orchestra's 1940 South American Tour." *American Music* 18, no. 3 (2000): 233–56.

Miller, Nicola. "The Historiography of Nationalism and National Identity in Latin America." *Nations and Nationalism* 12, no. 2 (2006): 201–21.

Miranda, Ricardo. *Ecos, Alientos y Sonidos: Ensayos sobre Música Mexicana*. Veracruz: Universidad Veracruzana and Fondo de Cultura Económica, 2001.

Mootz, William. "Critics Hear Orchestra and Open Workshop." *Courier-Journal*, (Louisville, Ky.), October 8, 1955.

Morgan, Robert P. *Twentieth-Century Music*. New York: Norton, 1991.

Moricz, Klara. *Jewish Identities: Nationalism, Racism, and Utopianism in Twentieth-Century Music*. Berkeley: University of California Press, 2008.

Morris, Nancy. "'Canto porque es necesario cantar': The New Song Movement in Chile, 1973–1983." *Latin American Research Review* 21, no. 2 (1986): 117–36.

Morris, William, ed. *The American Heritage Dictionary of the English Language*. Boston: American Heritage and Houghton Mifflin, 1969.

Moulard, Barbara L. *Tabula Rasa: Art of the Mexican Viceroyalty*. Mesa, Ariz.: Mesa Southwest Museum, 1988.

Mujica, Francisco. *History of the Skyscraper*. New York: Da Capo Press, 1977.

Mumford, Lewis. "Orozco in New England." *New Republic* 80 (October 10, 1934): 231–35.

Munoz, Peggy. "Dallapiccola Program Stirs Controversy in Mexico City." *Musical America* 77, no. 13 (1952): 6, 24.

Munro, Lisa. "Investigating World's Fairs: An Historiography." *Studies in Latin American Popular Culture* 28 (2010): 80–94.

Munson, Gorham. *Waldo Frank: A Study*. New York: Boni and Liveright, 1923.

Murphy, John P. *Music in Brazil*. New York: Oxford University Press, 2006.

Museu Villa-Lobos. *Villa-Lobos, Sua Obra*. Rio de Janeiro: Museu Villa-Lobos, 1965.

"Music in the Air." *New York Times*, December 14, 1941.

"Music: Not for Squares." *Newsweek*, May 28, 1967, 90.

Napp, Cornelia. *Personal Representatives in Musikverlegerischerin Kulturbeziehungen: Die Vertretung von Heitor Villa-Lobos in den USA*. Remagen-Rolandswerth, Germany: Max Brockhaus Musikverlag, 2003.

Neiburg, Federico, and Mariano Plotkin, compilers. *Intelectuales y expertos: La constitución del conocimiento social en la Argentina*. Buenos Aires: Paidós, 2004.

Nettl, Bruno. *The Study of Ethnomusicology: Twenty-nine Issues and Concepts*. Urbana: University of Illinois Press, 1983.

Neustadt, Robert. "Music as Memory and Torture: Sounds of Repression and Protest in Chile and Argentina." *Chasqui: Revista de literatura latinoamericana* 33, no. 1 (2004): 128–37.

Neves, José María. *Música contemporânea brasileira*. São Paulo: Ricordi Brasileira, 1981.

"New Orchestra Opens Series at Popular Prices." *New York Herald Tribune*, November 2, 1932.

The New York World's Fair Illustrated by Camera. New York: Manhattan Post Card Publishing, 1939.

Newton, Ronald C. *The "Nazi Menace" in Argentina, 1931–1947.* Stanford: Stanford University Press, 1992.

Nicholls, David. "Transethnicism and the American Experimental Tradition." *Musical Quarterly* 80, no. 4 (1996): 569–94.

Ninkovitch, Frank A. *The Diplomacy of Ideas: U.S. Foreign Policy and Cultural Relations, 1938–1950.* Cambridge: Cambridge University Press, 1981.

"No deseamos lanzar un manifiesto." *Índice* 12, no. 119 (1958): 28.

Noriega, Chon. "Citizen Chicano: The Trials and Titillations of Ethnicity in the American Cinema, 1935–1962." In Clara E. Rodríguez, ed., *Latin Looks: Images of Latinos and Latinas in the U.S. Media.* Boulder, Colo.: Westview Press, 1997, 121–41.

Novak, Barbara. *American Painting of the Nineteenth Century: Realism, Idealism and the American Experience.* New York: Praeger, 1976.

Novo, Salvador. "Nueva York (Continente vacío)." In *Toda la prosa.* Mexico City: Empresas Editoriales, 1964, 231–35.

Nunes, Benedito. "Anthropophagic Utopia, Barbarian Metaphysics." In Mari Carmen Ramírez and Héctor Olea, eds., *Inverted Utopias: Avant-Garde Art in Latin America.* New Haven: Yale University Press, 2004, 57–61.

Oboler, Suzanne. "'So Far from God, So Close to the United States': The Roots of Hispanic Homogenization." In Mary Romero, Pierette Hondagneu-Sotelo, and Vilma Ortíz, eds., *Challenging Fronteras: Structuring Latina and Latino Lives in the U.S.* New York: Routledge, 1997, 31–54.

O'Brien, Eileen. *The Racial Middle: Latinos and Asian Americans Living beyond the Racial Divide.* New York: New York University Press, 2008.

O'Connell, Patrick L. "Narrating History through Memory in Three Novels of Post-Pinochet Chile." *Hispania* 84, no. 2 (2001): 181–92.

O'Connor, Francis V. "The Usable Future: The Role of Fantasy in the Promotion of a Consumer Society for Art." In Helen A. Harrison, ed., *Dawn of a New Day.* New York: Queens Museum, 1980, 57–71.

"Oedipus Rex Gets American Premiere: Special to the New York Times." *New York Times,* April 11, 1931.

O'Gorman, Edward. "Philharmonic in Brazilian Program at World's Fair." *New York Post,* May 5, 1939.

Oja, Carol J. "Bernstein Meets Broadway: Race, the Blues, and *On the Town* (1944)." AMS–Library of Congress Lecture Series. February 7, 2011, http://www.ams-net.org/LC-lectures.

———. "The Copland-Sessions Concerts and Their Reception in the Contemporary Press." *Musical Quarterly* 65, no. 2 (1979): 212–29.

———. *Making Music Modern.* New York: Oxford University Press, 2000.

Olmstead, Andrea. "The Copland-Sessions Letters." *Tempo* 175 (1990): 2–5.

———. *The Correspondence of Roger Sessions.* Boston: Northeastern University Press, 1992.

Olsen, Dale A., and Daniel E. Sheehy, eds. *South America, Mexico, Central America, and the Caribbean: Garland Encyclopedia of World Music.* Vol. 2. New York: Garland, 1998.

O'Neil, Brian. "The Demands of Authenticity: Addison Durland and Hollywood's Latin Images During World War II." In Daniel Bernardi, ed., *Classic Hollywood, Classic Whiteness.* Minneapolis: University of Minnesota Press, 2001, 359–85.

Orbón, Julián. "Las Sinfonías de Carlos Chávez." In Julio Estrada, ed., *En la escencia de los estilos y otros ensayos*. Madrid: Colibrí, 2000, 148–58.

"Organize to Foster Artistry in Mexico." *New York Times*, December 10, 1930.

Orozco, Gilberto. *Tradiciones y leyendas del Istmo de Tehuantepec*. Mexico City: Revista Musical Mexicana, 1946.

Orrego-Salas, Juan. "La nueva canción chilena: Tradición, espíritu y contendio de su música." *Literatura chilena en el exilio* 4, no. 2 (1980): 2–7.

———. "The Young Generation of Latin American Composers: Background and Perspectives." *Inter-American Music Bulletin* 38 (1963): 1–10.

Pach, Walter. "The Art of the American Indian." *Dial* 68 (January 1920): 57–66.

———. "The Greatest American Artists." *Harper's Magazine* 148, no. 884 (1924): 252–62.

Packenham, Robert A. *The Dependency Movement: Scholarship and Politics in Development Studies*. Cambridge: Harvard University Press, 1992.

———. *Liberal America and the Third World*. Princeton: Princeton University Press, 1973.

Palmer, Steven. "Central American Encounters with Rockefeller: 1914–1921." In Gilbert M. Joseph, Catharine C. LeGrand, and Ricardo D. Salvatore eds., *Close Encounters of Empire: Writing the Cultural History of U.S.–Latin American Relations*. Durham, N.C.: Duke University Press, 1998, 311–32.

Paoli, Domenico de, Leigh Henry, Leonide Sbaneyeff, et al. *Lazare Saminsky: Composer and Civic Worker*. New York: Bloch, 1930.

Parakilas, James. "How Spain Got a Soul." In Jonathan Bellman, ed., *The Exotic in Western Music*. Boston: Northeastern University Press, 1998, 137–93.

Paraskevaídis, Graciela "Algunas reflexiones sobre música y dictadura en América Latina." October 2008, www.gp-magma.net/pdf/txt_e/sitio-MusyDicfinal2008.pdf.

———. "Edgar [sic] Varèse y su relación con músicos e intelectuales latinoamericanos de su tiempo: Algunas historias en redondo." *Revista Musical Chilena* 56, no. 198 (2002): 7–20.

———. "Música dodecafónica y serialismo en America Latina." *La del taller*, April–May 1985, 21–27, http://www.latinoamerica-musica.net/historia/para-dodecafonica.html#referencias. Translated in "An Introduction to Twelve-Tone Music and Serialism in Latin America," *Interface* 13 (Netherlands) (1984–85): 133–47.

Parker, Robert L. *Carlos Chávez: Mexico's Modern-Day Orpheus*. Boston: Twayne, 1983.

———. "Carlos Chávez and the Ballet: A Study in Persistence," *Dance Chronicle* 8, nos. 3–4 (1985): 179–210.

———. "Carlos Chávez's Aztec Ballets." *Choreography and Dance* 3, no. 4 (1994): 81–87.

———. "Copland and Chávez: Brothers-in-Arms." *American Music* 5, no. 4 (1987): 433–44.

———. "De música incidental a sinfonía: La *Antígona* de Chávez." *Heterofonía* 113 (July–September 1995): 4–12.

———. "A Recurring Melodic Cell in the Music of Carlos Chávez." *Latin American Music Review* 12, no. 2 (1991): 160–72.

Party, Daniel. "Beyond 'Protest Song': Popular Music in Pinochet's Chile (1973–1990)." In Roberto Illiano and Massimiliano Sala, eds., *Music and Dictatorship in Europe and Latin America*. Turnhout, Belgium: Brephols, 2009, 671–84; http://sites.google.com/site/dparty/publications-1/beyondprotest.

Patrick, Corbin. "Sevitzky's Current Bill Features Crisp Playing." *Indianapolis Star*, January 25, 1954.

Paul, David C. "From American Ethnographer to Cold War Icon: Charles Ives through the Eyes of Henry and Sidney Cowell." *Journal of the American Musicological Society* 59, no. 2 (2006): 399–457.

Payne, Alyson. "Creating Music of the Americas During the Cold War: Alberto Ginastera and the Inter-American Music Festivals." *Music Research Forum* 22 (2007): 57–79.

Paz, Juan Carlos. "Bach y la música de hoy." *Sur* 17 (February 1936): 77–82.

——. *La Música en los Estados Unidos.* Mexico City: Fondo de Cultura Económica, 1952.

Pease, Allison. *Modernism, Mass Culture, and the Aesthetics of Obscenity.* Cambridge: Cambridge University Press, 2000.

Pellettieri, Osvaldo. *Cien años de teatro argentino: 1886–1990.* Buenos Aires: Galerna, Instituto Internacional de Teoría y Crítica de Teatro Latinoamericano, 1991.

Peppercorn, Lisa. "Some Aspects of Villa-Lobos' Principles of Composition." *Music Review* 4, no. 1 (1943): 28–34.

——. "Villa-Lobos 'Ben Trovato.'" *Tempo*, no. 177 (June 1991): 32–35, 38–39.

——. *The World of Villa-Lobos in Pictures and Documents.* Aldershot, U.K.: Scolar Press, 1996.

Pérez Firmat, Gustavo. "Latunes: An Introduction." *Latin American Research Review* 43, no. 2 (2008): 180–203.

Pérez-Torres, Rafael. "Mestizaje in the Mix: Chicano Identity, Cultural Politics, and Postmodern Music." In Ronald Radano and Philip V. Bohlman, eds., *Music and the Racial Imagination.* Chicago: University of Chicago Press, 2000, 206–30.

Perkins, Francis D. "Brazil's Music Is Interpreted by Rubinstein." *New York Herald Tribune*, October 21, 1940.

——. "Carlos Chávez Directs First of 6 Concerts." *New York Herald Tribune*, February 12, 1937.

——. "Music." *New York Herald Tribune*, April 18, 1940.

——. "NBC Symphony Concert Led by Boult, of BBC." *New York Herald Tribune*, May 15, 1938.

——. "Philharmonic Plays Brazilian Music at Fair." *New York Herald Tribune*, May 5, 1939.

Pernet, Corinne A. "For the Genuine Culture of the Americas." In Jessica C. E. Gienow-Hecht, ed., Decentering America. New York: Berghahn Books, 2007, 132–68.

Peyser, Joan. *The Memory of All That: The Life of George Gershwin.* New York: Simon & Schuster, 1993.

"Philadelphia Hears Premieres of Works by Antheil and Chávez." *Musical America* 52, no. 6 (1932): 27.

Pickard, John. Review [Untitled]. *Tempo*, n.s. no. 210 (October 1999): 47–48.

Pike, Frederick B. *The United States and Latin America: Myths and Stereotypes of Civilization and Nature.* Austin: University of Texas Press, 1992.

Pisani, Michael V. *Imagining Native America in Music.* New Haven: Yale University Press, 2005.

Plotkin, Mariano Ben. *Freud in the Pampas: The Emergence and Development of Psychoanalytic Culture in Argentina.* Stanford: Stanford University Press, 2001.

Podalsky, Laura. "Patterns of the Primitive: Sergei Eisenstein's *Que Viva México!*" In John King, Ana M. López, and Manuel Alvardo, eds., *Mediating Two Worlds.* London: BFI, 1993, 25–39.

Pollack, Howard. *Aaron Copland: The Life and Work of an Uncommon Man.* New York: Henry Holt, 1999.

——. *George Gershwin: His Life and Work.* Berkeley: University of California Press, 2006.

——. *Harvard Composers: Walter Piston and His Students from Elliot Carter to Frederic Rzewski.* Metuchen, N.J.: Scarecrow Press, 1992.

Ponce, Manuel. "S.M. el Fox." *México Moderno* 1, no. 9 (1921): 180–81.

Poovey, Mary. "Accommodating Merchants: Accounting, Civility, and the Natural Laws of Gender." *differences* 8, no. 3 (1996): 1–20.

Porter, Andrew. "Musical Events Most Select and Generous." *New Yorker*, December 7, 1987, 155–56, 162–64.

Potter, Pamela M. "From Jewish Exile in Germany to German Scholar in America: Alfred Einstein's Emigration." In Reinhold Brinkmann and Christoph Wolff, eds., *Driven into Paradise: The Musical Migration from Nazi Germany to the United States*. Berkeley: University of California Press, 1999, 298–321.

———. *Most German of the Arts: Musicology and Society from the Weimar Republic to the End of Hitler's Reich*. New Haven: Yale University Press, 1998.

Pound, Ezra. *Personae: The Collected Poems of Ezra Pound*. New York: New Directions, 1926.

Powell, Philip. *Tree of Hate: Propaganda and Prejudices Affecting United States Relations with the Hispanic World*. New York: Basic Books, 1971.

"The Programs of the Week." *New York Times*, December 8, 1946.

Prunières, Henri. "Les Concerts: Oeuvres de Villa-Lobos." *La Revue Musicale* 9, no. 3 (1928): 258–59.

Prutsch, Ursula. *Creating Good Neighbors? Die Kultur- und Wirtschaftspolitik der USA in Lateinamerika, 1940–1946*. Stuttgart: Franz Steiner Verlag, 2008.

Puri, Michael J. "Dandy Interrupted: Sublimation, Repression, and Self-Portraiture in Maurice Ravel's *Daphnis et Chloé* (1909–1912)." *Journal of the American Musicological Society* 59, no. 2 (2006): 488–501.

Quirk, Tom. *Bergson and American Culture: The Worlds of Willa Cather and Wallace Stevens*. Chapel Hill: University of North Carolina Press, 1990.

Rabe, Stephen G. *Eisenhower and Latin America: The Foreign Policy of Anti-Communism*. Chapel Hill: University of North Carolina Press, 1988.

Radano, Ronald, and Philip V. Bohlman, eds. Introduction to *Music and the Racial Imagination*. Chicago: University of Chicago Press, 2000.

Radice, Mark A. "'Futurismo': Its Origins, Context, Repertory, and Influence." *Musical Quarterly* 73, no. 1 (1989): 1–17.

"Radio Concerts." *New York Times*, February 24, 1946.

Radway, Janice. "What's in a Name? Presidential Address to the American Studies Association, November 20, 1998." *American Quarterly* 51 (1999): 1–32.

Ramírez, Mari Carmen. "A Highly Topical Utopia: Some Outstanding Features of the Avant-Garde in Latin America." In Mari Carmen Ramírez and Héctor Olea, eds., *Inverted Utopias: Avant-Garde Art in Latin America*. New Haven: Yale University Press, 2004, 1–15.

Ramirez Berg, Charles. "Stereotyping and Resistance: A Crash Course on Hollywood's Latino Imagery." In Chon A. Noriega, ed., *The Future of Latino Independent Media: A NALIP Sourcebook*. Los Angeles: UCLA Chicano Studies Research Center, 2000, 3–14.

Ramos, Julio. *Divergent Modernities: Culture and Politics in Nineteenth-Century Latin America*. Trans. John D. Blanco. Durham, N.C.: Duke University Press, 2001.

Raymond, Gregory A. *Salvador Allende and the Peaceful Road to Socialism*. Pew Case Studies in International Affairs, Case 451, part A. Washington, D.C.: Georgetown University Institute for the Study of Diplomacy, 1992.

Redfield, Robert. *Tepotzlan: A Mexican Village*. Chicago: University of Chicago Press, 1930.

Reich, Steve. *Writings about Music*. Halifax: Press of the Nova Scotia College of Art and Design and New York University Press, 1976.

Reid, John T. "The Rise and Decline of the Ariel-Caliban Antithesis in Spanish America." *Americas* 34 (1977–78): 345–55.

Reiman, Karen Cordero. "Prometheus Unraveled: Readings of and from the Body. Orozco's Pomona College Mural." In Renato González Mello and Diane Miliotes, eds., *José Clemente Orozco in the United States, 1927–1934*. Hanover, N.H.: Hood Museum of Art, 2002, 98–117.

Reiss, Robert. "'H.P.' Presentation Is Swell Occasion but Lacks Timely Proletarian Touch." *Philadelphia Record*, April 1, 1932.

"Report on the Teaching of Latin American History." *Bulletin of the Pan American Union* 61 (June 1927): 547–51.

"Resolución Final del Encuentro de la Canción Protesta." *Casa de las Américas* 45 (November–December 1967): 143–44.

Reuss, Richard A., and JoAnne C. Reuss. *American Folk Music and Left-Wing Politics, 1927–1957*. Lanham, Md.: Scarecrow Press, 2000.

"Review of 1939 New York World's Fair." *Architectural Review* 86 (August 1939): 54–92.

Revilla, Manuel G. *El arte en México*. 2nd ed. Mexico City: Librería Universal de Porrua Hermanos, 1923.

"Reviving Mayan Architecture." *New York Times*, January 30, 1927.

Rey García, Marta. *Stars for Spain: La guerra civil española en los Estados Unidos*. A Coruña, Spain: Edicios do Castro, 1997.

Reyes, Luis, and Peter Rube. *Hispanics in Hollywood: A Celebration of 100 Years in Film and Television*. Hollywood: Lone Eagle, 2000.

Reyes Matta, Fernando. "The 'New Song' and Its Confrontation in Latin America." In Cary Nelson and Lawrence Grossberg, eds., *Marxism and the Interpretation of Culture*. Urbana: University of Illinois Press, 1998, 447–60.

Reynolds, Christopher A. *Motives for Allusion: Context and Content in Nineteenth-Century Music*. Cambridge: Harvard University Press, 2003.

———. "*Porgy and Bess*: 'An American *Wozzeck*.'" *Journal of the Society for American Music* 1, no. 1 (2007): 1–28.

Rickover, Hyman G. *How the "Maine" Was Destroyed*. Washington, D.C.: Department of the Navy, 1976.

Ricoeur, Paul. *Memory, History, Forgetting*. Trans. Kathleen Blamey and David Pallauer. Chicago: University of Chicago Press, 2004.

Rink, Jonathan. "Opposition and Integration in the Piano Music." In Michael Musgrave, ed., *The Cambridge Companion to Brahms*. Cambridge: Cambridge University Press, 1999, 79–97.

Rios, Fernando. "Bolero Trios, Mestizo Panpipe Ensembles, and Bolivia's 1952 Revolution: Urban La Paz Musicians and the Nationalist Revolutionary Movement." *Ethnomusicology* 54, no. 2 (2010): 281–318.

Rivas, Darlene. *Missionary Capitalist: Nelson Rockefeller in Venezuela*. Chapel Hill: University of North Carolina Press, 2002.

Rivera, Diego. "Dynamic Detroit—An Interpretation." *Creative Art* 12, no. 4 (1933): 289–95.

———. *Arte y política*. Ed. Raquel Tibol. Mexico City: Editorial Grijalbo, 1979.

R.L. "Novelties Played by Orchestrette." *New York Times*, May 4, 1943.

Roa Bárcena, José María. *The View from Chapultepec: Mexican Writers on the Mexican-American War*. Trans. Cecil Robinson. Tucson: University of Arizona Press, 1989.

Robbins, Bruce. "Introduction: Part I: Actually Existing Cosmopolitanism." In Pheng Cheah and Bruce Robbins, eds., *Cosmopolitics: Thinking and Feeling beyond the Nation*. Minneapolis: University of Minnesota Press, 1998, 1–19.

Roberts, John Storm. *The Latin Tinge: The Impact of Latin American Music on the United States*. 2nd ed. New York: Oxford University Press, 1999.

Roberts, Shari. "'The Lady in the Tutti-Frutti Hat': Carmen Miranda, a Spectacle of Ethnicity." In Steven Cohan, ed., *Hollywood Musicals: The Film Reader*. London: Routledge, 2002, 143–53.

Robertson, Nan. "*Bomarzo*: Sex, Violence, Hallucination." *New York Times*, May 28, 1967.

Robinson, Suzanne. "'A Ping, Qualified by a Thud': Music Criticism in Manhattan and the Case of Cage (1943–58)." *Journal of the Society for American Music* 1, no. 1 (2007): 79–139.

Rockwell, John. *All American Music: Composition in the Late Twentieth Century*. New York: Knopf, 1983.

———. "The Pop Life." *New York Times*, November 18, 1977.

Rodó, José Enrique. *Ariel*. Trans. Margaret Sayers Peden. Austin: University of Texas Press, 1988.

Rodríguez, Antonio. *Guia de los murales de Diego Rivera en la Secretaría de Educación Pública*. Mexico City: Secretaría de Educación Pública, 1984.

Rodríguez, Clara E. *Changing Race: Latinos, the Census, and the History of Ethnicity in the United States*. New York: New York University Press, 2000.

Roosevelt, Theodore. *Theodor Roosevelt: An Autobiography with Illustrations*. 1913. New York: Charles Scribner's Sons, 1920.

Root, Deane L. "The Pan American Association of Composers (1928–1934)." *Yearbook for Inter-American Musical Research* 8 (1972): 49–70.

Ros-Fábregas, Emilio. "Nicolas Slonimsky (1894–1995) y sus escritos sobre música en Latinoamérica: Reivindicación de un 'fishing trip.'" In María Gembero Ustárroz and Emilio Ros-Fábregas, eds., *La Música y el Atlántico: Relaciones musicales entre España y Latinoamérica*. Granada: University of Granada, 2007, 153–80.

Rosen, Charles. "Influence: Plagiarism and Inspiration." *19th-Century Music* 4, no. 2 (1980): 87–100.

Rosenberg, Emily S. *Financial Missionaries to the World: The Politics and Culture of Dollar Diplomacy, 1900–1930*. Cambridge: Harvard University Press, 1999.

——— *Spreading the American Dream: American Economic and Cultural Expansion, 1890–1945*. New York: Hill and Wang, 1982.

———. "Turning to Culture." In Gilbert M. Joseph, Catherine C. LeGrand, and Ricardo Salvatore, eds., *Close Encounters of Empire*. Durham, N.C.: Duke University Press, 1998, 497–514.

Rosenfeld, Paul. "Aaron Copland's Growth." *New Republic* 67 (May 27, 1931): 46–47.

———. "American Composers, VIII: Carlos Chávez." *Modern Music*, May–June 1932, 153–59.

———. "American Premieres." *New Republic* 70 (April 20, 1932): 273–74.

———. "Bach Conquers Musical America." *American Mercury* 50, no. 199 (1940): 314–19.

———. *By Way of Art*. 1928. Freeport, N.Y.: Books for Libraries Press, 1967.

———. "Current Chronicle: Szymanowski—Villa Lobos." *Musical Quarterly* 25, no. 4 (1939): 513–18.

———. "D. H. Lawrence." *New Republic* 32 (September 27, 1922): 125–26.

————. *Discoveries of a Music Critic*. New York: Harcourt, Brace, 1936.

————. "Folksong and Cultural Politics." *Modern Music* 17, no. 1 (1939): 18–24.

————. *An Hour with American Music*. Philadelphia: Lippincott, 1929.

————. "Musical Chronicle." *Dial* 82 (February 1927): 175–77.

————. "Neo-Classicism and Paul Hindemith." *New Republic* 62 (April 2, 1930): 193–94.

————. "The New American Music," *Scribner's Magazine*, 89, no. 6 (1931): 624–32.

Rowe, William, and Vivian Schelling. *Memory and Modernity: Popular Culture in Latin America*. London: Verso, 1991.

Rowland, Donald W. *History of the Office of the Coordinator of Inter-American Affairs*. Washington, D.C.: Government Printing Office, 1947.

Rozwenc, Edwin C. "Edmundo O'Gorman and the Idea of America." *American Quarterly* 10, no. 2, part 1 (1958): 99–115.

R.P. "Work by Berlioz Heard at Concert." *New York Times*, February 22, 1957.

Rubio, Héctor, et al. *La música en el Di Tella: Resonancias de la modernidad*. Buenos Aires: Secretaria de la Cultura, 2011.

Ruitenbeek, Hendrik M. *Freud and America*. New York: Macmillan, 1966.

————, ed. *Varieties of Personality Theory*. New York: Dutton, 1964.

Rumpf, Stephen. "A Kingdom Not of This World: The Political Context of E. T. A. Hoffmann's Beethoven Criticism." *19th-Century Music* 19, no. 1 (1995): 50–67.

Runciman, W. G., ed. *Max Weber: Selections in Translation*. Cambridge: Cambridge University Press, 1978.

Russell, Craig H. *From Serra to Sancho: Music and Pageantry in the California Missions*. Currents in Latin American and Iberian Music. Ed. Walter A. Clark. New York: Oxford University Press, 2009.

Ryan, James G. *Earl Browder: The Failure of American Communism*. 2nd ed. Tuscaloosa: University of Alabama Press, 2005.

Rydell, Robert. *World of Fairs: The Century of Progress Expositions*. Chicago: University of Chicago Press, 1993.

S. "Works of Latin Americans Heard." *Musical America* 53, no. 17 (1933): 27, 29.

Saavedra, Leonora. "The American Composer in the 1930s: The Social Thought of Seeger and Chávez." In Bell Yung and Helen Rees, eds., *Understanding Charles Seeger: Pioneer in American Musicology*. Urbana: University of Illinois Press, 1999, 29–63.

————. "Los escritos periodísticos de Carlos Chávez: Una fuente para la historia de la música en México." *Inter-American Music Review* 10, no. 2 (1989): 77–91.

————. "Of Selves and Others: Historiography, Ideology, and the Politics of Modern Mexican Music." Ph.D. diss., University of Pittsburgh, 2001.

Sabin, Robert. "Villa-Lobos, Man of Action, Pays First Visit to U.S." *Musical America* 65, no. 1 (1945): 7.

Saborit, Antonio. "Mexican Gaities: Carlos Chávez en la Babilonia de hierro." In Yael Bitrán and Ricardo Miranda, eds., *Diálogo de resplendores: Carlos Chávez y Silvestre Revueltas*. Mexico City: Teoría y Práctica del Arte, 2002, 139–58.

Safire, William. *Safire's Political Dictionary*. 1993. New York: Oxford University Press, 2008.

Said, Edward. *Culture and Imperialism*. New York: Vintage Books, 1993.

Salvatore, Ricardo D. *Imágenes de un imperio: Estados Unidos y las formas de representación de América Latina*. Buenos Aires: Editorial Sudamericana, 2006.

Salzman, Eric. "Eartha Kitt Sings Stadium Program." *New York Times*, July 11, 1960.

————. "*Modern Music* in Retrospect." *Perspectives of New Music* 2, no. 2 (1964): 14–20.

————. "Peripatetic Philharmonic." *New York Herald Tribune*, October 4, 1963.

———. "Records: Chávez." *New York Times*, April 17, 1960.

Samaroff, Olga. "Music." *New York Evening Post*, November 29, 1926.

Saminsky, Lazare. "In the Argentine." *Modern Music* 18, no. 1 (1940): 31–36.

———. *Living Music of the Americas*. New York: Howell, Soskin and Crown, 1949.

———. "South American Report." *New York Times*, September 8, 1940.

San Juan, Epifanio. *Beyond Postcolonial Theory*. New York: St. Martin's Press, 1998.

Sanborn, Pitts. "Boston Orchestra Honors Composer." *New York World-Telegram*, November 19, 1938.

———. "Gershwin Sets Mark in Stadium: Draws 21,000 Musical Persons to Concert All His Own." *New York World-Telegram*, August 17, 1932.

———. "Honors of the Season." *League of Composers Review* 1, no. 2 (1924): 3–8.

Sandoval Sánchez, Alberto. "*West Side Story*: A Puerto Rican Reading of 'America.'" In Clara E. Rodríguez, ed., *Latin Looks: Images of Latinos and Latinas in the U.S. Media*. Boulder, Colo.: Westview Press, 1997, 164–79.

Santa Cruz, Domingo. "Prólogo para Gustavo Bercera, músico de su tiempo." *Revista Musical Chilena* 26, nos. 119–20 (1972): 4–7.

Santomasso, Eugene A. "The Design of Reason: Architecture and Planning at the 1939/40 New York World's Fair." In Helen A. Harrison, ed., *Dawn of a New Day*. New York: Queens Museum, 1980, 29–41.

Sapir, Edward. *Selected Writings of Edward Sapir in Language, Culture, and Personality*. Ed. D. G. Mandelbaum. Berkeley: University of California Press, 1949.

Sargeant, Winthrop. "Musical Events: Spooked Duke." *New Yorker*, March 23, 1968, 126.

Saunders, Frances Stonor. *The Cultural Cold War: The CIA and the World of Arts and Letters*. New York: New Press, 1999.

Scarabino, Guillermo. *Alberto Ginastera: Técnicas y Estilo (1935–1950)*. Buenos Aires: Instituto de Investigación Musicológica Carlos Vega, 1996.

———. *El Grupo Renovación (1929–1944) y la "nueva música" en la Argentina del siglo XX*. Buenos Aires: Ediciones de la Universidad Católica Argentina, 1999.

Schacter, Daniel L. *The Seven Sins of Memory*. Boston: Houghton Mifflin, 2001.

Schallert, Edwin. "Huge Ovation for Rodzinski." *Los Angeles Times*, July 30, 1931.

Schebera, Jürgen. *Kurt Weill: An Illustrated Life*. New Haven: Yale University Press, 1995.

Schechter, John M., ed. *Music in Latin American Culture: Regional Traditions*. New York: Schirmer Books, 1999.

Schlesinger, Stephen C. *Bitter Fruit: The Story of the American Coup in Guatemala*. Cambridge: Harvard University Press, 1982.

Schmidt, Henry C. *The Roots of "Lo Mexicano": Self and Society in Mexican Thought, 1900–1934*. College Station: Texas A&M University Press, 1978.

Schmitz, Nancy Brooks. "A Profile of Catherine Littlefield: A Pioneer of American Ballet." Ph.D. diss., Temple University, 1986.

Schobeß, Rainer. "Review: Bernard Bessière, *La nouvelle Chanson chilienne en exil (1980)*." *Jahrbuch für Volksliedforschung* 30 (1985): 205–6.

Schonberg, Harold C. "*Bomarzo*: Once the Shock Value, Such As It Is, Has Worn Off . . ." *New York Times*, March 24, 1968.

———. "Music: City Opera Company Sparkles in Its Rich, New Setting." *New York Times*, February 23, 1966.

———. "Music: Some Moderns." *New York Times*, December 15, 1978.

———. "The Opera: Ginastera's Not-So-Wicked *Bomarzo* Arrives Here." *New York Times*, March 15, 1968.

———. "7 Modern Works Heard in South." *New York Times*, October 10, 1955.

Schopenhauer, Arthur. *The World as Will and Representation*. 2 vols. Trans. E. F. J. Payne. New York: Dover, 1966.

Schumann, Robert. *On Music and Musicians*. Ed. Konrad Wolff. Trans. Paul Rosenfeld. New York: Norton, 1946.

Schwartz, Charles. *Gershwin: His Life and Music*. Indianapolis: Bobbs-Merrill, 1973.

Schwartz, David. "Postmodernism, the Subject, and the Real in John Adams's *Nixon in China*." *Indiana Theory Review* 13, no. 2 (1992): 107–35.

Schwartz, K. Robert. "Steve Reich: Music as a Gradual Process." *Perspectives of New Music* 19 (1980–81): 373–92.

Schwartz, Rosalie. *Flying Down to Rio: Hollywood, Tourists, and Yankee Clippers*. College Station: Texas A&M University Press, 2004.

Schwartz-Kates, Deborah. *Alberto Ginastera: A Research and Information Guide*. New York: Routledge, 2010.

———. "Alberto Ginastera, Argentine Cultural Construction, and the Gauchesco Tradition." *Musical Quarterly* 86, no. 2 (2002): 248–81.

———. "The Correspondence of Alberto Ginastera at the Library of Congress." *Notes* 68, no. 2 (2011): 284–312.

———. "The *Gauchesco* Tradition as a Source of National Identity in Argentine Art Music (ca. 1890–1955)." Ph.D. diss., University of Texas at Austin, 1997.

———. "Ginastera, Alberto (Evaristo)." Oxford Music Online, http://www.oxfordmusiconline.com/subscriber/article/grove/music/11159 (accessed April 13, 2010).

Schweitzer, Vivien. "Donizetti Returns, Offering Plenty of Chemistry and Nine High C's." *New York Times*, February 8, 2010.

Schwerké, Irving. "A Brazilian Rabelais." *League of Composers' Review* 2, no. 1 (1925): 28–30.

Seeger, Charles. "Grass Roots for American Composers." *Modern Music* 16, no. 3 (1939): 143–49.

———. "On Proletarian Music." *Modern Music* 11, no. 3 (1934): 121–27.

Segal, Howard. "Utopian Fairs." *Chicago History* 12, no. 3 (1983): 7–9.

Seldes, Gilbert. *The Seven Lively Arts*. New York: A. S. Barnes, 1962.

———. "Thompson's Panorama, the Woolworth Building, and Do It Now: Can a Purely American Art Be Created out of These Elements?" *Vanity Fair*, December 1924, 39, 108, 118.

Sessions, Roger. "Music and Nationalism: Some Notes on Dr. Göbbel's Letter to Furtwängler." *Modern Music* 11, no. 1 (1933): 3–12.

———. "On the American Future." *Modern Music* 17, no. 2 (1940): 71–75.

Seton, Marie. *Sergei Eisenstein*. New York: Grove Press, 1960.

"Sex and the Strait-Laced Strongman." *Time*, August 18, 1967, 33.

Shale, Richard. *Donald Duck Joins Up: The Walt Disney Studio During World War II*. Ann Arbor, Mich.: UMI Research Press, 1987.

Shaw, Lisa. *The Social History of Brazilian Samba*. Aldershot, U.K.: Ashgate, 1999.

———. "Vargas on Film: From the Newsreel to the *Chanchada*." In Jens R. Hentschke, ed. *Vargas and Brazil: New Perspectives*. New York: Palgrave Macmillan, 2006, 208–25.

Sheehy, Daniel. *Mariachi Music in America*. New York: Oxford University Press, 2006.

Shepard, John. "The Legacy of Carleton Sprague Smith: Pan-American Holdings in the Music Division of the New York Public Library for the Performing Arts." *Notes* (second series) 62, no. 3 (2006): 621–62.

Sherman, Robert. "Politics and Music by Chilean Group." *New York Times*, March 23, 1975.

Shreffler, Anne C. "Ideologies of Serialism." In Karol Berger and Anthony Newcomb, eds., *Music and the Aesthetics of Modernity*. Cambridge: Harvard Publications in Music, 2005, 217–45.

————. "The Myth of Empirical Historiography: A Response to Joseph N. Straus." *Musical Quarterly* 82, no. 1 (2000): 30–39.

Shumway, Nicolas. *The Invention of Argentina*. Berkeley: University of California Press, 1991.

Sigmund, Paul E. *The Overthrow of Allende and Politics of Chile, 1964–1976*. Pittsburgh: University of Pittsburgh Press, 1977.

Silet, Charles L. P. *The Writings of Paul Rosenfeld*. New York: Garland, 1981.

Simms, Bryan. *Music of the Twentieth Century*. New York: Schirmer Books, 1986.

Siqueiros, David Alfaro. "Rivera's Counter-Revolutionary Road." *New Masses* 11, no. 9 (1934): 16–19.

Sisman, Elaine. "Memory and Invention at the Threshold of Beethoven's Late Style." In Scott Burnham and Michael P. Steinberg, eds., *Beethoven and His World*. Princeton: Princeton University Press, 2000, pp. 51–87.

————. "Variations." Oxford Music Online, http://www.oxfordmusiconline.com/subscriber/article/grove/music/29050 (accessed July 12, 2010).

Skidmore, Thomas E., and Peter H. Smith. *Modern Latin America*. 5th ed. New York: Oxford University Press, 2001.

Skinner, Thomas E. *Black into White: Race and Nationality in Brazilian Thought*. New York: Oxford University Press, 1974.

Slonimsky, Nicolas. *Music of Latin America*. New York: Thomas Y. Crowell, 1945.

————. "A Visit with Villa-Lobos." *Musical America* 61, no. 15 (1941): 7, 10.

Smith, Amanda. Interview with Alexis Dolinoff. May 1979. Typescript, MGZMT 5–670, New York Public Library, Dance Division.

Smith, Carleton Sprague. "Alberto Ginastera's 'Duo for Flute and Oboe.'" *Latin American Music Review* 6, no. 1 (1985): 85–93.

————. "The Composers of Chile." *Modern Music* 19, no. 1 (1941): 26–31.

————. "Music Libraries in South America." *Notes* 11 (1941): 19–31.

————. "Song of Brazil." *Américas* 2, no. 10 (1950): 14–16, 43–44.

————. "What Not to Expect in South America." *Musical America* 61, no. 3 (1941): 217, 220.

Smith, Catherine Parsons. "'A Distinguishing Virility': Feminism and Modernism in American Art Music." In Susan C. Cook and Judy S. Tsou, eds., *Cecilia Reclaimed: Feminist Perspectives on Gender and Music*. Urbana: University of Illinois Press, 1994, 90–106.

————. *William Grant Still*. Urbana: University of Illinois Press, 2008.

Smith, Henry Nash. *Virgin Land: The American West as Symbol and Myth*. 1950. Cambridge: Harvard University Press, 1970.

Smith, Julia. *Aaron Copland: His Work and Contribution to American Music*. New York: Dutton, 1955.

Smoodin, Eric. *Animating Culture: Hollywood Cartoons from the Sound Era*. New Brunswick, N.J.: Rutgers University Press, 1993.

Soames, Wood. "*Magdalena* Superb Opera by Top Cast." *Oakland Tribune*, n.d. New York Public Library clippings file.

Solberg, Carl. *Hubert Humphrey: A Biography*. New York: Norton, 1984.

Solie, Ruth A. "The Living Work: Organicism and Musical Analysis." *19th-Century Music* 4, no. 2 (1980): 147–56.

————, ed. *Musicology and Difference: Gender and Sexuality in Music Scholarship*. Berkeley: University of California Press, 1993.

Squeff, Enio and José Miguel Wisnik, eds. *Musica: O Nacional e o Popular na Cultura Brasileira*. São Paulo: Brasiliense, 1982.

Stallings, Stephanie N. "Collective Difference: The Pan American Association of Composers and Pan American Ideology in Music, 1925–1945." Ph.D. diss., Florida State University, 2008.

Stam, Robert. *Tropical Multiculturalism: A Comparative History of Race in Brazilian Cinema and Culture*. Durham, N.C.: Duke University Press, 1997.

Stearns, Harold E., ed. *Civilization in the United States: An Inquiry by Thirty Americans*. New York: Harcourt, Brace, 1922.

Stein, Louise K. *Songs of Mortals, Dialogues of the Gods: Music and Theatre in Seventeenth-Century Spain*. Oxford: Clarendon Press, 1993.

Steinberg, Michael. *Nights in the Gardens of Spain: Symphonic Impressions for Piano and Orchestra*. Program booklet, New York Philharmonic, November 4, 1995.

Steinfirst, Donald. "Final Festival Concerts Draw Fair Attendance." *Pittsburgh Press*, December 1, 1952, 32.

Stevenson, Robert M. "Brazilian Report of Villa-Lobos's First Los Angeles Visit." *Inter-American Music Review* 9, no. 1 (1987): 9–10.

———. "Carlos Chávez's United States Press Coverage." *Inter-American Music Review* 3, no. 2 (1981): 125–31.

———. "Heitor Villa-Lobos's Los Angeles Connection: A Centennial Tribute." *Inter-American Music Review* 9, no. 1 (1987): 1–8.

———. *Music in Mexico: A Historical Survey*. New York: Thomas Y. Crowell, 1952.

———. "Nino Marcelli, Founder of the San Diego Symphony Orchestra." *Inter-American Music Review* 10, no. 1 (1988): 113–23.

———. "Opera Beginnings in the New World." *Musical Quarterly* 45, no. 1 (1959): 8–25.

Stocking, George W., Jr. "The Enthographical Sensibility of the 1920s and the Dualism of the Anthropological Tradition." In George W. Stocking Jr., ed., *Romantic Motives: Essays on Anthropological Sensibility*. Madison: University of Wisconsin Press, 1989, 208–76.

Stokes, Richard L. "Realm of Music." *Evening World* (New York), April 23, 1928.

"Stokowski Directs *H.P.* in First Dress Rehearsal as Stock Attacks Moderns." *Philadelphia Record*, March 27, 1932.

"Stokowski to Give Chávez Ballet." *Musical America* 52, no. 2 (1932): 6.

Straus, Joseph N. "The Myth of Serial 'Tyranny' in the 1950s and 1960s." *Musical Quarterly* 83, no. 3 (1999): 301–43.

———. "A Response to Anne C. Shreffler." *Musical Quarterly* 82, no. 1 (2000): 40.

———. "A Revisionist History of Twelve-Tone Serialism in American Music." *Journal of the Society for American Music* 2, no. 3 (2008): 355–95.

———. *Twelve-Tone Music in America*. Cambridge: Cambridge University Press, 2009.

Strauss, Theodore. "Donald Duck's Disney." *New York Times*, February 7, 1943.

Stravinsky, Igor, and Robert Craft. *Conversations with Igor Stravinsky*. 1959. Berkeley: University of California Press, 1980.

Strohm, Reinhard. "Looking Back at Ourselves: The Problem with the Musical Work Concept." In Michael Talbot, ed., *The Musical Work: Reality or Invention?* Liverpool: Liverpool University Press, 2000, 128–52.

Stuckenschmidt, H. H. "Machines—A Vision of the Future." *Modern Music* 4, no. 3 (1927): 8–14.

Sturman, Janet L. *Zarzuela: Spanish Operetta, American Stage*. Urbana: University of Illinois Press, 2000.

Suárez Urtubey, Pola. *Alberto Ginastera*. Buenos Aires: Ediciones Culturales Argentinas, 1967.

———. *Alberto Ginastera en cinco movimientos*. Buenos Aires: Editorial Victor Leru, 1972.

———. "La *Cantata para América mágica*." *Revista Musical Chilena* 84 (June–July 1983): 19–35.

———. *Ginastera: Veinte años después*. Buenos Aires: Academia Nacional de Bellas Artes, 2003.

———. "Ginastera's *Bomarzo*." *Tempo* 84 (Spring 1968): 14–21.

Summers, William. "New and Little Known Sources of Hispanic Music from California." *Inter-American Music Review* 11, no. 2 (1991): 13–24.

———. "Spanish Music in California, 1769–1840: A Reassessment." In *Report of the Twelfth Congress of the International Musicological Society, Berkeley, 1977*. Kassel, Germany: Bärenreiter, 1981, 360–80.

Susman, Warren I. *Culture as History: The Transformation of American Society in the Twentieth Century*. New York: Pantheon Books, 1984.

Suzuki, Shinichi. *Nurtured by Love: The Classic Approach to Talent Education*. Trans. Waltraud Suzuki. 2nd ed. Miami: Warner Brothers, Summy Birchard, 1983.

Swan, Annalyn. "The Spell of Philip Glass." *New Republic* 189 (December 12, 1983): 27–32.

Sweet, William Warren. *A History of Latin America*. New York: Abingdon Press, 1919.

Szulc, Tad. "Beneath the Boiling-Up in South America." *New York Times*, May 25, 1958.

Tabor, Michelle. "Alberto Ginastera's Late Instrumental Style." *Latin American Music Review* 15, no. 1 (1994): 1–31.

Taffet, Jeffrey F. "'My Guitar Is Not for the Rich': The New Chilean Song Movement and the Politics of Culture." *Journal of American Culture* 20, no. 2 (1997): 91–103.

"Talk of the Town: Villa-Lobos." *New Yorker*, February 10, 1945, 16.

Tarasti, Eero. *Heitor Villa-Lobos: The Life and Works, 1887–1959*. Jefferson, N.C.: McFarland, 1987.

Taruskin, Richard. "Back to Whom? Neoclassicism as Ideology." *19th-Century Music* 16 (1993): 286–302.

———. *The Danger of Music and Other Anti-Utopian Essays*. Berkeley: University of California Press, 2009.

———. "Colonialist Nationalism." Oxford Music Online, http://www.oxfordmusiconline.com/subscriber/article/grove/music/50846 (accessed March 6, 2011).

———. *The Oxford History of Western Music*. 6 vols. Oxford: Oxford University Press, 2005.

———. "Russian Folk Melodies in *The Rite of Spring*." *Journal of the American Musicological Society* 33, no. 3 (1980): 501–43.

———. *Stravinsky and the Russian Traditions: A Biography of the Works through "Mavra."* 2 vols. Berkeley: University of California Press, 1996.

Tashjian, Dickran. *Skyscraper Primitives: Dada and the American Avant-Garde, 1910–1925*. Middletown, Conn.: Wesleyan University Press, 1975.

Taubman, Howard [H.T.]. "In Time to Come? Twelve-Tone Influence Is Major Influence but Public Has Not Yet Accepted It." *New York Times*, March 23, 1958.

———. "Mexican Composers: Carlos Chávez Discusses the Creative Work of His Countrymen." *New York Times*, January 26, 1936.

———. "Mexican Novelty Offered by Iturbi." *New York Times*, June 28, 1934.

———. "Music: Little Orchestra Society." *New York Times*, October 18, 1955.

———. "Music: 17,000 Hear Gershwin Program." *New York Times*, August 17, 1932.

———. "Musical Theatre: Fine Score Not Enough to Carry the Day." *New York Times*, September 26, 1948.

———. "Three New Works Heard in Capital." *New York Times*, April 20, 1958.

Taylor, Timothy D. *Beyond Exoticism: Western Music and the World*. Durham, N.C.: Duke University Press, 2007.

Taylor, W. S. "A Critique of Sublimation in Males: A Study of Forty Superior Single Men." *Genetic Psychology Monographs* 13, no. 1 (1933): 3–115.

Taylor Gibson, Christina. "The Music of Manuel M. Ponce, Julián Carrillo, and Carlos Chávez in New York, 1925–1932." Ph.D. diss., University of Maryland, College Park, 2008.

"Text of Address by President Eisenhower at Pan American Union." *New York Times*, April 13, 1953.

Thomas, Susan. *Cuban Zarzuela: Performing Race and Gender on Havana's Lyric Stage*. Urbana: University of Illinois Press, 2009.

Thompson, Oscar. "Brazilian Music Given at Museum." *New York Sun*, October 17, 1940.

———. "Burle Marx Conducts with Soprano and Two Pianists as Soloists." *New York Sun*, May 5, 1939.

———. "Fly-Wheel Opera." *Modern Music* 7, no. 1 (1929–30): 39–42.

———. "Music: Musicians' Symphony Begins New Series of Concerts with George Gershwin in Triple Role." *New York Evening Post*, November 2, 1932.

———. "Own Works Led by Villa-Lobos." *New York Sun*, February 13, 1945.

———. "Philadelphia Gives Chávez Ballet, *H.P.*, in World Premiere." *Musical America* 52, no. 7 (1932): 1, 7.

———. "Two *Choros* Led by Villa-Lobos." *New York Sun*, February 9, 1945.

Thomson, Virgil. "Aaron Copland." *Modern Music* 9, no. 2 (1932): 71–72.

———. "Music." *New York Herald Tribune*, February 24, 1947.

———. "Music: Children's Day." *New York Herald Tribune*, February 9, 1945.

———. "Music: Heavy Hands across Caribbean." *New York Herald Tribune*, October 17, 1940.

———. "Music: More Brazil." *New York Herald Tribune*, October 19, 1940.

———. *A Virgil Thomson Reader*. New York: Dutton, 1984.

"Throng Hears Concert." *New York Times*, February 22, 1928.

Tick, Judith. "Charles Ives and Gender Ideology." In Ruth A. Solie, ed., *Musicology and Difference: Gender and Sexuality in Music Scholarship*. Berkeley: University of California Press, 1993, 83–106.

"To Latin America." *New York Times*, August 10, 1941.

Tomlinson, Gary. *The Singing of the New World: Indigenous Voice in the Era of European Contact*. Cambridge: Cambridge University Press, 2007.

Toor, Frances ed. *Cancionero Mexicano*. Mexico City: Mexican Folkways, 1931.

"Topics of the Times." *New York Times*, April 15, 1933.

Torgovnick, Mariana. *Gone Primitive: Savage Intellects, Modern Lives*. Chicago: University of Chicago Press, 1990.

Torres, Rodrigo, ed. *Victor Jara Obra Musical Completa*. Santiago, Chile: Fundación Víctor Jara, 1996.

Trippett, David. "Composing Time: Zeno's Arrow, Hindemith's *Erinnerung*, and Satie's *Instantaneisme*." *Journal of Musicology* 24, no. 4 (2007): 522–80.

Turino, Thomas. "Nationalism and Latin American Music: Selected Case Studies and Theoretical Considerations." *Latin American Music Review* 24, no. 2 (2003): 169–209.

Tyron, Winthrop P. "Two American Modernists." *Christian Science Monitor*, April 26, 1928.

Tyrrell, Sarah. "M. Camargo Guarnieri and the Influence of Mário de Andrade's Modernism." *Latin American Music Review* 29, no. 1 (2008): 43–63.

Van den Toorn, Pieter. *Stravinsky and the Rite of Spring: The Beginnings of a Musical Language*. Berkeley: University of California Press, 1987.

Vasconcelos, José. "Bolivarismo y Monroismo." In *Obras completas*. Vol. 2. Mexico City: Libreros Mexicanos Unidos, 1958, 1305–493.

———. "Indología: Una interpretación de la cultura iberoamericana." In *Obras completas*. Vol. 2. Mexico City: Libreros Mexicanos Unidos, 1958, 1069–303.

———. "El monismo estético." In *Obras completas*. Vol. 4. Mexico City: Liberos Mexicanos Unidos, 1961, 9–92.

———. "La raza cósmica." In *Obras completas*. Vol. 2. Mexico City: Liberos Mexicanos Unidos, 1958, 903–1068.

Vasconcelos, José, and Manuel Gamio. *Aspects of Mexican Civilization*. Chicago: University of Chicago Press, 1926.

Vásquez, Genaro. *Música popular y costumbres regionales del estado de Oaxaca*. Lecture for Alumnos del Instituto de Ciecias y Artes del Estado de Oaxaca, 1917. Mexico City: n.p., 1924.

Vassberg, David E. "Villa-Lobos: Music as a Tool of Nationalism." *Luso Brazilian Review* 6, no. 2 (1969): 55–65.

Vega, Aurelio de la. "Latin American Composers in the United States." *Latin American Music Review* 1, no. 2 (1980): 162–75.

Venn, Edward. "Rethinking Russolo." *Tempo* 64, no. 251 (2010): 8–16.

Verhaalen, Marion. *Camargo Guarnieri, Brazilian Composer*. Bloomington: Indiana University Press, 2005.

Vila, Pablo. "Argentina's 'Rock nacional': The Struggle for Meaning." *Latin American Music Review* 10, no. 1 (1989): 1–28.

———. "Rock nacional and Dictatorship in Argentina." *Popular Music* 6, no. 2 (1987): 129–48.

Villa-Lobos, Heitor. *O ensino popular de música no Brasil*. Rio de Janeiro: Oficina Grafica da Secretaria Geral de Educacão e Cultura, 1937.

Viñao, Alejandro. "An Old Tradition We Have Just Invented." *Electroacoustic Music* 4, nos. 1–2 (1989): 33–43.

Vincent, John. "New Opera in Buenos Aires." *Inter-American Music Bulletin* 44 (November 1964): 1–4.

Wagenknecht, Edward. "W. H. Hudson's South American Idyll in a New Edition." *New York Times*, November 21, 1943.

Wagner, Richard. *Richard Wagner's Prose Works*. Vol. 1: *The Artwork of the Future*. Ed. William Ashton Ellis. 2nd ed. London: Kegan, Paul, Trench, Trübner, 1895.

Wallace, David Edward. "Alberto Ginastera: An Analysis of His Style and Techniques of Composition." Ph.D. diss., Northwestern University, 1964.

Wallaschek, Richard. *Primitive Music: An Inquiry into the Origin and Development of Music, Songs, Instruments, Dances, and Pantomimes of Savages*. London: Longmans, Green, 1893.

Walsh, Michael. "The Heart Is Back in the Game." *Time*, September 20, 1982, 60–61.

Warshow, Robert. "The Legacy of the 1930s." In *The Immediate Experience: Movies, Comics, Theatre and Other Aspects of Popular Culture*. Garden City, N.Y.: Anchor Books, 1964, 33–48.

Waseen, Amber. "Carlos Chávez and the Corrido." Master's thesis, Bowling Green State University, 2005.

Wason, Robert W. "Tonality and Atonality in Frederic Rzewski's *Variations on 'The People United Will Never Be Defeated!'*" *Perspectives of New Music* 26, no. 1 (1988): 108–43.

Watkins, Glenn. *Proof through the Night: Music and the Great War*. Berkeley: University of California Press, 2003.

———. *Pyramids at the Louvre: Music, Culture, and Collage from Stravinsky to the Postmodernists*. Cambridge: Belknap Press of Harvard University Press, 1994.

Watkins, Mary F. "Chávez's Ballet 'H.P.' Has Debut in Philadelphia: Mexican Composer Typifies Interrelation of North and South in Symphony." *New York Herald Tribune*, April 1, 1932.

Weine, Stephen. *Testimony after Catastrophe: Narrating the Traumas of Political Violence*. Evanston, Ill.: Northwestern University Press, 2006.

Weinstock, Herbert. "America: *Bomarzo* Fails to Shock." *Opera* 19, no. 5 (1968): 467.

———. "Carlos Chávez." *Musical Quarterly* 22, no. 4 (1936): 435–45.

———. *Carlos Chávez: North American Press 1936–1950*. New York: Herbert Barrett, 1951.

———, annotator. *Mexican Music. Concerts Arranged by Carlos Chávez as Part of the Exhibition: Twenty Centuries of Mexican Art*. New York: William E. Rudge's Sons, 1940.

Weissmann, Adolph. "Race and Modernity." *League of Composers' Review* 1, no. 1 (1924): 3–6.

———. "The Tyranny of the Absolute." *League of Composers' Review* 2, no. 2 (1925): 17–20.

Wellens, Ian. *Music on the Frontline: Nicolas Nabokov's Struggle against Communism and Middlebrow Culture*. Aldershot, U.K.: Ashgate, 2002.

Wertenbaker, Charles. *A New Doctrine for the Americas*. New York: Viking Press, 1941.

Whitaker, Arthur P. *The Western Hemisphere Idea*. Ithaca, N.Y.: Cornell University Press, 1954.

White, Eric Walter. *Stravinsky and His Works*. 2nd ed. Berkeley: University of California Press, 1979.

Whitworth, Walter. "Symphony and Guest Pianist in Top Form." *Indianapolis News*, January 25, 1954.

Williams, Daryle. *Culture Wars in Brazil: The First Vargas Regime, 1930–1945*. Durham, N.C.: Duke University Press, 2001.

Williams, Virginia S. *Radical Journalists, Generalist Intellectuals, and U.S.–Latin American Relations*. Lewiston, N.Y.: Edwin Mellen Press, 2001.

Williams, William Appleman. *Empire as a Way of Life*. New York: Oxford University Press, 1980.

Williams, William Carlos. *In the American Grain*. Norfolk, Conn.: New Directions, 1925.

Wilson, Edmund. "Imaginary Conversation: Mr. Paul Rosenfeld and Mr. Matthew Josephson." *New Republic* 38 (April 9, 1924): 179–81.

Winterer, Caroline. *The Culture of Classicism: Ancient Greece and Rome in American Intellectual Life, 1780–1910*. Baltimore: Johns Hopkins University Press, 2002.

Wisnik, José Miguel. *O coro dos contrários: A música em torno da semana de 22*. São Paulo: Livraria Duas Cidades, 1977.

Wolff, Christian. Liner notes for *The People United Will Never Be Defeated!* Ursula Oppens, piano. Vanguard 1978.

Woll, Allen L. *The Latin Image in American Film*. Revised ed. Los Angeles: UCLA Latin American Center Publications, 1997.

Woodmansee, Martha. *The Author, Art, and the Market*. New York: Columbia University Press, 1994.

"Words and Music: Sir Adrian Boult Conducts N.B.C. Orchestra Expertly." *New York Post*, May 16, 1938.

Wright, Simon. *Villa-Lobos*. Oxford: Oxford University Press, 1992.

————. "Villa-Lobos and the Cinema: A Note." *Luso-Brazilian Review* 19 (1982): 243–50.

Yellis, Kenneth A. "Prosperity's Child: Some Thoughts on the Flapper." *American Quarterly* 21, no. 1 (1969): 44–64.

"Young Composers [*sic*] Work Opens Concert Series." *New York Herald Tribune*, April 23, 1928.

Young, Mary. "The West and American Cultural Identity: Old Themes and New Variations." *Western Historical Quarterly* 1, no. 2 (1970): 137–60.

Zimmerman, Walter. *Desert Plants: Conversations with 25 American Musicians.* Vancouver: ARC Publications, 1976.

Zuck, Barbara A. *A History of Musical Americanism.* Ann Arbor, Mich.: UMI Research Press, 1980.

■ INDEX

A

absolute music 26, 40, 44, 48, 77, 79, 191
adaptation, Spanish missionaries 203n55
"Adios, muchachos" 69
adjectivization 4, 5, 190
Adler, Larry 227n130
Adorno, Theodor W. 7, 76, 119–20, 170
    sublimation and 156–57
Advis, Luis 175
    Santa María de Iquique 175
Aeolian Hall 23, 60
"African" rhythm 4–5, 11, 87, 106–7
Agawu, Kofi 4, 106
Alencar, José de 85
Alex, Joe 90
Alsogaray, Álvaro 142
Allende, Salvador 171–72, 175,
    176, 179
    nueva canción and 173–74
    art music and 186, 237n38
Alliance for Progress (AFP) 143–44, 166,
    172
Allied Chemical 151
Altamira 151
Álvarez, Alejandro 19
Álvarez Quintero, Serafín and Joaquín 22
Amado, Jorge 97
Amaral, Tarsila do (Tarsila) 88
Amengual, René Astuburuaga 130
America, naming of 15
American Association of Teachers of
    Spanish and Portuguese 37
American Ballet Caravan 114, 131
American Council of Learned Societies
    222n21
American Institute of Architects 101
American Mercury 122
"American" rhythm 11, 106–8, 123, 187
Amsterdam, Morey 153
Amsterdam Opera House 22
Anaconda Copper Mining Company 173
Anderson, Benedict 6
Andrade, Mário de 86, 88

Andrade, Oswald de 88–89, 110, 134
    Manifesto Antropófago (Cannibalist
    Manifesto) 89
Andrews Sisters 153, 222n15
Angell, James B. 17
Anglo-Saxon superiority, notions of 16, 20, 88
Antheil, George 50, 53
    Ballet Mécanique 52, 74
    surrealism and 209n20
anthropology 8, 26, 32, 46
    "Apollonian" anthropologists, 1920s
    33–34
anti-communism 79, 143, 144, 175
    see also Paine, Frances Ford
anti-Mexican sentiment 21, 22, 32
antinationalism 11, 115, 129, 141, 144–46,
    154, 187
    see also Lange, Francisco Curt
anti-US sentiment 10, 19, 144, 173
Antonioni, Michelangelo 166
Antorcha, La 206n154
Apel, Willi 241n15
"Apollonians" (see anthropology)
Arbenz, Jacobo 143
Architectural Review 101
Ardévol, José 8, 128–29
Argentina 18, 19, 22, 27, 59, 68, 142, 144,
    186
    fears of Axis infiltration 112, 113
    post-Perón period 158–59
    U.S. press coverage of, Cold War 165–66,
    167
"Argentina, La" (Antonia Mercé y Luque)
    22
Argentine Embassy 142, 159
Argentine Nights 222n15
Arlington National Cemetery 241n29
Armstrong, Louis 213n107
Art Deco 34
Arthur, Chester A. 16
Atkinson, Brooks 227n142
Attali, Jacques 7
Avramoff, Arseny 209n22